√ × √ × √ × √ × √ × √ × √ × √ ×

ABC of Common Grammatical Errors

√ × √ × √ × √ × √ × √ × √ × √ ×

Nigel Turton

Macmillan Heinemann English Language Teaching
Between Towns Road, Oxford OX4 3PP
A division of Macmillan Publishers Limited
Companies and representatives throughout the world

ISBN 0 333 56734 X

First published 1995

This book is printed on paper suitable for recycling and
made from fully managed and sustained forest sources.

A catalogue record for this book is available from the
British Library.

Printed in Hong Kong

2003 2002 2001
14 13 12

To Alberto and Noemi

Acknowledgements

I would like to thank all those who read and made useful comments on the text during the course of its preparation. Deserving special mention are: Barbara Applin, Adam Brown, Graeme Cane, Kevin Dunseath, Connor Ferris, Brian Heaton, Alex Henry, Peter Martin, Gloria Poedjosoedarmo, Wendy Preston, Agneta Svalberg and John Swan.

My thanks are also extended to Alison Hubert for overseeing the project and to Jody Linsell for advising on American English usage.

Contents

Introduction

What is the purpose of the book?

The *ABC of Common Grammatical Errors* is a practical reference book for learners and teachers of English as a second or foreign language. Its main purpose is to provide intermediate and advanced learners with easy access to the information they need in order to correct their grammatical errors. Up until now, this information has been spread across grammar reference books, usage guides and learners' dictionaries. In the *ABC*, it is available for the first time within a single volume.

For teachers of English, the *ABC* provides a comprehensive checklist of learners' grammatical errors, together with clear explanations of the relevant grammatical points. (See *A note for teachers* below.)

Which errors are dealt with?

The *ABC* deals with the grammatical errors that learners make again and again. It covers errors in *system* grammar and errors in *word* grammar. System grammar includes such areas as subject–verb agreement, tense use, the passive, question forms. Word grammar, sometimes called 'usage', consists of rules that control the use of particular words. For example, we *allow* someone *to do* something, but we *let* someone *do* something (without *to*). We *hope* that someone *will* do something, but we *wish* that someone *would* do something. We open our *letters* (with-*s*), but we open our *mail* (without -*s*). We can say '*It* seems that she likes you' but not '*She* seems that she likes you'. System errors and word errors are combined in the *ABC* within a single alphabetical arrangement.

The *ABC* contains 'common' errors. A common error is one that is made frequently by learners of various language backgrounds. An error that is made, for example, only by Italian learners of English is not included.

The errors have been gathered from a large corpus of written texts produced by learners at intermediate and advanced levels of proficiency. In view of this proficiency range, some of the errors in the *ABC* may seem surprisingly elementary (e.g. 'She live in Paris' instead of 'She lives in Paris'). It should be remembered, however, that even advanced learners sometimes make basic mistakes.

The model of correct usage employed in the *ABC* is standard British English. Differences between British English and American English usage are described at the relevant entries.

How do I find the information I need?

When you need information about a word error, you look for the information in the same way that you would look for it when using a normal dictionary. For example, if you do not know whether to say 'I look forward *to see* you' or 'I look forward *to seeing* you', you just turn to the entry for **look forward to**.

Entries dealing with system errors are also arranged alphabetically. For example, imagine that you have made a mistake in the use of the present perfect tense (× 'I *have bought* a new computer last week'). In the ABC you will find the information you need at the entry for **present perfect tense: use** in its usual alphabetical position among the '**p**' errors.

If you try to use a traditional grammar book for the purpose of error correction, you encounter a number of difficulties. The main problem is that you usually do not know where to look. For example, in the case of 'I *have bought* a new computer last week', the relevant information will probably be shown in the section dealing with the **past simple tense**. However, if you know that the information you need is to be found under this heading, it is questionable whether you would have made the mistake in the first place. The error-based organization of the ABC gives you a better chance of finding the information you need, and finding it quickly. When you make an error in the use of a particular tense, you just look up the entry for that same tense.

present perfect tense: use **617**

1

×	√
× I have seen the film in London last week.	√ I saw the film in London last week.
× In France the death penalty has been abolished in 1981.	√ In France the death penalty was abolished in 1981.

When we mention something which took place at a particular time in the past (e.g. 'last week', 'in 1981', 'yesterday', 'two months ago'), we use the past simple tense, NOT the present perfect. ⇨ 583.1–4

Unlike word errors, many system errors may be classified in more than one way. For example, the error 'I *have bought* a new computer last week' could be placed under the headings **tense, present perfect tense** or **have + -ed**. In view of this, before you begin to use the ABC, it is recommended that you spend just a few minutes examining the list of entries for system errors at the back of the book. This list shows you at a glance all the major categories of system error, including their names and where to find them. At the same time, once you have begun to use the ABC, you will discover that the entries for system errors and word errors are often closely linked.

last **443**

1

×	√
× I have arrived in England last July.	√ I arrived in England last July.

With 'last night', 'last week', etc, we usually use the past simple tense. ⇨ 617.1

What do the entries contain?

Although the *ABC* is a reference book, it also provides opportunities for active learning. For this reason, the normal sequence of 'explanation' followed by 'examples' has been deliberately reversed. The entries in the *ABC* begin with examples of incorrect and correct usage. Each pair of sentences contains a type of puzzle, which you are invited to solve by carefully comparing the error sentence and the correction. If you are successful in 'solving the puzzle', i.e. in working out the rule for yourself, what you have learned by your own efforts is more likely to be remembered.

Each of the error sentences contains just one error. To avoid confusion, additional errors that were present in the source material have been corrected.

Below the examples of incorrect and correct usage, there is normally an explanation of the rule which has been broken. However, some of the word entries have a cross-reference to another part of the book, where the explanation is located.

As with all reference materials that deal with grammar, the use of technical terms has been unavoidable. The technical terms used in the *ABC* are explained in the *Glossary*.

How is the warning sign used?

Most of the examples of learner usage in the *ABC* are clearly ungrammatical. These 'learner English' sentences are marked with a cross (×) as incorrect. However, instead of a cross, there is sometimes a warning sign (!). This sign has three functions:

1 Some examples of learner usage are grammatical in American English – e.g. 'accommodations' (with *-s*) – but ungrammatical in British English. The warning sign draws attention to such cases.

2 The warning sign also draws attention to examples of usage which are unacceptable if used in the wrong circumstances. For example, the use of *for* as a conjunction, although grammatical, is restricted to formal or literary styles.

3 The third function of the warning sign is to mark areas of usage that are influenced by opinions, passed down from one generation to the next, about what is 'good' grammar and what is 'bad'. One of these opinions, for example, is that a sentence should not begin with a coordinating conjunction, such as ***and*** or ***but***. In formal styles, we tend to follow these so-called 'prescriptive rules', since we do not wish to seem 'uneducated'. Otherwise, we take little notice of them.

A note for teachers

As teachers of English know only too well, some learners are in the habit of asking searching questions about specific points of usage, e.g. 'Which is correct: *Each pair of shoes* **was** *too big* or *Each pair of shoes* **were** *too big*?' Most grammar reference books begin their descriptions at the system level (e.g. subject–verb agreement) and work down towards the word level. More often than not, however, the description stops short of the particular word that the learner needs to know about, such as ***pair***.

The *ABC* begins at the word level and works upwards. It takes as its starting point not just the words that learners actually use, but the words that time and time again cause them difficulty. As a result of this 'bottom up' orientation, the book contains answers to many of the 'awkward' questions.

I should be very pleased to hear from teachers who come across gaps in the *ABC*. Please write to me c/o Macmillan Education Ltd, Houndmills, Basingstoke, Hampshire RG21 2XS, England.

Glossary

abstract noun An abstract noun is a noun that refers to a concept or feeling, e.g. *danger, hope, courage, luck, happiness, peace, strength, success.*

active See PASSIVE

adjective An adjective is a word that tells us what a person, thing, place, etc. is like: 'a *tall* woman', 'a *blue* scarf', 'The questions were *difficult*.'

adjective phrase An adjective phrase is a group of words in which the main word is an adjective: 'The floor was *very dirty*.' 'These shoes are *far too expensive*.' 'She isn't *old enough*.'

adverb An adverb is a word which tells us 'how', 'when', 'how often', 'where', etc, something happens: 'I closed the door *quietly*.' 'We saw her *yesterday*.' 'They *often* go *there*.' Adverbs also tell us about the degree or extent of something: '*very* old', '*too* quickly', '*fairly* important', '*quite* a good idea'. See also LINKING ADVERB, DISJUNCT

adverbial An adverbial is a word, phrase or clause which tells us 'how', 'when', 'where', 'why', etc., something happens: 'He arrived *yesterday*.' 'He arrived *about a week ago*.' 'He had arrived *before I reached the station*.'

adverbial clause An adverbial clause is a type of subordinate clause which tells us *how, when, where, why,* etc., something happens: '*While I was having breakfast*, the telephone rang.' 'I've come to England *to improve my English*.'

adverbial phrase An adverbial phrase is a group of words in which the main word is an adverb: 'He should drive *more carefully*.' 'She'll be back *fairly soon*.'

affirmative A statement which contains a word such as *not, never, rarely* is said to be 'negative': 'I don't like coffee.' A statement which does not contain a negative word is said to be 'affirmative': 'I like coffee.'

agreement When we say that two words in a sentence must 'agree', we mean that they must have the same grammatical features. For example, if the subject of a sentence is plural, the verb must also be plural: 'The *girls* in my class *are* French.' Similarly, if the subject of a sentence is third person singular, we have to use a third person singular pronoun to refer back to it: '*Mr Jones* is a good teacher, but *he* always arrives late.' The pronoun *he* shares the same grammatical features as *Mr Jones*.

antecedent An antecedent is the word or phrase that a pronoun or determiner refers back to: 'Tim likes *onions* but his wife hates *them*.' In this sentence, the pronoun *them* refers back to (and agrees with) *onions*, which is the antecedent.

apposition To give more information about someone or something, we sometimes follow a noun phrase with a second noun phrase: '*Mr Williams, the headmaster*, used to play rugby for Wales.' The two noun phrases are said to be 'in apposition'.

attributive When we use the words 'attributive' and 'predicative', we are talking about adjectives and their positions in a sentence. An adjective that is placed before a noun is said to be in attributive position: 'He gave me the *correct* answer'. An adjective that is placed after a linking verb such as *be* is said to be in predicative position: 'His answer *was correct*.'

auxiliary verb An auxiliary verb (e.g. *be, have, do, can, must, will*) is used before a main verb to make tenses, questions, passive forms, etc: 'She ***has** lost* her passport.' '***Did*** you *go* to the meeting?' 'The new furniture ***will be** delivered* tomorrow.' See also MAIN VERB, VERB PHRASE

bare infinitive See INFINITIVE

clause A clause is usually either a sentence ('*She arrived an hour late.*') or a major part of a sentence ('She arrived an hour late + *because her car broke down.*') See also MAIN CLAUSE, SUBORDINATE CLAUSE

collective noun A collective noun is a word which refers to a group, e.g. *crowd, family, team.* When it is singular, a collective noun may normally be used with a singular or plural verb: 'The *committee has/have* finally reached a decision.'

comparative A comparative is the form of an adjective or adverb that ends in *-er* or that begins with *more/less*: 'My car is *older* than yours.' 'The leather bag is *more expensive* than the plastic one.' See also SUPERLATIVE

complement A complement (sometimes called a 'subject complement') is normally a word or phrase which describes the subject: '*This apple* is ***delicious***.' '*His wife* became ***a music teacher***.' '*Smoking* is **bad for your health**.' Similarly, an object complement describes the object: 'I found *his new book* ***very interesting***.' 'The film made *her* ***famous*** almost overnight.'

compound A compound is a combination of two or more words that we use as a single word: 'a *teacup*', 'a *two-week* holiday', 'a *six-year-old* child', 'a *police officer*'.

conditional A conditional clause (also called an '*if*-clause') is a type of subordinate clause that begins with *if, unless,* etc: '*If Mary had arrived on time*, we would have caught the train.' Less frequently, a conditional clause may begin with subject-verb inversion: '*Had I known that you were ill*, I would have come to see you.' A conditional sentence is one that contains a conditional clause.

conjunction A conjunction is a word such as *and, or, but, because, if, when, although* which joins two parts of a sentence, or shows how they are related: 'Would you like *tea* **or** *coffee*?' 'There are *two apples* **and** *three oranges*.' '*She likes you* **because** *you never get angry*.' '***Although** it was late, the shops were still open*.'

consonant A consonant (or consonant sound) is a speech sound that is made by blocking or partly blocking the air from the lungs. For example, the sounds at the beginning of *take, fight* and *see* are consonants.

context When a word is used in speech or writing, there are normally words before it and words after it. These surrounding words are known as the 'context'. Context also means the social situation in which language is used.

contracted A contracted form (or 'contraction') is the short form of a word that we use in everyday conversation. For example, instead of saying 'I *have* done it', we normally say 'I'*ve* done it'.

coordinating conjunction A coordinating conjunction (e.g. *and, or, but*) is used to link two equal parts of a sentence: 'Would you like tea ***or*** coffee?' 'I invited him to come in *and* sit down.' 'Tom plays football *but* Peter prefers tennis.'

coordination Coordination is the linking of equal grammatical units, usually by means of *and, or, but.*

countable noun A countable noun (or count noun) is a noun with both singular and plural forms: e.g. 'a *chair*' – 'two *chairs*', 'a *child*' – 'six *children*'. See also UNCOUNTABLE NOUN

defining See RELATIVE CLAUSE

demonstrative The demonstratives *this/these* and *that/those* tell us whether something is near the speaker or at a distance from the speaker. These words are used as both determiners and pronouns.

determiner A determiner is a word that is frequently used at the beginning of a noun phrase, e.g. *a/an, the, this, that, these, my, your, their, some, any, more, many, all, both, each, every.*

direct object See OBJECT

direct speech See INDIRECT SPEECH

disjunct A disjunct is a word or phrase that we use to express our attitude to what we are about to say, e.g. *unfortunately, luckily, of course, naturally, on the whole, in short, to be precise.*

double genitive A double genitive is a structure in which *of* is followed by a possessive form: 'a friend *of my father's*', 'a neighbour *of mine*'.

empty subject/object The term 'empty subject' refers to the use of *it* and *there* in sentences like 'It's getting late.' 'It's cold in here.' 'It would be quicker to do the job yourself.' 'There's a hole in your sleeve.' 'There's someone waiting to see you.' 'There's been an accident.' In these sentences, *it* and *there* are 'empty of meaning'; they merely fill the subject position. Similarly, *it* is sometimes used as an 'empty object', e.g. 'You may find *it* difficult to obtain the tickets.' 'I like *it* when I'm busy.'

finite A finite verb is a verb which has a tense: 'They *are* waiting for you.' 'She *sent* me a postcard.' '*Have* you seen my keys?' A finite clause is a clause that contains a finite verb.

A non-finite verb does not have a tense: 'I heard someone *coming* in.' 'We went *to see* a film *called* "Midnight Express".' A non-finite clause is a clause that contains a non-finite verb.

first person See PERSON

fixed A fixed expression is one whose form cannot be changed in any way: e.g. *on the whole, needless to say, could do with, a couple of* (NOT 'one couple of', 'couples of', etc.).

formal Formal styles are those in which words and structures are carefully chosen. Such styles are used in business letters, academic textbooks, news broadcasts, public ceremonies, etc. Informal styles are those in which language is used spontaneously, as in everyday conversation.

gender In some languages, each noun has a grammatical gender. In French, for example, the word for 'house' is feminine whereas the word for 'sky' is masculine. In English, nouns do not have grammatical gender.

genitive The genitive (or 'possessive') form of a noun ends with *-'s* (apostrophe + s) or *-s'* (s + apostrophe): '*Tom's* bicycle', 'a *girls'* school'. Genitive forms often express a relationship of possession ('my wife's car'), but they express a number of other relationships as well. For example, they are commonly used with time words: 'a month's salary', 'today's lesson', 'in three weeks' time'.

We do not normally use the *-'s/-s'* genitive with inanimate nouns. Instead, we tend to use the *of*-genitive: 'the end *of the road*', 'the back *of the house*'.

gradable A gradable adjective is one that can be used with *very, too,* etc. It also has comparative/superlative forms: 'James is a *very tall* boy, much *taller* than Mark, but John is the *tallest.*' Unlike *tall,* adjectives such as *medical* and *dead* are ungradable. We do not normally say 'very dead' or 'more medical'.

head The head of a phrase is the word that is modified/qualified by all the other words in the phrase: *'The two* ***books*** *that you lent me* were *extremely interesting.'*

***if*-clause** See CONDITIONAL

imperative The imperative form of a verb is the same as the bare infinitive: '*Come* here.' '*Have* a seat.' '*Try* one of these cakes.' Imperative clauses begin with a verb in the imperative. We use them for commands, suggestions, invitations, etc.

indefinite pronoun Indefinite pronouns are words such as *somebody, something, anyone, nobody, everything.* They are 'indefinite' because they do not refer to a particular person or thing.

indirect object See OBJECT

indirect speech Direct speech is speech that is written down without changing the words of the speaker. These words are usually enclosed within inverted commas: *'Don't be late.'* Indirect speech (or 'reported speech') is speech that is reported in the words of the reporter: *She told him not to be late.*

infinitive The infinitive (sometimes called the 'present infinitive') is the base form of a verb: *(to) be, (to) go, (to) know,* etc. The base form is used sometimes with to ('He wants *to stay* in bed') and sometimes without *to* ('He should *stay* in bed'). The form with *to* is called a '*to*-infinitive'; the form without *to* is called a 'bare infinitive'. See also PERFECT INFINITIVE

infinitive clause An infinitive clause is a type of subordinate clause which begins with an infinitive: 'I've come to England *to visit my sister.*' 'It was good *to see you again.*' 'All you can do is *ask for your money back.*'

infinitive marker The infinitive marker is *to.* We use it to make a *to*-infinitive: 'I'd like *to meet* them again.'

informal See FORMAL

***-ing* clause** An *-ing* clause is a type of subordinate clause in which the first verb is an *-ing* form: '*Playing the piano* can be very relaxing.' 'She hates *saying goodbye to anyone.*' 'The man *sitting next to me* started to laugh.'

***-ing* form** An *-ing* form is the form of a verb that ends in *-ing*: 'He's *finishing* his dinner.' 'I like *listening* to the news.' '*Sitting* behind me were two German girls.'

intensifier An intensifier is a type of adverb which 'strengthens' the meaning of the following word: '*very* strange', '*extremely* disappointed', '*absolutely* amazing'.

interrogative An interrogative clause is a clause that has the form of a question: *'Have you seen my umbrella anywhere?'* '*Where does he live?*' Note, however, that interrogative clauses are not always questions: 'If you are going out, *would you post this letter for me?*' (= a request)

intransitive See TRANSITIVE

irregular See REGULAR

linking adverb Linking adverbs are words such as *therefore, however, moreover, nevertheless.* We use these words to show the connection between what we are about to say and what we have just said. 'Most criminals realize that they may be caught. *Nevertheless,* they are prepared to take the risk.'

linking verb A linking verb (e.g. *be, become, seem, look*) links the subject with one or more words which describe the subject: 'My mother *is* a doctor.' 'The children *looked* tired and hungry.'

main clause A main clause is a clause that may be used on its own as a sentence: 'Someone has taken my umbrella.' 'She arrived an hour late.' For this reason, a main clause is sometimes called an 'independent clause'. See also SUBORDINATE CLAUSE

main verb A main verb (e.g. *lose, go, deliver, forget*) is the last verb in a verb phrase: 'She *has **lost*** her passport.' 'We *didn't **buy*** anything.' 'The new furniture *will be **delivered*** tomorrow.' If there are no auxiliary verbs (e.g. *be, have, do, can, must, will*), the main verb is the only verb: 'Then we ***went*** home.' 'She ***has*** a bad cold.' See also AUXILIARY VERB, VERB PHRASE

middle position A middle position (or 'mid-position') adverb is an adverb that normally comes immediately before the main verb: 'She *often* writes to me.' 'I had *almost* fallen asleep.'

modal verb A modal verb (e.g. *can, could, may, might, will, should, must*) is a type of auxiliary verb which expresses the speaker's attitude. It comes right at the beginning of a verb phrase: 'You ***should** see* a doctor.' 'They ***must** have missed* the train.' '***Would*** you *like* a drink?'

modifier In a phrase, a modifier is a word or group of words which makes the meaning of the main word (the head) more specific. For example, in the phrase 'two silk ties from Italy', the main word 'ties' has three modifiers: 'two', 'silk' and 'from Italy'. A modifier which comes after the main word, such as 'from Italy', is sometimes called a 'qualifier'. See also QUALIFIER

negative See AFFIRMATIVE

non-defining See RELATIVE CLAUSE

non-finite See FINITE

noun A noun is a word that refers to a person, place, thing, idea, etc: 'My *sister* is writing a long *essay* about the *life* of *Napoleon*.' Most nouns can be used after a determiner.

noun phrase A noun phrase is a group of words in which the main word is a noun or pronoun: '*The shop assistant* showed me *several expensive watches* and then *some cheaper ones*.' '*Our guide* told us about *the history of London* and *the places that we were going to visit*.' (the last main word = *places*)

number Number involves the contrast between words which are singular (e.g. *this, boy, he*) and words which are plural (e.g. *these, boys, they*). Two words are said to agree in number when they refer to the same thing and are both singular or both plural. See also AGREEMENT

object The object (also called the 'direct object') of a sentence is the person or thing that is affected by the action of the verb: 'I took *George* to the airport.' 'She closed *the door* quietly.'

An indirect object is normally the person or thing that receives the direct object: 'She gave *the boy* an apple.' 'I sent *him* a postcard.' 'He told *the doctor* that he couldn't sleep.'

object complement See COMPLEMENT

participle See PRESENT PARTICIPLE, PAST PARTICIPLE

participle clause A participle clause is a type of subordinate clause which begins with a participle. '***Dried** in the sun*, the leaves had turned brown.' '***Not wanting** to disturb them*, I waited outside.'

passive The subject of a clause is usually the 'doer' of the action expressed by the verb: e.g. 'Alex has typed the letter.' In such cases, we say that the verb and the clause are 'active'. Sometimes, however, the subject of a clause is the 'receiver' of the action: e.g. 'The letter has been typed.' When this is the case, we say that the verb and the clause are 'passive'.

Passive verb forms are made with *be* + past participle: 'The car *has been repaired.*' 'More trees *are being planted.*' Since a passive clause begins with the 'receiver' of the action, only transitive verbs (i.e. verbs which take an object) can be used in the passive.

past participle The past participle is the form of a verb that is used in perfect tenses ('Someone *has/had* ***broken*** the window'), in passive structures ('My computer *is being* ***repaired***'), and in some non-finite clauses ('***Driven*** *carefully*, the car will last you a lifetime'). Past participles are also used as adjectives: 'an *excited* audience', 'a *lost* child'.

The past participle form of a regular verb ends with *-ed*: 'I have *opened* a bank account.' For the past participle forms of irregular verbs, see 419.

past perfect The past perfect tense has two forms: the past perfect simple ('She *had written* to him') and the past perfect progressive ('She *had been writing* to him'). When people talk about 'the past perfect', they normally mean the simple form. See also PAST PERFECT SIMPLE, PAST PERFECT PROGRESSIVE

past perfect progressive The past perfect progressive tense is made with *had* + *been* + *-ing*: 'Previously, he *had been working* for a newspaper.'

past perfect simple The past perfect simple tense is made with *had* + past participle: 'He told me that he *had left* his suitcases at the airport.'

past progressive The past progressive tense is made with *was/were* + *-ing*: 'When I arrived, they *were sitting* in the garden.'

past simple The past simple tense of a regular verb ends in *-ed*: 'I *knocked* on the door, and then *opened* it.' For the past simple forms of irregular verbs, see 419.

past tense The past tense has two forms: the past simple ('She *laughed*') and the past progressive ('She *was laughing*'). When people talk about 'the past tense', they normally mean the past simple form. See PAST SIMPLE, PAST PROGRESSIVE

perfect infinitive The perfect infinitive is made with *(to) have* + past participle: 'The train should *have arrived* by now.' 'She is known *to have been* a keen tennis player.'

person As a grammatical term, 'person' involves the contrast between words which show that we are talking about ourselves (e.g. *I, we* = 'first person'), words which show that we are talking about the listener (e.g. *you* = 'second person'), and words which show that we are talking about someone or something else (e.g. *he, she, it, the tree, they, the girls* = 'third person').

personal pronoun The personal pronouns are *I, me, you, he, him, she,* etc.

phrasal verb A phrasal verb is a verb which consists of two or three parts: 'If I come to London, I'll *look* you *up.*' (= verb + adverb); 'Who *looks after* the children?' (= verb + preposition); 'I *look forward to* seeing you.' (= verb + adverb + preposition).

phrase A phrase is a group of words, one of which is the 'head' (the main word): e.g. 'the best hotel in London', 'much too expensive', 'as quickly as possible'. See also NOUN PHRASE, VERB PHRASE, ADJECTIVE PHRASE, ADVERBIAL PHRASE, PREPOSITIONAL PHRASE

plural A plural form refers to two or more people or things: 'books', 'children', 'these', 'we', 'many'.

plural count noun A plural count noun is a countable noun that is used in the plural: 'two *tables*', 'several *books*'. See also PLURAL NOUN

plural noun A plural noun is a noun which is always plural and does not have a singular form, e.g. *trousers, clothes, scissors, sunglasses.*

possessive See GENITIVE

possessive determiner The possessive determiners are *my, your, his, her, its, our, their, whose*: 'Have you seen *their* new house?'

possessive pronoun The possessive pronouns are *mine, yours, his, hers, ours, theirs.*

predicate The predicate is the whole of a clause apart from the subject: 'His wife *is writing a book about wild flowers.*' In other words, the predicate is everything that we say about the subject.

predicative See ATTRIBUTIVE

preposition A preposition is a word that comes at the beginning of a phrase telling us *when, where, why, how,* etc: 'I'll meet you *on* Monday *at* six o'clock *outside* the cinema.' Prepositions are also used as linking words: 'I was given a book *about* birds.' 'She refuses to talk *to* me.' 'Smoking is bad *for* you.' Note that some prepositions consist of more than one word, e.g. *because of, in spite of, as a result of.*

prepositional phrase A prepositional phrase is a group of words which begins with a preposition and ends with a noun or pronoun: '*In the afternoon* I went *to the airport* to meet a friend *of mine.*'

present infinitive See INFINITIVE

present participle The present participle is the *-ing* form of a verb. It is used in progressive tenses ('She *was **singing***'), in some non-finite clauses ('***Feeling** tired*, I went to bed'), and as an adjective ('a ***boring*** lesson').

present perfect The present perfect tense has two forms: the present perfect simple ('She *has written* to him') and the present perfect progressive ('She *has been writing* to him'). When people talk about 'the present perfect', they normally mean the simple form. See also PRESENT PERFECT SIMPLE, PRESENT PERFECT PROGRESSIVE

present perfect progressive The present perfect progressive tense is made with *have/has* + *been* + *-ing*: 'I*'ve been looking* for you everywhere.' 'He *has been working* in a bank.'

present perfect simple The present perfect simple tense is made with *have/has* + past participle: 'They *have gone* on holiday.' Nobody *has applied* for the job.'

present progressive The present progressive tense is made with *am/are/is* + *-ing*: 'They *are waiting* outside.' 'I*'m doing* my homework.'

present simple With the exception of *be*, the present simple tense is the same as the base form of the verb: 'My parents *live* in Rome.' However, when the subject is third person singular, the verb takes an *-s* or *-es* ending: 'I *like* football but my sister *hates* it.'

present tense The present tense has two forms: the present simple ('She *plays* the guitar') and the present progressive ('She *is playing* the guitar'). When people talk about 'the present tense', they normally mean the present simple form. See PRESENT SIMPLE, PRESENT PROGRESSIVE

progressive Each tense has two forms, a 'progressive' (or 'continuous') form and a 'simple' form. Progressive tenses are made with *be* + *-ing*: e.g. 'is working', 'has been working'. They are used for actions and situations that are viewed by the speaker as incomplete or temporary: e.g. 'The children *were digging* a hole in the sand.' 'She *is living* in London.' Simple (or 'non-progressive') tenses are used for actions and situations that are viewed by the speaker as complete or permanent: e.g. 'The children *dug* a hole in the sand.' 'She *lives* in London.'

pronoun A pronoun is a word that is used in place of a noun or noun phrase: 'Did *my wife* tell you where ***she*** was going?' 'I've typed *the letters* but I haven't posted ***them***.' See also PERSONAL PRONOUN, REFLEXIVE PRONOUN, RELATIVE PRONOUN, POSSESSIVE PRONOUN, INDEFINITE PRONOUN

qualifier In a phrase, a qualifier is a word or group of words which comes after the main word (the head) and makes its meaning more specific: 'a book *about computers*', 'the oldest building *in France*', 'the best book *I have ever read*', 'much cheaper *than a new one*'. See also MODIFIER

quantifier A quantifier is a word or phrase which tells us 'how many' or 'how much': e.g. '*most* people', '*several* of my friends', '*a few* problems', '*some* money', '*a little* milk'.

question tag A question tag is a short question form that we sometimes add to the end of a statement: 'They've gone on holiday, *haven't they?*' 'He isn't too old, *is he?*' 'She works for IBM, *doesn't she*?'

real subject A real subject is the part of a sentence that is replaced by an empty subject. In the sentence 'It's a pity that you cannot stay longer', the real or 'logical' subject is *that you cannot stay longer* and the grammatical subject is empty *it*. See also PREPARATORY SUBJECT

reflexive pronoun The reflexive pronouns are *myself, himself, themselves,* etc: 'We all enjoyed *ourselves*.' 'She has bought *herself* a new computer.'

reflexive verb A reflexive verb is a verb that is used with a reflexive pronoun, e.g. *myself, himself, themselves*: 'Be careful or you will *cut yourself*.' 'Just relax and *enjoy yourselves*.'

regular/irregular A regular form is one which follows the normal rules. For example, to make the past simple tense of a verb, we normally add *ed/-d* to the base form: *kicked, jumped, danced.* However, the past simple tense of an irregular verb is not made in this way: e.g. *went, did, gave, wrote.* An irregular form does not follow the normal rules.

relative adverb The relative adverbs *where*, *when* and *why* are used at the beginning of a relative clause: 'We spent two days in Bristol, ***where*** *we stayed with my brother.*' 'I shall never forget the day ***when*** *I arrived in England.*'

relative clause A relative clause is a type of subordinate clause that begins with *who, that, which,* etc. A 'defining' relative clause tells us which person or thing the speaker is talking about: 'The man *who stole the money* has been caught.' A 'non-defining' relative clause provides further information about someone or something: 'My youngest child, *who is only three*, is learning to read.'

relative pronoun We use a relative pronoun (e.g. *who, which, that*) at the beginning of a relative clause: 'Have you found the book ***that*** *you were looking for?* See also RELATIVE CLAUSE

reported clause A reported clause is a clause that is introduced by a reporting verb (e.g. *say, tell, ask*): 'She said *that she had a headache.*' 'I told them *to wait outside.*' 'He asked me *why I was late.*'

reported speech See INDIRECT SPEECH

reporting verb A reporting verb is used to introduce indirect/reported speech: 'She *said* that she wanted to see you.' 'They *asked* me where you were.'

second person See PERSON

sentence A sentence is the largest grammatical unit, containing at least one main clause. It begins with a capital letter and ends with a full stop. See also MAIN CLAUSE

simple See PROGRESSIVE

singular A singular form refers to just one person or thing: 'book', 'child', 'this', 'she', 'is'.

stative A stative verb (e.g. *know, contain, own*) refers to a state (not an action). For this reason, stative verbs are not normally used in progressive tenses. For example, we can say 'I know the answer' but NOT 'I am knowing the answer'. See also PROGRESSIVE

subject The subject of a sentence is the person or thing that the sentence is about: '*Those shoes* look too small for you.' 'Last week *the car* broke down three times.'

subject complement See COMPLEMENT

subordinate clause A subordinate clause provides part of a main clause, telling us 'why', 'when', 'where', 'how', 'what' etc: 'She arrived an hour late *because her car broke down*.' '*While we were having dinner*, the doorbell rang.' 'I've come here *to ask your advice*.' 'He told me *that he had lost your address*.' '*Working in Oxford Street,* I meet a lot of tourists.'

A subordinate clause may also provide part of a phrase: 'The person *that I feel sorry for* is his brother.' 'Do you recognise the man *sitting in the back of the car?*'

Unlike a main clause, a subordinate clause cannot be used on its own as a sentence. For this reason, it is sometimes called a 'dependent clause'. See also MAIN CLAUSE

subordinating conjunction A subordinating conjunction is a word such as *because, if, when, although* which joins a subordinate clause to a main clause: 'She went to bed *because* she was tired.' '*Although* he was ill, he insisted on helping me.'

superlative A superlative is the form of an adjective or adverb that ends in *-est* or that begins with *most/least*: 'This is the *tallest* building in the city.' 'The third question was by far the *most difficult*.' See also COMPARATIVE

syllable A syllable is a part of a word (or sometimes a whole word) that is pronounced as one unit. *Pear* has one syllable, *apple* has two syllables, and *banana* has three syllables.

tense A tense is a form of the verb which indicates, for example, the time of an action, and whether it is complete or in progress.

***that*-clause** A *that*-clause is a type of subordinate clause which begins (or which could begin) with the conjunction *that*: 'He said *(that) he wanted to see you*.' 'I'm surprised *(that) they didn't wait for you*.' 'She was so busy *(that) she didn't stop for lunch*.'

third person See PERSON

***to*-clause** A *to*-clause is a type of subordinate clause that begins with a *to*-infinitive: 'He's gone out *to do some shopping*.' 'It's good *to see you again*.'

'It was too dark *to see where we were going.*' '*To win first prize* would be a marvellous achievement.'

***to*-infinitive** See INFINITIVE

transitive/intransitive Transitive verbs (e.g. *buy, find*) take an object: 'She *bought* some apples.' 'They *found* their passports.' Intransitive verbs (e.g. *laugh, come*) do not take an object: 'Everyone *laughed.*' 'The train *is coming.*' Some verbs have both transitive and intransitive uses: 'He was reading (a book).'

uncountable noun An uncountable noun (also called a 'mass noun') is a noun that does not have a plural form (e.g. *furniture, homework, advice, equipment, information*): 'We need more *information.*' 'There was very little *furniture* in the room.' Some nouns which are normally uncountable also have countable meanings: 'I never drink *coffee.*' (= uncountable) 'The waiter brought two *coffees* and a glass of water.' (= countable) See also COUNTABLE NOUN

ungradable See GRADABLE

unit noun A unit noun is a noun that we use to talk about a particular quantity of something: 'a *piece* of furniture', 'two *sheets* of writing paper', 'one and a half *slices* of bread'.

verb A verb is a word which refers to an action or state, and which can show tense: 'He *went* to Italy.' 'She *speaks* three languages.' See also AUXILIARY VERB, MAIN VERB, VERB PHRASE

verb phrase A verb phrase consists of a main verb (e.g. *write, drink, think, go*) preceded by one or more auxiliary verbs (e.g. *be, have, do, can, must, will*): 'He *has written* another book.' 'The car *is being repaired.*' 'She *must have gone* home.' '*Have* you *seen* my keys anywhere?'

vowel A vowel (or vowel sound) is a speech sound that is made without blocking the air from the lungs. For example, the sounds at the beginning of *egg, old* and *artist* are vowels.

***wh*-clause** A *wh*-clause is a type of subordinate clause that begins with a *wh*-word: 'Do you know *what he wants*?' '*Where she has gone* remains a mystery.' 'This is *what you have to do.*'

***wh*-question** A *wh*-question is a question that begins with a *wh*-word: '*Who* is he?' '*What* did she say?' '*Where* are they going?'

***wh*-word** A *wh*-word is a question word beginning with *wh*-: *who, which, when, where,* etc. Note that *how* is also in this group.

word classes The term 'word classes' (sometimes called 'parts of speech') refers to the groups into which words are placed according to their grammatical functions. The major word classes are nouns, verbs, adjectives, adverbs, prepositions, conjunctions, and determiners.

***yes/no* question** A *yes/no* question is a question form which invites a 'yes' or 'no' answer: 'Have you seen Alex today?' 'Did you remember to post the letters?'

ABC of Common Grammatical Errors

a/an: form 1

1

× Sending young people to prison is a enormous mistake.	√ Sending young people to prison is an enormous mistake.
× All applicants must possess an university degree.	√ All applicants must possess a university degree.

Before a vowel sound, we use ***an***. Otherwise, we use ***a***.

a + CONSONANT SOUND	***an*** + VOWEL SOUND
a banana	an orange
a chicken	an egg

In most cases, the letters 'e', 'o' and 'u' are pronounced as vowels but sometimes they are pronounced as consonants:

a + CONSONANT SOUND	***an*** + VOWEL SOUND
a European	an English lesson
a one-way street	an only child
a university	an umbrella

2

× It takes me about a hour to get to work.	√ It takes me about an hour to get to work.
× He had never been inside an hospital before.	√ He had never been inside a hospital before.

When the next word begins with the letter 'h', we use ***a*** if the 'h' is pronounced and ***an*** if the 'h' is silent. This means that we follow the same rule as above: ***a*** before consonant sounds and ***an*** before vowels.

a + CONSONANT SOUND	***an*** + VOWEL SOUND (silent 'h')
a hard question	an honest answer
a huge house	an hour's delay

Nowadays, very few words begin with a silent 'h'. The most common are *heir, honest, honour, hour* and all the words which come from these, e.g. *heiress, heirloom, honorary, honourable, hourly*. Some people still pronounce *hotel, historian* and *habitual* with a silent 'h', but this usage is disappearing.

3

× I'm studying for a MA in history.	√ I'm studying for an MA in history.
× I always use a HB pencil.	√ I always use an HB pencil.
× He had spelt the word with a 's' instead of a 'p'.	√ He had spelt the word with an 's' instead of a 'p'.

We use ***an*** before an abbreviation or letter beginning with a vowel sound and ***a*** before an abbreviation or letter beginning with a consonant sound:

a + CONSONANT SOUND	***an*** + VOWEL SOUND
a BSc	an MSc
a VIP	an RAF pilot
a UK passport	an IOU
a 'b'	an 's'
a 'k'	an 'n'
a 'u'	an 'e'

The letters which begin with a vowel sound are: 'a', 'e', 'f', 'h', 'i', 'l', 'm', 'n', 'o', 'r', 's', 'x'. All other letters begin with a consonant sound.

4

×	√
× After the wedding, there was a 8-course meal.	√ After the wedding, there was an 8-course meal.

We use ***an*** before a number beginning with a vowel sound and ***a*** before a number beginning with a consonant sound:

a + CONSONANT SOUND		***an*** + VOWEL SOUND	
a '3'	/θriː/	an '8'	/eɪt/
a '5'	/faɪv/	an '11'	/ɪ'levən/
a '12'	/twelv/	an '18'	/eɪ'tiːn/

a/an: use 2

1

×	√
× She needs a good advice about choosing a career.	√ She needs some good advice about choosing a career.
× They couldn't give me a detailed information.	√ They couldn't give me any detailed information.
× I don't like driving in a heavy traffic.	√ I don't like driving in heavy traffic.
× To teach young children, you need a patience.	√ To teach young children, you need patience.

We do not use ***a/an*** before uncountable nouns, e.g. 'advice', 'information', 'traffic', 'patience'. When we talk about an indefinite quantity of something, we normally use ***some***: 'She poured ***some milk*** into a tall glass.' 'I'd like ***some information*** about medical insurance.'

In questions and negative sentences, we usually replace ***some*** with ***any***: 'Is there ***any milk*** left?' 'We don't have ***any information*** about medical insurance.'

When an uncountable noun refers to something in general, it is used without a determiner: 'Most babies like ***milk***.' 'Computers make it very easy to transfer ***information***.'

2

×	√
× His lawyer produced an important new evidence.	√ His lawyer produced a piece of important new evidence.

Many uncountable nouns can be 'made countable' with phrases such as ***a piece of, a bit of, a drop of, a glass of, an item of, a sheet of, a slice of, a packet of***: 'two pieces of cheese', 'a few pieces of furniture', 'several items of clothing', 'a loaf of bread'

The head of these phrases is a countable noun, e.g. *piece, item, loaf.*

3

✗	✓
× In the old days, many children did not go to a school.	√ In the old days, many children did not go to school.
× We had a breakfast in the hotel restaurant.	√ We had breakfast in the hotel restaurant.

⇨ 532: 2-3

4

✗	✓
× Luckily, only a person was injured.	√ Luckily, only one person was injured.
× A girl said that she liked the book, but the others hated it.	√ One girl said that she liked the book, but the others hated it.

When we need to emphasize 'how many', we use ***one***. (NOT ***a/an***) Compare:
Luckily, only ***one saucer*** was broken. (not two, three, etc.)
Luckily, only ***a saucer*** was broken. (not a cup, plate, etc.)

5

✗	✓
× She telephoned the police and told them that her daughter had not come home. They asked her to describe a missing child.	√ She telephoned the police and told them that her daughter had not come home. They asked her to describe the missing child.

We use ***a/an*** when we mention someone or something for the first time. To show that we are talking about the same person or thing that we have mentioned before ('her daughter'), we use ***the*** ('the missing child'). Compare: 'Last Saturday I bought ***a*** new dining table and four chairs. When ***the*** furniture was delivered, I noticed that ***the*** table had been badly scratched.'

6

✗	✓
× The children were playing outside in a garden.	√ The children were playing outside in the garden.

When we are sure that the listener/reader will understand which person or thing we are talking about, we use ***the***: 'There's someone outside ***the door***.' (= the door of this room) 'Whose turn is it to bath ***the baby***?' (= our baby) ⇨ 783.2

a/an: wrongly omitted 3

1

×	✓
× In the classroom, the children were having arithmetic lesson.	✓ In the classroom, the children were having an arithmetic lesson.
× Last year the company had record turnover of $5 million.	✓ Last year the company had a record turnover of $5 million.

A singular count noun (e.g. 'lesson', 'turnover') cannot be used without a determiner (e.g. *a/an, the, this, each, my*). When we mention someone or something for the first time, we normally use ***a/an***.

2

×	✓
× My brother is electrical engineer.	✓ My brother is an electrical engineer.
× St Andrews is private school and the fees are very high.	✓ St Andrews is a private school and the fees are very high.

When we define or classify someone or something, we use ***a/an*** + singular count noun: 'Her husband is ***a builder***.' 'Their dog is ***an Alsatian***.' 'Our new video camera is ***a Sony***.'

Note that when we are talking about more than one person or thing, we use a plural count noun without a determiner. Compare: 'My mother is ***a teacher***.' 'Both my parents are ***teachers.'***

3

×	✓
× The war lasted almost hundred years.	✓ The war lasted almost a hundred years.

⇨ 538.1

able 4

×	✓
× He said that the money was not able to be refunded.	✓ He said that he was unable to refund the money.
	✓ He said that the money could not be refunded.

The subject of ***be able/unable to*** is usually a person, not a thing.

about 5

×	✓
× I usually arrive home about at 6 o'clock.	✓ I usually arrive home at about 6 o'clock.

When ***about*** means 'approximately', it normally goes after a preposition (*at, in, with,* etc): 'I'll be there ***in about*** an hour's time.' '***With about*** ten minutes to go, United has taken the lead.'

about to 6

1

× I was about getting into the bath when I heard a strange noise.	√ I was about to get into the bath when I heard a strange noise.

We say that someone is ***about to do*** something: 'When I arrived, she was just ***about to*** go out.'

2

× The building is about to be pulled down next year.	√ The building is going to be pulled down next year.

If something is ***about to*** happen, it is going to happen immediately or very soon:
I was just ***about to*** go to bed when the telephone rang.
We had to return to our seats because the plane was ***about to*** land.

To refer to something that is planned or expected to happen, we use ***going to***. With ***going to***, we often mention the time of the action (e.g. 'next year', 'tomorrow', 'on Tuesday'), but not with ***about to***.

above 7

× There must have been above twenty cars outside the house.	√ There must have been over twenty cars outside the house.

When we mean 'more than', we normally use ***over***: '***over*** two weeks', '***over*** 20 pages', '***over*** 2 million signatures'.

When we mean 'higher than a particular level', we can normally use either word: 'temperatures ***over/above*** 100 degrees centigrade', 'children ***over/above*** the age of eight'.

absent 8

× Anyone absent at work has to get a medical certificate.	√ Anyone absent from work has to get a medical certificate.

We say that someone is ***absent from*** class, school, work, etc.

absolutely 9

× A car can be absolutely useful when you are in a hurry.	√ A car can be very useful when you are in a hurry.

We use ***absolutely*** before adjectives which already contain 'very' as part of their meaning: 'absolutely awful' (*awful* = 'very bad'), 'absolutely fascinating' (*fascinating* = 'very interesting').

With other adjectives, we use ***very*** or ***extremely***. ⇨ 405.2

accommodation

10

! Accommodations for overseas students can be arranged.	√ Accommodation for overseas students can be arranged.

The plural form ***accommodations*** is used in American English but not in British English. In British English, ***accommodation*** is an uncountable noun and does not have a plural form: 'The hostel provides ***accommodation*** for 238 students.'

according to

11

1

× According to Professor Newman, he says that management is a science.	√ According to Professor Newman, management is a science. √ Professor Newman says that management is a science.

We do not introduce a reported clause twice. We can use EITHER an ***according to*** phrase OR a subject + reporting verb, but not both together.

2

× According to me, all nuclear weapons should be destroyed.	√ In my opinion, all nuclear weapons should be destroyed.

We can say 'According to you/her/him/them' but NOT 'According to me/us'. We use ***according to*** to report another person's opinion or statement, not our own.

3

× According to Erica's opinion, the forests should be left alone.	√ According to Erica, the forests should be left alone. √ In Erica's opinion, the forests should be left alone.

We do not use ***opinion*** after ***according to***.

accuse

12

× She accused me for not telling the truth.	√ She accused me of not telling the truth.

We ***accuse*** someone ***of*** (doing) something.

accustom/accustomed

13

1

× It took her a long time to accustom to living alone.	√ It took her a long time to get accustomed to living alone.

Nowadays, we normally use ***be/get accustomed to*** something. The alternative, ***accustom oneself to*** something, is disappearing.

Note that ***be/get accustomed to*** is used mainly in formal styles. In informal styles, ***be/get used to*** sounds more natural: 'I'm not ***used to*** having so much free time.'

2

×	√
× I am not accustomed to see boys and girls in the same classroom.	√ I am not accustomed to seeing boys and girls in the same classroom.

⇨ 837

adjectives: form **14**

1

×	√
× I was too frighten to move.	√ I was too frightened to move.
× Several banks have shown interest in the propose development.	√ Several banks have shown interest in the proposed development.

Many adjectives are past participles, e.g. *frightened, scared, pleased, proposed, relaxed, retired, united*. The past participle of a regular verb ends in ***-ed***.

2

×	√
× We stayed in some excellents hotels.	√ We stayed in some excellent hotels.
× She thinks she is very importante.	√ She thinks she is very important.

The form of an adjective does not change for number or gender. Compare:
an ***excellent*** hotel – two ***excellent*** hotels (without ***-s***)
a ***clever*** boy – a ***clever*** girl (without ***-e***)

3

×	√
× I am very interesting in problems caused by pollution.	√ I am very interested in problems caused by pollution.
× It was such a bored film that I fell asleep.	√ It was such a boring film that I fell asleep.

The two participle forms of a verb are often used as adjectives. The ***-ed*** form usually describes how someone feels: 'By the end of the trip I felt completely ***exhausted***.' The ***-ing*** form describes the person or thing that causes the feeling: 'It was an ***exhausting*** trip and I was glad to get home.' Compare:
We were all ***bored*** (by the lesson). – The lesson was ***boring***.
She was ***excited*** (by the news). – The news was ***exciting***.

adjectives: comparison 15

1

×	✓
× Gas is usually more cheap than electricity.	✓ Gas is usually cheaper than electricity.

Most one-syllable adjectives form their comparatives and superlatives with ***-er/-est***: 'My brother is ***younger*** than I am.' 'This is the ***tallest*** building in Montreal.'

Participles used as adjectives are exceptions: 'I've never felt ***more bored*** in all my life.' 'The two front tyres look ***more worn***.'

2

×	✓
× He is one of the most rudest men I've ever met.	✓ He is one of the rudest men I've ever met.
× The medicine made me feel much more better.	✓ The medicine made me feel much better.

We do not use an ***-er/-est*** form and ***more/most*** together. 'Rudest' is a superlative form and is not used with ***most***. 'Better' is a comparative form and is not used with ***more***. Note the comparative and superlative forms of ***good*** and ***bad***:

	COMPARATIVE	SUPERLATIVE
good	better	(the) best
bad	worse	(the) worst

3

×	✓
× It is oldest university in Europe.	✓ It is the oldest university in Europe.

Before a superlative adjective ('oldest'), we normally use ***the*** or a possessive determiner (*my, her, their,* etc.): 'This is ***the tallest*** building in Boston.' 'Have you read ***her latest*** novel?'

When the noun phrase ends with a qualifier ('in Europe'), we use ***the***: 'She is ***the youngest*** girl in my class.' 'It is ***the worst*** film that I've ever seen.'

4

×	✓
× My most favourite subject is history.	✓ My favourite subject is history.
× Cheap products are often more inferior.	✓ Cheap products are often inferior.

Some adjectives are not normally used either with ***-er/-est*** or with ***more/most*** because they have a comparative/superlative meaning already. Someone's 'favourite' subject, for example, is the one that they like 'the most'.

Words which attract this type of error include:

complete, equal, favourite, ideal, inferior, perfect, superior, unique.

5

×	✓
× Singapore is cleaner than Hong Kong but Hong Kong is the most interesting.	✓ Singapore is cleaner than Hong Kong but Hong Kong is more interesting.

When we compare just two people or things, we use ***-er/more***, especially in formal styles. We use ***-est/most*** for more than two.

6

×	√
× There are so many good shops that it is easiest for people to buy what they want.	√ There are so many good shops that it is very easy for people to buy what they want.
× We must not forget that some criminals are the richest people.	√ We must not forget that some criminals are very rich people.

When we simply want to intensify an adjective, we use ***very, extremely,*** etc. We do not use ***-est/most*** unless we are making a comparison. Compare:

Simon's new computer is ***very easy*** to use.
Of the three computers, the XT2 is ***the easiest*** to use.

adjectives: position 16

1

×	√
× Some ill people refuse to take medicine.	√ Some sick people refuse to take medicine.
	√ Some people who are ill/sick refuse to take medicine.

Most adjectives can be used before a noun or after a linking verb (e.g. *be, become, look, seem*):

She has ***long/beautiful/black*** hair. (ATTRIBUTIVE position)
Her hair is ***long/beautiful/black***. (PREDICATIVE position)

However, some adjectives can be used in only one of these positions. For example, we can say 'the boy was ***alone***' but NOT 'the ***alone*** boy'. We can say 'the ***main*** road' but NOT 'the road is ***main***'.

Adjectives which are never or seldom used before a noun include:

afraid, alight, alike, alive, alone, ashamed, asleep, awake, aware, content, glad, ill, lit, ready, sorry, sure, upset, well (and ***unafraid, unaware, unwell,*** etc).

Adjectives which are never or seldom used after a linking verb include:

chief, drunken, elder, lighted, little, main, principal. ⇨ .2 below

2

×	√
× The country's main problem is economic.	√ The country's main problem is an economic one.
	√ The country's main problem concerns its economy.

We can say 'the ***economic*** crisis' but NOT 'the crisis is ***economic***'. Adjectives which classify usually go before a noun (NOT after a linking verb): 'an ***economic*** policy', '***atomic*** energy', 'a ***medical*** certificate', '***legal*** advice', 'the ***northern*** hemisphere', 'a ***weekly*** visit'.

Note, however, that adjectives of nationality, race and religion can be used in both positions: 'a ***French*** chef', 'her husband is ***French***'.

3

× The only thing that was damaged was the window of the opposite shop.	√ The only thing that was damaged was the window of the shop opposite.

Instead of saying 'the shop *that was opposite*', we can simply say 'the shop *opposite*'. Adjectives which may be used immediately after a noun include *concerned, involved, opposite, present* and *responsible.*

These adjectives may also be used before a noun, but then they have a different meaning. Compare:

The agreement was signed by everyone ***present***.
My ***present*** contract ends in September.

The person ***responsible*** should be punished.
Responsible parents do not let a child play with matches.

Henry has a flat above the bank and I live in the house ***opposite***.
The two families live at ***opposite*** ends of the street.

Further information will be sent to everyone ***concerned***.
A number of ***concerned*** parents wanted to know why the syllabus had been changed.

Both of the drivers ***involved*** managed to escape unhurt.
His new novel has a typically ***involved*** plot.

4

× Most of the visited government schools have very modern facilities.	√ Most of the government schools visited have very modern facilities.

When a past participle ('visited') refers more to an action than to a state, it normally comes after the noun. The verbal force of 'visited' becomes clear when we fill out the sentence: 'Most of the government schools ***(that we) visited*** have very modern facilities.'

When a past participle refers more to a state than to an action, it comes before the noun: 'a ***retired*** sales manager', 'two ***cracked*** glasses'.

5

× I would like a big enough house for my parents to live in.	√ I would like a house big enough for my parents to live in.

An adjective ('big') which has a qualifier ('enough for my parents to live in') normally goes after the noun.

adjectives: sequence 17

1

× Each child was given a red beautiful balloon.	√ Each child was given a beautiful red balloon.

When we use two or more adjectives before a noun, we normally put those which express opinions and impressions ('beautiful') before those which express facts ('red'): 'an ***unusual pink*** dress', 'a ***wonderful Italian*** pizza'.

2

× She has married a young tall Australian accountant.	√ She has married a tall young Australian accountant.
× It has black short hair and very sharp teeth.	√ It has short black hair and very sharp teeth.

Adjectives which express facts normally go in the following sequence:

	SIZE	AGE	SHAPE	COLOUR	ORIGIN	MATERIAL	PURPOSE	
an		old		green			kitchen	table
a	small		round			plastic		bowl
a		new			German		car	shampoo
a	long			white		silk		scarf

3

× The tree was a great comfort during the midday scorching sun.	√ The tree was a great comfort during the scorching midday sun.

A noun used as an adjective ('midday') goes immediately before the noun ('sun'): 'an exciting ***detective*** story', 'expensive ***leather*** shoes', 'an excellent ***evening*** meal'.

When there are two nouns used as adjectives, we put MATERIAL before PURPOSE: 'a ***nylon swimming*** costume', 'a cheap ***plastic medicine*** cupboard', 'a long ***steel exhaust*** pipe'.

4

× We bought six handmade very old wine glasses.	√ We bought six very old handmade wine glasses.

Gradable adjectives (i.e. those that can be used with ***very***) normally come before ungradable adjectives: 'a ***famous medical*** school', 'an ***old carved*** picture frame', 'a ***beautiful embroidered*** dressing gown'.

adjectives: use 18

1

× I answered her as casual as I could.	√ I answered her as casually as I could.
× When I first got the camera, it worked perfect.	√ When I first got the camera, it worked perfectly.

When we want to say 'how', we normally use an adverb ('casually'), NOT an adjective ('casual'). An adverb adds a detail to the meaning of a verb:

	VERB		ADVERB	
She	speaks	English	fluently.	
He always	listens		patiently	to what you say.
It	rained		heavily	all day.

Note, however, that after a linking verb, we use an adjective: 'She was/looked/stayed very ***calm***.'

⇨ 28.1

2

×	√
× It was an unusual difficult question.	√ It was an unusually difficult question.
× Make sure that the spray is environmental friendly.	√ Make sure that the spray is environmentally friendly.

To modify an adjective ('difficult', 'friendly'), we use an adverb: e.g. '***unusually*** clever', '***perfectly*** correct', '***remarkably*** talented'.

3

×	√
× World peace is a very common debated subject.	√ World peace is a very commonly debated subject.
× These severe handicapped children need special help.	√ These severely handicapped children need special help.

To modify a participle used as an adjective ('debated', 'handicapped'), we use an adverb: e.g. 'a ***frequently*** discussed proposal', 'a ***badly*** managed company', '***poorly*** ventilated rooms', 'an ***amazingly*** boring lecture'.

adjectives: used as nouns 19

1

×	√
× She has spent most of her life helping the poors.	√ She has spent most of her life helping the poor.

Instead of saying 'poor people' we often say 'the poor', using the adjective as a noun. Adjectives used as nouns (and ***-ed*** forms used as nouns) do not take a plural ending: 'He is collecting money for ***the blind***.' '***The injured*** have been taken to hospital.'

2

×	√
× His younger sister is a disabled.	√ His younger sister is disabled.
× By acting as an insane, he managed to escape the death penalty.	√ By acting insane, he managed to escape the death penalty.

Some adjectives are used as nouns ('the poor', 'the blind', 'the insane') and some past participles are used as nouns ('the retired', 'the disabled', 'the uneducated'). These words are nearly always used with ***the*** and refer to all the members of a class or group.

Why do ***the deaf*** receive such little sympathy? (= all deaf people)
The injured were taken to hospital. (= all the people who were injured)

We cannot use them with determiners that have a singular meaning, e.g. *a/an, another, each.*

adjective patterns 20

× I'll be ready for leaving by five o'clock.	√ I'll be ready to leave by five o'clock.
× In my country it is very common that women go out to work.	√ In my country it is very common for women to go out to work.

Adjectives are used in a number of different patterns. Some of the more common patterns are illustrated below.

She is ***keen*** + ***to have*** her own bank account. (+ ***to***-infinitive)
The drawer was ***full*** + ***of*** photographs. (+ preposition + noun)
He is ***interested*** + ***in buying*** a new car. (+ preposition + ***-ing*** form)
She is ***busy*** + ***finishing*** her thesis. (+ ***-ing*** form)
We were ***amazed*** + ***that*** you managed to find us. (+ ***that***-clause)
It would be ***better*** + ***to buy*** a large packet. (***It*** ... + ***to***-infinitive)
It is quite ***obvious*** + ***that*** she doesn't want to go. (***It*** ... + ***that***-clause)

Many adjectives may be used in several different patterns:

She is ***pleased*** + ***with*** her exam results.
She is ***pleased*** + ***about/at passing*** the exam.
She is ***pleased*** + ***that*** she has passed.
She is ***pleased*** + ***to see*** that she has passed.

In some cases, however, only one or two patterns are possible: 'She is ***busy*** + ***with*** her homework.' 'She is ***busy*** + ***doing*** her homework.'

Unfortunately, there are no rules to help us choose the correct pattern. Adjectives of similar meaning often take the same pattern:
They are ***keen/eager/anxious*** + ***to hear*** the latest news.

But there are many exceptions:

He is ***unable*** + ***to do*** the job.
He is ***incapable*** + ***of doing*** the job. (NOT ***to do***)

He is ***determined*** + ***to have*** the operation.
He is ***intent*** + ***on having*** the operation. (NOT ***to have***)

Special care is needed with adjectives that have more than one meaning. Each meaning may have its own pattern:

He is ***afraid*** + ***of getting*** lost.
Students should not be ***afraid*** + ***to ask*** questions.

She is not ***interested*** + ***in coming*** with us.
I'd be ***interested*** + ***to know*** what they said.

In this book, common errors involving adjective patterns are shown at the entry for the adjective, e.g. ***afraid***. If you cannot find what you are looking for, look up the word in a good dictionary, paying particular attention to the examples of usage.

adjectives with prepositions 21

× This part of Greece used to be full with trees.	√ This part of Greece used to be full of trees.
× His daughter is married with a doctor.	√ His daughter is married to a doctor.
× I'm sorry for all the mistakes in this letter.	√ I'm sorry about all the mistakes in this letter.

Most adjectives may be followed by a preposition:
The bottle is ***full*** + ***of*** water.
We're still ***interested*** + ***in*** the idea.
She is quite ***capable*** + ***of*** passing the exam.

Unfortunately, there are no general rules to help us decide which preposition to use after a particular adjective. Adjectives of similar meaning often take the same preposition:
Why is she so ***angry with*** you?
Why is she so ***annoyed with*** you?

However, there are many exceptions:
The new design is much ***better than*** the old one.
The new design is far ***superior to*** the old one.

To complicate matters, the different meanings of an adjective often require different prepositions:
Peter is very ***good to*** his mother. (= kind)
Apples are ***good for*** you. (= beneficial)
Helen is ***good at*** languages. (= proficient)
Derek is very ***good with*** his hands. (= skilful)
The tyres are ***good for*** another six months. (= usable)

Even when an adjective has just one meaning, different contexts may require different prepositions: 'I was ***annoyed with*** John.' (*with* someone) 'I was ***annoyed about*** the delay.' (*about/at* something)

Common errors involving the choice of preposition after an adjective are shown in this book at the entry for the adjective. If you cannot find what you are looking for, look up the adjective in a good dictionary, paying particular attention to the examples of usage.

adverbial clauses of purpose 22

1

× I want to go to France for learning how to cook.	√ I want to go to France to learn how to cook.
× For testing the new microphone, I tried to record my voice.	√ To test the new microphone, I tried to record my voice.

We use ***for*** + ***-ing*** when we mention the purpose of an object: 'This camera is ***for taking*** underwater photographs.' 'This knife is ***for cutting*** bread.'

When we mention the purpose of an action, we normally use a ***to***-clause: 'I bought the camera + ***to take*** underwater photographs.' 'I'm going to the post office + ***to buy*** some stamps.'

2

× He telephoned me for to tell me about his new job.	√ He telephoned me to tell me about his new job.

We never use ***for*** immediately before a *to*-infinitive.

3

× I promised to go with her that she wouldn't be nervous.	√ I promised to go with her so that she wouldn't be nervous.

To introduce a clause of purpose, we can use ***so that*** or (in formal styles) ***in order that***, but NOT ***that*** by itself: 'Take a map with you *so that* you don't get lost.' 'I hid behind the door *so that* she wouldn't see me.'

Compare:

She was *so* nervous + ***that I promised to go with her***.
They ran *so* quickly + ***that I couldn't keep up***.
He is *such* a kind man + ***that everyone likes him***.

In these ***so/such*** structures, the ***that***-clause expresses result.

adverbial clauses of reason 23

1

! I can't buy it for I don't have any money.	√ I can't buy it because I don't have any money.

Nowadays, the use of ***for*** to introduce a clause of reason occurs mainly in formal and literary styles. Instead of ***for***, we normally use ***because, as*** or ***since***.

2

× Since we were late, so we decided to go by taxi.	√ Since we were late, we decided to go by taxi. √ We were late, so we decided to go by taxi.

We do not use ***since*** and ***so*** together in the same sentence. To link two clauses, we use just one conjunction (NOT two). ⇨ 169.2

adverbial clauses of result 24

1

× If a country has no natural resources, so it has to rely on imports. × Since I couldn't sleep, so I got up and went downstairs.	√ If a country has no natural resources, it has to rely on imports. √ Since I couldn't sleep, I got up and went downstairs. √ I couldn't sleep, so I got up and went downstairs.

We do not use ***if/since*** and ***so*** together in the same sentence. To link two clauses, we use just one conjunction (NOT two). ⇨ 169.2

2

×	✓
× She shouted too loudly that the children began to cry. × I was very nervous that I couldn't say anything.	✓ She shouted so loudly that the children began to cry. ✓ I was so nervous that I couldn't say anything. ✓ I was too nervous to say anything.

Before a ***that***-clause of result, we use ***so*** + adjective/adverb (NOT ***very/too*** + adjective/adverb): 'He was ***so tired*** + ***that he fell asleep in the chair.***' 'I laughed ***so much*** + ***that my sides began to ache***.'

Note that instead of using a ***that***-clause with a negative verb, we sometimes use a different pattern with ***too***. Compare: 'It was ***so dark*** + ***that we couldn't see anything.***' 'It was ***too dark*** + ***(for us) to see anything.***'

3

×	✓
× It was a very good film that we watched it again.	✓ It was such a good film that we watched it again.

When a ***that***-clause of result comes after a noun phrase, the noun phrase begins with ***such*** (NOT ***very***): 'I was having ***such*** a good time + ***that I stayed an extra day.***' 'It was ***such*** an amazing story + ***that nobody believed it.***'

Note also the pattern ***so*** + ***much/many/few*** + noun + ***that***-clause: 'She had ***so many*** children + ***that she didn't know what to do.***'

adverbial clauses of time 25

×	✓
× I'll telephone you when I will reach London. × I have to stay here until they will come back.	✓ I'll telephone you when I reach London. ✓ I have to stay here until they come back.

When we refer to the future in an adverbial clause of time, we normally use the present simple tense (NOT *will* or *shall*): 'Wait here ***until I come back.***' 'I'll bring her to your office ***the moment she arrives.***'

Instead of using the present simple tense, we sometimes use the present perfect. This tense expresses a sense of completion: '***As soon as I've finished the job,*** I'm going home.' '***Once you've seen the film***, you'll want to see it again.'

In many cases, we can use either the present simple or the present perfect with very little difference in meaning: 'I'm not leaving ***until I see/have seen the manager***.'

Note that the same applies to ***if***-clauses with future reference: '***If she arrives before Friday***, I'll bring her to see you. (NOT ***will arrive***)

⇨ 163.2

adverbs: form **26**

1

× When I first got the camera, it worked perfect.	√ When I first got the camera, it worked perfectly.
× I don't understand how she could treat him so bad.	√ I don't understand how she could treat him so badly.

When we want to say 'how', we normally use an adverb. Most adverbs end in ***-ly***: e.g. *calmly, happily, peacefully, economically*.

2

× He behaved rather silly.	√ His behaviour was rather silly.
	√ He behaved in a rather silly way.
	√ He behaved rather stupidly.

Some words ending in ***-ly*** are adjectives (NOT adverbs). Common ***-ly*** adjectives include:

brotherly, cowardly, elderly, fatherly, friendly/unfriendly, likely/unlikely, lively, lonely, lovely, manly, motherly, silly, sisterly, ugly, womanly.

Since these ***-ly*** adjectives do not have corresponding adverbs, we have to use either a different structure (e.g. 'in a rather silly way/manner') or an adverb with a similar meaning (e.g. 'stupidly').

3

× He has worked hardly today.	√ He has worked hard today.

Some adverbs have two forms, one with ***-ly*** and one without ***-ly***, e.g. *hard/hardly, late/lately*. Most of these pairs have either different meanings or different uses. Compare:

I've been working ***hard*** all day. (= with a lot of effort)
She ***hardly*** noticed me. (= almost not)

The train arrived ***late.*** (= after the usual time)
I haven't seen John ***lately.*** (= recently)

Common adverbs with two forms include:

clear/clearly, close/closely, dear/dearly, deep/deeply, direct/directly, easy/easily, fine/finely, first/firstly, flat/flatly, free/freely, hard/hardly, high/highly, just/justly, last/lastly, late/lately, loud/loudly, near/nearly, rough/roughly, sharp/sharply, short/shortly, strong/strongly, thick/thickly, thin/thinly, tight/tightly, wide/widely.

The different meanings and uses of these pairs can be found in a good dictionary.

adverbs: comparison 27

1

× She arrived more late than we had expected.	√ She arrived later than we had expected.

Most one-syllable adverbs form their comparatives and superlatives with ***-er/-est:*** 'Gloria works ***harder*** than anyone I know.' 'Who can run the ***fastest***?'

2

× I usually play more better when nobody is watching me.	√ I usually play better when nobody is watching me.
× On the day of the test I drove more worse than a beginner.	√ On the day of the test I drove worse than a beginner.

We do not use ***more*** with a form which is already comparative.

	COMPARATIVE	SUPERLATIVE
fast	faster	(the) fastest
badly	worse	(the) worst
well	better	(the) best
far	farther/further	(the) farthest/furthest

Compare: 'On the day of the test I drove ***more carefully.***'

adverbs: use 28

1

× She always looks beautifully.	√ She always looks beautiful.
× It seemed clearly to me that the man was guilty.	√ It seemed clear to me that the man was guilty.

When we say how an action is performed, we use an adverb:

SUBJECT	+ VERB	+ ADVERB
She	sings	*beautifully.*
He	answered	*correctly.*

After a linking verb, however, we use an adjective (NOT an adverb) because we are describing the subject, not the action.

SUBJECT	+ LINKING VERB	+ ADJECTIVE
Her voice	is	*beautiful.*
His answer	sounded	*correct.*

The main linking verbs are listed below.

appear, be, become, fall ('she fell ill'), ***feel, get*** (= become: 'the engine got too hot'), ***go*** (= become: 'he is going bald'), ***grow*** (= become: 'the children were growing tired'), ***keep*** (= remain: 'I keep fit by walking everywhere'), ***look*** (= appear: 'you look cold'), ***prove*** ('their advice proved very useful'), ***remain, seem, smell, sound, stay*** (= remain: 'you must try to stay calm'), ***taste, turn*** (= become: 'the weather turned warm')

Note that, with the exception of ***be*** and ***become***, the verbs in this list are not always linking verbs. Compare: 'Plants ***grow*** very ***quickly*** in a tropical climate.' 'After twenty minutes, we began to ***grow impatient.***'

When ***grow*** means 'develop', it takes an adverb. When ***grow*** means 'become', it is a linking verb and takes an adjective.

2

× I pulled the string tightly.	√ I pulled the string tight.

If the word that follows an object describes the object, we use an adjective. Compare:

SUBJECT	+	VERB	+	OBJECT	+	ADJECTIVE
She		painted		the kitchen		white.
His answer		made		my wife		angry.

SUBJECT	+	VERB	+	OBJECT	+	ADVERB
She		painted		the kitchen		quickly.
He		closed		the door		quietly.

An adverb tells us how an action is performed.

3

× Many new roads have been built therefore it is much easier to travel from one place to another.	√ Many new roads have been built. Therefore, it is much easier to travel from one place to another. √ Many new roads have been built and therefore it is much easier to travel from one place to another.

Therefore is a linking adverb (NOT a conjunction). A linking adverb often comes at the beginning of a sentence:

> Most criminals realize that they may be caught. ***Nevertheless***, they are prepared to take the risk.

When a linking adverb comes between two main clauses, a conjunction (***and*** or ***but***) is required:

> Most criminals realize that they may be caught ***but nevertheless*** they are prepared to take the risk.

Alternatively, the first clause may end with a semi-colon:

> Most criminals realize that they may be caught; ***nevertheless***, they are prepared to take the risk.

Linking adverbs that are sometimes used wrongly (as if they were conjunctions) include:

> ***accordingly, also, as a result, besides, consequently, furthermore, hence, however, in fact, meanwhile, moreover, nevertheless, nonetheless, on the other hand, otherwise, still, then, therefore, thus***.

Note that linking adverbs are sometimes called 'conjuncts'.

4

× I shall return back to Athens at the end of August.	√ I shall return to Athens at the end of August.

For a list of verbs which are sometimes used wrongly with an adverb ⇨ 840

adverbs/adverbials: position 29

1

× Always he arrives late.	√ He always arrives late.
× I have difficulty often in understanding her.	√ I often have difficulty in understanding her.

Some adverbs normally go immediately before the main verb:

	(AUXILIARY)	ADVERB	MAIN VERB	
She		*usually*	stays	at the Hilton.
He		*almost*	fell	off the ladder.
They	have	*probably*	got	lost again.
You	should	*always*	lock	the door.

Adverbs that go in this position are called 'middle position adverbs'. The group includes:

almost, already, also, always, barely, certainly, definitely, even, ever, frequently, generally, hardly, hardly ever, just, merely, nearly, never, normally, obviously, occasionally, often, once, only, probably, rarely, really, scarcely, seldom, simply, sometimes, soon, still, suddenly, usually.

Note that some of these adverbs may also come at the beginning or end of the clause, especially when we wish to emphasize them: 'I'm surprised that Tina is late. ***Usually*** she arrives early.' 'Don't worry. I'm sure that she'll be here ***soon.***'

⇨ .2–4 below

2

× The rest of my family still is in France.	√ The rest of my family is still in France.
× I shall introduce you to Kumar, who also is a member of the Debating Society.	√ I shall introduce you to Kumar, who is also a member of the Debating Society.

When the main verb is ***be*** (and there are no auxiliary verbs) a middle position adverb normally goes immediately after it (NOT before it):

	BE	ADVERB	
The trains	are	*usually*	on time.
She	is	*almost*	sixteen.

3

× My letters still are being sent to the wrong address.	√ My letters are still being sent to the wrong address.
× My family will be soon joining me in London.	√ My family will soon be joining me in London.

When there is more than one auxiliary verb, a middle position adverb normally goes immediately after the first one:

	FIRST AUXILIARY	ADVERB	SECOND AUXILIARY	MAIN VERB	
We	are	*always*	being	asked	to work overtime.
They	could	*probably*	have	done	the job themselves.

4

× You have to usually pay for the tickets in advance.	√ You usually have to pay for the tickets in advance.

A middle position adverb normally goes immediately before ***have to, ought to*** and ***used to***:

You	*really*	ought to see a doctor.
My father	*sometimes*	used to take me to work with him.

5

! He was too busy unfortunately to see me yesterday.	√ Unfortunately, he was too busy to see me yesterday.

Some adverbs/adverbials express our attitude to what we are about to say, e.g.
sadly, unfortunately, surprisingly, luckily, undoubtedly, frankly, apparently, naturally, of course, on the whole, in short, to be precise.

These 'disjuncts' normally come at the beginning of the sentence:
Apparently her car broke down and she had to come by train.
Of course, we would all be delighted if you could stay longer.

Many of them can also be used like middle position adverbs:
We would ***naturally*** be delighted if you could stay longer.
St. Paul's is ***undoubtedly*** one of the finest buildings in London.

6

× He told us to read carefully the questions. × I like very much living in England.	√ He told us to read the questions carefully. √ I like living in England very much.

An adverb/adverbial does not normally come between a verb and its object.

VERB	+	OBJECT	+	ADVERB/ADVERBIAL
read		the questions		*carefully*
like		living in England		*very much*

7

× I shall be every afternoon available. × Children cannot be expected to keep all the time quiet.	√ I shall be available every afternoon. √ Children cannot be expected to keep quiet all the time.

An adverb/adverbial does not normally come between a verb and a complement.

VERB	+	COMPLEMENT	+	ADVERB/ADVERBIAL
be		available		*every afternoon*
keep		quiet		*all the time*

Note, however, the following pattern:

SUBJECT +	BE +	MIDDLE POSITION ADVERB +	COMPLEMENT
She	is	always	very helpful.
They	are	often	late.

⇨ .2 above

8

× Last August I went with some friends camping.	√ Last August I went camping with some friends.
× He likes in the summer to play golf.	√ In the summer he likes to play golf.

We do not normally put an adverb/adverbial between a main verb + ***-ing*** form (e.g. 'went camping') or a main verb + ***to***-infinitive ('likes to play').

9

× We would like to eventually buy our own house.	√ Eventually, we would like to buy our own house. √ We would like to buy our own house eventually.
× I told him to not be so impatient.	√ I told him not to be so impatient.

Although it is sometimes unavoidable, we do not normally separate the two parts of a ***to***-infinitive.

Note that ***not*** and ***never*** go before the ***to***: 'She promised ***never to do*** it again.'

10

! Rubber became one of the most important materials in the world after the motor car was invented.	√ After the motor car was invented, rubber became one of the most important materials in the world.

The first sentence above is grammatical, but it fails to communicate the writer's main point ('rubber became one of the most important materials in the world'). Normally, we arrange the parts of a sentence so that the most important information comes last. ⇨ 387.3

adverbs/adverbials: sequence 30

1

! It's cheaper to go by train to the airport.	√ It's cheaper to go to the airport by train.
! I waited for two whole hours in the queue.	√ I waited in the queue for two whole hours.

There are no firm rules for putting adverbials in the correct order. Instead of using rules, we follow general principles. The main principle is that the adverbial containing the most important new information goes at the end.

	LEAST IMPORTANT INFORMATION →	MOST IMPORTANT INFORMATION
I waited	in the queue	for two whole hours.
It's cheaper to go	to the airport	by train

2

× She tore the paper into two halves neatly.	√ She tore the paper neatly into two halves.

Unless there is a reason for using a different order (⇨ .1 above) we normally put a shorter adverbial before a longer one. This means that we put an adverb before a phrase, and a phrase before a clause.

	ADVERB →	PHRASE →	CLAUSE
She tore the paper	neatly	into two halves.	
They arrived		at one o'clock	while I was having lunch.
He went	back	to the office	to make a phone call.

3

× We arrived just after midnight in Singapore.	√ We arrived in Singapore just after midnight.
× She has to stay for one more week in hospital.	√ She has to stay in hospital for one more week.

Unless there is a reason for using a different order (⇨ .1 and .2 above), we normally put these adverbials in the following order:

	MANNER →	PLACE →	TIME
The boat moved	slowly	across the lake.	
We arrived		in Singapore	just after midnight.
United played	quite well	at Villa Park	last week.

4

! I'm staying near Cambridge in a youth hostel.	√ I'm staying in a youth hostel near Cambridge.
× She is coming back next week on Tuesday or Wednesday.	√ She is coming back on Tuesday or Wednesday next week.

When there are two adverbials of the same type at the end of a sentence (e.g. PLACE + PLACE), the one which helps to define the other normally goes last.

5

× We went to Kuching last year three times.	√ We went to Kuching three times last year.
! I shall be visiting Paris in July for a few days.	√ I shall be visiting Paris for a few days in July.

When there are two or more adverbials of TIME at the end of a sentence, the usual order is DURATION (how long?), FREQUENCY (how often?), TIME (when?).

	DURATION →	FREQUENCY →	TIME WHEN
We went to Kuching		three times	last year.
I shall be visiting Paris	for a few days		in July.

6

! I was not allowed to go out on my own after dark as a child.	√ As a child, I was not allowed to go out on my own after dark.

For reasons of style, we try to avoid an unnecessarily long string of adverbials, especially when they all have the same grammatical form (e.g. prepositional phrase + prepositional phrase + prepositional phrase). When one of the adverbials provides a 'background' for the sentence, we normally place it at the beginning.

adverbs/adverbials: word order 31

1

× Not once he complained about anything.	√ Not once did he complain about anything.
× Only under special circumstances permission will be given.	√ Only under special circumstances will permission be given.

Some adverbs/adverbials have a negative meaning. The group includes:

barely, hardly, neither, never, nor, only, rarely, scarcely, seldom, not once, at no time, on no account, under no circumstances.

If a clause begins with a negative expression, the word order changes to that of a question. Compare:

SUBJECT		AUXILIARY				
I	+	*have*	+	***never***	+	heard such a ridiculous excuse.
		AUXILIARY		SUBJECT		
Never	+	*have*	+	*I*	+	heard such a ridiculous excuse.

When there is no auxiliary verb, we use ***do***. Compare: 'They never mentioned the cost of the project.' '***Not once did they mention*** the cost of the project.' However, we do not use ***do*** if the main verb is ***be***: 'Rarely ***was he*** in his office when you needed him.'

For information about conjunctions (*not only, no sooner, neither, nor*) and changes in word order ⇨ 169.5

2

× Only if the two sides talk to each other war can be avoided.	√ Only if the two sides talk to each other can war be avoided.
× Only when the cat had kittens we realized it was female.	√ Only when the cat had kittens did we realize it was female.

Sometimes, mainly in formal styles, we begin an adverbial clause with ***only*** + conjunction, e.g. *only if, only when, only once*. When a sentence begins in this way, the word order in the main clause changes to that of a question. Compare:

After she had met him, ***she knew*** that she could trust him.

Only after she had met him ***did she know*** that she could trust him.

3

× Down the rain came, and we all ran back to the house.	√ Down came the rain, and we all ran back to the house.

When we place an expression of direction at (or near) the beginning of a clause, the subject and verb change places. Compare:

SUBJECT	VERB	ADVERBIAL
A white Mercedes	came	round the corner.
ADVERBIAL	VERB	SUBJECT
Round the corner	came	a white Mercedes.

Since the subject is in an unusual position, it receives special emphasis: 'At that very moment, into the room walked ***Melissa***.'
Note that when the subject is a pronoun, the subject and verb stay in their normal positions. Compare: 'Here ***comes Sue*** in her new car.' 'Here ***she comes*** in her new car.' (NOT 'Here ***comes she*** ...')

advertisement 32

× On page 3 there is an advertisement about a new video camera.	√ On page 3 there is an advertisement for a new video camera.

We talk about an ***advertisement for*** something.

advice 33

1

× My headmaster gave me a good advice on choosing a career.	√ My headmaster gave me some good advice on choosing a career.

Advice is an uncountable noun and is not used with ***a/an***. ⇨ 2.1

2

× I would like your advice for how to keep fit.	√ I would like your advice on how to keep fit.

We ask for ***advice on/about*** (how to do) something.

3

× He adviced me to start looking for another job.	√ He advised me to start looking for another job.

⇨ 882.5

advise 34

× I shall never forget my headmaster's advise.	√ I shall never forget my headmaster's advice.

⇨ 882.5

affect 35

× He described some of the harmful affects of smoking.	√ He described some of the harmful effects of smoking.

Affect is nearly always a verb. The noun is normally ***effect***. Compare:
The new tax laws are likely to ***affect*** exports.
The new tax laws are likely to have an ***effect*** on exports. ⇨ 251.1

afford 36

1

× We do not afford to eat in restaurants nowadays.	√ We cannot afford to eat in restaurants nowadays.

Afford is normally used with ***can/could*** or (especially when talking about the future) ***able to***:

How ***can*** you ***afford*** to waste so much time?
I'm surprised that she ***could afford*** a new car.
We'll never be ***able to afford*** a trip like this again.

2

× Some students cannot afford paying regular shop prices.	√ Some students cannot afford to pay regular shop prices.

We say that someone can or cannot ***afford to do*** something, NOT ***doing***.

3

× Not even a short holiday can be afforded by some people.	√ Some people cannot afford even a short holiday.

Afford is not normally used in the passive.

afraid 37

1

× The little boy was lost and spoke in an afraid voice.	√ The little boy was lost and spoke in a frightened voice.

Afraid is not used before a noun. ⇨ 16.1

2

× Many of them are afraid to lose their jobs.	√ Many of them are afraid of losing their jobs.

If we are ***afraid to do*** something, we would like to do it but we dare not do it because we fear what might happen as a result: 'It was so windy that I was ***afraid to open*** the umbrella.'

If we are ***afraid of doing*** something, we do not want to do it or we do not want it to happen: 'He was ***afraid of hurting*** his back.' 'She was ***afraid of missing*** the plane.'

3

× Don't be afraid. There's nothing to be afraid for.	√ Don't be afraid. There's nothing to be afraid of.

If we are ***afraid for*** someone, we feel worried about what might happen to them: 'We felt ***afraid for*** the child and told her to keep away from strangers.'

If we are ***afraid of*** someone or something, we feel frightened: 'Many children are ***afraid of*** the dark.'

4

× Some of the students afraid to ask questions.	√ Some of the students are afraid to ask questions.

The subject of a sentence must always have a verb. ***Afraid*** is an adjective (NOT a verb).

⇨ 96.1

after 38

1

× After three weeks I am going back to France.	√ In three weeks I am going back to France.
× The new offices will be available for occupation after two months' time.	√ The new offices will be available for occupation in two months' time.

When we mean 'at the end of (a period of time which starts now)', we use ***in***: 'Can you come back ***in*** about thirty minutes?'

2

× He came to see me after and apologized.	√ He came to see me afterwards and apologized.
× Five minutes after, the lights came on again.	√ Five minutes later, the lights came on again.

After is not normally used as an adverb. Instead, we use ***afterwards*** or ***later***.

3

× Anyone after sixty should be made to retire.	√ Anyone over sixty should be made to retire.

When we mention someone's age, we normally use ***over***: 'All my friends are ***over*** eighteen.'

4

× After it will stop raining, we can go out.	√ After it stops raining, we can go out.

⇨ 25

again 39

×	✓
× I went again back to the shop.	✓ I went back to the shop again.
× When I got home, I read again the instructions.	✓ When I got home, I read the instructions again.

Again normally goes at the end of a clause: 'His back is troubling him ***again***.' 'I told him not to do it ***again***.'

ago 40

1

×	✓
× It is six months ago since we last saw each other.	✓ It is six months since we last saw each other.

Ago is not used before ***since***. Note the alternative: 'We last saw each other six months ***ago***.'

2

×	✓
× I have seen her in the canteen about ten minutes ago.	✓ I saw her in the canteen about ten minutes ago.

With ***ago***-phrases, we use the past tense (NOT the present perfect).

⇨ 617.1

agree 41

1

×	✓
× I didn't agree some of the things she said.	✓ I didn't agree with some of the things she said.

If we have the same opinion as someone, we ***agree with*** them.

2

×	✓
× I don't agree to send three-year-olds to school.	✓ I don't agree with sending three-year-olds to school.

If we approve of an action or proposal, we ***agree with*** (***doing***) it.

3

×	✓
× Both sides have at last agreed with a United Nations plan to end the fighting.	✓ Both sides have at last agreed to a United Nations plan to end the fighting.

If we accept a plan or proposal, we ***agree to*** it.

4

×	✓
× She agreed waiting for one more week.	✓ She agreed to wait for one more week.

When we say that we will do what someone has asked us to do, we ***agree to do*** it: 'I ***agreed to help*** her with her essay.'

5

×	✓
× I am agree that too much money is spent on weapons.	✓ I agree that too much money is spent on weapons.

Agree is a verb, not an adjective. Compare:

It was ***agreed*** that both applicants should be interviewed. (= it was decided)
Since we are all ***agreed*** on this matter, there is no need for further discussion. (= since we all have the same opinion)

agreement: pronoun/determiner and antecedent **42**

1

×	✓
× This report looks at teaching aids and how it helps teachers.	✓ This report looks at teaching aids and how they help teachers.
× Pupils sometimes suffer in a test when the questions are written in a language which is not his mother tongue.	✓ Pupils sometimes suffer in a test when the questions are written in a language which is not their mother tongue.

Personal pronouns and their related forms agree in number with the antecedent (i.e. the word or phrase they refer back to). Compare:

ANTECEDENT ↓	SUBJECT PRONOUN ↓		POSSESSIVE DETERMINER ↓	
The *tree* was dying.	*It*	had begun to lose	*its*	leaves.
The *trees* were dying.	*They*	had begun to lose	*their*	leaves.

2

×	✓
× The jewellery was given to Mary, who sold them for $6,000.	✓ The jewellery was given to Mary, who sold it for $6,000.
× We get a lot of homework and it is often difficult to finish them.	✓ We get a lot of homework and it is often difficult to finish it.

When the antecedent is an uncountable noun (e.g. *jewellery, homework, furniture, equipment*), we use the singular forms ***it*** and ***its***.

3

×	✓
× Paul and her wife have separated.	✓ Paul and his wife have separated.
× I visited the local library with her collection of rare books.	✓ I visited the local library with its collection of rare books.

When the antecedent refers to a man, boy or male animal, we use ***he/him/his***. When the antecedent refers to a woman, girl or female animal, we use ***she/her/hers***. Compare:

Arthur is now living with ***his*** mother.
Angela is now living with ***her*** mother.

If the antecedent does not refer to a male or female, we use ***it/its***.

4

! An incentive scheme encourages a worker to produce more than his or her colleagues.	√ An incentive scheme encourages workers to produce more than their colleagues.
! Each pupil was told to write their name at the top of the paper.	√ All the pupils were told to write their name at the top of the paper.

When we are talking about a person who could be either male or female, or about a group comprising both sexes, the choice of personal pronoun (*he/she/they*) and possessive determiner (*his/her/their*) is often a problem.

For many centuries, writers have used ***he*** and its related forms to include both sexes: 'If ***anyone*** requires more information, ***he*** should write to this office, remembering to include ***his*** name, address and telephone number.'

Since the 1960s, this use of ***he*** has been criticized by some people for being sexist. To avoid such criticism, some writers today use ***he*** or ***she***, ***his*** or ***her***, etc. However, this usage tends to sound very awkward, especially when it is repeated: 'If ***anyone*** requires more information, ***he*** or ***she*** should write to this office, remembering to include ***his*** or ***her*** name, address and telephone number.'

Many writers prefer to use ***they*** and its related forms: 'If ***anyone*** requires more information, ***they*** should write to this office, remembering to include ***their*** name, address and telephone number.'

This use of ***they*** is very common. However, some careful users insist that singular forms (e.g. *anyone*) cannot be used with plural forms (e.g. *they, their*), especially in formal styles. In formal styles, therefore, it is advisable to avoid possible criticism by making all the forms plural, restructuring the sentence as necessary: '***Those*** requiring more information should write to this office, remembering to include ***their*** name, address and telephone number.'

5

× The company is trying to solve their problem by reducing expenditure.	√ The company is trying to solve its problem by reducing expenditure. (not acceptable in AmE) √ The company are trying to solve their problem by reducing expenditure.

⇨ 147.3

agreement: subject and complement **43**

1

× My two English teachers are also a good friend of mine.	√ My two English teachers are also good friends of mine.
× The country's chief export is oil and gas.	√ The country's chief exports are oil and gas.

The subject and the subject complement normally agree in number.

SUBJECT		SUBJECT COMPLEMENT
My mother	is	a teacher.
My parents	are	teachers.

Note, however, that the agreement rule does not apply if the subject complement has an adjectival function: 'Our history lessons are a bore.' (= are boring) 'These drivers are a danger to society.' (= are dangerous)

Similarly, the rule does not apply when a plural subject has a singular meaning: 'Computers are a recent invention.' (= The computer is a recent invention.)

2

×	√
× The Japanese couple at the back of the coach was obviously newly-weds.	√ The Japanese couple at the back of the coach were obviously newly-weds.

In British English, the verb after a collective noun (e.g. *couple, team, committee*) can be singular or plural: 'The British couple ***were/was*** disqualified.' 'The committee ***have/has*** reached a decision.'

However, when the complement is plural (e.g. 'newly-weds'), the verb is normally plural: 'The British couple ***were*** obviously ***amateurs***.' 'The committee ***are*** firm ***believers*** in the right to strike.'

agreement: subject and verb **44**

1

×	√
× My mother write to me three times a week.	√ My mother writes to me three times a week.
× What happen to the balloon when you let it go?	√ What happens to the balloon when you let it go?

⇨ 620.1

2

×	√
× Even the tall girl were unable to reach it.	√ Even the tall girl was unable to reach it.
× I think that tutorials is quite important.	√ I think that tutorials are quite important.

When the subject is singular, the verb must be singular. When the subject is plural, the verb must be plural. Compare: 'My ***sister is*** married.' 'Both my ***sisters are*** married.'

Note that *-s/-es* at the end of a noun normally means that the noun is plural, while *-s/-es* at the end of a verb means that the verb is singular.

3

×	✓
× An example of these substances are tobacco.	✓ An example of these substances is tobacco.
× The effectiveness of teaching and learning depend on several factors.	✓ The effectiveness of teaching and learning depends on several factors.
× One of the most serious problems that some students have are lack of motivation.	✓ One of the most serious problems that some students have is lack of motivation.

The verb must agree with the 'head' of the subject (the word that the rest of the subject describes or qualifies). In the above sentences, the head of each subject is singular and so the verb must be singular:

SUBJECT = An example of these substances
HEAD = example

SUBJECT = The effectiveness of teaching and learning
HEAD = effectiveness

SUBJECT = One of the most serious problems that some students have
HEAD = One

Errors in subject–verb agreement often occur when the head of the subject is separated from the verb.

4

×	✓
× It was always the brightest students who was asked to answer the question.	✓ It was always the brightest students who were asked to answer the question.
× Some countries do not have enough skilled workers, which cause serious problems.	✓ Some countries do not have enough skilled workers, which causes serious problems.

⇨ 670.2–3

5

×	✓
× All interest are paid without deduction of tax.	✓ All interest is paid without deduction of tax.

When the head of the subject is an uncountable noun (e.g. 'interest'), the verb is singular. ⇨ .12 below

6

×	✓
× The police is investigating the incident.	✓ The police are investigating the incident.

Some nouns which look singular (e.g. 'police') are in fact plural and take a plural verb. ⇨ 531

7

×	✓
× The news are always bad nowadays.	✓ The news is always bad nowadays.

Some nouns which look plural (e.g. 'news') are in fact singular and take a singular verb.

⇨ 530

8

× The crowd outside the gates of the palace were enormous.	√ The crowd outside the gates of the palace was enormous.
× The class was all working hard during the lesson.	√ The class were all working hard during the lesson.

⇨ 147

9

× Getting letters from old friends give me a lot of pleasure.	√ Getting letters from old friends gives me a lot of pleasure.
× To see her again after so many years were wonderful.	√ To see her again after so many years was wonderful.

When the subject is an ***-ing*** clause ('Getting letters from old friends') or a ***to***-clause ('To see her again after so many years'), the following verb is singular. Compare: 'Cigarettes + ***are*** bad for you.' 'Smoking twenty cigarettes a day + ***is*** bad for you.'

10

× Ten years are a long time to spend in prison.	√ Ten years is a long time to spend in prison.
× 90 miles an hour were over the speed limit.	√ 90 miles an hour was over the speed limit.

When the subject is a period of time, an amount, a distance, a speed, etc., the verb is singular.

11

× The house had been broken into but nothing were missing.	√ The house had been broken into but nothing was missing.
× Were anybody hurt in the accident?	√ Was anybody hurt in the accident?

The following pronouns are singular and take a singular verb:

another, anybody, anyone, anything, everybody, everyone, everything, nobody, no one, nothing, somebody, someone, something, what, whatever

Note that although these pronouns take a singular verb, many of them are used with ***they***, ***their***, etc, especially in informal styles: '***Someone*** has forgotten ***their*** umbrella.'

⇨ 42.4

12

× Some of the fruit were going bad.	√ Some of the fruit was going bad.
× Two thirds of the money were spent on laboratory equipment.	√ Two thirds of the money was spent on laboratory equipment.

When the subject consists of ***all, a lot of, any, more, most, some,*** a fraction or percentage + noun, the verb agrees with the noun. Compare:

Most/Three quarters of the ***machinery*** + ***was*** old-fashioned.
Most/Three quarters of the ***letter*** + ***was*** about her holiday.
Most/Three quarters of the ***books*** + ***are*** in the library.

13

× Neither letter were properly addressed.	√ Neither letter was properly addressed.
× Every one of us were given a prize.	√ Every one of us was given a prize.
! Neither of the governments are willing to give way.	√ Neither of the governments is willing to give way.

Each (***of***), ***every*** (***one of***), ***either*** (***of***) and ***neither*** (***of***) normally take a singular verb:

Neither child ***is*** interested in music.
Neither is interested in music.
Neither of our children ***is*** interested in music.

Note that ***neither of*** and ***either of*** may also be used with a plural verb, but NOT in formal styles. In formal styles, the verb is singular. ⇨ 523.2

14

× How many children do Angela have?	√ How many children does Angela have?
× Among her achievements are winning a medal in the last Olympics.	√ Among her achievements is winning a medal in the last Olympics.

Errors in subject–verb agreement sometimes occur when the subject is not in its normal position (i.e. immediately before the verb).

In questions, the subject normally goes after the first auxiliary verb. This means that, in the first sentence above, ***do*** has to agree with 'Angela', NOT with 'children'.

When a sentence begins with an adverbial expression, the subject and verb sometimes change places. The subject of the second sentence above is 'winning a medal in the last Olympics', NOT 'her achievements'.

15

× Italy and India has signed a three-year trade agreement.	√ Italy and India have signed a three-year trade agreement.

When the subject consists of two parts joined by ***and*** (or by ***both*** ... ***and***), the verb is normally plural. ⇨ .16 below

16

× Bread and butter were all we had to eat.	√ Bread and butter was all we had to eat.

Sometimes two nouns joined by ***and*** form the name of a single thing or idea, e.g.

'fish and chips', 'bread and butter' (= bread with butter on it), 'law and order'. After subjects of this type, the verb is singular.

17

×	✓
× For most writers, a typewriter or a word processor are indispensable.	✓ For most writers, a typewriter or a word processor is indispensable.

When the subject consists of two singular count nouns linked by ***or***, the verb is singular.

18

×	✓
× Either the landlord or his wife were not telling the truth. × Neither the principal nor his assistants is in favour of the proposal.	✓ Either the landlord or his wife was not telling the truth. ✓ Neither the principal nor his assistants are in favour of the proposal.

In formal styles, when the subject consists of two nouns joined by ***or, either** … **or,*** or ***neither** … **nor,*** the verb usually agrees with the second noun. In the first sentence above, 'wife' is singular and so the verb is singular. In the second sentence, 'assistants' is plural and so the verb is plural.

When just one of the nouns is plural, it is usually placed last: 'Either the child or the parents ***have*** to adjust.' (NOT 'Either the parents or the child has to adjust.')

Note that in everyday conversation many speakers use a plural verb, even when the last noun is singular.

19

×	✓
× There is two countries that I have always wanted to visit. × In the kitchen there were a table and two chairs.	✓ There are two countries that I have always wanted to visit. ✓ In the kitchen there was a table and two chairs.

⇨ 786.3

aid 45

×	✓
× Poorer countries in the region are to receive more foreign aids.	✓ Poorer countries in the region are to receive more foreign aid.

When ***aid*** means 'money, equipment, food,' etc, it is an uncountable noun and does not have a plural form.

aim 46

1

×	✓
× The medical team has been sent with the aim to train local staff.	✓ The medical team has been sent with the aim of training local staff.

An action is taken ***with the aim of doing*** something. Compare: 'Their aim is to train local staff.' 'They aim/are aiming to train local staff.'

2

× When I turned round, he was aiming a gun to me.	√ When I turned round, he was aiming a gun at me.

We ***aim*** a weapon ***at*** someone or something.

aircraft 47

× The museum contains some of the oldest aircrafts in the world.	√ The museum contains some of the oldest aircraft in the world.

The plural form of ***aircraft*** is the same as the singular form: 'one aircraft', 'two aircraft'.

⇨ 181.5

alive 48

× Inside the basket there was an alive snake.	√ Inside the basket there was a live snake.

We do not use ***alive*** in front of a noun (⇨ 16.1) Instead, we use ***live*** when we are talking about animals or things: 'a *live* mouse', 'a *live* broadcast', 'a *live* match'. When we are talking about people, we use ***living***: 'He is the world's greatest *living* opera singer.'

all 49

1

× By the end of the race, all the runners was exhausted.	√ By the end of the race, all the runners were exhausted.

It is the noun after ***all*** that decides the number of the verb. Since 'runners' is plural, the verb must be plural. Compare: 'All the ***tickets have*** been sold.' 'All the ***money has*** been spent.'

⇨ 44.12

2

× I meet all the kinds of people in my work. × All of the living creatures need food.	√ I meet all kinds of people in my work. √ All living creatures need food.

We do not use ***the*** or ***of the*** after ***all*** when we refer to people or things in general.

⇨ 640.2

3

× All of computers have been repaired.	√ All (of) the computers have been repaired.

⇨ 640.1

4

×	✓
× Thank you again for all.	✓ Thank you again for everything.
× All thanked me and called me a hero.	✓ Everyone thanked me and called me a hero.

All is not normally used on its own (i.e. as a pronoun) to mean 'everything' or 'everyone'. When used as a pronoun, ***all*** is followed by a qualifier: 'Thank you again for ***all you have done.***' '***All I'm trying to do*** is help you.'

5

×	✓
× All the letter was about her holiday in Italy.	✓ The whole/entire letter was about her holiday in Italy.

All is not normally used with a singular count noun ('letter'). Compare:

All the money has been spent. ('money' = uncountable)
He answered ***all*** the questions. ('questions' = plural count noun)
I read the ***whole/entire*** book in one day. ('book' = singular count noun)

Note, however, the use of ***all*** + singular count noun in time expressions: 'The baby cried ***all night***.' '***All my life*** I have wanted to live by the sea.'

6

×	✓
× We gave all them a present.	✓ We gave them all a present.
	✓ We gave all of them a present.

⇨ 640.6

7

×	✓
× The children all were very excited.	✓ The children were all very excited.
× We all have seen a road accident at some time in our lives.	✓ We have all seen a road accident at some time in our lives.

⇨ 640.7–8

8

×	✓
× All of the trees didn't have any leaves.	✓ None of the trees had any leaves.

⇨ 512.6

allow 50

1

×	✓
× The driver would not allow that I take the goat on the bus.	✓ The driver would not allow me to take the goat on the bus.

We ***allow*** someone ***to do*** something.

⇨ 839.1

2

×	√
It is not allowed to talk during the examination.	You are not allowed to talk during the examination.

We do not use ***it*** as an empty subject with ***be*** *(not)* ***allowed***: 'Only the goalkeeper *is* ***allowed*** to handle the ball.' 'Bringing drinks into the classroom ***is*** not ***allowed.***'

almost 51

1

×	√
She almost has decided to give up teaching.	She has almost decided to give up teaching.
One of the cars for sale almost was new.	One of the cars for sale was almost new.

⇨ 29.1–2

2

×	√
There was so much smoke that I almost couldn't breathe.	There was so much smoke that I could hardly breathe.
It was very late at night and there was almost no traffic.	It was very late at night and there was hardly any traffic.

Almost is not normally used with negative words (e.g. *not, no, never, nobody*)

INCORRECT	CORRECT
almost not	hardly
almost never	hardly ever
almost no	hardly any
almost nobody	hardly anybody

3

×	√
Almost all the classrooms are not air-conditioned.	Hardly any of the classrooms are air-conditioned.

⇨ 512.6

already 52

1

×	√
She already went back to France.	She has already gone back to France.

With ***already***, we normally use the present perfect tense. ⇨ 583.3

2

×	√
Joo Teik has left already for London.	Joo Teik has already left for London.
The taxi already was outside the house.	The taxi was already outside the house.

⇨ 29.1–2

also 53

1

×	✓
× The car had also four new tyres.	✓ The car also had four new tyres
× I also have invited Lisa's brother.	✓ I have also invited Lisa's brother.
× There also are people who do not want to get married.	✓ There are also people who do not want to get married.

⇨ 29.1–2

2

×	✓
× I don't like cricket and I don't like baseball also.	✓ I don't like cricket and I don't like baseball either.

After a negative word (e.g. *no, not, never, rarely*), we use ***either***, NOT ***also, as well*** or ***too***. Compare: 'He speaks French and he ***also*** speaks German.' 'He doesn't speak French and he doesn't speak German ***either***.'

Note the alternative with ***neither/nor***: 'I don't like cricket and ***neither/nor*** do I like baseball.' This is slightly more formal.

although 54

1

×	✓
× Although it is only a small town, but it is very popular with tourists.	✓ Although it is only a small town, it is very popular with tourists.
	✓ It is only a small town, but it is very popular with tourists.

We do not use ***although*** and ***but*** together in the same sentence. To link two clauses, we use just one conjunction (NOT two). ⇨ 169.2

2

×	✓
× Although all these problems, I have continued to work on my thesis.	✓ Despite all these problems, I have continued to work on my thesis.
	✓ Although I have had all these problems, I have continued to work on my thesis.

Although is a conjunction, NOT a preposition. ⇨ 882.7

always 55

1

×	✓
× I know always when it is going to rain.	✓ I always know when it is going to rain.
× He always is asking if he can borrow something.	✓ He is always asking if he can borrow something.

⇨ 29.1

2

× Mr Lim always does not leave the office before five o'clock.	√ Mr Lim never leaves the office before five o'clock.

Instead of saying 'always ... not', we use ***never***.

amaze 56

× I amazed when I heard that he was out of prison.	√ I was amazed when I heard that he was out of prison.

The verb ***amaze*** requires an object: 'The news that he was out of prison ***amazed me.***' (⇨ 838.1) To describe how someone feels, we use ***be amazed***: 'The team of inspectors ***were amazed*** at what they saw.'

amount 57

1

× The amount of tourists increases every year.	√ The number of tourists increases every year.

Before the plural form of a countable noun ('tourists'), we use ***number of***. We use ***amount of*** before uncountable nouns. Compare: 'The ***amount of traffic*** has been steadily increasing, especially the ***number of cars***.'

2

× Since the death penalty was abolished, the amount of crime in Hong Kong have almost doubled.	√ Since the death penalty was abolished, the amount of crime in Hong Kong has almost doubled.

After ***an amount of*** and ***the amount of***, the verb is singular. Compare: 'Large *amounts* of paper *are* being wasted every day.'

and 58

1

× She never ate and slept properly after her husband died. × Taboos abound during Lunar New Year – no crying, quarrelling and accidents.	√ She never ate or slept properly after her husband died. √ Taboos abound during Lunar New Year – no crying, quarrelling or accidents.

After ***no, not, never,*** etc, we normally use ***or*** (NOT ***and***).

Note that ***and*** may be used after a negative when the linked items are closely related or are considered as a single thing: 'We didn't bring any knives *and* forks.' 'The regulation does not apply to husbands *and* wives.'

2

× He said he was looking for a tall and blond girl called Anna.	√ He said he was looking for a tall blond girl called Anna.
× Inside the box there was a cheap and plastic watch.	√ Inside the box there was a cheap plastic watch.

When two adjectives are used before a noun, they are linked with ***and*** only if they belong to the same class. Compare:

	blue ***and*** white sheets	(colour + colour)
	cotton ***and*** nylon sheets	(material + material)
BUT	blue nylon sheets	(colour + material)

For more information about linking parts of a sentence with ***and***, ⇨ 178

angry 59

× His parents were getting more and more angry at him.	√ His parents were getting more and more angry with him.

⇨ 60

annoyed 60

× I was annoyed about John for arriving late.	√ I was annoyed with John for arriving late.

We are ***annoyed/angry about/at*** something but ***with*** someone. Compare: 'I was ***annoyed about*** wasting so much time.' 'I was ***annoyed with*** him for wasting my time.'

another 61

1

× We need another information before we can reach a decision.	√ We need more information before we can reach a decision.

We use ***another*** with countable nouns (NOT with uncountable nouns): '***another*** chair' BUT '***more*** furniture'; '***another*** fact' BUT '***more/further*** evidence'. Compare: 'We need ***another*** *piece of* information before ...' ⇨ 2.2

2

× This is another steps along the road towards peace.	√ This is another step along the road towards peace.

Another ('one more') cannot come immediately before a plural form. Compare:

Another glass has been broken.
Another of the glasses has been broken.

3

× Apart from the fish market, there are another developments being planned for the area.	√ Apart from the fish market, there are other developments being planned for the area.

We use ***another*** ('one other') before a singular form. Before a plural form, we use ***other***. Compare: 'She has ***another reason*** for giving up the job.' 'She has ***other reasons*** for giving up the job.'

answer 62

× I always answer to your letters as soon as I can. × There are answers for all the questions at the back of the book.	√ I always answer your letters as soon as I can. √ There are answers to all the questions at the back of the book.

We ***answer*** a person, letter, question, etc, (WITHOUT ***to***). Compare: 'I received ***an answer to*** my letter today.' We use ***to*** after the noun but not after the verb.

⇨ 677

anxious 63

1

× I was getting anxious for the long delay.	√ I was getting anxious about the long delay.

When something causes us to feel worried or nervous, we are ***anxious about*** it (NOT ***for*** it): 'They are ***anxious about*** the shortage of drinking water.'

2

× She was anxious for getting home before dark.	√ She was anxious to get home before dark.

If we want to do something very much, we are ***anxious to do*** it.

any 64

1

× You can use my computer if you don't have any.	√ You can use my computer if you don't have one.

We use ***any*** with plural count nouns (e.g. 'chairs', 'computers') and uncountable nouns (e.g. 'furniture', 'milk'). With singular count nouns (e.g. 'chair', 'computer'), we normally use ***one***.

2

× Do you have any ticket for the concert?	√ Do you have a ticket for the concert? √ Do you have any tickets for the concert?

Any is not normally used with a singular count noun ('ticket'). It is normally used with plural count nouns (e.g. *tickets*, *books*) and uncountable nouns (e.g. *traffic, information*).

When we use ***any*** with a singular count noun, it means 'it doesn't matter which': '***Any doctor*** is better than no doctor.' 'You can borrow ***any book*** you like.'

anybody/anyone 65

×	✓
× Were anybody hurt in the accident?	✓ Was anybody hurt in the accident?

⇨ 44.11

apologize 66

×	✓
× I apologized her for arriving so late.	✓ I apologized to her for arriving so late.
× He apologized all the trouble he had caused.	✓ He apologized for all the trouble he had caused.

We ***apologize*** (***to*** someone) (***for*** something).

appeal 67

×	✓
× I didn't know that you appealed to classical music.	✓ I didn't know that classical music appealed to you.

When ***appeal*** means 'to be attractive to someone', we put the source of the attraction in subject position. Instead of saying 'I like the idea of being my own boss', we might say 'The idea of being my own boss ***appeals*** to me.' Compare: 'The police have ***appealed*** to witnesses to come forward with information.'

appear 68

1

×	✓
× There is appearing to be a shortage of skilled staff.	✓ There appears to be a shortage of skilled staff.

When ***appear*** means 'to seem', it is not used in progressive tenses. ⇨ 627.3

2

×	✓
× In some hospitals appears to be a shortage of beds.	✓ In some hospitals there appears to be a shortage of beds.

Appear must always have a subject. When we mention the existence of something, we use ***there*** as an empty subject. ⇨ 787

3

× In 1991 appeared a much stronger battery.	√ In 1991 there appeared a much stronger battery. √ In 1991 a much stronger battery appeared.

When ***appear*** means 'to become available', we sometimes use ***there*** as an empty subject and put the real subject after the verb. If we do not use ***there***, the real subject must come before the verb.

4

× Making punishments more severe doesn't appear that it makes any difference.	√ Making punishments more severe doesn't appear to make any difference. √ It appears that making punishments more severe doesn't make any difference.

⇨ 708.2

apply 69

1

× They asked about my reasons for applying the job.	√ They asked about my reasons for applying for the job.

We ***apply for*** a job, licence, scholarship, etc.

2

× This paint should be applied on clean surfaces only.	√ This paint should be applied to clean surfaces only.

We ***apply*** paint, varnish, etc., ***to*** a surface.

appreciate 70

× I would appreciate if you could let me know when you receive this letter.	√ I would appreciate it if you could let me know when you receive this letter.

⇨ 838.3

approach 71

× As we approached to the cage, the monkeys got very excited.	√ As we approached the cage, the monkeys got very excited.

We ***approach*** someone or something (WITHOUT ***to***). Compare: 'As we ***went up to*** the cage, the monkeys got very excited.'

approve 72

× Neither of my parents approved my new girlfriend.	√ Neither of my parents approved of my new girlfriend.

When we think that something is good, we ***approve of*** it: 'I don't *approve of* sending young children to boarding school.'

When ***approve*** is used without ***of***, it means 'officially accept': 'The council is unlikely to *approve* the building plans.' 'We are pleased to inform you that your application for renewal of contract has been *approved*.'

Arabic 73

× To my surprise, his friend was an Arabic too.	√ To my surprise, his friend was an Arab too.

Arabic is the name of a language: 'She is learning *Arabic*.' A person whose first language is Arabic is an ***Arab***.

arithmetic 74

× My arithmetics are not very good.	√ My arithmetic is not very good.

Arithmetic (without ***-s***) is an uncountable noun and takes a singular verb.

arrival 75

1

× At my arrival in London, all the banks were closed.	√ On my arrival in London, all the banks were closed.

The phrase is ***on*** (*someone's*) ***arrival***, NOT ***at***.

⇨ 87.4

2

× On my arrival at Brussels, I went straight to the nearest hospital.	√ On my arrival in Brussels, I went straight to the nearest hospital.

⇨ 76

arrive 76

1

× It was very late when we arrived London.	√ It was very late when we arrived in London.
× He will be arriving to Heathrow at 11 o'clock.	√ He will be arriving at Heathrow at 11 o'clock.

We normally ***arrive in*** a town, city or country, especially when it is the end of our journey and we intend to stay there. We ***arrive at*** an airport, bank, hotel, office, school, station, etc.

We use ***arrival in*** and ***arrival at*** in the same way.

2

×	√
× The summit was arrived at just before dawn.	√ The summit was reached just before dawn. √ We arrived at the summit just before dawn.

When ***arrive*** means 'come to a place at the end of a journey', it is intransitive and cannot be used in passive structures. ⇨ 575.5

as **77**

1

×	√
× As I knew she was interested in tennis, so I decided buy her a book about Wimbledon.	√ I knew she was interested in tennis, so I decided buy her a book about Wimbledon. √ As I knew she was interested in tennis, I decided to buy her a book about Wimbledon.

We do not use ***as*** and ***so*** together in the same sentence. To link two clauses, we use just one conjunction (NOT two). ⇨ 169.2

2

×	√
× As I arrived home, I phoned the police	√ When I arrived home, I phoned the police.

In the above sentence, the first action ('arrived') happens before the second action ('phoned'). When there are two actions and one happens before the other, we join the two clauses with ***when, once, as soon as*** or ***after***.

We use ***as*** to show that two actions take place at exactly the same time: ('Henry came in ***as*** Philip went out.') or to show that two actions take place over the same period of time: ('***As/While*** I was cooking the dinner, Rubiah was having a bath.') or to show that one action takes place while another action is in progress: ('***As/While*** I was driving to work, I saw a serious road accident.')

3

×	√
× Suddenly I heard a terrible noise, as a bomb exploding.	√ Suddenly I heard a terrible noise, like a bomb exploding.

When we are making a comparison, we normally use ***like*** (NOT ***as***): 'Helen is very intelligent, just ***like*** her mother.'

We use ***as*** in comparisons when it is part of the structure ***as*** + adjective/adverb + ***as***: 'Helen is ***as*** intelligent ***as*** her mother.'

4

× In some countries, as England, the police do not carry firearms.	√ In some countries, such as England, the police do not carry firearms.

When we give an example, we use ***such as*** or (in informal styles) ***like***.

⇨ 456.2

5

× In Denmark, it is always hotter in July as in September.	√ In Denmark, it is always hotter in July than in September.

After a comparative form ('hotter'), we use ***than***. Compare: 'It is not ***as*** hot in September ***as*** in July.'

as if and as though **78**

! He has been treated as if he was a criminal.	√ He has been treated as if he were a criminal.

In formal styles we use ***were*** (NOT ***was***) after ***as if*** and ***as though***. In informal styles, both ***was*** and ***were*** are commonly heard. However, some careful users insist that ***was*** is always incorrect.

as long as **79**

× We're going to the beach tomorrow as long as it won't rain.	√ We're going to the beach tomorrow as long as it doesn't rain.

⇨ 163.2

as soon as **80**

× I will telephone you as soon as I will reach London.	√ I will telephone you as soon as I reach London.

⇨ 25

as well **81**

× She didn't want to see him again but she didn't want to hurt his feelings as well.	√ She didn't want to see him again but she didn't want to hurt his feelings either.

In negative contexts we use ***either***, NOT ***as well***. ⇨ 53.2

as well as

82

1

× The accident ruined our holiday, as well as cost us a lot of money.	√ The accident ruined our holiday, as well as costing us a lot of money.

When we use a verb after ***as well as***, we use the ***-ing*** form: '***As well as giving*** piano lessons, she teaches French.' ⇨ 882.7

2

! The driver as well as the two passengers were taken to hospital.	√ The driver, as well as the two passengers, was taken to hospital.

When two nouns are linked by ***as well as***, careful users insist that the verb should agree with the first noun ('driver'). In informal styles, however, a plural verb is fairly common.

3

× Bettina plays both the piano as well as the guitar.	√ Bettina plays both the piano and the guitar.

Both is followed by ***and***.

ashamed

83

1

× The ashamed look on her face made me feel sorry for her.	√ The look of shame on her face made me feel sorry for her.

Ashamed is not used before a noun. ⇨ 16.1

2

× I am ashamed of saying that I am very lazy.	√ I am ashamed to say that I am very lazy.

When someone is unwilling to do something because of what people will think or say, they are *(too)* ***ashamed to do*** it: 'He was ***ashamed to admit*** that he couldn't read or write, and tried to keep it a secret.'

When someone feels bad because of something that they have done, they are ***ashamed of/about doing*** it: 'He feels ***ashamed about neglecting*** his family for all these years.'

ask

84

1

× I asked to the air hostess if there were any empty seats.	√ I asked the air hostess if there were any empty seats.

We ***ask*** someone something (NOT ***to*** someone): 'We ***asked the driver*** where he was taking us.' '***Ask her*** how long it will take.'

⇨ 390.3

2

× I asked him how far was it to the nearest town.	√ I asked him how far it was to the nearest town.

⇨ 389.1

3

× The woman asked me a cigarette .	√ The woman asked me for a cigarette.

We ***ask*** someone ***for*** something that we would like to have: 'He ***asked*** me ***for*** my name and address.'

4

× I asked for them to change the shoes for a larger size.	√ I asked them to change the shoes for a larger size.

We ***ask*** someone ***to do*** something (WITHOUT ***for***).

5

× He asked for using my car.	√ He asked if he could use my car.

We ***ask*** (someone) ***if/whether*** we can do or have something.

assist 85

× Our sales staff will be pleased to assist you to make the right choice.	√ Our sales staff will be pleased to assist you in making the right choice.

We ***assist*** someone ***in doing*** something. Compare: 'Will you ***help*** me ***(to) move*** the piano?'

associate 86

× He does not wish to be associated to any political party.	√ He does not wish to be associated with any political party.

After ***associate*** and ***associated***, we use ***with*** (NOT ***to***): 'Most people ***associate*** Stratford ***with*** Shakespeare.'

at 87

1

× We spent the first two weeks at London.	√ We spent the first two weeks in London.

We live, work, or spend a period of time ***in*** a town, city, country or region:

'I live *in* Amsterdam.' 'We spend our holidays *in* France.' 'He has been working *in* the Middle East.'

2

× At the day I planned to travel, I got up very early.	√ On the day I planned to travel, I got up very early.

Something happens ***on*** a particular day or date: '*on* Monday', '*on* New Year's Day', '*on* the following day', '*on* 26th June'. ⇨ 549.1

3

× At the winter we always go skiing.	√ In the winter we always go skiing.

Something happens ***in*** a particular month, season, year, decade or century: '*in* June', '*in* the spring', '*in* 1994', '*in* the 1990s', '*in* the twentieth century'.

4

× At my arrival in Brussels, I went straight to the nearest hospital.	√ On my arrival in Brussels, I went straight to the nearest hospital.

When we mean 'at the same moment as' or 'just after', we use ***on*** (in formal contexts ***upon***):

On my return to Bali, I noticed that many things had changed.
The goods will be despatched *upon* receipt of payment.

5

! Call us during office hours at 733 4593.	√ Call us during office hours on 733 4593.

Users of British English ***call/ring/phone/reach*** someone ***on*** a particular number. To ***call*** someone ***at*** a number is American English.

attend 88

× Most of the people who attended at the book exhibition were teachers.	√ Most of the people who attended the book exhibition were teachers.

We ***attend*** a meeting, exhibition, concert, etc., (WITHOUT ***at***). Compare: 'I'm sorry that I couldn't ***be present at*** the meeting.'

attention 89

1

× Teachers should give slow learners more attentions.	√ Teachers should give slow learners more attention.

Attention is an uncountable noun and does not have a plural form.

2

× She didn't pay attention on what I was saying.	√ She didn't pay attention to what I was saying.

We ***pay attention to*** something.

attitude 90

× Some people have a very poor attitude for work.	√ Some people have a very poor attitude to work.

We talk about someone's ***attitude to*** or ***towards*** something.

avoid 91

× You cannot avoid to speak to someone when you both live in the same house.	√ You cannot avoid speaking to someone when you both live in the same house.

We ***avoid doing*** something (NOT ***to do*** something).

baby 92

× She is going to have baby.	√ She is going to have a baby.

⇨ 3.1

bad 93

× I don't understand how she could treat him so bad.	√ I don't understand how she could treat him so badly.

Bad is an adjective: 'He received very ***bad*** treatment.' ⇨ 26.1

baggage 94

× She had no money to pay for all the excess baggages.	√ She had no money to pay for all the excess baggage.

Baggage is an uncountable noun and does not have a plural form.

be: use 95

1

× She is goes to Spain every year.	√ She goes to Spain every year.

When we use ***be*** as an auxiliary verb, the next verb is either an ***-ing*** form or a past participle. Compare:

This year he ***is going*** to Florence.	(***be*** + *-ing*)
Last year he ***was sent*** to Rome.	(***be*** + past participle)
Next year he ***is being sent*** to Turin.	(***be*** + *-ing* + past participle)

2

× The woman is waiting to see you looks rather angry.	√ The woman (who is) waiting to see you looks rather angry.

⇨ 670.1

be: wrongly omitted 96

1

× My sister now eager to start her new job.	√ My sister is now eager to start her new job.
× Listening to the radio while you are driving often dangerous.	√ Listening to the radio while you are driving is often dangerous.

To join a subject and a complement, we use a linking verb. The most common linking verb is ***be***:

SUBJECT	BE	(ADVERB)	COMPLEMENT
My sister	is	now	eager to start her new job.
Listening to ... driving	is	often	dangerous.

This error is particularly common when there is an adverb before the complement.

2

× A small country like ours must alert to such dangers.	√ A small country like ours must be alert to such dangers.

A modal verb ('must') cannot come immediately before an adjective ('alert'). Between the modal and the adjective there has to be a linking verb. This is normally ***be***: 'The letter ***should be ready*** for posting by now.' 'She ***may be reluctant*** to come without her husband.

because 97

1

× Because I had forgotten my watch, so I didn't know the time.	√ Because I had forgotten my watch, I didn't know the time. √ I had forgotten my watch, so I didn't know the time.

We do not use ***because*** and ***so*** together in the same sentence. To link two clauses, we use just one conjunction (NOT two). ⇨ 169.2

2

× Because the bad weather, we stayed at home.	√ Because of the bad weather, we stayed at home. √ Because the weather was bad, we stayed at home.

Because is a conjunction, NOT a preposition. ⇨ 882.7

3

! The reason I didn't take the exam was because I didn't think I would pass.	√ The reason I didn't take the exam was that I didn't think I would pass.

Careful users insist that ***reason*** (or ***reason why***) should be followed by a ***that***-clause (NOT ***because***). The meaning of ***because*** is included in the word ***reason***.

because of 98

× Because of I had no money, I had to walk home.	√ Because I had no money, I had to walk home.

Because of is a preposition, NOT a conjunction. ⇨ 882.7

bed 99

! I jumped out of my bed and ran over to the window.	√ I jumped out of bed and ran over to the window.

⇨ 532.2

before 100

1

× I came to England about two months before.	√ I came to England about two months ago.

When we talk about a past event in relation to *now* (the moment of speaking), we use ***ago***: 'Her birthday was two days ***ago***.' (= If it is now Wednesday, her birthday was on Monday.)

We use ***before*** when we talk about a past event in relation to *then* (a time in the past): I saw her last December in Rome but our first meeting was two years ***before*** in Monaco. (= our first meeting was two years before last December)

Ago means 'before now'; ***before*** means 'before then'.

2

× The woman sitting before us turned round and told us to be quiet.	√ The woman sitting in front of us turned round and told us to be quiet.

When talking about position, we normally use ***in front of***: 'His car was parked ***in front of*** the house.' 'I wish you wouldn't stand ***in front of*** the television.' We can use ***before*** (or ***in front of***) when talking about order: 'There were six people ***before*** me in the queue.'

3

× I want to have their bedrooms ready before they will arrive.	√ I want to have their bedrooms ready before they arrive.

⇨ 25

begin 101

1

× He stood in the middle of the room and begun to cry.	√ He stood in the middle of the room and began to cry.

Begin (infinitive), ***began*** (past simple), ***begun*** (past participle).

2

× I am beginning writing a book about my father.	√ I am beginning to write a book about my father.
! It's about time they began considering the possibility of further tax relief.	√ It's about time they began to consider the possibility of further tax relief.

⇨ 839.8

behaviour 102

× Society is no longer prepared to tolerate such a violent behaviour.	√ Society is no longer prepared to tolerate such violent behaviour.

Behaviour is an uncountable noun and is not used with ***a/an***. ⇨ 2.1

behind 103

1

× The fighting started behind of the far goal.	√ The fighting started behind the far goal.

We do not use ***of*** after ***behind***. Compare: 'She stood ***in front of*** the television so that he couldn't see.'

2

× I was so angry that I dropped my bags and ran behind the thief.	√ I was so angry that I dropped my bags and ran after the thief.

When we want to catch somebody, we run/drive/etc. ***after*** them. When we walk/drive/etc. ***behind*** someone, we keep a steady distance from them: 'We wondered why Mr Patel's wife always walked ***behind*** him.'

believe 104

1

× Her eyes showed that she was obviously not believing me.	√ Her eyes showed that she obviously did not believe me.

Believe is not used in progressive tenses. ⇨ 627.3

2

× I just couldn't believe in what he told me about her.	√ I just couldn't believe what he told me about her.

If we ***believe in*** something, we think that it exists or that it is good for us: 'I stopped ***believing in*** Father Christmas when I was five.' 'Philip and I don't ***believe in*** dieting.'

belong 105

1

× Do you mean that the whole building is belong to one man?	√ Do you mean that the whole building belongs to one man?

Belong is a verb, not an adjective.

2

× Nobody belonged the suitcase.	√ The suitcase belonged to nobody.

If we buy something, for example a suitcase, the suitcase ***belongs to*** us. Note the alternative: 'Nobody ***owned*** the suitcase.'

3

× All these houses belong His Majesty.	√ All these houses belong to His Majesty.

Something ***belongs to*** someone.

4

× Most of the books we use are belonging to the school.	√ Most of the books we use belong to the school.

Belong is not used in progressive tenses. ⇨ 627.3

beside 106

1

× Beside wasting my time, she was also rather rude.	√ Besides wasting my time, she was also rather rude.

When we mean 'in addition to', we use ***besides***. ***Beside*** (WITHOUT ***-s***) means 'next to': 'I sat ***beside*** the driver.'

2

×	√
The boy's mother went beside the lifeguard and thanked him.	The boy's mother went up to the lifeguard and thanked him.

When we go towards someone and stop in front of them, we go ***up to*** them. ***Beside*** means 'next to'. Compare: 'She went ***up to*** her father and stood ***beside*** him.' 'He walked along ***beside*** her.'

besides 107

1

×	√
I recognized the woman sitting besides him.	I recognized the woman sitting beside him.

When we mean 'next to', we use ***beside***. ***Besides*** (WITH ***-s***) means 'in addition to'.

2

×	√
Besides to like children, a teacher has to have a lot of patience.	Besides liking children, a teacher has to have a lot of patience.

When ***besides*** means 'in addition to', it is a preposition and is followed by an ***-ing*** form.

⇨ 837

3

×	√
He is a good-looking boy besides he is very polite.	He is a good-looking boy, besides being very polite. √ Besides being very polite, he is a good-looking boy.

Besides (= 'in addition to') is a preposition (NOT a conjunction) and cannot be followed by a finite clause (i.e. a clause with a subject and a finite verb).

⇨ 882.7

Compare the use of ***besides*** as an adverb: 'He is a good-looking boy. And ***besides***, he is very polite.' (= 'furthermore') 'I don't feel like going out tonight. ***Besides***, I want to finish my essay.' (= 'in any case')

best 108

×	√
I answered the questions as best as I could.	I answered the questions as best I could.

We say '***as well/fast/soon as*** I could', but we do not use ***as*** after ***as best***: 'She makes a living ***as best*** *she can*.'

better

109

1

×	√
× It is more better if one of the parents stays at home to look after the children.	√ It is better if one of the parents stays at home to look after the children.

Better is the comparative form of ***good/well*** and is not used with ***more***.

2

×	√
× I think you would better count the money again. × You better report the matter to the police.	√ I think you had better count the money again. √ You'd better report the matter to the police.

Had better (*not*) is a fixed expression:

We'***d better*** hurry up or we'll miss the train.
You'***d better*** not let me see you do that again!
Hadn't you ***better*** see a doctor?

3

×	√
× You had better not to tell her she can't go.	√ You had better not tell her she can't go.

Had better (*not*) is followed by a bare infinitive (NOT a ***to***-infinitive): 'You'***d better wait*** here until I get back.' Compare: 'It ***would be better to wait*** here ... .'

between

110

1

×	√
× Between all the photographs Minghui showed me, there was only one of his wife. × The little boy stood between all the people feeling very lost.	√ Among all the photographs Minghui showed me, there was only one of his wife. √ The little boy stood among all the people feeling very lost.

When three or more people or things are seen as a group or mass, we use ***among/amongst***. When there is someone/something on one side and someone/something on the other side, we use ***between***: 'The teacher walked up and down ***between*** the rows of desks.'

2

×	√
× There must have been between 40 to 50 people in the queue.	√ There must have been between 40 and 50 people in the queue. √ There must have been from 40 to 50 people in the queue.

After ***between*** we use ***and*** (NOT ***to***): '***Between*** 1983 ***and*** 1987 she worked for a newspaper.' 'What were you doing ***between*** eight ***and*** nine last night?'

3

× Is it necessary to show advertisements between a television programme?	√ Is it necessary to show advertisements during a television programme?

Something happens ***between*** two periods but ***during*** a single period. Compare: 'Advertisements should be shown ***between*** programmes, not ***during*** a programme.'

beware 111

× The sign on the gate said: 'Beware the dog.'	√ The sign on the gate said: 'Beware of the dog.'

Beware is normally intransitive: 'I told her to beware of pickpockets.' 'Beware, pickpockets!' As a transitive verb, it normally takes a ***wh***-clause: 'Beware how you answer her questions.'

a bit 112

1

× He has brown eyes and a bit crooked nose.	√ He has brown eyes and his nose is a bit crooked.

We cannot use ***a bit*** (or ***a little bit***) before an attributive adjective (i.e. an adjective which is followed by a noun). Note the alternative: 'He has brown eyes and a slightly crooked nose.'

2

× I like to do a bit housework while the children are at school.	√ I like to do a bit of housework while the children are at school.

Before a noun, we use ***a bit of***: 'Going out has been ***a bit of*** a problem since we sold the car.'

blame 113

× Please do not blame young people about these problems.	√ Please do not blame young people for these problems.

We ***blame*** someone ***for*** (doing) something.

bored/boring 114

× It was such a bored film that I fell asleep. × With nothing to do, you soon get very boring.	√ It was such a boring film that I fell asleep. √ With nothing to do, you soon get very bored.

If something is ***boring***, it makes you feel ***bored***.

⇨ 14.3

born — 115

×	√
× Both my sons have been born in hospital.	√ Both my sons were born in hospital.

When talking about the past, we normally use ***was/were born***: 'I *was born* in Athens.'

borrow — 116

×	√
× If he borrows you anything, you never get it back.	√ If he borrows anything from you, you never get it back.

We ***borrow*** something ***from*** someone: 'He has *borrowed* most of the money *from* his parents.' Compare: 'If you *lend* him anything, you never get it back.'

both — 117

1

×	√
× Our both countries get money from oil.	√ Both our countries get money from oil.
× First of all, the both families must agree to the wedding.	√ First of all, both the families must agree to the wedding.

Both goes before a determiner (*the/these/our* etc), not after it. Note that ***the*** is often omitted: 'First of all, ***both*** families must agree to the wedding.'

2

×	√
× Both of suitcases were completely empty.	√ Both of the suitcases were completely empty.

⇨ 640.1

3

×	√
× In my opinion, both you need a good holiday.	√ In my opinion, you both need a good holiday.
	√ In my opinion, both of you need a good holiday.

⇨ 640.6

4

×	√
× Both of the letters didn't arrive.	√ Neither of the letters arrived.

⇨ 512.6

5

×	✓
She looked very tired and her hands both were red and sore.	She looked very tired and her hands were both red and sore.

⇨ 640.7

6

×	✓
We both have come to England to improve our English.	We have both come to England to improve our English.

⇨ 640.8

7

×	✓
Both two stories are based on fact.	Both stories are based on fact.

Both is not used with ***two***.

8

×	✓
Bettina plays both the piano as well as the guitar.	Bettina plays both the piano and the guitar.

Both is followed by ***and*** (NOT ***as well as***).

9

×	✓
She didn't buy both of the dresses because they were too expensive.	She didn't buy either of the dresses because they were too expensive.

'She didn't buy ***both*** of the dresses' means that she bought just one of them. When we mean 'not the first one and not the second one', we use ***either***.

both ... and ... 118

1

×	✓
As far as I know, both Bettina and Mitsuko is having lessons in karate.	As far as I know, both Bettina and Mitsuko are having lessons in karate.

When the subject is a ***both*** ... ***and*** structure, the verb is plural.

2

×	✓
She both lost her money and her passport.	She lost both her money and her passport.
Some people are afraid both of bees and wasps.	Some people are afraid of both bees and wasps.

⇨ 178.9

3

×	√
I would like both more free time and to be given extra help with writing.	I would like both more free time and extra help with writing.
	I would like to be given both more free time and extra help with writing.

⇨ 178.10

bread 119

×	√
I love the smell of a fresh bread.	I love the smell of fresh bread.

We can say '*a fresh loaf*' or '*a fresh loaf of bread*' or '*fresh bread*', but NOT '*a fresh bread*'. **Bread** is an uncountable noun and cannot be used with ***a/an***.

⇨ 2.1

breakfast 120

×	√
There was no time to have a breakfast.	There was no time to have breakfast.

⇨ 532.3

bright 121

×	√
I was never very bright with maths.	I was never very bright at maths.

A clever student is ***bright at/in*** a subject.

British 122

×	√
The woman sitting next to me on the plane was a British.	The woman sitting next to me on the plane was British.

⇨ 504.1

build 123

×	√
A new road has been build along the coast.	A new road has been built along the coast.

Build (infinitive), ***built*** (past simple), ***built*** (past participle).

busy 124

× James is very busy in preparing for his trip to Moscow.	√ James is very busy preparing for his trip to Moscow.

Someone is ***busy doing*** something. There is no preposition before the *-ing* form.

but 125

1

× Although I was tired, but I couldn't sleep.	√ Although I was tired, I couldn't sleep. √ I was tired but I couldn't sleep.

We do not use ***but*** and ***although*** together in the same sentence. To link two clauses, we use just one conjunction (NOT two). ⇨ 169.2

2

× The next morning I was having breakfast in the hotel but was astonished to see the man from the train sitting at the next table.	√ The next morning I was having breakfast in the hotel and was astonished to see the man from the train sitting at the next table.

But is normally used to link two details or statements that are in contrast. It means 'in view of the last point, the next point will come as a surprise'. Compare: 'The car is very ***old but*** it's still reliable.' 'The car is very ***old and*** keeps breaking down.'

When the next point does not come as a surprise, we use ***and***.

For more information about linking parts of a sentence with **but**, ⇨ 178

by 126

1

× She cut the apple into two by a large knife.	√ She cut the apple into two with a large knife.

We do something ***with*** a tool or object: 'She attacked me ***with*** her umbrella.' 'He managed to open the lock ***with*** a knife.'

2

× There were six of us and so we had to go by two cars.	√ There were six of us and so we had to go in two cars.

When we mention a form of transport, we use ***by car***, ***by bus***, ***by train***, etc: 'Are they coming ***by car*** or or ***by train***?

However, we do not use ***by*** when we mention a particular vehicle. Compare:

He usually comes to work ***by car***.
This morning he came to work ***in his wife's car***.

We decided it would be quicker ***by train***.
We travelled ***on the 8.45 Leeds to London express***.

She doesn't like travelling ***by plane***.
I flew back to Singapore ***on a British Airways 737***.

Their children go to school ***by bus***.
You can get to Crystal Palace ***on a 137 bus***.

Note that instead of saying 'We walked', we sometimes say 'We went ***on foot***' (NOT *by foot*). ***By foot*** is used in American English.

3

× I will be at your house by an hour.	√ I will be at your house within an hour.

We say that we will arrive somewhere ***by*** a particular time ('I'll be at your house ***by*** seven o'clock.') or ***within*** a length of time. Compare: 'He said he'd be here ***within*** half an hour, ***by*** eight at the latest.'

4

× As you know by my postcard, I am now in New York.	√ As you know from my postcard, I am now in New York.

When we mention the basis of a judgement or conclusion, we use ***from***:

From this report, it seems that the company is in serious trouble. (= the report makes me conclude that the company is in serious trouble)
You could see *from* his face that he was not at all well.
From what I have heard about her, I'd say that Mrs Jones is bound to get the job.

5

× The policeman thought I had stolen the wallet by someone.	√ The policeman thought I had stolen the wallet from someone.

We take something ***from*** a person or place:

I would never borrow money *from* Denise.
She got her new car *from* the Volvo dealer.
These books are *from* the library.
She slowly removed the letter *from* the envelope.

call 127

1

× I told him that if he didn't go away, I would call to the police.	√ I told him that if he didn't go away, I would call the police.

When we telephone someone (or shout to someone because we want them to come), we ***call*** them (NOT ***to*** them).

2

× Spitzer calls these people as "social junk".	√ Spitzer calls these people "social junk".

We do not use ***as*** after ***call***: 'My friends ***call*** me Joe.' 'Her new novel has been ***called*** a literary masterpiece.' Compare: 'Spitzer ***thinks of/regards*** these people *as* "social junk".'

can/could 128

1

× Some students can not afford the tuition fees.	√ Some students cannot afford the tuition fees.

Cannot is written as one word in British English. It is often written as two words in American English.

2

× She said that she could not to go straight home after school because she had to wait for her father to collect her.	√ She said that she could not go straight home after school because she had to wait for her father to collect her.

Can and ***could*** (modal verbs) are followed by a bare infinitive (NOT a ***to***-infinitive).

⇨ 495.2

3

× The squealing of brakes is quite deafening and could be heard whenever the buses stop.	√ The squealing of brakes is quite deafening and can be heard whenever the buses stop.

In statements, ***could*** refers to the past: 'The squealing of brakes *was* quite deafening and ***could*** be heard whenever the buses ***stopped***. To refer to the present or future, we use ***can***.

4

× I set off at midnight and, by driving non-stop, I could reach Kuala Lumpur by 6 o'clock the following morning.	√ I set off at midnight and, by driving non-stop, I was able to reach Kuala Lumpur by 6 o'clock the following morning.
× The visit was worthwhile since we could gain first-hand knowledge of how a school operates.	√ The visit was worthwhile since we were able to gain first-hand knowledge of how a school operates.

We use ***could*** when we talk about someone's general ability: 'By the age of five, Martha ***could*** swim three lengths of the pool.' When we talk about someone managing to do something on a particular occasion, we use ***be able*** or ***manage***: 'By checking her essay carefully, she ***was able/managed*** to correct several mistakes.'

5

× If the beaches are covered in oil, we could say goodbye to our tourists.	√ If the beaches are covered in oil, we can say goodbye to our tourists.

We use ***could*** to suggest a possible outcome: 'If you aren't careful, you ***could*** have an accident.' To predict a certain or likely outcome, we use ***can***.

6

× As you can know, we have only two weeks to write the report. × According to the latest information available, the detainees can be released at the end of the month.	√ As you may know, we have only two weeks to write the report. √ According to the latest information available, the detainees may be released at the end of the month.

To express possibility, we use ***may*** (possible), ***might*** (possible but slightly doubtful) or ***could*** (possible but doubtful). ***Can*** is not used for this purpose.

7

× With a fresh coat of paint, the school can look much nicer.	√ With a fresh coat of paint, the school could look much nicer.

When we are talking about an imaginary situation, we use ***could*** (NOT ***can***): 'If it stopped raining, we *could* go for a walk.' ⇨ 163.5

capable/incapable 129

× There are machines capable to produce more noise than people can tolerate.	√ There are machines capable of producing more noise than people can tolerate.

A person or machine is ***capable/incapable of doing*** something. Compare: 'She was ***unable to*** talk to anyone.' 'She was ***incapable of*** talking to anyone.

care 130

1

× These irresponsible people do not care for dropping litter.	√ These irresponsible people do not care about dropping litter.

If we feel that something is important, we ***care about*** it: 'All he ***cares about*** is having a good time.' Compare: 'Her mother is being ***cared for*** in hospital.' (= is being looked after) 'Would you ***care*** *for* a chocolate?' (= Would you like ... ?)

2

× The child had never received a proper care.	√ The child had never received proper care.

When ***care*** means 'provision of everything a person needs to keep them healthy and happy', it is an uncountable noun and cannot be used with ***a/an***. ⇨ 2.1

in case 131

1

× Let's go to the airport now just in case her plane will arrive early.	√ Let's go to the airport now just in case her plane arrives early.

To refer to something which may happen in the future, we normally use the present simple tense after ***in case*** (NOT ***will***).

Note the alternative: 'Let's go to the airport now *in case* her plane *should arrive* early.' ***In case*** + ***should*** is slightly more formal.

2

! In case I fail the examination, I shall have to repeat the course.	√ If I fail the examination, I shall have to repeat the course.

If and (***just***) ***in case*** are often interchangeable in American English but NOT in British English. In British English, we use ***(just) in case*** when we are talking about something that we do as a precaution: 'Let's take the umbrella with us *in case* it rains.' 'I always take a book to bed with me *just in case* I can't sleep.'

When we are talking about something that will happen as a result of something else, we use ***if***: '*If* it rains on Saturday, I shall bring an umbrella.' (NOT ***In case*** ...) '*If* you come by train, I'll meet you at the station.' (NOT ***In case*** ...)

catch 132

× I was very lucky that day and catched a lot of fish.	√ I was very lucky that day and caught a lot of fish.

Catch (infinitive), ***caught*** (past simple), ***caught*** (past participle).

cater 133

× I suggest that an extra lane is built to cater to cyclists.	√ I suggest that an extra lane is built to cater for cyclists.

In British English, ***cater to*** means 'try to satisfy needs or desires which are generally considered to be undesirable or depraved': 'Some film makers *cater to* man's animal instincts.' 'I refuse to *cater to* his childish whims.' When the needs or desires are normal, ***cater for*** is used: 'The hotel does not *cater for* children.'

Note that in American English, ***cater to*** is used with both of the above meanings. ***Cater for*** is used in connection with the provision of food and drink: 'Our chefs are not used to *catering for* such large numbers.'

cause 134

× The cause for the accident is still being investigated.	√ The cause of the accident is still being investigated.

We talk about the ***reason for*** something but the ***cause of*** something.

⇨ 655.1

certain 135

× He seems quite certain to be offered the job.	√ He seems quite certain of being offered the job.

When we say that something is ***certain/sure to happen***, we mean that it will definitely happen: 'The new property tax is *certain to meet* public opposition.'

If someone feels certain that they will do something, we say that they feel ***certain/sure of doing*** it: 'The team feel *certain of getting* through to the final.'

chance 136

1

× There is little chance to see her again before she leaves.	√ There is little chance of seeing her again before she leaves.
× The chances of a newborn baby to survive are much better now.	√ The chances of a newborn baby surviving are much better now.

When ***chance*** means 'the degree to which something is possible or likely', it is normally followed by ***of*** + ***-ing***: 'What are the team's *chances of winning* the cup?' 'How much *chance* is there *of finding* them alive?'

2

× In San Antonio I didn't have the chance of speaking much English because everyone speaks Spanish.	√ In San Antonio I didn't have the chance to speak much English because everyone speaks Spanish.

When ***chance*** means 'opportunity', it is normally followed by a ***to***-infinitive: 'I hope that we'll have a *chance to visit* the water village.' 'My parents didn't have the *chance to go* to university.'

change 137

× I asked the salesman if I could change the faulty camera with another one.	√ I asked the salesman if I could change the faulty camera for another one.

We ***change*** something that we don't want ***for*** something that we do want (NOT ***with***): 'I'd like to *change* this shirt *for* a larger size.'

charge 138

× An inexperienced nurse should not be left incharge of a busy ward.	√ An inexperienced nurse should not be left in charge of a busy ward.

In charge is written as two words.

⇨ 883.1

cheque 139

×	✓
× I enclose a cheque of $245.	✓ I enclose a cheque for $245.

We write/receive a ***cheque for*** an amount of money.

children 140

×	✓
× Give your childrens a holiday they will never forget.	✓ Give your children a holiday they will never forget.

Children is the plural form of ***child***. ⇨ 181.5

china 141

×	✓
× They packed all the glasses and chinas in a separate box.	✓ They packed all the glasses and china in a separate box.

China (= cups, saucers, plates, etc.) is an uncountable noun and does not have a plural form.

choose 142

×	✓
× They certainly choosed the right person for the job.	✓ They certainly chose the right person for the job.
× We've chose two very old castles for you to visit.	✓ We've chosen two very old castles for you to visit.

Choose (infinitive), ***chose*** (past simple), ***chosen*** (past participle).

class 143

×	✓
× I am attending evening classes of philosophy and fine art.	✓ I am attending evening classes in philosophy and fine art.

We attend ***classes in*** a subject. Compare: 'Mrs Williams has a ***class of*** 30 pupils.' 'The hotel offers three ***classes of*** accommodation.'

close 144

×	✓
× An assistant came close to me and asked me what I wanted.	✓ An assistant came up to me and asked me what I wanted.

When we go towards someone and stop in front of them, we go ***up to*** them. We normally use ***close to*** when there is no movement: 'The post office is ***close to*** the bank.' 'Our seats were ***close to*** the exit.'

clothes 145

× For the wedding, we all had to buy a new clothes.	√ For the wedding, we all had to buy (some) new clothes.

Clothes is a plural noun.

⇨ 603

clothing 146

× Full-time students are entitled to a 20% discount on all clothings.	√ Full-time students are entitled to a 20% discount on all clothing.

Clothing is an uncountable noun and does not have a plural form.

collective nouns 147

1

× The crowd outside the gates of the palace were enormous.	√ The crowd outside the gates of the palace was enormous.

A collective noun (e.g. *crowd, family, team*) may often be used with either a singular verb or a plural verb: 'The ***team is/are*** playing better this season.'

However, when we consider a crowd, family, team, etc. as a group, we use a singular verb: 'The ***team has*** been banned from playing in Europe.'

When we consider a crowd, family, team, etc. as a number of separate individuals, we use a plural verb: 'The ***team were*** all running towards the referee.'

Collective nouns in common use include:

> ***audience, class, committee, company, crew, crowd, family, gang, government, group, jury, majority, minority, population*** (in the general sense of 'people living in an area'), ***staff, team***.

The names of teams, committees, organizations, etc, also tend to be collective nouns: e.g. ***Leeds United, the BBC, the United Nations.***

Note that, in American English, the verb after a collective noun is normally singular.

2

× I work for a company which make personal computers.	√ I work for a company which makes personal computers.

When a collective noun is used with a singular determiner (e.g. *a/an, each, its, this*), the verb is singular: '***This class is*** getting a new teacher next week.'
When a singular collective noun is used with a plural determiner (e.g. *their*), the verb is plural: 'The ***class were*** asked to stay in ***their*** seats.'

3

×	✓
× The company is trying to solve their problem by reducing expenditure.	✓ The company is trying to solve its problem by reducing expenditure. ✓ The company are trying to solve their problem by reducing expenditure.

When the verb after a collective noun is singular ('is'), all other forms which refer to the noun are singular ('its'). When the verb after a collective noun is plural ('are'), all other forms which refer to the noun are plural ('their').

college 148

×	✓
× My parents couldn't afford to send me to a college.	✓ My parents couldn't afford to send me to college.

⇨ 532.2

collide 149

×	✓
× The two cars in front almost collided into each other.	✓ The two cars in front almost collided with each other.

Two people or things ***collide with*** each other. However, most people would simply say: 'The two cars in front of me almost ***collided***.' Compare: 'The two cars in front almost ***crashed into*** each other.' ⇨ 187

colour 150

×	✓
× He was dressed in a smart blue colour suit.	✓ He was dressed in a smart blue suit.

Colour is not normally used after ***blue***, ***yellow***, ***red***, etc. We use ***colour*** after a colour name only when we are trying to describe a colour which is a mixture, e.g. 'The head and beak of the king parrot are an ***orangy-red colour***.'

coloured 151

1

×	✓
× On the wall was a large coloured photograph of their children.	✓ On the wall was a large colour photograph of their children.

When we want to say that something is not just black and white but has or uses different colours, we use ***colour***: 'a colour television', 'colour printing'. ***Coloured*** is not very common and is used mainly in compounds, e.g. ***flesh-coloured*** (whose colour is like the colour of flesh), ***brightly-coloured***.

2

× She was knitting a blue-coloured cardigan.	√ She was knitting a blue cardigan.

Coloured is not normally used in compounds with ***blue***, ***red***, ***orange***, etc. 'Blue-coloured' means 'having a colour similar to blue, but not really blue'.

combat 152

× We should all try to help the police in their efforts to combat against crime.	√ We should all try to help the police in their efforts to combat crime.

We ***combat*** something (NOT ***against*** something).

come 153

× My father heard me scream and come running into my room.	√ My father heard me scream and came running into my room.

Come (infinitive), ***came*** (past simple), ***come*** (past participle).

come from 154

× My name is Paula and I am coming from Italy.	√ My name is Paula and I come from Italy.
× Some of the best apples are coming from New Zealand.	√ Some of the best apples come from New Zealand.

When ***come from*** means 'be born/grown/made in', it is always in the present simple tense: 'Siti *comes from* Malaysia.' 'These oranges *come from* Spain.' When ***come from*** is used in a progressive tense, it means 'travel from': 'Renata is *coming from* Frankfurt and won't be here until Tuesday.'

common 155

× In my country it is very common that women go out to work.	√ In my country it is very common for women to go out to work.

It is ***common for*** someone ***to do*** something.

compare 156

1

! He was tired of being compared to his elder brother.	√ He was tired of being compared with his elder brother.
× Several writers have compared people with flies.	√ Several writers have compared people to flies.

When we draw attention to the similarities and/or differences between A and B, it is safer to use ***compare with***, especially in formal styles: 'This report ***compares*** the latest figures ***with*** those for the last five years.' '***Compared with*** the new models, my computer is very slow.'

When we are trying to show what someone or something is like, we use ***compare to***: 'In terms of its social impact, the computer could be ***compared to*** the wheel.'

2

×	✓
× Comparing with other countries in the region, ours is very small.	✓ Compared with other countries in the region, ours is very small.

When the meaning is passive, we use ***compared***. ⇨ 397.7

complain 157

1

×	✓
× I complained the assistant that the machine had ruined my clothes.	✓ I complained to the assistant that the machine had ruined my clothes.

We ***complain to*** someone: 'If I were you, I'd take it back to the shop and *complain to* the manager.'

2

×	✓
× They had come to complain of all the noise.	✓ They had come to complain about all the noise.
× The letter complained against solicitors' fees.	✓ The letter complained about solicitors' fees.

We ***complain about*** something that we consider unreasonable or unacceptable.

3

×	✓
× He had often complained about pains in the chest.	✓ He had often complained of pains in the chest.

When we tell someone that we have a pain or an unpleasant feeling, we ***complain of*** it: 'She's been complaining of backache.'

completely 158

×	✓
× I was completely disappointed with the results.	✓ I was very/extremely disappointed with the results.

⇨ 405.2

comprise 159

1

!	✓
! Malaysia comprises of thirteen states.	✓ Malaysia comprises thirteen states.

In British English we do not use ***of*** after ***comprise***. Compare:

Malaysia ***consists of*** thirteen states.
Malaysia ***is composed of*** thirteen states.
Malaysia ***is made up of*** thirteen states.

Comprise of is used in American English.

2

! The second prize was comprised of a six-day holiday for two.	√ The second prize comprised a six-day holiday for two.

Comprise and ***consist*** are not used with ***be***. ⇨ 172.2

concern 160

1

× The book concerns about the destruction of the rain forests.	√ The book concerns the destruction of the rain forests. √ The book is concerned with the destruction of the rain forests.

We can say either 'X ***concerns*** Y' or 'X ***is concerned with*** Y'. Note that is it often more natural just to say 'X ***is about*** Y': 'The book ***is about*** the destruction of the rain forests.'

2

× As far as I concern, the cost of the repair is your responsibility.	√ As far as I am concerned, the cost of the repair is your responsibility.

As far as is followed by ***be concerned***: '***As far as*** my parents ***are concerned***, I can stay in England until I finish my course.'

3

× Some parents have expressed concern for the amount of homework their children have to do.	√ Some parents have expressed concern about the amount of homework their children have to do.

We express ***concern about/at/over*** a situation that worries or interests us: 'The government has expressed considerable ***concern about*** the latest crime figures.' We express ***concern for*** a person, especially someone that we love and care about: 'How can you show such little ***concern for*** your child's future?'

4

× What they do with the statistics is not concerning me.	√ What they do with the statistics does not concern me.

Concern is not used in progressive tenses. ⇨ 627.3

concerned **161**

×	√
× That afternoon I took the camera back to the shop and spoke to the concerned salesperson.	√ That afternoon I took the camera back to the shop and spoke to the salesperson concerned.

When ***concerned*** means 'involved or connected', it goes immediately after the noun it describes. Placed before the noun, it means 'anxious'. ⇨ 16.3

condition **162**

1

×	√
× Apart from a few scratches, the chairs were in perfect conditions.	√ Apart from a few scratches, the chairs were in perfect condition.

When we describe the state or quality of something, we use the uncountable noun ***condition*** (WITHOUT ***-s***): 'The engine is still ***in good condition***.'

2

×	√
× These poor people live in a terrible condition.	√ These poor people live in terrible conditions.

When we refer to the circumstances in which someone or something exists, we use the plural noun ***conditions***.

conditionals **163**

1

×	√
× If you will turn on the radio, it makes a strange noise.	√ If you turn on the radio, it makes a strange noise.

When ***if*** means 'every time' or 'whenever', we normally use the present simple tense in both parts of the sentence (the ***if***-clause and the main clause): '***If*** the water ***gets*** too hot, the kettle ***switches off*** automatically.'

In the main clause, it is usually possible to use ***will*** instead of the present simple: '***If*** the water gets too hot, the kettle ***will switch off*** automatically.

In this type of conditional sentence (sometimes called the *present conditional*), ***will*** is never used in the ***if***-clause.

2

×	√
× If you will go to London, you can stay with my uncle.	√ If you go to London, you can stay with my uncle.
× We're going to the beach tomorrow as long as it won't rain.	√ We're going to the beach tomorrow as long as it doesn't rain.
× Anyone who will get all the answers correct will receive a special prize.	√ Anyone who gets all the answers correct will receive a special prize.

When we are talking about something in the future which may well happen (i.e. there is a good possibility that it will happen), we use a *Type 1* conditional. In this pattern, we normally use the present simple in the ***if***-clause (NOT *will* or *shall*): '***If he passes the test***, I'll be amazed.' 'She'll never know about it ***unless you tell her***.'

Will + bare infinitive (sometimes called the *simple future tense*) is very common in the main clause. (⇨ .3 below) When this form is used in the ***if***-clause, ***will*** expresses the idea of willingness:

> ***If*** you'***ll wait*** here with the suitcases, I'll go and find a trolley.
> ***If*** you ***will take*** a seat, Dr Cook will be with you very shortly.
> ***If*** George ***won't help*** you, you'll have to ask somebody else.

3

×	✓
× If I find your pen, I send it to you.	✓ If I find your pen, I'll send it to you.

In a *Type 1* conditional (⇨ .2 above) the main clause normally has a modal verb + bare infinitive. The modal verb is often ***will*** (***'ll***), which expresses the idea of certainty: '***If*** you go by car, you***'ll get*** stuck in a traffic jam.'

However, other modal verbs are very common: '***If*** you go by car, you ***could/might get*** stuck in a traffic jam.' '***If*** you post the letter today, it ***should/might get*** there by Friday.'

We use the present simple in the ***if***-clause, but not in the main clause.

4

×	✓
× If I would have a lot of money, I would buy my parents a house.	✓ If I had a lot of money, I would buy my parents a house.
× If I would be a journalist, I would be able to travel a lot.	✓ If I were a journalist, I would be able to travel a lot.

When we are talking about an imaginary situation or about something which is unlikely to happen, we use a *Type 2* conditional. In this pattern, the verb in the *if*-clause is usually in the past tense: '***If*** I ***knew*** their address, I would send them a postcard.' '***If*** I ***asked*** him to return the money, he would give it to me.'

Note that we often use ***were*** instead of ***was***, especially in formal styles: '***If*** I ***was/were*** in charge, I would make everyone work harder.'

Also, we sometimes use ***were*** + ***to***-infinitive in formal styles, instead of the past tense: '***If*** they ***arrived/were to arrive*** late, they would have to sleep on the floor.'

Would is very common in the main clause (⇨ .5 below) but not in the ***if***-clause. When used in the ***if***-clause, ***would*** (***'d***) expresses the idea of willingness: '***If*** they ***would sign*** the contract, we could start work.

⇨ .8 below

5

×	✓
× If you had proper lessons, you will make more progress.	✓ If you had proper lessons, you would make more progress.
× If I were to start again, my choice of career would have been the same.	✓ If I were to start again, my choice of career would be the same.

In a *Type 2* conditional (⇨ .4 above) the main clause normally has a modal verb + bare infinitive. The modal verb is often ***would***, which expresses a feeling of certainty: '***If*** you married him, you ***would regret*** it.

Could, ***might*** and ***should*** are also very common: '***If*** you married him, you ***might regret*** it.' '***If*** they left home at two o'clock, they ***could/should be*** here soon.'
Will is used in *Type 1* conditionals.

⇨ .2–3 above

6

× If I would have answered one more question, I would have passed.	√ If I had answered one more question, I would have passed.
× If you watered the plant regularly, it wouldn't have died.	√ If you had watered the plant regularly, it wouldn't have died.

When we are talking about something which might have happened in the past but which did not happen, we use a *Type 3* conditional. In this pattern, the verb in the ***if***-clause is normally in the past perfect tense (***had*** + past participle): '***If*** she ***hadn't resigned***, she would've had her own office by now.'

We often use ***would have*** + past participle in the main clause (⇨ .7 below), but this form is not used in the ***if***-clause.

The past simple tense ('watered') is used in *Type 2* conditionals.

⇨ .4–5 above

7

× If he had been driving more slowly, he would be able to stop in time.	√ If he had been driving more slowly, he would have been able to stop in time.
× If you had spoken to the receptionist, she could tell you where I was.	√ If you had spoken to the receptionist, she could have told you where I was.

In a *Type 3* conditional (⇨.6 above), the main clause normally has a modal verb + ***have*** + past participle. The modal verb is normally ***would*** (***'d***), which expresses a feeling of certainty: '***If*** we'd gone by taxi, we ***would have been*** there an hour ago.'

Could, ***might*** and ***should*** are also very common: '***If*** I'd had the right tools, I ***could have done*** the job myself.'

The modal verb is always followed by ***have*** + past participle, which places the action in the past.

8

× I will be grateful if you answer my letter as soon as possible.	√ I should/would be grateful if you would/could answer my letter as soon as possible.

In polite formal requests, we normally use ***should/would*** in the main clause and ***would/could*** in the ***if***-clause: 'We ***would be*** grateful ***if*** you ***could inform*** us of your decision by Tuesday 27 March.' 'I ***should be*** most grateful ***if*** you ***would look into*** this matter.'

Note that the ***if***-clause normally goes at the end of the sentence.

conduct 164

× The surgeon has been charged with an unprofessional conduct.	√ The surgeon has been charged with unprofessional conduct.

Like ***behaviour***, ***conduct*** is an uncountable noun and is not used with ***a/an***.

⇨ 2.1

confess 165

1

× I am surprised that he has confessed the crime.	√ I am surprised that he has confessed to the crime.

We ***confess to*** a crime or misdeed.

2

× She confessed to have forged his signature on the cheque.	√ She confessed to having forged his signature on the cheque.

We ***confess to doing/having done*** something. Note the alternative: 'She *confessed that* she had forged his signature on the cheque.'

confide 166

1

× There are only two people that I know well enough to confide with.	√ There are only two people that I know well enough to confide in.

We ***confide in*** someone (NOT ***with***).

2

× She confided me that Gianni had asked her to marry him.	√ She confided to me that Gianni had asked her to marry him.

We ***confide*** a secret ***to*** someone.

congratulate 167

× My teachers congratulated me for my success.	√ My teachers congratulated me on my success.

We ***congratulate*** someone ***on*** (doing) something.

congratulations 168

×	√
× Congratulations for another fine performance!	√ Congratulations on another fine performance!

We offer someone our ***congratulations on*** (doing) something: '*Congratulations on* your engagement.' '*Congratulations on* passing all your examinations.'

conjunctions 169

1

×	√
× Although his apology, we were still angry.	√ Despite his apology, we were still angry. √ Although he apologized, we were still angry.
× Because the bad weather, we stayed at home.	√ Because of the bad weather, we stayed at home. √ Because the weather was bad, we stayed at home.

For information about conjunctions and prepositions which are sometimes confused, ⇨ 882.7

2

×	√
× Although I was tired, but I couldn't sleep.	√ Although I was tired, I couldn't sleep. √ I was tired but I couldn't sleep.
× Since we were late, so we decided to go by taxi.	√ Since we were late, we decided to go by taxi. √ We were late, so we decided to go by taxi.
× If a country has no natural resources, so it has to rely on imports.	√ If a country has no natural resources, it has to rely on imports.

To link two clauses, we use just one conjunction (NOT two). If the first clause begins with ***although, though, even if*** or ***even though***, the second clause cannot begin with ***but*** or ***yet***. If the first clause begins with ***if, as, since*** or ***because***, the second clause cannot begin with ***so***.

For information about a similar error in the use of ***therefore***, ⇨ 788.2

3

×	√
× We were unable to visit her. Because we did not have her address.	√ We were unable to visit her because we did not have her address.

In most varieties of written English, a clause beginning with a subordinating conjunction (e.g. ***because***, ***since***, ***although***, ***while***) cannot be used on its own as a sentence.

4

! He wants to go to university. But he doesn't want to leave home.	√ He wants to go to university but he doesn't want to leave home.

In most varieties of written English, the coordinating conjunctions ***and***, ***or*** and ***but*** are not placed at the beginning of a sentence.

5

× Not only computers are faster today, but they are also cheaper.	√ Not only are computers faster today, but they are also cheaper.

If a clause begins with ***not only***, ***no sooner***, ***neither*** or ***nor***, the subject and auxiliary verb normally change places. Compare: '***They have lost*** their jobs and they have lost their house as well.' '***Not only have they lost*** their jobs, they have lost their house as well.'

When there is no auxiliary verb, we use ***do***. Compare: '***He likes her*** and wants to marry her.' '***Not only does he like her*** but he wants to marry her.'

A negative adverbial at the beginning of a clause has the same effect on word order. ⇨ 31.1

consider 170

× Until then, I had never considered to choose teaching as a career.	√ Until then, I had never considered choosing teaching as a career.

We ***consider doing*** something (NOT ***to do*** something).

consideration 171

× I assure you that your letter of application will be given full considerations.	√ I assure you that your letter of application will be given full consideration.

When ***consideration*** means 'careful thought', it is an uncountable noun and does not have a plural form.

consist 172

1

× The book consists eight chapters and an introduction.	√ The book consists of eight chapters and an introduction.

Something ***consists of*** a number of parts or members. Compare: 'The book ***comprises*** eight chapters and an introduction.'

2

× The tool kit is consist of just two spanners, two screw drivers and a jack.	√ The tool kit consists of just two spanners, two screw drivers and a jack.

Consist of and ***comprise*** are not used with ***be***. We cannot say 'is consist/comprise of' or 'is consisted/comprised of'. Compare:

The team ***consists of*** two girls and two boys.
The team ***comprises*** two girls and two boys.

The team ***is composed of*** two girls and two boys.
The team ***is made up of*** two girls and two boys.

3

× The board is consisting of a chairman and twelve directors.	√ The board consists of a chairman and twelve directors.

Consist of is not used in progressive tenses. ⇨ 627.3

consult 173

× They decided to consult with a marriage guidance counsellor.	√ They decided to consult a marriage guidance counsellor.

Users of British English ***consult someone*** (NOT ***with*** someone). In American English, ***with*** is optional.

contact 174

× I shall contact with you again as soon as the dates of the trip have been confirmed.	√ I shall contact you again as soon as the dates of the trip have been confirmed.

We ***contact*** someone (NOT ***with*** someone). Compare: 'I suggest that you get ***in contact with*** one of our local agents.'

contain 175

× Both bottles were containing sulphuric acid.	√ Both bottles contained sulphuric acid.

Contain is not used in progressive tenses. ⇨ 627.3

control 176

1

× The driver must have lost the control of the car.	√ The driver must have lost control of the car.

In the phrases ***take/gain/lose control of***, ***in control***, ***out of control***, ***under control***, there is no determiner before ***control***: 'Iacocca *took control of* Chrysler in 1978.' 'Everything is now *under control*.'

2

× We are no longer able to control over our eldest child.	√ We are no longer able to control our eldest child.

We ***control*** someone/something (WITHOUT ***over***). Compare: 'We have no *control over* our eldest child.' We use ***over*** after the noun but not after the verb.

cooperation 177

× The principal stressed the importance of a good cooperation between teachers and parents.	√ The principal stressed the importance of good cooperation between teachers and parents.

Cooperation is an uncountable noun and is not used with ***a/an***. ⇨ 2.1

coordination 178

1

× The walls were covered with pictures, cards, posters. × I prefer men who are lively, handsome, amusing.	√ The walls were covered with pictures, cards and posters. √ I prefer men who are lively, handsome and amusing.

When a sentence or part of a sentence consists of two equal units, we link the two units or 'coordinates' with ***and***, ***or*** or ***but***: 'Would you like *tea* ***or*** *coffee*?' 'She chased him *out of the house* ***and*** *down the street*.'

When there are three or more coordinates, we link the last two: 'Would you like *milk, orange juice, tea* ***or*** *coffee*?' 'She chased him *down the stairs, out of the house* ***and*** *down the street*.'

2

! I enjoy jogging and I enjoy playing the piano.	√ I enjoy jogging and playing the piano.

When we link parts of a sentence, we normally omit any words that would produce unnecessary repetition.

I enjoy	jogging
	and
(*I enjoy*)	playing the piano.

Note, however, that words are sometimes repeated deliberately to give emphasis, especially in informal styles: '*I don't like* cricket ***and I don't like*** football ***either***.'

3

! He never washes or polishes his car.	√ He never washes his car or polishes it.

When we omit words to avoid repetition, we have to make sure that the final sentence is not ambiguous. 'He never washes or polishes his car' has two possible meanings:

either He never washes (himself). He never polishes his car.
or He never washes his car. He never polishes his car.

The intended meaning is often clear from the context, but this is not always the case.

4

× I hope that you will enjoy your stay and to visit us again soon.	√ I hope that you will enjoy your stay and visit us again soon.
× Mr Leggitt allowed us to interrupt and asking questions.	√ Mr Leggitt allowed us to interrupt and ask questions.

Whenever we omit words to avoid repetition, it should always be possible to 'replace the missing words' and produce a grammatical sentence:

She is packing her bags and (***she is***) ***going*** on holiday.
She should pack her bags and (***she should***) ***go*** on holiday.
She could have packed her bags and (***she could have***) ***gone*** on holiday.

When we replace the missing words in the error sentences above, the sentences that we produce are not grammatical: ' ... and (***I hope that you will***) ***to visit*** us again soon.' ' ... and (***Mr Leggitt allowed us to***) ***asking*** him questions.'

5

! She invited me to sit down and to have something to drink.	√ She invited me to sit down and have something to drink.
× She told me to go and to buy her some tissues.	√ She told me to go and buy her some tissues.

Compare the two patterns below:

Pattern A

	sit down
He invited me ***to***	and
	have something to drink.

Pattern B

	to sit down
He invited me	and
	to have something to drink.

Although both patterns are grammatical, Pattern A is more common, especially in informal styles.

When two actions are considered as a single event ('go and buy'), only Pattern A is possible: 'I've invited them to ***come and see*** us.'

After ***have to***, ***ought to*** and ***used to***, we normally use Pattern A:

He used to | *sleep* in the daytime and *work* at night.

6	
× Interviewees should be encouraged to relax, talk freely about themselves, and to ask the panel questions.	√ Interviewees should be encouraged to relax, talk freely about themselves, and ask the panel questions.
× I am interested in history, politics and in music.	√ I am interested in history, politics and music.

Having chosen Pattern A or Pattern B (⇨ .5 above) we have to keep to it. Compare:

Interviewees should be encouraged to *relax*, *talk* freely about themselves, and *ask* the panel questions.

Interviewees should be encouraged *to relax*, *to talk* freely about themselves, and *to ask* the panel questions.

The same principle of consistency applies to the use of prepositions. Compare:

I am interested *in* *history*, *politics* and *music*.

I am interested *in* history, *in* politics and *in* music.

As with the infinitive marker ***to***, a preposition should be used before the first coordinate only, or before each coordinate.

7	
× He told us about the history of the school, the school curriculum, and a brief speech about his job as principal.	√ He told us about the history of the school, the school curriculum, and his job as principal. √ He told us about the history of the school and the school curriculum, and he made a brief speech about his job as principal.

If we replace the missing words in the error sentence above, the sentence that we produce is grammatical but the last part is illogical:

He told us about the history of the school,
(*he told us about*) the school curriculum,
× and (*he told us about*) a brief speech about his job as principal.

To correct the sentence, we can edit the last of the three linked units to fit 'He told us about'. The sentence is then a single clause with three linked noun phrases:

He told us about
the history of the school,
the school curriculum,
and
his job as principal.

Alternatively, by adding 'he made', we can make the last noun phrase a clause. The sentence then has two linked clauses, the first clause having two linked noun phrases.

He told us about
the history of the school
and
the school curriculum,
and
he made a brief speech about his job as principal.

8

× We found the hotel very convenient and was not too expensive.	√ We found the hotel very convenient and not too expensive. √ We found the hotel very convenient and it was not too expensive.

Linked units must be grammatically equal. For example, we can say: 'She is ***very young*** and ***extremely intelligent***' (adjective phrase + adjective phrase) but we cannot say 'She is ***very young*** and ***an extremely intelligent girl*** (adjective phrase + noun phrase).

In the error sentence, an adjective phrase ('very convenient') is wrongly linked with a predicate ('was not too expensive'). To correct the sentence, we can simply delete 'was', leaving two linked adjective phrases.

We found the hotel
very convenient
and
not too expensive.

Alternatively, we can add *it* to the second unit so that it becomes a clause. The sentence then consists of two linked clauses.

We found the hotel very convenient
and
it was not too expensive.

9

× She both lost her money and her passport. × The visitor can either choose the normal train or the express which stops only at major stations. × The watch is either broken or it needs a new battery.	√ She lost both her money and her passport. √ The visitor can choose either the normal train or the express which stops only at major stations. √ Either the watch is broken or it needs a new battery.

Sometimes two units are linked with a pair of conjunctions, e.g. ***both** ... **and***, ***either** ... **or***, ***neither** ... **nor***, ***whether/if** ... **or***, ***not only** ... **but (also)***. Linking with a pair of conjunctions follows the same basic rule as linking with a single conjunction: it must be possible to replace the missing words and produce a grammatical sentence. This means that the linked units must be grammatically equal.

The most common error is to put the first conjunction in the wrong place. Compare:

	She	***both***	
		lost her money	
		and	
×	(*she*)	her passport.	('she her passport' is ungrammatical)
	She lost	***both***	
		her money	
		and	
	(*she lost*)	her passport.	('she lost her passport' is grammatical)

The two other sentences above display the same fault. When we replace the missing words (the words before the first conjunction), we get:

× (*the visitor can*) the express which stops only at major stations.
× (*the watch is*) it needs a new battery.

To correct each sentence, we move the first conjunction to make the linked units grammatically equal (noun phrase + noun phrase; clause + clause).

10

×	√
× I would like both more free time and to be given extra help with writing.	√ I would like both more free time and extra help with writing. √ I would like to be given both more free time and extra help with writing.

Sometimes unbalanced co-ordination cannot be corrected just by moving the position of the first conjunction (⇨ .9 above) In the first sentence above, a noun phrase ('more free time') is awkwardly linked with a clause ('to be given extra help with writing'). To improve the sentence, we can reduce the clause to a noun phrase in one of the two ways shown.

11

×	√
× The cheese looks and smells of rubber.	√ The cheese looks like and smells of rubber.
× Their children are the ones that I feel worried and sorry for.	√ Their children are the ones that I feel worried about and sorry for.

When we link two units that both end with a preposition, we can omit the first preposition if both prepositions are the same: 'The cheese ***tastes of*** and ***smells of*** rubber.' 'The cheese ***tastes*** and ***smells of*** rubber.'

We cannot omit the first preposition if it is different from the second one: 'The cheese ***looks like*** and ***smells of*** rubber.'

The same principle applies when we link more than two units. As long as all the prepositions are the same, all except the last one may be omitted.

12

× The building is very old and beginning to fall down.	√ The building is very old and is beginning to fall down.

When we link two clauses, we do not omit ***be*** when it is used as a main verb in the first clause ('The building is very old') and as an auxiliary verb in the second clause ('is beginning'). The same rule applies to ***have*** and ***do***:

× She ***has*** a car and ***taken*** her driving test.
√ She ***has*** a car and ***has taken*** her driving test.

13

× My friend had been to London before, but I didn't.	√ My friend had been to London before, but I hadn't.

When there is an auxiliary verb in the first clause ('had'), we use the same auxiliary in the second clause:

Helga ***is*** arriving on Monday and so ***is*** Lucy.
My sister ***can*** swim, but I ***can't***.

We use ***do*** in the second clause only when there is no auxiliary in the first clause:
My friends all bought a copy of the book, but I ***didn't***.
Singapore imports cars from Japan, and so ***does*** Malaysia.

14

× Many of us travel to countries where meals require the use of a fork and knife.	√ Many of us travel to countries where meals require the use of a knife and fork.

When certain pairs of nouns are linked, they always occur in the same sequence, e.g. 'bread and butter', 'a knife and fork', 'a cup and saucer', 'a bucket and spade', 'father and son'.

corner 179

× You should write your address on the top right-hand corner.	√ You should write your address in the top right-hand corner.

Something is ***in the corner*** of an envelope, form, sheet of paper, etc (NOT ***on***)

cost 180

1

× I couldn't understand why the meal had costed so much.	√ I couldn't understand why the meal had cost so much.

Cost (infinitive), ***cost*** (past simple), ***cost*** (past participle).

2

× A child's education can cost to parents a lot of money.	√ A child's education can cost parents a lot of money.

Something ***costs*** someone an amount of money (NOT ***to*** someone).

⇨ 387.1

3

×	✓
× The cost for repairing the car was almost $1000.	✓ The cost of repairing the car was almost $1000.

We talk about the ***cost of*** (doing) something.

countable nouns: form 181

1

×	✓
× Every summer Venice is full of tourist.	✓ Every summer Venice is full of tourists.
× How many question did you answer?	✓ How many questions did you answer?

Most countable nouns have a singular form and a plural form. To make the plural form, we normally add **-s**, e.g. *tourist*, *tourists*; *answer*, *answers.*

2

×	✓
× The suitcase was full of stolen watchs.	✓ The suitcase was full of stolen watches.
× In the city centre there are two new shopping complexs.	✓ In the city centre there are two new shopping complexes.

If a countable noun ends in ***-ch***, ***-s***, ***-sh***, ***-x*** or ***-z***, we form the plural by adding ***-es***, e.g. *match*, *matches*; *bus*, *buses*; *dish*, *dishes*; *box*, *boxes.*

3

×	✓
× The hospital is for women who are about to have babys.	✓ The hospital is for women who are about to have babies.
× Oil has made Brunei one of the richest country in Southeast Asia.	✓ Oil has made Brunei one of the richest countries in Southeast Asia.

If a countable noun ends in a consonant + ***-y***, we form the plural by changing the ***-y*** to ***-ies***, e.g. *hobby*, *hobbies*; *party*, *parties.*

4

×	✓
× Most of the shelfs in the library are empty.	✓ Most of the shelves in the library are empty.
× The two women have spent their lifes helping the poor.	✓ The two women have spent their lives helping the poor.

To form the plural of a countable noun ending in ***-f*** or ***-fe***, we normally just add ***-s***: e.g. *handkerchief*, *handkerchiefs*; *roof*, *roofs*. However, with some countable nouns ending in ***-f*** or ***-fe***, we change the ***-f*** or ***-fe*** to ***-ves***. This group includes ***calf, calves; half, halves; knife, knives; leaf, leaves; life, lives; loaf, loaves; shelf, shelves; thief, thieves; wife, wives; wolf, wolves.***

5

×	√
× The fields were full of cows and sheeps.	√ The fields were full of cows and sheep.
× Give your childrens a holiday they will never forget.	√ Give your children a holiday they will never forget.

Some nouns have irregular plural forms (i.e. they do not take *-s*, *-es* or *-ies*). This group includes:

aircraft, aircraft; child, children; deer, deer; fireman, firemen; fish, fish; foot, feet; gentleman, gentlemen; goose, geese; grandchild, grandchildren; grouse, grouse; hovercraft, hovercraft; mackerel, mackerel; man, men; mouse, mice; offspring, offspring; ox, oxen; penny, pence/pennies; person, people/persons; postman, postmen; salmon, salmon; sheep, sheep; spacecraft, spacecraft; tooth, teeth; trout, trout; woman, women; workman, workmen.

In addition, some nationality words have the same form for both singular and plural reference, e.g. ***a Vietnamese, two Vietnamese*** ⇨ 504.4

6

×	√
× We still don't have explanations for such phenomenons.	√ We still don't have explanations for such phenomena.
× The medias, especially television, have a very powerful influence.	√ The media, especially television, have a very powerful influence.

Some nouns, usually of Greek or Latin origin, have kept the plural form of the original language. This group includes:

analysis, analyses; basis, bases; crisis, crises; criterion, criteria; curriculum, curricula; diagnosis, diagnoses; hypothesis, hypotheses; larva, larvae; medium, media; neurosis, neuroses; oasis, oases; parenthesis, parentheses; phenomenon, phenomena; stimulus, stimuli; stratum, strata; thesis, theses; vertebra, vertebrae.

countable nouns: use **182**

1

×	√
× In my country it is too cold to grow the bananas.	√ In my country it is too cold to grow bananas.
× It is sometimes said that the teachers have a very easy life.	√ It is sometimes said that teachers have a very easy life.

When we mean bananas in general, we say 'bananas', NOT 'the bananas' or 'some bananas'. A plural count noun used for general reference does not have a determiner. Compare:

Bananas are good for you. (general reference)
Some bananas have thick skins; others have thin skins.
The bananas you bought this morning aren't ripe.

Teachers spend a lot of time preparing lessons. (general reference)
Some teachers do a lot of work at home.
The teachers at my school are very friendly.

2

× Incorrect	√ Correct
× Suddenly I had good idea.	√ Suddenly I had a good idea.
× My father is teacher.	√ My father is a teacher.
× Doctor told me to go home and rest.	√ The doctor told me to go home and rest.

A singular count noun (e.g. 'idea', 'teacher', 'doctor') cannot be used without a determiner, e.g. *a/an*, *the*, *this*, *each*, *my*, *which*. The two articles, ***a/an*** and ***the***, are often wrongly omitted. ⇨ 3.1–2, 783.2

3

× Incorrect	√ Correct
× Each school is surrounded by the brick wall.	√ Each school is surrounded by a brick wall.
× She telephoned the police and told them that her daughter had not come home. They asked her to describe a missing child.	√ She telephoned the police and told them that her daughter had not come home. They asked her to describe the missing child.

When we mention someone or something for the first time, we normally use ***a/an***. When we mention the same person or thing a second time, we use ***the***.
⇨ 782.2–4

4

× Incorrect	√ Correct
× There are as much advantages as disadvantages.	√ There are as many advantages as disadvantages.
× There are too many people for too little jobs.	√ There are too many people for too few jobs.

Some quantifiers (e.g. 'much, little') cannot be used before countable nouns.
⇨ 640.3, 202.1

couple 183

1

× Incorrect	√ Correct
× Couple of days was not long enough to see all the sights.	√ A couple of days was not long enough to see all the sights.
× The train should have arrived a couple hours ago.	√ The train should have arrived a couple of hours ago.

A couple of (*two* or *few*) is a fixed phrase.

2

× Incorrect	√ Correct
× I gave him a couple of dollars, which were enough to buy something to eat.	√ I gave him a couple of dollars, which was enough to buy something to eat.

⇨ 44.10

3

× The Japanese couple at the back of the coach was obviously newly-weds.	√ The Japanese couple at the back of the coach were obviously newly-weds.

⇨ 43.2

courage 184

× The girl showed a great courage for someone so young.	√ The girl showed great courage for someone so young.

Courage is an uncountable noun and is not used with ***a/an***. ⇨ 2.1

course 185

1

× I am doing an evening course on computer programming.	√ I am doing an evening course in computer programming.

We do/take a ***course in*** a particular subject (NOT ***on*** or ***of***).

2

! Most of the students in my course speak very good English.	√ Most of the students on my course speak very good English.

Users of British English talk about the students ***on*** a ***course***. Users of American English talk about the students ***in*** a ***course***.

covered 186

× The boot of the car was covered by sand.	√ The boot of the car was covered with sand.

If a surface has a layer of sand/dust/oil/snow/etc all over it, we say that it is ***covered in*** or ***with*** something: 'The table was ***covered in*** dust.'

crash 187

× The car had crashed the back of a petrol tanker.	√ The car had crashed into the back of a petrol tanker.

In a road accident, a moving vehicle ***crashes into*** something. Compare: 'Did you know that Alan has ***crashed*** his new car? Apparently, it went off the road and ***crashed into*** a tree.' ⇨ 149

crazy 188

×	✓
× Some of my friends are crazy for keeping fit.	✓ Some of my friends are crazy about keeping fit.

If someone is very enthusiastic about something, we say that they are ***crazy about*** it, NOT ***for*** it. This expression is not used in formal styles.

criteria 189

×	✓
× One important criteria is staff workload.	✓ One important criterion is staff workload.
× These new criterias make it more difficult for people to emigrate.	✓ These new criteria make it more difficult for people to emigrate.

Criteria (without **-*s***) is the plural form of ***criterion***. ⇨ 181.6

criticize 190

×	✓
× My teachers used to criticize me that I didn't try hard enough.	✓ My teachers used to criticize me for not trying hard enough.

We ***criticize*** someone ***for doing*** something.

crockery 191

×	✓
× 'Whizzo' removes stains from ovens, pots and crockeries.	✓ 'Whizzo' removes stains from ovens, pots and crockery.

Crockery (cups, plates, bowls, etc) is an uncountable noun and does not have a plural form.

crowded 192

×	✓
× The room was crowded of people.	✓ The room was crowded with people.

An area or enclosed space is ***crowded with*** people. Compare: 'A large crowd of people had gathered round the speaker.'

cry 193

×	✓
× Whenever I put the baby down, she cryed.	✓ Whenever I put the baby down, she cried.

Cry (infinitive), ***cried*** (past simple), ***cried*** (past participle). ⇨ 666.2

cure 194

×	✓
× It is doubtful whether he will ever be cured from the disease.	✓ It is doubtful whether he will ever be cured of the disease.

A person is ***cured of*** a disease.

damage 195

×	✓
× The recent floods have caused considerable damages to property.	✓ The recent floods have caused considerable damage to property.

In its common meaning, ***damage*** is an uncountable noun and does not have a plural form.

dance 196

×	✓
× The room is too small for us to dance this kind of music.	✓ The room is too small for us to dance to this kind of music.
× We like dancing with disco music.	✓ We like dancing to disco music.

We ***dance to*** (a type of) music.

danger 197

1

×	✓
× I realized that the little girl was in a great danger.	✓ I realized that the little girl was in great danger.

In the phrases ***in*** *(adjective)* ***danger*** and ***out of danger***, ***danger*** is an uncountable noun and is not used with ***a/an***. ⇨ 532.4

2

×	✓
× These forests are in danger to be destroyed.	✓ These forests are in danger of being destroyed.

The phrase ***in danger*** is followed by ***of*** + ***-ing*** form: 'She is ***in danger of losing*** her job.'

dare 198

1

×	✓
× She dared me follow her across the bridge.	✓ She dared me to follow her across the bridge.

If we challenge someone to do something, we ***dare*** them ***to do*** it.

2

×	I daren't to tell her that I've lost her keys.	√	I daren't tell her that I've lost her keys.
×	How dare they to accuse you of cheating!	√	How dare they accuse you of cheating!

When ***dare*** means 'to have enough courage', it can be used either as a modal verb or as a main verb. As a modal verb, it takes a bare infinitive: 'She ***daren't walk*** home alone at night.' (NOT ***to walk***) 'How ***dare*** you ***speak*** to me like that!' (NOT ***to speak***)

As a main verb, it takes either a bare infinitive or a ***to***-infinitive: 'I don't/wouldn't ***dare (to) tell*** her that I've lost her keys.'

dates 199

1

×	I am going to Athens at 20th December.	√	I am going to Athens on 20th December.

Something happens ***on*** a particular ***date***: 'on 7th April', 'on October 3rd'.

2

×	My holiday begins on March the 8th.	√	My holiday begins on March 8th.
×	I arrived in England on the 14th of June, 1990.	√	I arrived in England on 14th June, 1990

When we write the date, we do not use 'the' or 'of'. We use 'the' and 'of' only when we say the date.

3

×	22th July, 1994	√	22nd July, 1994

When we write the day of the month, we do not add the letters ***-th*** to ***1***, ***2*** or ***3*** or to numbers ending in ***1***, ***2*** or ***3***.

We add ***-st*** (fir***st***) to ***1***, ***21***, ***31***: 1st, 21st, 31st
We add ***-nd*** (seco***nd***) to ***2*** and ***22***: 2nd, 22nd
We add ***-rd*** (thi***rd***) to ***3*** and ***23***: 3rd, 23rd
We add ***-th*** (four***th***, fif***th***, etc) to all other numbers: e.g. 4th, 5th, 11th

Note that the day of the month can be written without letters after the number: '22 July 1994', 'July 22, 1994'.

day 200

1

×	Unfortunately, my sister's party is at the same day.	√	Unfortunately, my sister's party is on the same day.

Something happens ***on*** a particular day: 'on Saturday', 'on New Year's Day', 'on my birthday', 'on the following day', 'on the day before the meeting'. ⇨ 549.1

2

× How many of us clean our teeth three times in a day?	√ How many of us clean our teeth three times a day?

⇨ 383.1

3

× Unemployment is a major problem in these days.	√ Unemployment is a major problem these days.

⇨ 383.6

dead 201

× The driver of the green car was dead on the way to hospital.	√ The driver of the green car died on the way to hospital.

When we mean 'to stop being alive', we use the verb ***die*** (past tense and past participle ***died***): 'My grandfather ***died*** before I was born.'

We use ***dead*** (an adjective) to describe the state of someone or something that is no longer alive: 'If there are no leaves on the tree, it must be ***dead***.'

⇨ 220

deal 202

1

× We've already received a great deal of enquiries about it.	√ We've already received a large number of enquiries about it.
× The children were busy making a great deal of sandcastles.	√ The children were busy making a lot of sandcastles.

A great/good deal of is used only with uncountable nouns: '***a great deal of*** money', '***a good deal of*** patience'.

⇨ 640.3

2

× The book deals about castles in Scotland.	√ The book deals with castles in Scotland.
× The play deals in the struggle of a married couple to live their own lives.	√ The play deals with the struggle of a married couple to live their own lives.

A book, film, lecture, etc. ***deals with*** a particular subject, NOT ***about*** or ***in***. Compare: 'The book ***is about*** castles in Scotland.'

3

×	✓
× An established motor trading company dealing with popular Japanese cars requires two additional salesmen.	✓ An established motor trading company dealing in popular Japanese cars requires two additional salesmen.

A company ***deals in*** something that it buys and sells, NOT ***with***.

decrease 203

×	✓
× The decrease of the infant mortality rate is the result of better health care services.	✓ The decrease in the infant mortality rate is the result of better health care services.

We talk about a **decrease/*increase in*** something, NOT ***of***.

delay 204

1

×	✓
× I'm sorry that I delayed to answer your last letter.	✓ I'm sorry that I delayed answering your last letter.

We ***delay doing*** something, NOT ***to do***.

2

×	✓
× There are several reasons for our delay to reprint the book.	✓ There are several reasons for our delay in reprinting the book.

We talk about a ***delay in doing*** something: 'We would like to apologize for the ***delay in despatching*** the goods.'

delighted 205

×	✓
× I was very delighted to see my name on the list.	✓ I was (absolutely) delighted to see my name on the list.

⇨ 405.1

demand 206

1

×	✓
× Some employers demand for very high qualifications.	✓ Some employers demand very high qualifications.

We ***ask for*** something but we ***demand*** something (WITHOUT ***for***): 'The staff who have lost their jobs are ***demanding*** compensation.' Compare: 'There is a growing ***demand for*** part-time teachers.' We use ***for*** after the noun, but not after the verb.

2

×	√
They have demanded all copies of the book to be destroyed.	They have demanded that all copies of the book (should) be destroyed.

We ***demand that*** someone (***should***) ***do*** something, or ***that*** something (***should***) ***be done***.
⇨ 839.9

demonstratives 207

1

×	√
These photograph was taken at my grandparents' house.	This photograph was taken at my grandparents' house.
	These photographs were taken at my grandparents' house.
The school's outdoor facilities are better than that of many country clubs.	The school's outdoor facilities are better than those of many country clubs.

A demonstrative determiner/pronoun agrees with the number of the noun that it precedes or replaces.

SINGULAR	PLURAL
this	these
that	those

2

×	√
Who is responsible for the maintenance of these equipment?	Who is responsible for the maintenance of this equipment?
All junk food, especially those sold at the canteen, should be avoided.	All junk food, especially that sold at the canteen, should be avoided.

When a demonstrative precedes or replaces an uncountable noun ('equipment', 'food'), we use a singular form (***this/that***).

deny 208

1

×	√
He denied to open the letter and I believed him.	He denied opening the letter and I believed him.

We ***deny doing*** something, NOT ***to do*** something.

2

×	√
I was sure that one of them had taken the watch, even though they all denied.	I was sure that one of them had taken the watch, even though they all denied it.

Deny is a transitive verb and must have an object.
⇨ 838.1

3

×	✓
× The chairman strongly denies knowing something about the report.	✓ The chairman strongly denies knowing anything about the report.

⇨ 733.3

depart 209

×	✓
× With tears in our eyes, we watched her train slowly depart the platform.	✓ With tears in our eyes, we watched her train slowly depart from the platform.

We ***depart from*** the place that we leave (***for*** our destination).

departure 210

×	✓
× The flight departures from Athens airport at 9.30 a.m.	✓ The flight departs from Athens airport at 9.30 a.m.

Departure is a noun: 'The ***departure*** of SQ398 was delayed as a result of technical problems.' 'We waited in the ***departure*** lounge.' The verb is ***depart***.

depend 211

1

×	✓
× The cost of the trip depends whether we can get everybody into one coach.	✓ The cost of the trip depends on whether we can get everybody into one coach.
× Nowadays a lot of people depend from machines.	✓ Nowadays a lot of people depend on machines.

Something ***depends on/upon*** something else. The only time that we can omit ***on/upon*** after ***depend*** is when we use the fixed expression: ***It depends***: 'How much will the trip cost?' 'I'm not sure. ***It depends***.'

2

×	✓
× Your child's future is depend on your decision.	✓ Your child's future depends on your decision.

Depend is a verb. Compare: 'He is ***dependent*** on his parents for financial support.'

3

×	✓
× I think depends on how much you trust the person.	✓ I think it depends on how much you trust the person.

Depend (on/upon) must have a subject. In the absence of a real subject, we normally use ***it***.

4

×	✓
× Your choice of hotel is depending on how much you want to pay.	✓ Your choice of hotel depends on how much you want to pay.

When ***depend*** means 'to be decided by', it is not used in progressive tenses. (⇨ 627.3) Note that ***depending on*** is a preposition: 'The journey should take about three hours, ***depending on*** how many stops we make.'

describe 212

1

×	✓
× In her first book she describes about her childhood.	✓ In her first book she describes her childhood.

We ***talk about*** or ***write about*** something, but we ***describe*** something (NOT ***about*** something).

2

×	✓
× I described her exactly what had happened.	✓ I described (to her) exactly what had happened.

With ***describe***, we use ***to*** before an indirect object, even when the indirect object comes before the direct object. ⇨ 387.1

Note, however, that an indirect object is often unnecessary: 'He *described* all the places he had visited.' We do not have to say 'She *described to us* … .'

description 213

×	✓
× The book begins with a long description on a team manager's responsibilities.	✓ The book begins with a long description of a team manager's responsibilities.

We give a ***description of*** someone or something.

desire 214

×	✓
× He promised to give her anything she desired for.	✓ He promised to give her anything she desired.

We ***ask for*** something but we ***desire*** something (without ***for***). Compare: 'They have begun to express a growing ***desire for*** independence.' We use ***for*** after the noun, but not after the verb.

desperate 215

×	✓
× When the doors wouldn't open, I began to feel very desperate.	✓ When the doors wouldn't open, I began to feel desperate.

⇨ 405.1

despite 216

1

× Despite he is much older than our other teachers, he makes us all laugh.	√ Although he is much older than our other teachers, he makes us all laugh. √ Despite the fact that he is much older than our other teachers, he makes us all laugh. √ Despite (his) being much older than our other teachers, he makes us all laugh.

Despite and ***in spite of*** are prepositions, NOT conjunctions. ⇨ 882.7

2

× Despite of the heavy traffic, we arrived on time.	√ Despite the heavy traffic, we arrived on time. √ In spite of the heavy traffic, we arrived on time.

We do not use ***of*** after ***despite***.

detail 217

1

× At the police station I described in details what I had seen.	√ At the police station I described in detail what I had seen.

In the phrase ***in detail***, ***detail*** is an uncountable noun and does not have a plural form.

2

× I am sending you the details for my travel arrangements.	√ I am sending you the details of my travel arrangements.

The noun ***details*** is followed by ***of*** (NOT ***for***): 'Further ***details of*** the agreement are yet to be released.'

deter 218

× These reports have deterred some women to have the operation.	√ These reports have deterred some women from having the operation.

If something makes us decide not to do what we had intended to do, it ***deters*** us ***from doing*** it, NOT ***to do*** it. ⇨ 841.3

die 219

× People say that she died with pneumonia.	√ People say that she died of pneumonia.

We ***die of*** or ***from*** a disease, hunger, natural causes, etc.

died 220

× The woman in the front passenger seat was already died.	√ The woman in the front passenger seat was already dead.

To describe the state of someone or something that has stopped living, we use the adjective ***dead***. ***Died*** is the past tense and past participle of the verb ***die***, 'to stop living'.

⇨ 201

differ 221

× Lambroso's ideas about criminals differ to Sheldon's in a number of ways.	√ Lambroso's ideas about criminals differ from Sheldon's in a number of ways.

Something ***differs from*** something else, NOT ***to***.

different 222

1

× My new boyfriend is very different than the last one.	√ My new boyfriend is very different from the last one.

Careful users of British English prefer ***different from***, although ***different to*** is quite common, especially in informal styles.

Different than occurs mainly in American English but is sometimes used in British English to avoid awkwardness. Compare: 'Her mother was ***different than*** I had expected.' 'Her mother was ***different from*** the person that I had expected.'

2

× The new government is not different from the last one.	√ The new government is no different from the last one.

When ***different*** is used in predicative position, we make it negative with ***no***. (Usually, we use ***no*** only with comparative forms: 'Their house is ***no bigger*** than ours.')

3

× People's ideas about what makes a good holiday are different.	√ People have different ideas about what makes a good holiday.

When ***different*** means 'various', it goes before the noun that it refers to: 'There are ***different*** ways of looking at the problem.'

Note the alternative: 'People's ideas about what makes a good holiday ***vary***.'

difficulty **223**

1

×	√
× Her family had great difficulty to get her transferred to another hospital.	√ Her family had great difficulty in getting her transferred to another hospital.

Someone has ***difficulty in doing*** something. In informal style, ***in*** is often omitted: 'Let me know if you have any ***difficulty obtaining*** the book.'

2

×	√
× A lot of people in Athens have a difficulty in breathing.	√ A lot of people in Athens have difficulty in breathing.

⇨ 532.4

3

×	√
× You won't have any difficulties in recognizing him.	√ You won't have any difficulty in recognizing him.

In the phrase ***have difficulty (in)***, ***difficulty*** is an uncountable noun and does not have a plural form.

dirt **224**

×	√
× He had dirts all over his face and hands.	√ He had dirt all over his face and hands.

Dirt is an uncountable noun and does not have a plural form.

disagree **225**

1

×	√
× Weber disagreed to Marx about the need to abolish private ownership.	√ Weber disagreed with Marx about the need to abolish private ownership.

When we do not have the same opinion as someone, we ***disagree with*** them (***about/on*** something).

2

×	√
× I completely disagree to pay women less than men.	√ I completely disagree with paying women less than men.

When we think that (doing) something is wrong or unjust, we ***disagree with (doing)*** it.

disallow 226

× The new rule will disallow accountants to charge what they like.	√ The new rule will stop accountants from charging what they like.

We ***allow*** someone ***to do*** something but we ***disallow*** something: 'The court has *disallowed* the claim.' 'The goal was *disallowed*.'

Disallow (to refuse to accept or recognize) is followed by an object (NOT an object + *to*-infinitive).

disappeared 227

× When I turned round, the woman was disappeared.	√ When I turned round, the woman had disappeared.

Disappeared is not used as an adjective and cannot come after ***be***. Compare: 'When I turned round, the woman ***was gone***.'

discourage 228

× Let us consider some of the factors which discourage Singaporeans to marry and produce babies.	√ Let us consider some of the factors which discourage Singaporeans from marrying and producing babies.

We ***encourage*** someone ***to do*** something but ***discourage*** someone ***from doing*** something.

discuss 229

1

× We will be discussing about the role of television in education.	√ We will be discussing the role of television in education.

We ***discuss*** something, NOT *about* something. Compare: 'We had a long ***discussion about*** the role of television in education.' We use *about* after the noun, but not after the verb.

⇨ 841.1

2

× I have discussed with Jean and we agree that the books should be no longer than 32 pages.	√ I have discussed the matter with Jean and we agree that the books should be no longer than 32 pages.
× If a mother doesn't have a job, she has more time to discuss with her children about their problems.	√ If a mother doesn't have a job, she has more time to talk to her children about their problems.
× Union leaders spent the morning discussing with the Prime Minister.	√ Union leaders spent the morning in discussion with the Prime Minister.

Discuss is a transitive verb and must have an object. Compare: 'Union leaders spent the morning ***discussing*** their grievances with the Prime Minister.'

dispose 230

× How am I going to dispose all this rubbish?	√ How am I going to dispose of all this rubbish?

We ***dispose of*** something that we do not want or cannot keep.

disregard 231

× Some drivers disregard to road signs.	√ Some drivers disregard road signs.

We ***disregard*** something, NOT ***to*** something. Compare: 'Some drivers pay ***no regard to*** road signs.'

divide 232

× The library is divided in two sections.	√ The library is divided into two sections.

We ***divide*** something ***into*** a number of parts or sections.

divorce 233

× His parents are always fighting and have decided to divorce.	√ His parents are always fighting and have decided to get divorced.

When a husband and wife decide to end their marriage, they decide to ***get divorced*** or ***get a divorce***.

do: auxiliary verb 234

1

× The main problem is that the radio do not work.	√ The main problem is that the radio does not work.
× They doesn't have any matches to light the fire.	√ They don't have any matches to light the fire.

In the present simple tense, when the subject is third person singular, we use ***does/does not/doesn't***. With all other subjects, we use ***do/do not/don't***.

2

×	✓
× I did not observed very much student–teacher interaction.	√ I did not observe very much student-teacher interaction.
× Why did she told you to go away?	√ Why did she tell you to go away?
× She doesn't wants to disappoint her parents.	√ She doesn't want to disappoint her parents.

After ***do***, the main verb is always a bare infinitive: '***I didn't see*** anybody go out. (NOT ***saw***) '***Did you find*** the book you wanted?' (NOT ***found***)

3

×	✓
× Teachers are responsible for making sure that their pupils do behave properly.	√ Teachers are responsible for making sure that their pupils behave properly.
× Some of my friends do say that I spoil my children.	√ Some of my friends say that I spoil my children.

The auxiliary ***do*** is used in questions and negative clauses. It is not normally used in positive clauses. Compare:

Do their pupils ***behave*** properly?
Their pupils ***do not behave*** properly.
Their pupils ***behave*** properly.

We use ***do*** in a positive clause only when we wish to express emphasis or contrast:

I ***do like*** these grapes. Where did you get them?
Ann doesn't play tennis, but she ***does play*** badminton.
Do come and see us when you visit London.

4

×	✓
× Do you know where does he live?	√ Do you know where he lives?
× Do you know who did write the poem?	√ Do you know who wrote the poem?

⇨ 389.1

5

×	✓
× She warned him don't go near the dog.	√ She warned him not to go near the dog.

We use ***do not/don't*** in direct speech: 'Please ***don't wake*** the baby.'
In indirect speech, ***do not/don't*** becomes ***not*** + ***to***-infinitive: 'She told him ***not to wake*** the baby.'

6

×	✓
× Kevin hasn't been to London before, but Peter did.	√ Kevin hasn't been to London before, but Peter has.

⇨ 178.13

7

× Do you like some coffee?	√ Would you like some coffee?

⇨ 457.2

do: main verb 235

1

× They asked him to return the book but he refused to do that.	√ They asked him to return the book but he refused to do so.
× The men ordered us to get out of the car. We did it immediately.	√ The men ordered us to get out of the car. We did so immediately.

To refer back precisely to an action that has just been mentioned ('return the book', 'get out of the car'), we use ***do so*** (NOT ***do that/this/it***): 'If you haven't reserved a seat yet, I would advise you to ***do so*** without delay.' (reserve a seat) 'She accepted the invitation but now she wishes that she hadn't ***done so***.' (accepted the invitation)

Do so is used mainly in formal styles. In informal styles, it is usually omitted: 'She accepted the invitation, but now wishes she hadn't.'

2

× The iron doesn't work and I'd like to know what you intend to do for it.	√ The iron doesn't work and I'd like to know what you intend to do about it.
× Something will have to be done for improving the situation.	√ Something will have to be done about improving the situation.

When there is a problem, we try to ***do*** something ***about*** it (NOT ***for*** it): 'What are you going to ***do about*** (repairing) your watch?'

3

× I'm sure that the problem has to do something with the battery.	√ I'm sure that the problem has something to do with the battery.

Note the word order in the expression ***have something/nothing/anything to do with*** (to be connected with): 'The tax increase ***has nothing to do with*** helping the poor.'

4

× I can do with a cold drink.	√ I could do with a cold drink.

If we need something, we ***could do with*** it (NOT ***can***). ***Could do with*** is a fixed expression: 'She ***could do with*** a little help.' 'The car ***could do with*** a service.'

doubt 236

× There is little doubt whether he will have to remain in hiding for the rest of his life.	√ There is little doubt that he will have to remain in hiding for the rest of his life.

When ***doubt*** is used in an expression of certainty or near certainty, it is followed by a *that*-clause: 'There is ***no/little/not much doubt*** that the accused is guilty.' It can also be followed by a clause beginning with ***who*** or ***which***: 'There is *not much doubt* who did it.'

We use a *whether*-clause after ***doubt*** in expressions of uncertainty: 'There is considerable *doubt as to whether* Collins will be fit enough for the match on Saturday.'

downstairs 237

×	✓
× I ran to downstairs and opened the front door.	✓ I ran downstairs and opened the front door.

⇨ 802.2

dozen 238

×	✓
× We packed three bars of soap and dozen toilet rolls.	✓ We packed three bars of soap and a dozen toilet rolls.
× You will need four litres of milk and two dozens of eggs.	✓ You will need four litres of milk and two dozen eggs.
× She smashed about a dozen of plates.	✓ She smashed about a dozen plates.

⇨ 538.1–3

dream 239

1

×	✓
× I used to dream to live in a warm climate.	✓ I used to dream of living in a warm climate.

⇨ 841.2

2

×	✓
× I don't dream of letting my children play in the street.	✓ I wouldn't dream of letting my children play in the street.

If we think that something is wrong, dangerous, foolish, etc, we ***would not/never dream of*** doing it: 'I *would never dream of* driving at that speed.'

dress 240

1

×	✓
× I dressed up very quickly and ran out of the house.	✓ I got dressed very quickly and ran out of the house.
	✓ I dressed very quickly and ran out of the house.

When we put on our clothes, we ***get dressed*** or we ***dress*** (WITHOUT ***up***). ***Get dressed*** is the usual expression. If we ***dress up***, we put on fancy dress for a party or very smart clothes for a special occasion.

2

×	√
Even though they have very little money, their children are always nicely dressed up.	Even though they have very little money, their children are always nicely dressed.

When we describe someone's usual appearance, we normally use an adverb + 'dressed': 'well dressed', 'neatly dressed', 'smartly dressed', etc. ***Dressed up*** (= wearing smart clothes for a special occasion or fancy dress for a party) cannot follow an adverb ('nicely').

3

×	√
The bridegroom was dressed with a dark blue suit.	The bridegroom was dressed in a dark blue suit.

We say that someone is ***dressed in*** certain clothes.

drink 241

1

×	√
Drink will be served during the interval.	Drinks will be served during the interval.

Drink (uncountable) is beer, wine, gin, etc., (i.e. things that contain alcohol). ***Drinks*** (plural countable) are all the things that people drink; they can be alcoholic or non-alcoholic.

2

×	√
He even drunk all the baby's milk.	He even drank all the baby's milk.
If she had drank the liquid, she could have died.	If she had drunk the liquid, she could have died.

Drink (infinitive), ***drank*** (past simple), ***drunk*** (past participle).

drunken 242

×	√
Either the driver fell asleep or he was drunken.	Either the driver fell asleep or he was drunk.

Drunken is not very common and is used only in attributive position: 'drunken drivers', 'drunken laughter'. In predicative position, we use ***drunk***. ⇨ 16.1

dry 243

×	✓
× After the jumper had dryed, it was too small for me.	✓ After the jumper had dried, it was too small for me.

Dry (infinitive), ***dried*** (past simple), ***dried*** (past participle). ⇨ 666.2

due to 244

1

×	✓
× I spent a lot of time with Helen due to we were staying at the same hotel.	✓ I spent a lot of time with Helen as we were staying at the same hotel.
× Due to the company's growth has been slower than expected, the workforce is to be reduced.	✓ Since the company's growth has been slower than expected, the workforce is to be reduced.

To join two clauses, we use ***as***, ***since*** or ***because*** (conjunctions), NOT ***due to*** (a preposition).

2

!	✓
! Some people arrived late due to the train drivers' strike.	✓ Some people arrived late because of the train drivers' strike.
! Due to the rain, the match was cancelled.	✓ Owing to the rain, the match was cancelled.

In everyday usage, ***due to*** is often used as a preposition, like ***because of*** or ***owing to***: '***Due to*** poor management, the company was forced to close.' 'All the cars had to slow down ***due to*** the roadworks.'

However, some careful users insist that ***due*** is an adjective and that ***due to*** may be used only after the verb ***be***: 'Her success *is* ***due to*** years of hard work.' 'Many of these errors *are* ***due to*** carelessness.'

For this reason, the use of ***due to*** as a preposition is best avoided, especially in formal styles. Use ***because of*** or ***owing to*** instead.

3

×	✓
× His illness may due to family problems.	✓ His illness may be due to family problems.

Due to normally goes after ***be***. It cannot be used as a verb.

during 245

1

×	✓
× Some of your guests will probably want to dance during they are listening to the records.	✓ Some of your guests will probably want to dance while they are listening to the records.

During is a preposition (NOT a conjunction). ⇨ 882.7

2

×	√
× During waiting for the bus, I try to learn a few new words.	√ While waiting for the bus, I try to learn a few new words.

Unlike most prepositions, ***during*** cannot introduce an *-ing* clause.

3

×	√
× The company has been operating during four years.	√ The company has been operating for four years.

When we are talking about 'how long', we use ***for***: 'I've been learning English ***for*** three years.' Compare: '***During*** the last twelve months, inflation has risen by four per cent.'

dust **246**

×	√
× The ventilation holes should be kept free of dusts and dirt.	√ The ventilation holes should be kept free of dust and dirt.

Dust is an uncountable noun and does not have a plural form.

each **247**

1

×	√
× Each students were given a new dictionary.	√ Each student was given a new dictionary. √ Each of the students was given a new dictionary.

⇨ 640.4

2

×	√
× Each of the six Asean countries were represented at the conference.	√ Each of the six Asean countries was represented at the conference.

The verb after ***each*** is normally singular. (⇨ 44.13) '***Each*** child ***was*** given a balloon.' '***Each*** of the children ***was*** given a balloon.'

The verb is plural only when ***each*** comes after the noun/pronoun it refers to: '***The children were each*** given a balloon.'

3

×	√
× They each were delighted with the photographs.	√ They were each delighted with the photographs.

⇨ 640.7

4

× I asked the girls if they each could describe the man.	√ I asked the girls if they could each describe the man.

⇨ 640.8

5

× Each of us didn't like the film.	√ None of us liked the film.

⇨ 512.6

each other 248

× We used to write to each others once a month.	√ We used to write to each other once a month.

Each other is always singular: 'We helped ***each other*** to answer the questions.' Compare: 'As children, we spent a lot of time at ***each other's*** house.'

eager 249

× I don't know why she is so eager for seeing you.	√ I don't know why she is so eager to see you.

Compare: 'The students are ***eager for*** their results.' 'The students are ***eager to receive*** their results.'

education 250

× Many students go overseas for the higher education.	√ Many students go overseas for higher education.

⇨ 782.3

effect 251

1

× Everyone knows that smoking effects your health.	√ Everyone knows that smoking affects your health.

Something either ***affects*** us or has an ***effect*** on us. ***Effect*** (with an **e**) is normally used as a noun. As a verb, it has a very different meaning. ⇨ 35

2

× The talk was about the effects of alcohol to the human body.	√ The talk was about the effects of alcohol on the human body.

Something has an ***effect on*** a person or thing.

effort 252

× Learning to play the piano requires a lot of efforts.	√ Learning to play the piano requires a lot of effort.

When ***effort*** means 'hard work', it is an uncountable noun and does not have a plural form.

either 253

1

× Either parents are able to sign the form.	√ Either parent is able to sign the form. √ Either of the parents is able to sign the form.

⇨ 640.4

2

! I am not sure whether either of these books are worth reading.	√ I am not sure whether either of these books is worth reading.

⇨ 44.13

either … or … 254

1

× The watch is either broken or it needs a new battery. × The visitor can either choose the normal train or the express which stops only at major stations.	√ Either the watch is broken or it needs a new battery. √ The visitor can choose either the normal train or the express which stops only at major stations.

The units that are linked by ***either*** … ***or*** must be grammatically equal.

⇨ 178.9

2

! Either the landlord or his wife were not telling the truth.	√ Either the landlord or his wife was not telling the truth.

⇨ 44.18

elder 255

× My sister is elder than my brother.	√ My sister is older than my brother.

We do not use ***elder*** in comparisons. ***Elder*** may be used before a noun ('my *elder* sister') or as a pronoun ('I thought that Patrick was *the elder* of the two.')

emphasize 256

×	√
The speaker emphasized on the importance of further research.	The speaker emphasized the importance of further research.

We ***emphasize*** something (NOT ***on*** something). Compare: 'There has been too little ***emphasis on*** research.' We use ***on*** after the noun, but not after the verb.

employment 257

×	√
Qualifications are of no use unless they prepare you for the employment.	Qualifications are of no use unless they prepare you for employment.

⇨ 532.1

energy 258

×	√
Our major source of the energy is oil.	Our major source of energy is oil.

⇨ 532.1

English 259

×	√
Her husband is a typical English.	Her husband is typically English. √ Her husband is a typical Englishman.

⇨ 504.1

enjoy 260

1

×	√
Some people do not enjoy just to sit and rest.	Some people do not enjoy just sitting and resting.

We ***enjoy doing*** something (NOT ***to do***): 'We both ***enjoyed having*** the children with us again.'

2

×	√
During the examination period there is no time to relax and enjoy.	During the examination period there is no time to relax and enjoy yourself/oneself.

Enjoy is a transitive verb.

⇨ 838.2

enough

261

1

×	✓
× The piece of wood was not enough thick.	✓ The piece of wood was not thick enough.
× The old man could not run enough fast.	✓ The old man could not run fast enough.
× I think that sending him to prison is an enough severe punishment.	✓ I think that sending him to prison is a severe enough punishment.

Adverbs of degree usually go BEFORE the adjective/adverb that they refer to: e.g. 'quite rich,' 'too softly'. However, ***enough*** always goes AFTER the adjective/ adverb.

2

×	✓
× I did not have money enough to buy a ticket.	✓ I did not have enough money to buy a ticket.

Enough normally goes in front of the noun it modifies. In this usage, it is a determiner like *some*, *any*, *more*, etc. ***Enough*** is placed after the noun only in literary styles.

3

×	✓
× We don't have enough time for visiting the museum.	✓ We don't have enough time to visit the museum.

We (don't) have ***enough*** time/money/etc. ***to do*** something, NOT ***for doing*** something. Compare: 'We don't have ***enough*** time ***for*** a visit to the museum.' (***enough*** time/money etc. ***for*** something)

4

×	✓
× There was not enough of snow to go skiing.	✓ There was not enough snow to go skiing.
× In fact, there is enough of food in the world to feed everyone.	✓ There is enough food in the world to feed everyone.

⇨ 640.1

5

×	✓
× If his sister wants to come too, the seats won't be enough.	✓ If his sister wants to come too, there won't be enough seats.

We do not normally use ***enough*** on its own as a complement. Instead, we begin the sentence with ***there*** and put ***enough*** before the noun it refers to.

Note that when ***enough*** is used on its own as a complement, the subject is normally ***there***, ***it***, ***that/this*** or a quantity: '***There*** isn't ***enough***.' '***Two litres*** isn't ***enough***.'

6

× Mr Yassin is tall enough and wears spectacles.	√ Mr Yassin is quite tall and wears spectacles.

Do not confuse ***enough*** with ***quite/fairly***. ***Enough*** means 'to a necessary or satisfactory degree'. Compare: 'Mr Yassin is ***quite*** tall. In fact, he's tall ***enough*** to be a policeman.'

7

× The number of offices available is not sufficient enough.	√ The number of offices available is not sufficient. √ The number of offices available is not enough.

Enough is not used after ***sufficient***. ***Sufficient*** means 'enough'.

enter 262

× As soon as he entered into the room, we all stood up. × The driver had entered in the opposite lane by mistake.	√ As soon as he entered the room, we all stood up. √ The driver had entered the opposite lane by mistake.

We ***enter*** a room, building or area (WITHOUT ***in*** or ***into***). Compare: 'Our client does not wish to ***enter into*** further negotiations.'

equal 263

× Lu is able to lift her companion, whose weight is nearly equal her own.	√ Lu is able to lift her companion, whose weight is nearly equal to her own.

When used as an adjective, ***equal*** is followed by ***to***: 'Your salary is ***equal to*** Jean's and mine put together.'

equipment 264

1

× We offer a full range of laboratory equipments.	√ We offer a full range of laboratory equipment.

Equipment is an uncountable noun and does not have a plural form.

2

× Dentists use a very expensive equipment.	√ Dentists use very expensive equipment.

Equipment is not used with ***a/an***.

⇨ 2.1

3

×	✓
The cargo handling equipment are mostly of Japanese origin.	The cargo handling equipment is mostly of Japanese origin.

Equipment takes a singular verb.

escape 265

×	✓
The prison has been escaped several times.	There have been several escapes from the prison.

When ***escape*** means 'manage to get out of a prison or a place in which you have been held', it is intransitive and cannot be used in passive structures.

⇨ 575.5

especially 266

1

×	✓
Most students try to get jobs in the summer. Especially girls like to earn some money.	Most students try to get jobs in the summer. Girls especially like to earn some money.

When ***especially*** refers to the subject of a sentence, the word order is: subject + ***especially*** + verb. A sentence cannot begin with ***especially***.

2

×	✓
There is no need to wait especially for me.	There is no need to wait specially for me.
These horses are especially bred for racing.	These horses are specially bred for racing.

For the difference between ***especially*** and ***specially***, ⇨ 747

even 267

1

×	✓
Even you know what the matter is, you should still see a doctor.	Even if you know what the matter is, you should still see a doctor.
It starts to play the other side of the tape, even the first side has not finished.	It starts to play the other side of the tape, even though the first side has not finished.

To join two clauses, we use ***even if*** or ***even though***. ***Even*** is not a conjunction.

2

×	✓
Her parents even say that she is lazy.	Even her parents say that she is lazy.

In writing, ***even*** is normally placed immediately before the word or phrase that it refers to. This helps to avoid possible confusion. 'Her parents ***even*** say that she is lazy' could mean that her parents do not just 'think' that she is lazy – they actually 'say' so.

3

×	√
× They even may decide to come by car.	√ They may even decide to come by car.
× Several of the guests even did not say goodbye.	√ Several of the guest did not even say goodbye.
× He even is too shy to answer the telephone.	√ He is even too shy to answer the telephone.

⇨ 29.1–2

even if 268

1

×	√
× Even if you are married or single, you will receive a warm welcome.	√ Whether you are married or single, you will receive a warm welcome.

To link two possibilities, we use ***whether*** ... ***or*** ...: '***Whether*** she is right ***or*** wrong, at least she has an opinion.' 'I am not interested in buying the car, ***whether*** he reduces the price ***or*** not.'

2

×	√
× Even if he is only 12, he is very trustworthy.	√ Even though he is only 12, he is very trustworthy.

Before a fact, we use ***even though***: '***Even though*** it's pouring with rain, I still have to go out.' We use ***even if*** before a possibility: '***Even if*** it pours with rain, I still have to go out.'

3

×	√
× Even if I could afford my own house, but I wouldn't buy one.	√ Even if I could afford my own house, I wouldn't buy one.

We do not use ***even if*** and ***but*** together in the same sentence. To link two clauses, we use just one conjunction (NOT two). ⇨ 169.2

even though 269

1

×	√
× Even though he had very little money, but he offered to pay for me.	√ Even though he had very little money, he offered to pay for me. √ He had very little money, but he offered to pay for me.

We do not use ***even though*** and ***but*** together in the same sentence. To link two clauses, we use just one conjunction (NOT two). ⇨ 169.2

2

×	√
× Even though Japan has a lot of imports, it can still compete with other countries.	√ Even though Japan has a lot of imports, it can still compete with other countries.

Even though is written as two words.

⇨ 883.1

ever 270

1

×	√
× She asked me if I ever had been to France.	√ She asked me if I had ever been to France.

⇨ 29.1

2

×	√
× It was the best wine that I had ever tasted before.	√ It was the best wine that I had ever tasted.

We do not use ***before*** after ***ever***.

3

×	√
× The Beatles will ever be my favourite pop group.	√ The Beatles will always be my favourite pop group.

Ever (at any time) is used mainly in questions. Compare: 'I have ***always*** wanted to visit France.' 'Have you ***ever*** wanted to visit France?'

every 271

1

×	√
× There is a flight to Bahrain every Mondays.	√ There is a flight to Bahrain every Monday.
× Every children need love and attention.	√ Every child needs love and attention.

When a noun comes immediately after ***every***, it is always singular.

⇨ 640.4

The noun is plural only when ***every*** is followed by a number: 'I visit the dentist *every six months*.'

2

×	√
× Every student have a chance to take the examination again.	√ Every student has a chance to take the examination again.
× Every one of the answers were wrong.	√ Every one of the answers was wrong.

After ***every***, the verb is always singular.

3

×	✓
× I usually visit my parents about three times every week.	✓ I usually visit my parents about three times a week.

When we are talking about frequency, price, speed, salary, etc., we normally use ***a/an***:

The airline flies to London five times **a** week.
Imported apples usually cost about five dollars **a** kilo.
The car was travelling at 60 miles ***an*** hour.

4

×	✓
× Every one of the lessons was not interesting.	✓ Not one of the lessons was interesting.

⇨ 512.6

5

×	✓
× Nowadays every one agrees that cigarettes are bad for you.	✓ Nowadays everyone agrees that cigarettes are bad for you.
× Every thing went according to plan.	✓ Everything went according to plan.

The pronouns ***everyone***, ***everybody*** and ***everything*** are written as one word.

⇨ 883.3

everybody/everyone 272

1

×	✓
× It was our first visit to Paris and everybody were impressed.	✓ It was our first visit to Paris and everybody was impressed.

Everybody and ***everyone*** take a singular verb. ⇨ 44.11

2

!	✓
! Everyone has to leave their bags outside the library.	✓ All bags have to be left outside the library.

⇨ 42.4

3

×	✓
× Everybody couldn't understand what he was saying.	✓ Nobody could understand what he was saying.

⇨ 512.6

everyday or every day ? 273

×	✓
× Everyday my mother made me practise for an hour.	✓ Every day my mother made me practise for an hour.

Everyday (written as one word) is an adjective: 'In the tropics, thunderstorms are an ***everyday*** occurrence.' The adverbial expression is ***every day*** (two words).

everyone or every one ? 274

×	√
× Everyone of the letters had been opened by someone.	√ Every one of the letters had been opened by someone.

Everyone and ***everybody*** are pronouns: '***Everyone*** needs a holiday now and again.' When we mean 'each', we use ***every one*** (two separate words). ⇨ 883.3

everything 275

1

×	√
× In a hospital everything have to be very clean.	√ In a hospital everything has to be very clean.

Everything takes a singular verb. ⇨ 44.11

2

×	√
× Everything had not been changed since my last visit.	√ Nothing had been changed since my last visit.

⇨ 512.6

evidence 276

1

×	√
× The research produced evidences that monolinguals perform better.	√ The research produced evidence that monolinguals perform better.

Evidence is an uncountable noun and does not have a plural form.

2

×	×
× His lawyer produced an important new evidence.	× His lawyer produce some important new evidence.

Evidence is not used with ***a/an***. We can say ***a piece of evidence*** but NOT ***an evidence***. ⇨ 2.1–2

except 277

1

×	√
× My parents would not let me go out except if my brother went with me.	√ My parents would not let me go out unless my brother went with me.

When we want to say *except if*, we use *unless*. Note the alternative with ***only if***: 'My parents would let me go out ***only if*** my brother went with me.

2

! I am allowed to do anything except to go out on my own at night.	√ I am allowed to do anything except go out on my own at night.

When ***except*** links two clauses, the second clause usually begins with a bare infinitive: 'I've done everything ***except feed*** the cat.'

3

× She was unhurt except a slight injury to her knee.	√ She was unhurt except for a slight injury to her knee.
× Except sausages, he doesn't eat meat.	√ Except for sausages, he doesn't eat meat.

We use ***except*** when the meaning is 'but not':

Everyone ***except*** Henry wants to go.
He eats everything ***except*** strawberries.
I saw him every day ***except*** on Sundays.

Otherwise, we use ***except for***.

4

× There was no sound and except this the picture was very poor.	√ There was no sound and besides this the picture was very poor.
× Except the records, I have a lot of good tapes.	√ Apart from the records, I have a lot of good tapes.

Prepositions which mean 'also' include ***besides***, ***in addition to***, ***as well as*** and ***apart from***, but not ***except***.

exciting 278

× I felt so exciting that I couldn't sleep.	√ I felt so excited that I couldn't sleep.

⇨ 14.3

experience 279

× For most good jobs you need qualifications and experiences.	√ For most good jobs you need qualifications and experience.

When ***experience*** means 'the knowledge and skill that someone gains from doing a job for a long time', it is an uncountable noun and does not have a plural form. Compare: 'He told us about his ***experiences*** in the desert.'

explain 280

1

×	√
× The old lady explained us that the bag was full of cheese.	√ The old lady explained (to us) that the bag was full of cheese.
× First, I would like to explain you the travel arrangements.	√ First, I would like to explain (to you) the travel arrangements.

With ***explain***, we use ***to*** before an indirect object, even when the indirect object comes before the direct object. ⇨ 387.1

Note, however, that an indirect object is often unnecessary: 'She ***explained*** that we would have to obtain a visa.' We do not have to say 'She ***explained to us*** ... .'

2

×	√
× She tried to explain about why she was crying.	√ She tried to explain why she was crying.

We ***explain*** something (NOT ***about*** something).

explanation 281

×	√
× He started his talk with an explanation on the difference between accent and dialect.	√ He started his talk with an explanation of the difference between accent and dialect.

An ***explanation of*** something helps people to understand it.

extremely 282

×	√
× I was extremely convinced that someone was following me.	√ I was absolutely convinced that someone was following me.

⇨ 405.1

face 283

×	√
× My dream is to buy a house which faces at the sea.	√ My dream is to buy a house which faces the sea.

Face is normally used as a transitive verb and is immediately followed by the direct object: 'The children were told to ***face*** the front of the class.' 'For the whole journey she sat ***facing*** me without saying a word.'

fact 284

×	√
× Politicians should recognize the fact people will not tolerate unemployment indefinitely.	√ Politicians should recognize the fact that people will not tolerate unemployment indefinitely.

When ***the fact*** is followed by a ***that***-clause, the word ***that*** cannot be omitted.

⇨ 838.7

faint 285

×	√
× When he saw the blood on his shirt, he was fainted.	√ When he saw the blood on his shirt, he fainted.

If we suddenly lose consciousness, we ***faint*** (past tense and past participle ***fainted***): 'I put my head between my knees to stop myself from ***fainting***.' If we feel that we are about to lose consciousness, we feel ***faint*** (adjective): 'She felt ***faint*** with hunger and exhaustion.'

fairly 286

1

×	√
× Her new book is fairly longer than her last one.	√ Her new book is rather longer than her last one.

We can say 'Her new book is ***fairly long***' but NOT ***fairly longer***. Before a comparative form (*-er*), we use ***rather***, NOT ***fairly*** or ***quite***.

2

×	√
× The results of the survey were fairly disappointing.	√ The results of the survey were rather disappointing.
× He shouted at me fairly angrily.	√ Her shouted at me rather angrily.

Before an adjective or adverb that expresses a negative idea (e.g. 'disappointing', 'angrily'), we use ***rather***. ***Fairly*** is normally used before a positive idea. Compare: 'Sales this year have been ***fairly*** satisfactory.' 'In the last examination, I did ***fairly*** well.'

⇨ 649.1

fall 287

×	√
x The film was so boring that I falled asleep.	√ The film was so boring that I fell asleep.

Fall (infinitive), ***fell*** (past simple), ***fallen*** (past participle).

familiarize 288

×	✓
× Hotel guests are advised to familiarize with the location of the nearest fire exits.	✓ Hotel guests are advised to familiarize themselves with the location of the nearest fire exits.

⇨ 838.2

far 289

1

×	✓
× The nearest telephone was far from the village.	✓ The nearest telephone was a long way from the village.

We use ***far*** in negative contexts and in questions: 'It's ***not*** very ***far*** to the station.' 'How ***far*** is it to the station?' In affirmative contexts, we use ***a long way***.

Note, however, that the phrases ***too far***, ***so far*** and ***far away*** may be used in all contexts: 'The hotel was ***too far*** from the city centre.'

2

×	✓
× The car stopped about two metres far from me.	✓ The car stopped about two metres (away) from me.
× The hotel is just three miles far from the beach.	✓ The hotel is just three miles (away) from the beach.

When we state a distance in units (e.g. 'two metres', 'three miles'), we do not use ***far***. Compare: 'The hotel is ***not*** very ***far*** from the beach.'

farther 290

×	✓
× For farther information, ring 02-376449.	✓ For further information, ring 02-376449.

When we mean 'more', we use ***further***. We use ***farther*** (or ***further***) when we are talking about distance: 'His house was ***further/farther*** than we had thought.'

fascinated 291

×	✓
× The child stood in front of the aquarium, very fascinated.	✓ The child stood in front of the aquarium, absolutely fascinated.

⇨ 405.1

fast 292

× He drives too fastly.	√ He drives too fast.

Fast is both an adjective and an adverb. Compare: 'He is a very ***fast*** swimmer.' (adjective) 'He can swim very ***fast***.' (adverb)

fatigue 293

× These exercises are for people suffering from stiffness or fatigues.	√ These exercises are for people suffering from stiffness or fatigue.

When ***fatigue*** means 'tiredness', it is an uncountable noun and does not have a plural form.

favour 294

× Could you do a favour to me?	√ Could you do me a favour?

We ***do*** someone *a* ***favour***. The indirect object ('me') goes immediately after ***do***.

favourite 295

× My most favourite season is the autumn.	√ My favourite season is the autumn.

Favourite has a superlative meaning already and is not normally used with ***most***.

⇨ 15.4

fed up 296

× A person who stays at home all the time soon gets fed up of everything.	√ A person who stays at home all the time soon gets fed up with everything.

Before a noun phrase, we normally use ***fed up with***, NOT ***of***: 'We're all ***fed up with*** his endless complaints.' 'You only bought the dress this morning. How can you be ***fed up with*** it already?'

Before an ***-ing*** form, both ***fed up with*** and ***fed up of*** are common: 'I'm getting ***fed up with/of*** having to walk home every day.'

However, many careful users regard ***fed up of*** as incorrect.

feel 297

1

×	√
× Some of us are feeling that we are given too much homework.	√ Some of us feel that we are given too much homework.

When ***feel*** means 'to think or consider', it is not used in progressive tenses.

⇨ 627.3

2

×	√
× I felt something to run across my pillow.	√ I felt something run across my pillow.

We ***feel*** someone/something ***do*** something (NOT ***to do***). ⇨ 839.3

feel like 298

×	√
× For a whole week I hadn't felt like to go out.	√ For a whole week I hadn't felt like going out.

We ***feel like doing*** something, (NOT ***to do*** something). ⇨ 837

feet 299

×	√
× Climbing a ten-feet wall is not easy, especially in the dark.	√ Climbing a ten-foot wall is not easy, especially in the dark.

⇨ 533.3

few 300

1

×	√
× I waited for few minutes and then rang again.	√ I waited for a few minutes and then rang again.

Few means 'hardly any': 'Most of these people are extremely poor and ***few*** can afford to pay for medical attention.' When we mean 'some but not many', we use ***a few***. ⇨ .2 below

2

×	√
× Unfortunately, a few of the passengers escaped injury.	√ Unfortunately, few of the passengers escaped injury.

A few means 'some' or 'several'. When we mean 'hardly any', we use **few**. Compare:

> ***A few*** people like to spend their holidays at home.
> ***Few*** people like to spend their holidays in hospital.

⇨ .1 above

3

×	✓
× He has very few chance of getting a good job.	✓ He has very little chance of getting a good job.
× These new cars will mean fewer pollution.	✓ These new cars will mean less pollution.

With uncountable nouns ('chance', 'pollution'), we use ***little/less***. We use ***few/fewer*** with plural count nouns. ⇨ 640.3

fill 301

×	✓
× It took me an hour to fill the application form.	✓ It took me an hour to fill in the application form.

In British English, we ***fill in*** (or sometimes ***fill out***) a form. We ***fill in*** a space in a form: '***Fill in*** the coupon below and return it in the reply paid envelope.' 'Remember to ***fill in*** your name and address in block capitals.'

In American English, ***fill out*** is more common than ***fill in***.

find 302

×	✓
× He finds to stop talking impossible.	✓ He finds it impossible to stop talking.

⇨ 838.4

finish 303

×	✓
× Have you finished to write the letter yet?	✓ Have you finished writing the letter yet?

We ***finish doing*** something (NOT ***to do*** something). ⇨ 839.1

first 304

×	✓
× At first, I'd like to thank you all for inviting me here today.	✓ First of all, I'd like to thank you all for inviting me here today.

To signal the stages of a talk, essay, etc., we use ***first (of all)/firstly***, ***second/secondly***, ***third/thirdly*** ... ***finally***.

At first is a time adverbial. It is used when there is a contrast between two situations in the past (an earlier situation and a later situation): '***At first*** we didn't know how we were going to get there. Then Carl arrived and said that we could borrow his car.'

first aid 305

×	✓
None of us knew anything about first aids.	None of us knew anything about first aid.

First aid is uncountable and does not have a plural form.

firstly 306

×	✓
Firstly, the watch worked perfectly but after two days it stopped.	At first, the watch worked perfectly but after two days it stopped.

⇨ 304

fish 307

×	✓
Some customers always smell the fishes to make sure that they are fresh.	Some customers always smell the fish to make sure that they are fresh.

The plural form of ***fish*** is usually ***fish***: 'one fish', 'three fish'. ***Fishes*** is mainly used in conversations with very young children, and in literature written for this age group. It is also used to refer to different species of fish.

flight 308

×	✓
He will be arriving by flight K335.	He will be arriving on flight K335.

We arrive/travel ***by*** plane but ***on*** (a particular) ***flight***.

fly 309

×	✓
As soon as the bird saw the cat, it flied away.	As soon as the bird saw the cat, it flew away.

Fly (infinitive), ***flew*** (past simple), ***flown*** (past participle).

food 310

×	✓
We took enough foods with us for three days.	We took enough food with us for three days.

Food is usually an uncountable noun. Use *foods* only when referring to particular types of food: 'health foods', 'baby foods'.

foot 311

! The best way to see the city is by foot.	√ The best way to see the city is on foot.

We go ***by car/bus/train/plane*** but ***on foot***. ***By foot*** is used in American English.

for 312

1

× I want to go to France for learning how to cook.	√ I want to go to France to learn how to cook.

When we mention the purpose of an action, we use a ***to***-clause.

⇨ 22.1

2

× I have come to England for to learn English.	√ I have come to England to learn English.

We do not use ***for*** in front of a ***to***-clause.

3

! I can't buy it for I don't have any money.	√ I can't buy it because I don't have any money.

Nowadays, the use of ***for*** to introduce a clause of reason occurs mainly in formal and literary styles. Instead of ***for***, we normally use ***because***, ***as*** or ***since***.

4

! It was very kind for you to invite me.	√ It was very kind of you to invite me.

When we use an ***it***-sentence to comment on someone's behaviour, the adjective is followed by an ***of***-phrase:

	ADJECTIVE	+	OF-PHRASE	+	TO-CLAUSE
It was	good		of your sister		to wait for us.
It was	rude		of them		not to reply.

Note also the related ***how***-pattern: 'How thoughtless + of him + not to tell us where he was going.'

5

× The food was much too rich to eat for me.	√ The food was much too rich for me to eat.
× The flat isn't big enough to live in for the six of us.	√ The flat isn't big enough for the six of us to live in.

A ***for***-phrase comes before a ***to***-infinitive, not after it. The ***for***-phrase contains the subject of the ***to***-infinitive and a subject normally comes before its verb.

	ADJECTIVE +	(FOR-PHRASE) +	TO-INFINITIVE
The address was	easy	for me	to remember.
The letters are	ready	for you	to post.

6

×	√
× For the last three weeks the shop is closed.	√ For the last three weeks the shop has been closed.
× He is working for Shell for over 12 years.	√ He has been working for Shell for over 12 years.

When a ***for***-phrase refers to a period of time which begins in the past and continues up to *now* (the moment of speaking), we use the present perfect tense.

⇨ 619.1

7

×	√
× For the last few years, many nuclear weapons have been destroyed.	√ During the last few years, many nuclear weapons have been destroyed.

When we refer to the period within which something takes place, we use ***during*** or ***over***. A time phrase beginning with ***for*** tells us how long an action or state continues: 'The two countries were fighting each other ***for*** almost five years.' '***For*** the last two weeks the telephone has been out of order.'

8

×	√
× On Saturday morning I usually go for shopping.	√ On Saturday morning I usually go shopping.

⇨ 331.3

9

×	√
× At half-time, the score was 3-1 for Brazil.	√ At half-time, the score was 3-1 to Brazil.

Before the name of the player or team that is winning, we use ***to***.

forbid 313

1

×	√
× The government has forbidden to drivers to enter the city centre during certain hours.	√ The government has forbidden drivers to enter the city centre during certain hours.

We ***forbid*** someone ***to do*** something (NOT ***to*** someone).

2

×	√
× My mother had forbidden me from going near the river.	√ My mother had forbidden me to go near the river.

We ***forbid*** someone ***to do*** something (NOT ***from doing*** something).

force 314

× Her parents forced her get married.	√ Her parents forced her to get married.

We ***make*** someone ***do*** something, but we ***force*** someone ***to do*** something.

⇨ 839.1

for ever 315

× He is for ever asking me to lend him more money.	√ He is forever asking me to lend him more money.

When we want to say 'for always', we can use either ***for ever*** or ***forever***: 'This time I intend to stop smoking ***forever/for ever***.'
When we want to say 'continually', we use ***forever***.

forget 316

1

× They have forgot what it is like to be young.	√ They have forgotten what it is like to be young.

Forget (infinitive), ***forgot*** (past simple), ***forgotten*** (past participle).

2

× Don't forget buying some milk while you are out.	√ Don't forget to buy some milk while you are out.

We use an *-ing* form after ***forget*** when we are talking about something which has already happened: 'I shall never ***forget seeing*** our baby born.'

When we are talking about something which has not yet happened, we use a *to*-infinitive: 'If you ***forget to write***, I'll be very disappointed.'

forgive 317

× My father never forgived her.	√ My father never forgave her.

Forgive (infinitive), ***forgave*** (past simple), ***forgiven*** (past participle).

fractions 318

1

× Two thirds of the money were spent on laboratory equipment.	√ Two thirds of the money was spent on laboratory equipment.

The verb agrees with the noun in the *of*-phrase. Compare: 'A quarter of the forest ***has*** been destroyed.' 'A quarter of the trees ***have*** been cut down.'

⇨ 44.12

2

×	√
× I bought two litres of milk and one quarter of a pound of cheese.	√ I bought two litres of milk and a quarter of a pound of cheese.
× The film lasted one and one half hours.	√ The film lasted one and a half hours.

Before ***quarter***, ***half***, ***eighth***, etc., we normally use ***a/an*** (NOT *one*):
'an hour and ***a quarter***', 'one and ***a quarter*** hours', 'two and ***a half*** kilometres'.

3

×	√
× The flight takes about one and a half hour.	√ The flight takes about one and a half hours.

After 'one and *a* half', 'two and *a* quarter', etc., the noun is plural.

frighten 319

1

×	√
× I was too frighten to move.	√ I was too frightened to move.

⇨ 14.1

2

×	√
× When I heard the scream, I frightened.	√ When I heard the scream, I was frightened.

Frighten (to make someone feel afraid) is a transitive verb and must have an object, e.g. 'The thought of growing old ***frightens*** some people.' (⇨ 838.1)
When there is no object, we use ***be/feel frightened*** or ***be/feel afraid***.

from 320

1

×	√
× Our holiday begins from the first day after the examinations.	√ Our holiday begins on the first day after the examinations.

Something happens ***on*** a particular day. ⇨ 87.2

2

×	√
× I have been working for Brunei Shell from 1987.	√ I have been working for Brunei Shell since 1987.

To refer to a period of time which begins in the past and continues up to 'now' (the moment of speaking), we use ***since***.

3

× It looked as if the burns had been made from a cigarette.	√ It looked as if the burns had been made with a cigarette.

When we mention the thing that is used to do something, we use a ***with***-phrase. Compare: 'He used a screwdriver to open the drawer.' 'He opened the drawer with a screwdriver.' 'The drawer was opened with a screwdriver.'

4

× I've just finished reading a novel from Norman Mailer.	√ I've just finished reading a novel by Norman Mailer.

Something is made/written/etc. ***by*** a certain person.

5

× The blouse was from silk and was very expensive.	√ The blouse was made of silk and was very expensive.

Something is ***made of*** a particular material, NOT ***from***. ⇨ 475

fruit 321

× During the next two weeks I ate nothing but fruits.	√ During the next two weeks I ate nothing but fruit.

When ***fruit*** refers to fruit in general, it is an uncountable noun and does not have a plural form: '***fruit*** and vegetables', 'a bowl of ***fruit***'.

We use ***fruit*** as a countable noun when we wish to refer to a particular type of fruit: 'Is cucumber ***a fruit*** or a vegetable?' 'Pineapples and mangoes are both tropical ***fruits***.'

full 322

× The suitcase was full with expensive-looking watches.	√ The suitcase was full of expensive-looking watches.

Full is normally followed by ***of***: 'The office was ***full of*** broken furniture.' 'The letter was ***full of*** bad news.'

Full (up) with is used mainly in informal styles to mean 'completely filled': 'The suitcase is already ***full up with*** the children's clothes.' ⇨ 21

fun 323

1

× I had never realized that sailing could be such a good fun.	√ I had never realized that sailing could be such good fun.

Fun is an uncountable noun and is not used with ***a/an***. ⇨ 2.1

2

×	✓
× All the groom's friends were making fun at him.	✓ All the groom's friends were making fun of him.

We ***laugh at*** someone but ***make fun of*** them.

furniture 324

1

×	✓
× Because of all the furnitures, it was difficult to move.	✓ Because of all the furniture, it was difficult to move.

Furniture is an uncountable noun and does not have a plural form.

2

×	✓
× The landlord provided a new furniture.	✓ The landlord provided (some) new furniture.

Furniture is not used with ***a/an***. However, we can say 'a piece of new furniture'.

⇨ 2.1–2

generally 325

×	✓
× Her lessons generally are very interesting.	✓ Her lessons are generally very interesting.

⇨ 29.2

get 326

×	✓
× It wasn't worth getting the watch repair.	✓ It wasn't worth getting the watch repaired.

⇨ 351.7

give 327

1

×	✓
× I'd like you to give my money back.	✓ I'd like you to give me my money back.

Give normally has two objects, a direct object and an indirect object.

⇨ 838.5

2

×	✓
× I shan't forget all the help you gave for me.	✓ I shan't forget all the help you gave me.

We ***give*** something ***to*** someone, NOT ***for*** someone. Note that when the object of ***give*** is used in a relative clause, ***to*** is often omitted before the indirect object ('me'): 'The answer that she ***gave*** (to) me was incorrect.'

3

×	✓
× I gave to the man all the money that was in my pocket.	✓ I gave the man all the money that was in my pocket.

⇨ 387.1

glad 328

×	✓
× It was wonderful to see so many glad faces.	✓ It was wonderful to see so many happy/cheerful faces.

Glad is not normally used in front of a noun. ⇨ 16.1

glass 329

×	✓
× The driver had just a few scratches from the broken glasses.	✓ The driver had just a few scratches from the broken glass.

When it means 'the material that is used to make windows, bottles, etc', ***glass*** is an uncountable noun and does not have a plural form. Compare: 'two glasses of orange juice', 'a set of wine glasses', 'I can't see without my glasses'.

glasses 330

1

×	✓
× She asked me if I had always worn such a thick glasses.	✓ She asked me if I had always worn such thick glasses.

Glasses, ***sunglasses*** and ***spectacles*** are plural nouns. ⇨ 603

2

×	✓
× When did you start wearing a pair of glasses?	✓ When did you start wearing glasses?

⇨ 567.4

go 331

1

×	✓
× I have gone to Scotland but I have never gone to Wales.	✓ I have been to Scotland but I have never been to Wales.
× I haven't gone to a party since last year.	✓ I haven't been to a party since last year.

When we mean that someone has gone somewhere and come back, we use ***been***. When we mean that someone has gone somewhere but has not come back, we use ***gone***. Compare: 'Lisa has *gone* to Frankfurt.' (= she has not come back yet) 'Lisa has *been* to Frankfurt.' (= she went and came back)

2

×	√
× Last December we went to ski in the French Alps.	√ Last December we went skiing in the French Alps.

When we are talking about a sport or pastime, we use ***go*** + *-ing*: 'They have invited me to *go **fishing/sailing/swimming*** with them tomorrow.' Compare: 'He's ***gone to see*** if the photographs are ready.' In this sentence, 'to see' introduces a clause of purpose.

3

×	√
× At one time I used to go for swimming every morning.	√ At one time I used to go swimming every morning.
× On Saturday morning I usually go for shopping.	√ On Saturday morning I usually go shopping.

We *go **swimming/go shopping, etc***, (WITHOUT *for*). Compare: 'He's ***gone for a*** *swim*.' 'Let's ***go for a jog***.'

4

×	√
× Last August I went with some friends camping.	√ Last August I went camping with some friends.

⇨ 29.8

5

×	√
× After my parents had went, I was all alone.	√ After my parents had gone, I was all alone.

Go (infinitive), ***went*** (past simple), ***gone*** (past participle).

go on 332

×	√
× After the short stories, she went on writing her first novel.	√ After the short stories, she went on to write her first novel.

When someone continues what they were doing before, they ***go on doing*** it: 'How much longer do you intend to ***go on working*** tonight?'

When there is a change of activity or topic, ***go on*** is followed by a ***to***-infinitive: 'Having introduced herself, she ***went on to explain*** why she had come.'

going to 333

× If you speak to the manager, I'm sure he is going to help you.	√ If you speak to the manager, I'm sure he will help you.

If we say that someone is ***going to*** do something, we can see that the action is about to happen ('Careful! You're ***going to*** spill your coffee.') or we know that they intend to do it ('Helen is ***going to*** be a doctor.')

When we say what we think or expect will happen, we normally use ***will*** + bare infinitive: 'If you leave now, you***'ll be*** back by six.' 'Do you think that Peter ***will get*** there in time?'

⇨ 163.1–3

2

× Don't worry! I'm going to be there as soon as I can.	√ Don't worry! I'll be there as soon as I can.

We use ***going to*** for a future action that has been decided before the moment of speaking. If the action is decided at the moment of speaking, we use ***will***. Compare the use of ***going to*** and ***will*** in the following dialogue:

Manager: You know that I***'m going to see*** Sinclair on Wednesday, don't you?
Secretary: But on Wednesday you have a meeting in London.
Manager: Oh, dear. In that case, I***'ll see*** Sinclair on Thursday.

The decision to see Sinclair on Wednesday has been made before the moment of speaking and so the speaker uses ***going to***. The decision to see Sinclair on Thursday is made at the moment of speaking and so the speaker uses ***will***.

⇨ 873.5

3

× The course is going to start on January 20th.	√ The course starts on January 20th. √ The course will start on January 20th.

When we refer to a scheduled future event, we normally use the present simple tense, NOT ***going to***:

Our coach ***leaves*** at half past five.
The concert ***begins*** at seven o'clock.
Tina's party ***is*** next Saturday.

In formal styles, we often use ***will***: 'The coach ***will leave*** at 5.30 p.m. and all passengers are requested to be punctual.'

golden 334

× I would never waste my money on a golden ring.	√ I would never waste my money on a gold ring.

Nowadays, ***golden*** is rarely used apart from in phrases such as 'a golden opportunity', 'a golden wedding anniversary', 'a golden rule'. In these phrases, ***golden*** is used figuratively. When we mean that something is made of gold or is the colour of gold, we use ***gold***: 'a gold watch', 'gold paint'.

good 335

1

×	✓
× I don't speak English very good.	✓ I don't speak English very well.
× Things did not turn out as good as we had expected.	✓ Things did not turn out as well as we had expected.

Good is an adjective. The adverb is ***well***. Compare: 'She is ***a very good*** swimmer.' 'She swims ***very well***.'

2

×	✓
× It's no good to have a piano if nobody can play it.	✓ It's no good having a piano if nobody can play it.

The expressions 'it is no good' and 'it is not much good' are followed by an *-ing* form.

3

×	✓
× There's no good trying to work if you feel tired.	✓ It's no good trying to work if you feel tired.

For information about 'there is no' and 'it is no' expressions, ⇨ 786.5.

4

×	✓
× In the market they were busy selling their good.	✓ In the market they were busy selling their goods.

Goods (= things for sale) is a plural noun. ⇨ 603

gossip 336

×	✓
× There had been a lot of gossips about the company going bankrupt.	✓ There had been a lot of gossip about the company going bankrupt.

When ***gossip*** means 'informal reports about someone, often unkind and not based on fact', it is an uncountable noun and does not have a plural form.

got 337

1

×	✓
× I got two sisters and one brother.	✓ I have two sisters and one brother.
	✓ I've got two sisters and one brother.

When we mean 'have', we use ***have*** or ***have got***, but not ***got***. Note that ***have got*** is far more common in British English than in American English.

2

! They had got a house in London and a flat in Brighton.	√ They had a house in London and a flat in Brighton.

When talking about the past, we normally use ***have***, NOT ***have got***.

3

× This year we have got two English lessons every day.	√ This year we have two English lessons every day.

When talking about something that happens repeatedly, we normally use ***have***, NOT ***have got***.

government 338

× British government should make sure that men and women are given the same opportunities.	√ The British government should make sure that men and women are given the same opportunities.

When ***government*** refers to the group of people who govern a particular country, it is a countable noun. The singular form requires a determiner. Compare the uncountable usage: '***Government*** is difficult when there is only a small majority.' 'In several countries, we have seen a swing to democratic ***government***.' ⇨ 529.4

grass 339

× The rain had made the grasses very wet.	√ The rain had made the grass very wet.

Grass is usually an uncountable noun and does not have a plural form: 'She was sitting on the ***grass***.' We use ***grass*** as a countable noun to refer to a particular type of grass: 'The taller ***grasses*** make attractive arrangements.' ⇨ 529.2

greenery 340

× Surrounded by greeneries, the school looks very attractive.	√ Surrounded by greenery, the school looks very attractive.

Greenery is an uncountable noun and does not have a plural form.

ground 341

1

× The headmaster showed us around the school ground.	√ The headmaster showed us around the school grounds.

To refer to the area of land which surrounds a building, we use the plural form ***grounds***: 'The house stands in six acres of ***grounds***.'

2

× On what ground has the film been banned?	√ On what grounds has the film been banned?

When we talk about the reason/s for doing something, we normally use the plural form ***grounds***:

She was given early retirement on medical ***grounds***.
They have no real ***grounds*** for suspecting him.
We accepted their offer on the ***grounds*** that something is better than nothing.

grow up 342

× Children should be grown up to respect nature.	√ Children should be brought up to respect nature.

Grow up is an intransitive verb: 'I ***grew up*** in a small town near Dresden.' The transitive equivalent is ***bring up***: 'My parents ***brought*** me ***up*** to believe that money isn't everything.' 'We ***brought up*** three children on just thirty pounds a week.'

hair 343

× This shampoo is ideal for people with dry hairs.	√ This shampoo is ideal for people with dry hair.

When ***hair*** means 'the mass of hair which grows on a person's head', it is an uncountable noun: 'He's gone to have his ***hair*** cut.' 'She doesn't like men with greasy ***hair***.' Compare: 'Turn round and I'll brush the ***hairs*** off your jacket.'

⇨ 529.2

half 344

1

× Use one capful to half bowl of water.	√ Use one capful to half a bowl of water.

Between ***half*** and the following noun, there is normally a determiner (*a/an*, *the*, *my*, etc.):

It takes me ***half an*** hour to get to work.
He spends ***half his*** time in bed.

2

× Last year there were so many apples that we had to give the half of them away.	√ Last year there were so many apples that we had to give half of them away.

We do not use ***the*** before ***half*** unless we wish to refer to a particular ***half***. Compare: 'We ate ***half*** the cake and put ***the other half*** back in the tin.'

For more information about fractions, ⇨ 318.

handful 345

× Only a handful people managed to finish the race.	√ Only a handful of people managed to finish the race.

⇨ 823.2

happen 346

1

× Last week happened to me something very strange.	√ Last week something very strange happened to me.

In a statement, we put the subject ('something very strange') before the verb ('happened'). The normal word order does not change when the verb is ***happen***.

2

× When I pressed the button, it happened something most peculiar.	√ When I pressed the button, something most peculiar happened.

When ***happen*** means 'take place', we use the normal word order, i.e. subject + verb.

When ***happen*** means 'to occur by chance', we often use the pattern ***it*** + ***happen*** + ***that***-clause: '***It happened that*** we both arrived in Helsinki on the same day.'

3

× It had happened a serious road accident.	√ There had been a serious road accident.

⇨ 421.3

4

× What has happened with your friend, Mohsen?	√ What has happened to your friend, Mohsen?

Something ***happens to*** someone/something: 'What's ***happened to*** the toaster? It's not working.'

hardly 347

1

× My mother and father have worked hardly all their lives.	√ My mother and father have worked hard all their lives.

⇨ 26.3

2

× The bag was so heavy that I couldn't hardly lift it.	√ The bag was so heavy that I could hardly lift it.

⇨ 512.9

3

× He was so exhausted that he hardly could stand up.	√ He was so exhausted that he could hardly stand up.

⇨ 29.1

4

× Hardly we had arrived than we had to leave again.	√ Hardly had we arrived than we had to leave again.

⇨ 31.1

hardware 348

× We stock a full range of general hardwares.	√ We stock a full range of general hardware.

Hardware is an uncountable noun and does not have a plural form.

harm 349

× A little meat will not do you a harm.	√ A little meat will not do you any harm.

Harm is an uncountable noun and is not used with ***a/an***. ⇨ 2.1

hate 350

× She hates to have nobody to talk to. × I would hate hurting the child's feelings.	√ She hates having nobody to talk to. √ I would hate to hurt the child's feelings.

For the difference between ***hate doing*** and ***hate to do***, ⇨ 839.6

have 351

1

× Mr Smart haven't returned to the office yet. × Are you sure that Rostinah have gone home?	√ Mr Smart hasn't returned to the office yet. √ Are you sure that Rostinah has gone home?

When the subject is third person singular subject, we use ***has/has not/hasn't***. All other subjects take ***have/have not/haven't***.

2

! Has he any sisters or brothers?	√ Does he have any sisters or brothers?
! We had not very much time to answer all the questions.	√ We didn't have very much time to answer all the questions.

When ***have*** is the main verb and there are no auxiliary verbs, we normally form questions and negative sentences with ***do***:

Do you *have* any books on bee-keeping?
Did you *have* any trouble finding your way here?

She ***doesn't have*** any money.
They ***didn't have*** the magazine I wanted.

Compare the use of ***have*** as an auxiliary verb: '***Hasn't*** he ***given up*** smoking?' 'The books you ordered ***haven't arrived*** yet.'

3

× These tests show whether someone is having an infection.	√ These tests show whether someone has an infection.

When ***have*** refers to a state, it is not used in progressive tenses: 'She ***has*** a headache.' 'The company ***has*** branches all over the country.' ⇨ 627.3

4

× I have to say only one thing.	√ I have only one thing to say.

The patterns ***have to do something*** and ***have something to do*** are both grammatical, but their meanings are not the same. We use ***have to do something*** to express obligation: 'If the traffic lights are red, you ***have to stop***.' (= you must stop)

Otherwise, we use ***have something to do***: 'On a long journey, I always like to ***have*** a good book ***to read***.'

In this pattern, the object of ***have*** is often an indefinite pronoun: 'He ***has nobody*** to talk to.' 'Do you ***have someone*** to help you?'

5

× We had him to put a new lock on the door.	√ We had him put a new lock on the door.

If we tell or order someone to do something, we ***have*** them ***do*** it, (NOT ***to do*** it). Compare: 'We ***got*** him ***to put*** a new lock on the door.'

Note the similar structure with ***doing***. 'She ***had*** us all ***thinking*** that there was going to be a test.' (= she caused us all to think that there was going to be a test) 'He soon ***had*** the television ***working*** again.'

6

× He was told not to return to school until he had cut his hair.	√ He was told not to return to school until he had had his hair cut.

If someone says 'I cut my hair', 'I repaired my car', 'I painted my house', they mean that they did these things themselves. However, most people do not do these things themselves; they employ someone to do them. To refer to a situation in which a person employs or causes someone to do something, we use the 'causative' structure ***have/get*** + object + past participle:

George ***had a tooth extracted*** yesterday.
How much will it cost to ***have the car repaired***?
We're ***having the house painted*** next week.
Where can *I* ***get this film developed***?

Note that the same structure can be 'non-causative': 'Mr Evans ***has had his car stolen***.' 'She ***got her fingers caught*** in the door.'

In these sentences, the subject is the victim of the action and does not cause it.

7

× I have my car service every six months.	√ I have my car serviced every six months.

When we pay someone to do a job for us, we ***have/get*** the job ***done*** (NOT ***do***), i.e. ***have/get*** + object + past participle. ⇨ .6 above

have to 352

1

× The patients have also to pay for medication.	√ The patients also have to pay for medication.

We use ***have to*** as if it were a single word; the two parts are inseparable. Adverbs normally come in front of it. ⇨ 29.4

2

× Had you to walk all the way home?	√ Did you have to walk all the way home?
× Most of us haven't to work on Sundays.	√ Most of us don't have to work on Sundays.

When ***have to*** is used in present simple and past simple tenses, questions and negative sentences are normally formed with ***do***: '***Do you have to*** get permission to leave the country?' 'I was delighted that I ***didn't have to*** wait.'

3

× You have to collect your bags and then to go through customs.	√ You have to collect your bags and then go through customs.

After ***have to***, we always use bare infinitives: 'I ***had to buy*** the food and ***cook*** it myself.' ⇨ 178.5

4

× Some people have said that I have to write a book about the journey.	√ Some people have said that I should write a book about the journey.

If a person in authority orders us to do something, or if something is a rule or law, we ***have to*** do it: 'You ***have to*** stop when the traffic lights are red.'

If someone simply suggests that we do something, they say that we ***should*** or ***ought to*** do it: 'He thinks that I ***should*** apply for the job.

With ***should*** or ***ought to***, we are free to decide. With ***have to***, we are not free to decide.

he 353

1

× Most of the villagers were much older than he.	√ Most of the villagers were much older than him/than he was.

⇨ 590.7

2

× The man with the camera he was taking photographs.	√ The man with the camera was taking photographs.

⇨ 591.1

3

! Everybody should stop smoking if he wants to improve his health.	√ People who want to improve their health should stop smoking.

⇨ 42.4

head 354

1

× Something hit me on my head.	√ Something hit me on the head.

⇨ 610.3

2

× The plane was heading to London.	√ The plane was heading for London.

When we go in the direction of a place, we ***head for*** or ***towards*** it.

headache 355

× I always get headache if I don't wear my glasses.	√ I always get a headache if I don't wear my glasses.

Headache is a countable noun. ⇨ 182.2

health 356

×	√
× If you want to have a good health, eat lots of vegetables.	√ If you want to have good health, eat lots of vegetables.
× I hope that you are both in a good health.	√ I hope that you are both in good health.

Health is an uncountable noun and is not used with ***a/an***. ⇨ 2.1

hear 357

1

×	√
× I heard someone to say that the driver was drunk.	√ I heard someone say/saying that the driver was drunk.

⇨ 839.3–5

2

×	√
× I was not hearing anyone go out.	√ I did not hear anyone go out.

Hear is not normally used in progressive tenses. ⇨ 627.3

3

×	√
× The engine was so quiet that I hardly heard it.	√ The engine was so quiet that I could hardly hear it.

When we want to say that we are able to ***hear*** something that continues over a period of time, we use ***can/could***. Compare: 'I ***heard*** a loud crash.' 'I ***could hear*** the radio from upstairs.'

help 358

1

×	√
× Two people stopped and helped me changing the wheel.	√ Two people stopped and helped me change the wheel.
	√ Two people stopped and helped me to change the wheel.

We ***help*** (someone) ***do*** or ***to do*** something, NOT ***doing***. ⇨ .2 below

2

×	√
× We were helped carry the piano upstairs by one or our neighbours.	√ We were helped to carry the piano upstairs by one of our neighbours.

Compare: 'One of our neighbours ***helped us carry/to carry*** the piano upstairs.'
⇨ 839.4

3

× I couldn't help to notice the hole in his trousers.	√ I couldn't help noticing the hole in his trousers.

A person ***cannot help doing*** something, NOT ***to do*** something: 'I ***can't help worrying*** about him.'

Note the alternative: 'I ***couldn't help but notice*** the hole in his trousers.' The expression ***cannot help but*** is followed by a bare infinitive ('notice').

4

× Thank you for all the help you have given me for my studies.	√ Thank you for all the help you have given me with my studies.

We give someone ***help with*** something: 'Do you need any ***help with*** the washing up?'

hence 359

× These people have no money hence they cannot afford proper medical attention.	√ These people have no money and so/therefore they cannot afford proper medical attention.

Hence is an adverb, not a conjunction, and cannot be used to link clauses.

⇨ 28.3

It is normally followed by a phrase: 'In many companies, women are required to do the same work as men and ***hence*** their insistence on equal pay.' 'He was involved in a serious road accident – ***hence*** the scars.'
Note that ***hence*** is used mainly in formal styles.

here 360

1

× Here is the magazines you asked me to get.	√ Here are the magazines you asked me to get.

⇨ 44.14

2

× Hurry up! Here the train comes.	√ Hurry up! Here comes the train.

⇨ 31.3

3

× A lot of tourists come to here, especially in the summer.	√ A lot of tourists come here, especially in the summer.

We do not use ***to*** before ***here*** unless we are pointing to something: 'Before she had it cut, her hair came right down ***to here***.' ⇨ 802.2

highlight 361

× This report highlights on the need for further research.	√ This report highlights the need for further research.

We ***highlight*** (= emphasize) something, WITHOUT ***on***.

him 362

! I fully understand him not wanting to pursue the matter.	√ I fully understand his not wanting to pursue the matter.

⇨ 590.8

his 363

× This morning you will visit the district of La Defense with his famous buildings.	√ This morning you will visit the district of La Defense with its famous buildings.
× Would you please send me some more information about your organization and his publications.	√ Would you please send me some more information about your organization and its publications.

⇨ 42.3

his or her 364

! An incentive scheme encourages a worker to produce more than his or her colleagues.	√ An incentive scheme encourages workers to produce more than their colleagues.

⇨ 42.4

hit 365

× He hitted her unintentionally.	√ He hit her unintentionally.

Hit (infinitive), ***hit*** (past simple), ***hit*** (past participle). ⇨ 419.1

holiday 366

× I first met him while I was on holidays in Scotland.	√ I first met him while I was on holiday in Scotland.
× Last year we went on holidays to Malta.	√ Last year we went on holiday to Malta.

Someone is ***on holiday*** or goes ***on holiday*** or returns ***from holiday***, NOT ***holidays***. The plural form ***holidays*** is used with a determiner: 'Where are you going for *your holidays* this year?'

home 367

× When I arrived at home, there was a letter waiting for me.	√ When I arrived home, there was a letter waiting for me.
× On my way to home, I stopped at the supermarket.	√ On my way home, I stopped at the supermarket.

After a verb or phrase of movement, we do not use a preposition before ***home***. Compare: 'Let's *go to my house*.' 'Let's *go home*.'

⇨ 802.2

homework 368

× As soon as I get home, I do my homeworks.	√ As soon as I get home, I do my homework.

Homework is an uncountable noun and does not have a plural form.

hope 369

1

× I hope that something could be done to improve the situation.	√ I hope that something can be done to improve the situation.
× We hope that you would consider our suggestion.	√ We hope that you will consider our suggestion.

When ***hope*** is in the present tense, it is followed by ***will/can*** (NOT ***would/could***). Compare:

I *hope/am hoping* that something *will/can* be done.
I *hoped/was hoping* that something *would/could* be done.

⇨ 874.1

2

× I hope to hearing from you again soon.	√ I hope to hear from you again soon.

We ***hope to do*** something (NOT ***to doing***). Note the alternative: 'I ***look forward to hearing*** from you again soon.'

3

× I hope you and Robert to be very happy in your new home.	√ I hope that you and Robert will be very happy in your new home.

Hope cannot be followed by a noun phrase + ***to***-infinitive. Instead, we use a ***that***-clause. Compare:

I ***hope*** + ***to visit*** London again.
× I ***hope*** + you + ***to visit*** London again.
I ***hope*** + ***that*** you will visit London again.

housework 370

× While I'm doing the houseworks, I like to listen to the radio.	√ While I'm doing the housework, I like to listen to the radio.

Housework is an uncountable noun and does not have a plural form.

how 371

1

× After leaving school, they suddenly discover how difficult is it to find a job.	√ After leaving school, they suddenly discover how difficult it is to find a job.

When ***how*** comes at the beginning of a subordinate clause, the word order does not change to that of a question. Compare:

How long is the film?
He wants to know ***how long the film is.*** (NOT 'how long is the film')

How much did you pay?
He asked me ***how much I paid***. (NOT 'how much did I pay') ⇨ 389.1

2

× They knew I had been to London and asked me how it was like.	√ They knew I had been to London and asked me what it was like.
× This is how the British High Commissioner's new $4 million residence will look like.	√ This is what the British High Commissioner's new $4 million residence will look like.

We ask or tell someone ***what*** a person, place or thing is ***like*** (NOT ***how***). Compare: '***How does it feel*** to have finished all your exams?' '***What does it feel like*** to have finished all your exams?'

however 372

×	✓
× The car was badly damaged, however none of the passengers was hurt.	✓ The car was badly damaged but none of the passengers was hurt. ✓ The car was badly damaged. However, none of the passengers was hurt.

To link two contrasting clauses, we use ***but***, ***although*** or (***and***) ***yet*** (conjunctions). ***However*** (an adverb) links sentences, not clauses.

hundred 373

×	✓
× The war lasted almost hundred years.	✓ The war lasted almost a hundred years.
× We were travelling at about two hundreds kilometres per hour.	✓ We were travelling at about two hundred kilometres per hour.
× The company employs over two hundreds of workers.	✓ The company employs over two hundred workers.

⇨ 538

I 374

1

×	✓
× I and my husband are the victims of inconsiderate neighbours.	✓ My husband and I are the victims of inconsiderate neighbours.
× I and my father did not talk to each other after that.	✓ My father and I did not talk to each other after that.

When we are talking about ourselves and another person, we normally mention ourselves last.

2

×	✓
× Nobody is allowed to use the computer but I.	✓ Nobody is allowed to use the computer but me.
× My sisters and brothers are all younger than I.	✓ My sisters and brothers are all younger than me. ✓ My sisters and brothers are all younger than I am.

⇨ 590.6–7

ideal 375

×	✓
× The most ideal way to learn English is to go and live in England.	✓ The ideal way to learn English is to go and live in England.

Ideal (= 'the most suitable') has a superlative meaning already and is not normally used with ***most***. ⇨ 15.4

if ⇨ **conditionals** (163)

if only 376

1

×	√
× If only I don't have to work tonight.	√ If only I didn't have to work tonight.
× If only they will stop phoning me.	√ If only they would stop phoning me.

To express a wish about something in the present or future, we use ***if only*** and the past tense ('would' is the past tense of 'will'). Compare: 'I wish I didn't have to work tonight.' 'I wish they would stop phoning me.'

2

×	√
× If only you came to me before, I could have helped you.	√ If only you had come to me before, I could have helped you.

To express a regret about something that happened or did not happen in the past, we use ***if only*** and the past perfect tense (***had*** + main verb). Compare: 'I wish that you ***had come*** to me before.' ⇨ 163.6

ignore 377

×	√
× They always ignore that their country attacked us first.	√ They always ignore the fact that their country attacked us first.

⇨ 838.7

ill 378

×	√
× Some ill people cannot afford to see a doctor.	√ Some people who are ill/sick cannot afford to see a doctor. √ Some sick people cannot afford to see a doctor.

⇨ 16.1

imagine 379

×	√
× I cannot imagine to live in a cold climate.	√ I cannot imagine living in a cold climate.

We ***imagine*** (someone) ***doing*** something (NOT ***to do*** something): 'I can't ***imagine*** Eric ***getting up*** at five in the morning just to go fishing.'

immediately 380

×	√
× They want me to phone them immediately the baby will be born.	√ They want me to phone them immediately the baby is born.

⇨ 25

importance 381

×	√
× Why do they attach such a great importance to the matter?	√ Why do they attach such great importance to the matter?

Importance is an uncountable noun and is not used with ***a/an***. ⇨ 2.1

important 382

×	√
× Winning has never been important for me.	√ Winning has never been important to me.

If we care about something, it is ***important to*** us: 'What the critics say is not ***important to*** some writers, but it is to me.' 'Our friendship is very ***important to*** me.'

in 383

1

×	√
× I visit my parents about two or three times in a year.	√ I visit my parents about two or three times a year.
× There should be a tutorial at least once in every two weeks.	√ There should be a tutorial at least once every two weeks.

When we mention frequency we do not use ***in***. Compare: '***In the last six months***, he has made three trips to London.'

2

×	√
× I am going to Athens in 20th December.	√ I am going to Athens on 20th December.

Something happens ***on*** a particular date or day: '*on* Tuesday', '*on* 22nd June'.

⇨ 549.1

3

×	√
× In the following morning he came to see me again.	√ On the following morning he came to see me again.

We do something '***in*** the morning/afternoon/evening' but '***on*** the following morning/afternoon/evening'. Note the alternative: 'The following morning he came to see me again.' This is slightly less formal.

4

×	✓
× I'm planning to visit England in the beginning of February.	✓ I'm planning to visit England at the beginning of February.

We do something ***in*** a particular month but ***at the beginning/end*** of a particular month. Compare: 'I'm planning to visit England ***in February***.'

5

×	✓
× It was the happiest time in my life.	✓ It was the happiest time of my life.

After a superlative ('the ***happiest*** time'), we normally use ***of*** + period: 'the ***busiest*** day ***of the week***', 'the ***coldest*** night ***of the year***'.

6

×	✓
× Unemployment is a major problem in these days.	✓ Unemployment is a major problem these days.

We do not use ***in*** (or any other preposition) before ***these days*** and ***nowadays***. However, compare: '***In those days*** my hair was very long.'

7

×	✓
× I live in 40 Alexandra Street.	✓ I live at 40 Alexandra Street.

When there is a number before the name of a street, road, etc., we use ***at***. Compare: 'She lives ***in*** Lime Tree Avenue.' 'She lives ***at*** 35 Lime Tree Avenue.'

8

×	✓
× You could smell the paint in the whole building.	✓ You could smell the paint all over building.

When we want to say that something is found/done/known in all the parts of a building, area, country, etc., we normally use ***all over*** or ***throughout***: 'These plants are found ***all over*** Japan.' 'His books are enjoyed by children ***throughout*** the world.'

inconvenience 384

×	✓
× We wish to apologize to local residents for any inconveniences caused.	✓ We wish to apologize to local residents for any inconvenience caused.

When it refers to problems or difficulties in general, ***inconvenience*** is an uncountable noun. Compare: 'Heavy traffic congestion was just one of several ***inconveniences*** caused by the road works.'

increase **385**

× There has been an increase of the number of people who suffer from heart disease.	√ There has been an increase in the number of people who suffer from heart disease.

We talk about an ***increase in*** something, NOT ***of***: 'These improvements have led to an ***increase in*** life expectancy.'

indeed **386**

× We knew little indeed about where we were going.	√ We knew very little indeed about where we were going.

When we use ***indeed*** at the end of a phrase, the phrase must begin with ***very***: 'Thank you ***very much indeed***.' 'I had a ***very good time indeed***.'

indirect objects **387**

1

× At bedtime, I always read to the children a story. × I gave to the man all the money that was in my pocket.	√ At bedtime, I always read the children a story. √ I gave the man all the money that was in my pocket.

When the indirect object comes before the direct object, we do not normally use ***to*** or ***for***. Compare:

He gave + the money + ***to Trevor***. (DIRECT OBJECT + INDIRECT OBJECT)
He gave + ***Trevor*** + the money. (INDIRECT OBJECT + DIRECT OBJECT)
I've got + some flowers + ***for her***. (DIRECT OBJECT + INDIRECT OBJECT)
I've got + ***her*** + some flowers. (INDIRECT OBJECT + DIRECT OBJECT)

For two exceptions to this rule ⇨ 280.1, 762.3

2

× I hadn't seen my aunt for a long time and decided to pay a visit to her.	√ I hadn't seen my aunt for a long time and decided to pay her a visit.

If one of the objects is a pronoun, the pronoun normally goes immediately after the verb: 'I think I'll send + ***it*** + to your parents.' 'Why don't you give + ***him*** + your address.'

With expressions such as ***pay (someone) a visit, give (someone) a chance, make (someone) an offer, tell (someone) the truth***, the direct object nearly always goes last: 'Why didn't you ***tell*** + them/your parents + ***the truth***?'

3

× He has bought a very expensive diamond necklace for his wife.	√ He has bought his wife a very expensive diamond necklace.

When the direct object is much longer than the indirect object, we put the indirect object immediately after the verb (without ***to/for***). Compare: 'We sent + a letter + to all the customers on our mailing list.' 'We sent + all our customers + a letter explaining the reasons for the price increases.'

In any sentence, short/simple units normally come before long/complex units. This principle of sentence arrangement is known as 'end-weight'.

4

×	✓
× What a lovely dress! Did someone make you it?	✓ What a lovely dress! Did someone make it for you?

When both the direct object and indirect object are pronouns, we normally separate them by using ***to*** or ***for*** with the indirect object and putting it last:

When did you lend + it + ***to him***?
She has offered to write + it + ***for me***.
I wouldn't tell + this + ***to everyone***.

indirect/reported speech: commands **388**

×	✓
× I told the driver let me out at the traffic lights.	✓ I told the driver to let me out at the traffic lights.
× She warned him don't go near the dog.	✓ She warned him not to go near the dog.

Imperative forms ('let', 'don't') are not used in indirect speech. Compare:

Turn right at the bank.
He told me ***to turn*** right at the bank.

Don't bother sending me an invitation.
She told me ***not to bother*** sending her an invitation.

When we report a command or warning, we use (***not***) + ***to***-infinitive.

indirect/reported speech: questions **389**

1

×	✓
× Can you remember what was she wearing?	✓ Can you remember what she was wearing?
× She asked me where did I learn to speak English.	✓ She asked me where I learned to speak English.

When a ***wh***-clause is part of another clause, the subject of the ***wh***-clause is placed before the verb. Compare:

Where ***has she*** gone?
He wants to know + where ***she has*** gone.

What time ***is it***?
Do you know + what time ***it is***?

We do not use ***do*** as an auxiliary verb. Compare: 'Where ***does he*** work?' 'Do you know + where ***he works***?'

2

×	✓
He asked me in what I was interested.	He asked me what I was interested in.

A preposition ('in') normally goes at the end of a *wh*-clause, not before the *wh*-word: 'She wants to know + ***what*** all the fuss is ***about***.' 'He asked me + ***who*** I was waiting ***for***.'

The preposition may come before the ***wh***-word only in very formal styles: 'I would like to know ***to whom*** the letter should be addressed.'

indirect/reported speech: reporting verbs **390**

1

×	✓
The doctor reassured that my problem was not serious.	The doctor reassured me that my problem was not serious.

After some reporting verbs, we have to mention the 'hearer'. This group includes ***advise, assure, convince, inform, notify, persuade, reassure, remind*** and ***tell.***

2

×	✓
She said the doctor that she was unable to sleep.	She told the doctor that she was unable to sleep.
She replied me that there was no hot water.	She replied that there was no hot water.

After some reporting verbs, we do not mention the 'hearer'. This group includes ***argue, deny, enquire, insist, reply*** and ***say***.

3

×	✓
She informed to her boss that she needed a larger office.	She informed her boss that she needed a larger office.
I asked to the air hostess if there were any empty seats.	I asked the air hostess if there were any empty seats.

After ***ask, assure, convince, inform, persuade, promise, remind*** and ***tell***, we do not use ***to*** before the 'hearer'.

indirect/reported speech: tenses **391**

1

×	✓
She told me that she is looking for the museum.	She told me that she was looking for the museum.
Mrs Lee wondered where her son has gone.	Mrs Lee wondered where her son had gone.
He thinks that output levels were likely to decline over the next twelve months.	He thinks that output levels are likely to decline over the next twelve months.
	He thought that output levels were likely to decline over the next twelve months.

If someone says 'I want to go home', we can report their words in two different ways:

PATTERN A	She ***says*** that she ***wants*** to go home.
PATTERN B	She ***said*** that she ***wanted*** to go home.

When we report what someone says immediately after they say it, we normally use Pattern A. In this pattern, the reporting verb is in the present tense ('says') and the verb in the reported clause ('wants') is in the same tense as in the direct speech ('want').

When we report what someone says some time after they say it, we normally use Pattern B. In this pattern, the reporting verb is in the past tense ('said') and we change the tense used by the original speaker. The tense used in direct speech is placed 'one step back' in time:

DIRECT SPEECH	INDIRECT SPEECH
I ***am*** late.	She said she ***was*** late.
I***'m*** going home.	She said she ***was*** going home.
I ***have***n't seen him before.	She said she ***had***n't seen him before.
Where ***has*** he gone?	She wondered where he ***had*** gone.

If the reporting verb is in the past tense, the tenses used by the original speaker normally have to be changed.

Note however that if the reported statement is still true at the time when it is reported, there is a choice of tense in the reported clause: 'She ***told*** me that she ***has/had*** two brothers.'

2

× The air hostess told the man to call her if he would feel ill again.	√ The air hostess told the man to call her if he felt ill again.

If the reporting verb is in the past tense ('told'), a present simple tense in direct speech ('Call me if you ***feel*** ill ...') normally becomes a past simple tense in indirect speech (if he ***felt***).

3

× I decided that once I would have finished secondary school, I would go to university.	√ I decided that once I had finished secondary school, I would go to university.

If the reporting verb is in the past tense ('decided'), a present perfect tense in direct speech (e.g. 'Once I ***have finished*** ...') normally becomes a past perfect tense in indirect speech ('once I ***had finished*** ...').

4

× She apologized and said that she won't do it again. × She wanted to know when she can go home.	√ She apologized and said that she wouldn't do it again. √ She wanted to know when she could go home.

If the reporting verb is in the past tense ('said', 'wanted to know'), a modal verb is normally changed to its past form:

DIRECT SPEECH	INDIRECT SPEECH
I ***can*** see her.	He said he ***could*** see her.
When ***can*** I go?	She wanted to know when she ***could*** go.
I ***'ll*** see you later.	He said he ***would*** see me later.
I ***won't*** do it again.	She said she ***wouldn't*** do it again.
I ***may*** be late.	He said he ***might*** be late.

5

×	√
× She threatened that if he does not leave her alone, she would call the police.	√ She threatened that if he did not leave her alone, she would call the police.

When we report a conditional sentence, we use the normal sequence of tenses. Compare:

She says that if she ***has*** the time, she ***will come.***
She said that if she ***had*** the time, she ***would come.***
She said that if she ***had had*** the time, she ***would have*** come. ⇨ 163

inferior **392**

1

×	√
× There is no reason at all for you to feel inferior than him.	√ There is no reason at all for you to feel inferior (to him).

When it is necessary to mention a person or thing after ***inferior***, we use a *to*-phrase, not ***than***. ⇨ 764

2

×	√
× Some women feel more inferior if they do not have a career.	√ Some women feel inferior if they do not have a career.

Inferior has a comparative meaning already and is not normally used with ***more***.
⇨ 15.4

infinitives: form **393**

1

×	√
× It cost the government $15 million to built the school.	√ It cost the government $15 million to build the school.
× I didn't want his mother to misunderstood me.	√ I didn't want his mother to misunderstand me.

The present infinitive (often referred to simply as 'the infinitive') is the base form of a verb. This is the form that we look up in a dictionary, e.g. ***be, go, build, misunderstand.***

Like all infinitive forms, the present infinitive is often used with the infinitive marker ***to***: *to be, to go, to build,* etc.

2

×	✓
× The train should arrive at 8.25, but it was almost an hour late.	✓ The train should have arrived at 8.25, but it was almost an hour late.
× Because the ball had burst, the air pressure may be too great.	✓ Because the ball had burst, the air pressure may have been too great.

When we refer to something that happened or was expected to happen *before now* (i.e. before the moment of speaking), we use a perfect infinitive ('have arrived', 'have been'), NOT a present infinitive ('arrive', 'be'). Compare: 'The letter should ***arrive*** tomorrow.' 'The letter should ***have arrived*** yesterday.'

3

×	✓
× The police made everyone to leave the building immediately.	✓ The police made everyone leave the building immediately.

⇨ 839.2

4

×	✓
× She felt that she could never to go home again.	✓ She felt that she could never go home again.

A modal verb (e.g. *could, may, must, should, will*) is followed by a bare infinitive (NOT a ***to***-infinitive). ⇨ 495.2

5

×	✓
× I advised her to not drink it.	✓ I advised her not to drink it.

We put ***not*** and ***never*** in front of the ***to*** of a ***to***-infinitive (NOT after it).

6

×	✓
× What you must never do is to give them your home address.	✓ What you must never do is give them your home address.
× All I could do was to cry.	✓ All I could do was cry.

To emphasize an action, we sometimes use the structure: ***what/all*** + subject + ***do*** + ***be*** + infinitive clause. Compare:

She closed all the windows.
What she ***did*** was ***(to) close all the windows.***

They put letters into envelopes.
All they ***do*** is ***(to) put letters into envelopes.***

Normally, the infinitive clause may begin with either a bare infinitive ('close') or a ***to***-infinitive ('to close'), although a bare infinitive is more common. When we use ***do*** after ***must***, ***should***, ***can***, ***will***, etc., only a bare infinitive is possible: 'What you ***shouldn't do*** is ***give*** him your address.' 'All I ***could do*** was just ***sit*** and ***wait***.'

7

! She invited me to sit down and to have something to drink.	√ She invited me to sit down and have something to drink.
× Interviewees should be encouraged to relax, talk freely about themselves, and to ask the panel questions.	√ Interviewees should be encouraged to relax, talk freely about themselves, and ask the panel questions.

⇨ 178.5–6

infinitives: use **394**

1

× I look forward to see you again.	√ I look forward to seeing you again.
× Instead of to buy books, I borrow them from the library.	√ Instead of buying books, I borrow them from the library.

After a preposition, we use the ***-ing*** form of a verb (NOT the infinitive).

⇨ 837

2

× I'll be lucky if I ever succeed to achieve my ambition.	√ I'll be lucky if I ever succeed in achieving my ambition.
× I enjoy to speak foreign languages.	√ I enjoy speaking foreign languages.

For information about verb + verb patterns, ⇨ 839

3

× After the second punch, he was incapable to stand up.	√ After the second punch, he was incapable of standing up.

For information about adjective + verb patterns, ⇨ 20

4

× The forests are in danger to be destroyed.	√ The forests are in danger of being destroyed.
× I had great difficulty to make him understand me.	√ I had great difficulty in making him understand me.

For information about noun + verb patterns, ⇨ 534

5

× To see the baby born is something I shall never forget.	√ Seeing the baby born is something I shall never forget.
× Clean your teeth regularly is very important.	√ Cleaning your teeth regularly is very important.

In subject position, we normally use an ***-ing*** clause, not a ***to***-clause: '***Cutting the grass*** is not my idea of relaxing.' '***Moving the piano*** is not going to be easy.'

When a ***to***-clause appears in subject position, it normally refers to something that has not actually happened: '***To ignore the invitation*** would be rude, wouldn't it?' A bare infinitive clause ('***Clean*** your teeth regularly') can never be the subject of a sentence.

6

×	✓
× My favourite pastime is play chess.	✓ My favourite pastime is playing chess.
× Their only regret was to not have children.	✓ Their only regret was not having children.

We do not normally use a bare infinitive clause ('play chess') after ***be***. In this position, we tend to use either a ***to***-clause or an ***-ing*** clause: 'My one ambition is ***to retire at the age of forty***.' 'My one regret was ***retiring at the age of forty***.'

When we are talking about an action which is in progress or which has already taken place, an ***-ing*** clause is more usual.

inform 395

1

×	✓
× We would be grateful if you could inform us your decision at the earliest opportunity.	✓ We would be grateful if you could inform us of your decision at the earliest opportunity.

We ***inform*** someone ***of*** something.

2

×	✓
× I am pleased to inform that your application has been approved.	✓ I am pleased to inform you that your application has been approved.

⇨ 390.1

information 396

1

×	✓
× This report is based on informations received from teachers and pupils.	✓ This report is based on information received from teachers and pupils.

Information is an uncountable noun and does not have a plural form.

2

×	✓
× We have just received a new information.	✓ We have just received some new information.

Information is not used with ***a/an***. However, we can say '***a piece of*** new information'.

⇨ 2.1–2

-ing forms 397

1

× Incorrect	√ Correct
× These scientists doing some very important research.	√ These scientists are doing some very important research.
× Advertisers sometimes trying to deceive the public.	√ Advertisers sometimes try to deceive the public.

The subject of a main clause is followed by a finite verb. An *-ing* form is non-finite. It cannot follow the subject of a main clause unless it is used with one or more auxiliary verbs. Examples:

SUBJECT	VERB PHRASE: FINITE	NON-FINITE			OBJECT
His wife	drives				a white Mercedes.
	was	***driving***			
	has	been	***driving***		
	would	have	been	***driving***	

An *-ing* form may be used without an auxiliary verb only in subordinate clauses. Examples:

Sitting at the back of the hall, we couldn't hear anything.
We saw his wife ***sitting in a white Mercedes.***
The girl ***sitting next to me*** suddenly started to scream.
Sitting on the floor can be very uncomfortable.
I don't like ***sitting on the floor***.

2

× Incorrect	√ Correct
× As soon as the little girl seeing me, she ran away.	√ As soon as the little girl saw me, she ran away.
× If you going to the market, can I come with you?	√ If you are going to the market, can I come with you?

When a subordinate clause has a subject ('the little girl', 'you'), the following verb is normally finite. Compare:

When ***travelling*** by train, she takes very little luggage.
When ***she travels*** by train, she takes very little luggage.

Before ***coming*** to England, he lived in Sweden.
Before ***he came*** to England, he lived in Sweden.

3

× Incorrect	√ Correct
× Some students cannot afford paying these prices.	√ Some students cannot afford to pay these prices.

⇨ 839.1

4

× Incorrect	√ Correct
× I'll be ready for leaving by five o'clock.	√ I'll be ready to leave by five o'clock.

⇨ 20

5

× In San Antonio I didn't have the chance of speaking much English.	√ In San Antonio I didn't have the chance to speak much English.

⇨ 534

6

× If you need someone helping you, I shall be free all day tomorrow.	√ If you need someone to help you, I shall be free all day tomorrow.

When we mention an imaginary situation or a future event (i.e. an event which has not happened at the moment of speaking), we normally use a ***to***-infinitive. Compare: 'There is someone ***to see*** you, Mr Evans.' 'There is someone ***seeing*** Mr Evans at the moment.'

7

× Comparing with other countries in the region, ours is very small.	√ Compared with other countries in the region, ours is very small.

When a participle clause has a passive meaning, it begins with a past participle (-*ed*). Compare: '***Used properly***, the camera will last a lifetime.' (PASSIVE) '***Using a telephoto lens***, she managed to get a good close-up.' (ACTIVE)

8

× I hope that you will all enjoy your visiting.	√ I hope that you will all enjoy your visit.
× He is not allowed to go out without his parents' consenting.	√ He is not allowed to go out without his parents' consent.

We do not normally use an ***-ing*** form as a noun when there is a noun with the same meaning available. Compare: 'The owner of the restaurant invited us to the ***reopening***.' There is no noun with which 'reopening' could be replaced.

For more information about ***-ing*** forms, ⇨ 626,627

ingredient 398

× What are the main ingredients to a happy marriage?	√ What are the main ingredients of a happy marriage?

Something is an ***ingredient of*** something else, (NOT ***to***): 'The basic ***ingredients of*** success are ambition and determination.'

injure 399

1

× While I was coming down the ladder, I fell and injured.	√ While I was coming down the ladder, I fell and injured myself.

⇨ 838.2

2

× Five minutes after the kick-off he injured.	√ Five minutes after the kick-off he was injured.

⇨ 575.1

inside 400

× Inside of the room I could hear someone laughing.	√ Inside the room I could hear someone laughing.

In British English, the preposition is nearly always ***inside*** (WITHOUT ***of***): 'She was sitting ***inside*** the car.' Compare: 'He never cleans ***the inside of*** the car.' (*the* + noun + *of*)

In American English, both ***inside*** and ***inside of*** are common. ⇨ 561

insist 401

1

× He insisted to drive me all the way to the airport.	√ He insisted on driving me all the way to the airport.

We ***insist on/upon doing*** something, NOT ***to do*** something.

2

× She insists you to stay until her husband comes home.	√ She insists that you stay until her husband comes home.

When the verb after ***insist*** has its own subject ('you'), we normally use a ***that***-clause. ⇨ 839.9

Note the more formal alternative: 'She ***insists on your staying*** until her husband comes home.'

in spite of 402

1

× In spite of the driver didn't stop, we managed to get the number of the car.	√ Although the driver didn't stop, we managed to get the number of the car.

In spite of and ***despite*** are prepositions, NOT conjunctions. ⇨ 882.7

2

× Inspite of her doctor's advice, she refuses to stop work.	√ In spite of her doctor's advice, she refuses to stop work.

In spite of is written as three words. ⇨ 883.1

instead 403

×	√
× Instead of to buy books, I borrow them from the library.	√ Instead of buying books, I borrow them from the library.

Instead of is a preposition and is followed by an *-ing* form. ⇨ 837

intend 404

×	√
× What are you intending to do about it?	√ What do you intend to do about it?

Intend is not normally used in progressive tenses. ⇨ 627.3

intensifiers 405

1

×	√
× I was very delighted to see my name on the list.	√ I was (absolutely) delighted to see my name on the list.

We do not use ***very*** or ***extremely*** before adjectives which contain 'very' as part of their meaning, e.g. *delighted* (very pleased), *enormous* (very big), *exhausted* (very tired), *fascinating* (very interesting), *filthy* (very dirty), *soaked* (very wet).

If we wish to intensify these adjectives, we use ***absolutely*** or ***completely***. Compare: 'They weren't just ***very pleased*** that you came – they were ***absolutely delighted***.'

2

×	√
× A car can be absolutely useful when you are in a hurry.	√ A car can be extremely useful when you are in a hurry.
× I am completely disappointed with the sound quality.	√ I am very disappointed with the sound quality.

We use ***absolutely*** and ***completely*** before adjectives that have 'very' as part of their meaning. For example, *delighted* means 'very pleased' and so we say 'absolutely delighted' (NOT 'very delighted').

Before adjectives which do not have 'very' as part of their meaning (e.g. *useful*, *disappointed*), we use ***very*** or ***extremely***.

3

×	√
× Your cooperation is very appreciated.	√ Your cooperation is much appreciated.

Very and ***extremely*** are intensifiers. We can use them before adjectives, including past participles used as adjectives: 'She was ***very happy***.' 'She was ***very pleased*** that we went to see her.'

We cannot intensify a past participle that is used as a verb. Compare: 'People ***admire*** his work.' (ACTIVE) 'His work ***is admired***.' (PASSIVE)

Instead of ***very*** or ***extremely***, we use a suitable adverb, e.g. ***much***, ***greatly***, ***widely***, ***universally***. 'His work is ***much admired*** in the medical world.' 'She is ***widely recognized*** to be an expert in her field.'

4

×	✓
× His hair was very in need of a good wash.	✓ His hair was very much in need of a good wash.

Before a prepositional phrase, we use ***very much***, NOT ***very*** on its own: 'Everyone is ***very much*** against the idea.' 'They are still ***very much*** in love with each other.'

intention 406

×	✓
× I have no intention to change my mind.	✓ I have no intention of changing my mind.

When ***intention*** has a negative modifier (e.g. *no/little/not the slightest*), it is followed by ***of*** + ***-ing***. Compare: 'It is their ***intention + to appeal*** against the decision.' 'They have ***no intention + of appealing*** against the decision.'

interest 407

1

×	✓
× My children have never shown any interest for sport.	✓ My children have never shown any interest in sport.

A person has/shows/takes/expresses (***an***) ***interest in*** something, (NOT ***for***): 'He has absolutely no ***interest in*** making money.' 'You should take more ***interest in*** your appearance.'

2

×	✓
× All interest are paid without deduction of tax.	✓ All interest is paid without deduction of tax.

When ***interest*** is used in its financial meaning, it is an uncountable noun and takes a singular verb.

interested 408

1

×	✓
× The course is for anyone who is interested to learn about computers.	✓ The course is for anyone who is interested in learning about computers.
× I was interested in hearing that Simon has found a job at last.	✓ I was interested to hear that Simon has found a job at last.

If we want to do something, we are ***interested in doing*** it: 'Douglas is ***interested in taking*** driving lessons.'

If we find something that we hear interesting, we say that we are ***interested to hear*** it: 'I'd be ***interested to know*** what you think about the idea.' Compare: 'I am ***interested to see*** that the government is ***interested in building*** more hospitals.'

2

× I am not interested about what other people think.	√ I am not interested in what other people think.

A person is ***interested in*** something: 'She's very ***interested in*** interior design.' 'I'm not ***interested in*** what they think.'

3

× His lessons are always very interested.	√ His lessons are always very interesting.

⇨ 14.3

interesting 409

× I am very interesting in problems caused by pollution.	√ I am very interested in problems caused by pollution.

⇨ 14.3

interfere 410

× I never let my work interfere my family life.	√ I never let my work interfere with my family life.

If something makes us change our plans, arrangements, routines, etc., it ***interferes with*** them: 'She doesn't let anything ***interfere with*** her child's education.' 'Nothing, not even having a baby, will ***interfere with*** my work.'

into 411

× He wanted to know what was into the parcel.	√ He wanted to know what was in the parcel.

Into normally expresses movement or a change of state:

We all ran *into* the garden.
I poured the milk *into* a jug.
The water had turned *into* ice.
The child burst *into* tears.

invest 412

×	√
× Businessmen invest vast amounts on these industries.	√ Businessmen invest vast amounts in these industries.
× They have invested over $1m into the company.	√ They have invested over $1m in the company.

We ***invest*** money ***in*** something.

investigate 413

×	√
× Each company should investigate into ways of increasing productivity.	√ Each company should investigate ways of increasing productivity.

We ***look into*** something but we ***investigate*** something (WITHOUT ***into***). Compare: 'The police are currently conducting ***investigations into*** the cause of the accident.' We use ***into*** after the noun but not after the verb.

investigation 414

×	√
× Investigations on the cause of the fire are still continuing.	√ Investigations into the cause of the fire are still continuing.

⇨ 413

invitation 415

×	√
× Thank you for your invitation for the party.	√ Thank you for your invitation to the party.

We receive or send someone an ***invitation to*** a party, wedding, etc., (NOT ***for***).

invite 416

1

×	√
× It was kind of you to invite me for your party.	√ It was kind of you to invite me to your party.

We ***invite*** someone ***to*** a place, party, wedding, etc: 'She *invited* us back ***to*** her apartment.'

We ***invite*** someone ***to*** or ***for*** a meal: 'They've *invited* us ***to/for*** dinner.'

We ***invite*** someone ***to*** a place ***for*** something. 'They've *invited* us over ***to*** their house ***for*** dinner.' 'He's *invited* us ***to*** his club ***for*** a game of tennis.'

2

× She has invited us for attending her daughter's wedding.	√ She has invited us to attend her daughter's wedding.

We ***invite*** someone ***to do*** something: 'He's ***invited*** us ***to play*** tennis.'

3

× The advertisement invites for married couples to apply.	√ The advertisement invites married couples to apply.

We ***invite*** someone ***to do*** something, NOT ***for*** someone.

involve 417

× Nowadays, many women involve in politics.	√ Nowadays, many women are involved in politics.

If we take part in something, we ***are involved in*** it: 'He is suspected of being ***involved in*** criminal activities.'

Involve is a transitive verb and must have an object: 'The protection of the environment ***involves everybody***.' ⇨ 838.1

involved 418

× Fortunately, all the involved people agreed to co-operate.	√ Fortunately, all the people involved agreed to co-operate.

When ***involved*** means 'taking part' or 'connected', it goes immediately after the noun it describes: 'Remember that there is ***a lot of money involved***.' Compare: 'He proceeded to give us a rather ***involved*** explanation as to why he could not attend.' (= hard to understand; complicated) ⇨ 16.3

irregular verbs 419

1

× He hitted her unintentionally.	√ He hit her unintentionally.

We can say 'The shoes ***fitted*** her' but we cannot say 'He ***hitted*** her'. Unlike ***fit***, ***hit*** is an irregular verb. It belongs to a small group of verbs whose infinitive, past simple and past participle forms are all the same.

INFINITIVE	PAST SIMPLE	PAST PARTICIPLE
bet	bet	bet
broadcast[1]	broadcast	broadcast
burst	burst	burst
cast	cast	cast
cost	cost	cost
forecast[1]	forecast	forecast
hit	hit	hit

INFINITIVE	PAST SIMPLE	PAST PARTICIPLE
hurt	hurt	hurt
let	let	let
put	put	put
quit	quit	quit
read[2]	read	read
rid	rid	rid
set	set	set
shed	shed	shed
shut	shut	shut
split	split	split
spread	spread	spread
thrust	thrust	thrust
upset	upset	upset
wet[1]	wet	wet

[1] These verbs also have regular ***-ed*** forms: 'The match will be ***broadcast/ broadcasted*** live from Wembley Stadium.'

[2] Note, however, the spoken forms: /ri:d/ /red/ /red/

2

× I was very lucky and catched a lot of fish.	√ I was very lucky and caught a lot of fish.
× She asked me to sent her my address.	√ She asked me to send her my address.

Catch and ***send*** belong to a group of irregular verbs whose past simple and past participle forms are the same.

INFINITIVE	PAST SIMPLE	PAST PARTICIPLE
bend	bent	bent
bind	bound	bound
bleed	bled	bled
breed	bred	bred
bring	brought	brought
build	built	built
burn[1]	burnt	burnt
buy	bought	bought
catch	caught	caught
cling	clung	clung
creep	crept	crept
deal	dealt	dealt
dig	dug	dug
dream[1]	dreamt	dreamt
dwell[1]	dwelt	dwelt
feed	fed	fed
feel	felt	felt
fight	fought	fought
find	found	found
flee	fled	fled
fling	flung	flung
get	got	got

INFINITIVE	PAST SIMPLE	PAST PARTICIPLE
grind	ground	ground
hang[2]	hung	hung
have	had	had
hear	heard	heard
hold	held	held
keep	kept	kept
kneel[1]	knelt	knelt
lay	laid	laid
lead	led	led
lean[1]	leant	leant
leap[1]	leapt	leapt
learn[1]	learnt	learnt
leave	left	left
lend	lent	lent
light[3]	lit	lit
lose	lost	lost
make	made	made
mean	meant	meant
meet	met	met
mislead	misled	misled
misunderstand	misunderstood	misunderstood
pay	paid	paid
say	said	said
seek	sought	sought
sell	sold	sold
send	sent	sent
shine[2]	shone	shone
shoot	shot	shot
sit	sat	sat
sleep	slept	slept
slide	slid	slid
sling	slung	slung
slink	slunk	slunk
smell[1]	smelt	smelt
speed	sped	sped
spell[1]	spelt	spelt
spend	spent	spent
spill[1]	spilt	spilt
spin	spun	spun
spit	spat	spat
spoil[1]	spoilt	spoilt
stand	stood	stood
stick	stuck	stuck
sting	stung	stung
strike	struck	struck
sweep	swept	swept
swing	swung	swung
teach	taught	taught
tell	told	told
think	thought	thought

INFINITIVE	PAST SIMPLE	PAST PARTICIPLE
understand	understood	understood
weep	wept	wept
win	won	won
wind /waɪnd/	wound	wound
wring	wrung	wrung

[1] These verbs also have regular ***-ed*** forms, e.g. 'You've ***spelt/spelled*** her surname incorrectly again.' In British English, the irregular ***-t*** forms are more common. American English uses the regular forms.

[2] In one of their meanings, ***hang*** and ***shine*** are regular verbs: 'The prisoner ***hanged*** himself in his cell.' 'She'd put polish on the shoes but she hadn't ***shined*** them.'

[3] See 454

[4] In American English, the past participle of ***get*** is usually ***gotten***.

3

✗	✓
× They choosed to stay at home.	√ They chose to stay at home.
× He stood in the centre of the room and begun to cry.	√ He stood in the centre of the room and began to cry.

Choose and ***begin*** belong to a group of irregular verbs whose past simple and past participle forms are different from each other. In most cases, all three forms are different.

INFINITIVE	PAST SIMPLE	PAST PARTICIPLE
arise	arose	arisen
awake	awoke	awoken
be	was/were	been
bear	bore	borne
beat	beat	beaten
become	became	become
begin	began	begun
bite	bit	bitten
blow	blew	blown
break	broke	broken
choose	chose	chosen
come	came	come
do	did	done
draw	drew	drawn
drink	drank	drunk
drive	drove	driven
eat	ate	eaten
fall	fell	fallen
fly	flew	flown
forbid	forbade	forbidden
foresee	foresaw	foreseen
forget	forgot	forgotten
forgive	forgave	forgiven
freeze	froze	frozen
give	gave	given
go	went	gone

INFINITIVE	PAST SIMPLE	PAST PARTICIPLE
grow	grew	grown
hide	hid	hidden
know	knew	known
lie[2]	lay	lain
mistake	mistook	mistaken
mow[1]	mowed	mown
prove[1]	proved	proven
ride	rode	ridden
ring	rang	rung
rise	rose	risen
run	ran	run
saw[1]	sawed	sawn
see	saw	seen
sew[1]	sewed	sewn
shake	shook	shaken
shear[1]	sheared	shorn
show	showed	shown
shrink	shrank	shrunk
sing	sang	sung
sink	sank	sunk
sow[1]	sowed	sown
speak	spoke	spoken
spring	sprang	sprung
steal	stole	stolen
stink	stank	stunk
stride	strode	stridden
swear	swore	sworn
swell[1]	swelled	swollen
swim	swam	swum
take	took	taken
tear	tore	torn
throw	threw	thrown
tread	trod	trodden
undertake	undertook	undertaken
wake	woke	woken
wear	wore	worn
weave	wove	woven
withdraw	withdrew	withdrawn
write	wrote	written

[1] These verbs also have regular -*ed* past participles.
[2] When ***lie*** means 'to deliberately say something which is not true', it is regular: 'He ***lied*** to me once and I will never trust him again.'

island 420

1

× We spent two weeks in a small island called Tioman.	√ We spent two weeks on a small island called Tioman.

We use ***on*** before ***island***, NOT ***in***. Note, however, that we use ***in*** before the name of an island that we regard as a country or city: 'She lives *in* Singapore.'

2

× We stayed on the island Rhodes.	√ We stayed on the island of Rhodes.

The name of an island is placed in an ***of***-phrase. Compare: '***the city of*** Dublin', '***the county of*** Kent'.

it 421

1

× This report looks at teaching aids and how it helps teachers.	√ This report looks at teaching aids and how they help teachers.
× Another advantage of contact lenses is that it can boost your confidence.	√ Another advantage of contact lenses is that they can boost your confidence.

A personal pronoun agrees in number with the the word or phrase that it replaces. ⇨ 42.1

2

× The men ordered us to get out of the car. We did it immediately.	√ The men ordered us to get out of the car. We did so immediately.

⇨ 235.1

3

× It was a small hole in the bucket.	√ There was a small hole in the bucket.
× It had happened a serious road accident.	√ There had been a serious road accident.

When we draw attention to the presence or existence of someone or something, we normally use ***there*** as an empty subject (NOT ***it***) and put the real subject after ***be***:

There are some more biscuits in the tin.
There were two men in the car.
There must be something wrong with the plug.

We use the same construction when we say that something has happened, may happen, is going to happen, etc. 'There have been a lot of complaints recently.' 'There must have been a fire.'

We use ***it*** as an empty subject when the real subject is a clause:

It was good ***to see you all again.***
It's a pity ***that you cannot stay a few more days.***
It's wonderful ***having my own computer.***
It's amazing ***how quickly the child has grown.*** ⇨ 423

Note also the use of ***it*** as an empty subject in expressions of time, distance, temperature, etc:

It's nearly eight o'clock.
It's Hilary's birthday tomorrow.

It's about two miles to the motorway.
It's terribly cold in here.
It's raining.

it: wrongly included **422**

1

× The research it will investigate some major traffic problems.	√ The research will investigate some major traffic problems.

⇨ 591.1

2

× The computer is very easy to use it.	√ The computer is very easy to use.

⇨ 591.3

3

× I wonder if Richard would like it to go to Zurich with me.	√ I wonder if Richard would like to go to Zurich with me.

When a verb ('like') already has an object ('to go to Zurich with me'), we do not use ***it*** as an empty object: 'He would like + ***to see the film again***.' (NOT *like **it***). 'I enjoyed + ***seeing all my old friends again***.' (NOT *enjoyed **it***).
Compare: 'He doesn't like ***it*** if you arrive late.' In this sentence, 'if you arrive late' is an adverbial, not an object. ⇨ 838.3

it: wrongly omitted **423**

1

× Nowadays is very expensive to run a car. × Always important is to know if there is a guarantee.	√ Nowadays it is very expensive to run a car. √ It is always important to know if there is a guarantee.

Compare the following patterns:

Pattern A ***To get there by six o'clock*** will be impossible.
Pattern B ***It*** will be impossible ***to get there by six o'clock***.

In Pattern A, the subject is a clause ('To get there by six o'clock'). In Pattern B, this clause has been moved to the end of the sentence, and in its place is the 'empty' subject ***it***. Here are some more examples of Pattern B:

IT +	LINKING VERB +	COMPLEMENT +	CLAUSE
It	is	very expensive	to run a car.
It	was	a pity	that they could not come.
It	seems	strange	having nobody to talk to.

Note that in this construction ***it*** has no meaning. It merely fills the subject position and makes the sentence complete.

2

× Some people find to stop smoking difficult.	√ Some people find it difficult to stop smoking.

For information about the use of ***it*** as an empty object, ⇨ 838.4

3

× She doesn't like when people criticize her.	√ She doesn't like it when people criticize her.

For information about the use of ***it*** as an empty object, ⇨ 838.3

it's or its ? 424

× The chair was cheap because one of it's legs was broken.	√ The chair was cheap because one of its legs was broken.
× The brain works at it's best at lower temperatures.	√ The brain works at its best at lower temperatures.

It's (with an apostrophe) is a short form of ***it is*** or ***it has***:

It's Tuesday today.
Do you think *it's* going to rain?
It's got four legs and a long tail.

The possessive determiner is ***its*** (without an apostrophe).

jargon 425

× I don't like books which are full of jargons.	√ I don't like books which are full of jargon.

Jargon is an uncountable noun and does not have a plural form.

jealous 426

× He has always been jealous for his sister.	√ He has always been jealous of his sister.

A person is ***jealous of*** someone or someone's achievements.

jealousy 427

× The jealousy can sometimes destroy a relationship.	√ Jealousy can sometimes destroy a relationship.

⇨ 782.3

jeans 428

×	✓
× I bought three jeans for just $60.	✓ I bought three pairs of jeans for just $60.
× When he arrives, he will be wearing a yellow jeans so that you can recognize him.	✓ When he arrives, he will be wearing yellow jeans so that you can recognize him.

Jeans is a plural noun. ⇨ 603

jewellery (American English jewelry) 429

×	✓
× Most of the stolen jewelleries have been recovered.	✓ Most of the stolen jewellery has been recovered.

Jewellery is an uncountable noun and does not have a plural form.

join 430

×	✓
× My nephew is going to join in the army when he leaves school.	✓ My nephew is going to join the army when he leaves school.

We ***join*** a team, club or organization, (WITHOUT ***in***): 'If you like singing, you could *join* the school choir.' We ***join in*** an activity: 'Watch what the other children are doing and then *join in*.'

junior 431

×	✓
× He doesn't want to work in an office where he is junior than everybody.	✓ He doesn't want to work in an office where he is junior to everybody.

A person is ***junior to*** someone who has a more important job or position, (NOT ***than***).

just 432

1

×	✓
× I just had finished my breakfast when the doorbell rang.	✓ I had just finished my breakfast when the doorbell rang.
× I want just to say thank you.	✓ I just want to say thank you.

⇨ 29.1

2

× The third language in Norway is Lappish, which is just spoken by the Lapps.	√ The third language in Norway is Lappish, which is spoken just by the Lapps.

To avoid ambiguity in written English, ***just*** is placed immediately before the word or phrase that is modifies. 'Lappish is ***just*** spoken by the Lapps' could mean that the Lapps speak Lappish but do not write it.

3

× The only present I received was just a pair of socks.	√ The only present I received was a pair of socks.

We do not use ***just*** if the same meaning is expressed elsewhere in the sentence. The use of ***only*** often makes ***just*** unnecessary.

keen 433

× Apart from gardening, she is very keen for golf.	√ Apart from gardening, she is very keen on golf.

If someone is enthusiastic about something, they are ***keen on*** it.

kilo 434

× Do not put more than two kilos clothes in the washing machine.	√ Do not put more than two kilos of clothes in the washing machine.

⇨ 823.1

kind 435

1

× It was very kind for you to invite me.	√ It was very kind of you to invite me.

⇨ 312.4

2

× She was always very kind with me when I was a child.	√ She was always very kind to me when I was a child.

We say that someone is ***kind/unkind to*** a person or animal: 'Children should be brought up to be ***kind to*** animals.'

3

× Would you be so kind to answer one more question.	√ Would you be so kind as to answer one more question.

When we ask someone to do something, we say 'Would you be ***kind enough to*** ...' or 'Would you be ***so kind as to*** ...' Both structures are used only in formal styles.

kind of 436

1

× These kind of animals should not be kept in cages.	√ These kinds of animal/s should not be kept in cages.
× There are several different kind of video camera.	√ There are several different kinds of video camera/s.

Kind is a countable noun. In formal styles, it is incorrect to use the singular form ('kind') after a plural determiner ('these', 'several'). The determiner and noun must agree in number:

this kind of camera
these kinds of camera/s

After ***kinds*** (plural), the noun in the ***of***-phrase may be singular or plural ('camera/s'). However, a plural form can sometimes sound awkward and careful users tend to prefer a singular form.

In informal styles, when the noun in the ***of***-phrase is plural, it is not unusual to hear people say: 'these ***kind of*** cameras'. Although this combination of singular and plural forms is fairly common, careful users regard it as incorrect.

The same is true for ***sort of*** and ***type of***.

2

× I don't like this kind of jobs, as you know.	√ I don't like this kind of job, as you know. √ I don't like jobs of this kind, as you know.

When a singular determiner is used before ***kind***, ***type*** or ***sort***, the noun in the ***of***-phrase cannot be plural: 'I haven't seen ***this kind of elephant*** before.' (NOT ***elephants***)

With ***kind*** and ***type***, we often use the alternative construction: 'I haven't seen ***elephants of this kind*** before.'

kindly 437

× Thank you again for your kindly invitation.	√ Thank you again for your kind invitation.

Nowadays, ***kindly*** is used mainly as an adverb: 'She has ***kindly*** offered to lend us her car.' 'Would you ***kindly*** take this to the post office for me?' When we need an adjective, we use ***kind***.

knock 438

× Someone suddenly knocked the door.	√ Someone suddenly knocked on/at the door.

We ***knock on/at*** a door when we want someone to open it. Compare: 'Be careful or you'll ***knock*** your head.' 'The baby keeps ***knocking*** her bowl onto the floor.'

know 439

1

× We have been knowing each other since we were children.	√ We have known each other since we were children.

Know is not used in progressive tenses.

⇨ 627.3

2

× Do you know where does she come from?	√ Do you know where she comes from?

⇨ 389.1

3

× I wish I knew swimming.	√ I wish I knew how to swim.

If we can do something, we ***know how to do*** it: 'Do you ***know how to play*** backgammon?'

4

× As we all know that there are people in the world who cannot read or write.	√ As we all know, there are people in the world who cannot read or write.

When ***know*** is part of an adverbial expression, e.g. 'as everyone knows', 'as far as I know', it is not followed by ***that***. Compare: 'Everyone ***knows that*** there are people in the world who cannot read or write.'

knowledge 440

1

× I want to improve my knowledge in English.	√ I want to improve my knowledge of English.

We have ***knowledge of*** something: 'His ***knowledge of*** financial matters is almost zero.'

2

× Scientists have little knowledges of what causes the disease.	√ Scientists have little knowledge of what causes the disease.

Knowledge is an uncountable noun and does not have a plural form.

lack 441

1

× My parents lacked of the funds to send me to college. × The country is lack of skilled workers.	√ My parents lacked the funds to send me to college. √ The country lacks skilled workers. √ The country has a lack of skilled workers.

Lack is used as a verb and as a noun. As a verb, it is followed immediately by an object: 'He ***lacks the ability*** to concentrate.' (NOT ***lacks of***) 'Sharing a flat means that you often ***lack privacy***.' (NOT ***lack of***)

As a noun, ***lack*** is followed by an ***of***-phrase: 'In some schools, there is a total ***lack of*** discipline.' 'The worst thing about sharing a flat is the ***lack of*** privacy.'

Note also the adjective ***lacking***, which is often followed by an ***in***-phrase: 'My present accommodation ***is lacking in*** privacy.' 'I like my new job, but I feel that something ***is lacking***.'

2

× Some people are lacking the ability to think clearly.	√ Some people lack the ability to think clearly.

The verb ***lack*** is not normally used in progressive tenses. ⇨ 627.3 Compare: 'The ability to think clearly is sometimes ***lacking***.' In this sentence, ***lacking*** is an adjective.

lake 442

× We stayed in a log cabin near the Lake Michigan.	√ We stayed in a log cabin near Lake Michigan.

We use ***the*** with the names of canals, rivers, seas and oceans, but not with the names of lakes. ⇨ 783.11

last 443

1

× I have arrived in England last July.	√ I arrived in England last July.

With 'last night', 'last week', etc, we usually use the past simple tense.

⇨ 617.1

2

× Last evening I went to see a friend in hospital.	√ Yesterday evening I went to see a friend in hospital.

We say 'last night' but not 'last evening'. Before *morning*, *afternoon*, *evening*, *lunchtime*, etc., we use ***yesterday***.

3

× At last I would like to end my talk with some suggestions for further reading.	√ Finally, I would like to end my talk with some suggestions for further reading.

To signal the last stage of a talk, essay, etc., we use ***finally***. Compare: 'The plane took off ***at last***, almost an hour behind schedule.' (= after a long delay) 'Do you mean that you've actually passed your driving test ***at last***?' ⇨ 304

late 444

× I was in a hurry because I didn't want to be late to school.	√ I was in a hurry because I didn't want to be late for school.

A person is/arrives ***late for*** school, work, an appointment, etc.

laugh 445

× Don't forget to laugh his jokes. × You must not laugh on them.	√ Don't forget to laugh at his jokes. √ You must not laugh at them.

We ***laugh at*** someone or something: 'Why is everybody ***laughing at*** me?'

laughter 446

× I love the sound of children's laughters.	√ I love the sound of children's laughter.

Laughter is an uncountable noun and does not have a plural form.

lay 447

1

× Two hours later he found himself laying in his own bed again.	√ Two hours later he found himself lying in his own bed again.

The verbs ***lay*** and ***lie*** are sometimes confused. ***Lay (laying, laid, laid)*** is a transitive verb and needs an object:

Why have the chickens stopped *laying* eggs? (= producing)
The waiters were busy *laying* the tables. (= preparing)
She *laid* the cards face down on the table. (= put)

When we are talking about the position of someone or something, we use ***lie*** (***lying**, **lay**, **lain***) + adverbial:

He spent the whole weekend *lying* under his car.
The dog *lay* motionless in the middle of the road.
I was so worried that I *lay* awake all night.
She has *lain* in bed for a week without speaking. (NOT She has laid …)

2

× This year the birds have layed eggs on the verandah.	√ This year the birds have laid eggs on the verandah.

Lay (infinitive), ***laid*** (past simple), ***laid*** (past participle).

learn 448

× How long does it take to learn playing the piano?	√ How long does it take to learn to play the piano?

We ***learn (how) to do*** something: 'He's been ***learning to drive*** for the last three years.'

leave 449

1

× She left from the building and got into a taxi.	√ She left the building and got into a taxi.

We ***leave*** a place (NOT ***from*** a place): 'I ***left*** home when I was eighteen.'
We use ***leave from*** only when we are talking about the place where a journey, trip or outing begins: 'We'll meet at midday and ***leave from*** the bus station.'

2

× We shall be leaving to France next Wednesday.	√ We shall be leaving for France next Wednesday.

We ***leave for*** a destination (NOT ***to***).

3

× She will be returning from leaves at the end of August.	√ She will be returning from leave at the end of August.

When ***leave*** means 'a period of time that someone spends away from his or her job', it is an uncountable noun and does not have a plural form: 'He is away on ***sick leave***.' ***Leaves*** is the plural form of ***leaf***.

less 450

1

× There are less monkeys in Brunei than in Sarawak.	√ There are fewer monkeys in Brunei than in Sarawak.

We use ***less*** before uncountable nouns and ***fewer*** before plural count nouns. Compare: '***Less*** traffic should lead to ***fewer*** accidents.'

In informal styles, some people use ***less*** instead of ***fewer***. However, careful users regard this as incorrect.

2

× Sue's examination results were less good than Mary's.	√ Sue's examination results were not as good as Mary's.

Instead of using ***less*** + adjective, we normally use ***not*** + ***as/so*** + adjective + ***as***. Compare:

× John is less tall than Christine.
√ John is***n't as*** tall ***as*** Christine.

× Peter writes less well than Henry.
√ Peter does***n't*** write ***as*** well ***as*** Henry.

3

× She asked me to watch her count the money less anyone should accuse her of stealing.	√ She asked me to watch her count the money lest anyone should accuse her of stealing.

When we mean 'in case', we can use ***lest*** (a conjunction).

let 451

× I thanked the shop assistant for letting me to look at the book.	√ I thanked the shop assistant for letting me look at the book.

We ***allow*** someone ***to do*** something but we ***let*** someone ***do*** something: 'She wouldn't *let* me *help* her.'

lied 452

× Goldilocks lied down on the bed and went straight to sleep.	√ Goldilocks lay down on the bed and went straight to sleep.

Do not confuse ***lie***, ***lying***, ***lied***, ***lied*** (= to say something which is not true) and ***lie***, ***lying***, ***lay***, ***lain*** + adverbial (= to be in or get into a resting position).

⇨ 447

life 453

× The two women have spent their lifes helping the poor.	√ The two women have spent their lives helping the poor.

The plural of ***life*** is ***lives***. ⇨ 181.4

lighted 454

1

× Our neighbourhood is very badly lighted.	√ Our neighbourhood is very badly lit.

The adjective ***lighted*** is normally used in attributive position: 'a lighted cigarette', 'a lighted candle', 'lighted windows'. ⇨ 16.1

2

× Once all the candles had been lighted, I turned the lights out.	√ Once all the candles had been lit, I turned the lights out.

For the past tense and past participle of ***light***, we use ***lit***. In some contexts it is possible to use ***lighted***, but ***lit*** is always correct.

like: conjunction 455

! My examination results were just like I expected.	√ My examination results were just as I expected.

Like is frequently used as a conjunction in informal styles: 'James thinks twice about running up to strangers, just ***like*** you'd expect.'

In formal styles, this usage is often considered to be incorrect, and is best avoided: 'The child tends to approach strangers with extreme caution, just ***as*** one would expect.'

like: preposition 456

1

× Like in many successful corporations, the link between the people and the policy-makers is an important one.	√ As in many successful corporations, the link between the people and the policy-makers is an important one.

When used as a preposition in formal styles, ***like*** is followed by a noun phrase, not by another preposition ('in'). Compare: 'January, ***like December***, was a good month for sales.' 'In January, ***as in December***, sales were high.'

2

×	✓
× The alleged offences include such non-violent crimes like theft and shoplifting.	✓ The alleged offences include such non-violent crimes as theft and shoplifting. ✓ The alleged offences include non-violent crimes like theft and shoplifting.

To introduce examples of a class, we use ***such*** + noun + ***as*** (NOT *such* + noun + *like*). Note the alternative: 'The alleged offences include non-violent crimes ***such as*** theft and shoplifting.'

3

×	✓
× They knew I had been to London and asked me how it was like.	✓ They knew I had been to London and asked me what it was like.

We ask/tell someone ***what*** a person, place or thing is ***like*** (NOT ***how***).

⇨ 371.2

like: verb **457**

1

×	✓
× 'Do you like England?' 'Yes, I like.'	✓ 'Do you like England?' 'Yes, I do.'

In answer to a 'Do you like ...' question, we say 'Yes, I do' or 'No, I don't.'
We do not use ***like*** unless we continue our answer, e.g. 'Yes, I ***like*** England very much, but not the weather.'

2

×	✓
× Do you like some coffee? × As a student, I like to know why there is no library in the college.	✓ Would you like some coffee? ✓ As a student, I would like to know why there is no library in the college.

When we mean 'want', we use either ***want*** or ***would like***. If we wish to sound polite, we use ***would like***: '***Would*** you ***like*** me to help you?' 'I'***d like*** to know how much it will cost.' Compare: '***Do*** you ***like*** cheese?' (= Are you fond of cheese?) '***Would*** you ***like*** some cheese?' (= Do you want some cheese?)

3

×	✓
× Would you like eating at a restaurant tonight? × I don't like to talk to strangers when I am travelling.	✓ Would you like to eat at a restaurant tonight? ✓ I don't like talking to strangers when I am travelling.

⇨ 839.6

4

!	✓
! Would you like to drink something?	✓ Would you like something to drink?

'***Would*** you ***like*** to drink something?' and '***Would*** you ***like*** something to drink?' are both grammatical. However, the first structure sounds unnatural. When there is a choice of structure, we normally avoid ending a sentence with an 'empty' word, such as an indefinite pronoun.

5

× We would like that you come and stay with us for a few days.	√ We would like you to come and stay with us for a few days.

Like cannot be followed by a ***that***-clause. When we want someone to do something, we ***would like*** them ***to do*** it.

6

× She doesn't like when people criticize her.	√ She doesn't like it when people criticize her.

⇨ 838.3

7

× I wonder if Richard would like it to go to Zurich with me.	√ I wonder if Richard would like to go to Zurich with me.

⇨ 422.3

8

× England likes him and he is looking forward to living there.	√ He likes England and he is looking forward to living there.

The subject of ***like*** is normally a person, animal or living thing. Compare: 'England ***appeals to*** him and he is looking forward to living there.'

9

× I like very much playing tennis.	√ I like playing tennis very much.

⇨ 29.6

likely 458

× The price of computers will likely to fall again.	√ The price of computers is likely to fall again.

We say that something ***is likely*** to happen in the future (NOT ***will likely***). Compare: 'The price of computers ***will probably*** fall again.'

listen 459

×	✓
× Every morning I listen the news on the radio.	✓ Every morning I listen to the news on the radio.
× Some parents are too busy to listen their children.	✓ Some parents are too busy to listen to their children.

We ***listen to*** someone or something. Compare: 'Have you ***heard*** the latest news?' 'Speak up! I can't ***hear*** you.'

litter 460

×	✓
× Many tourists comment on the fact that our streets are free of litters.	✓ Many tourists comment on the fact that our streets are free of litter.

When ***litter*** means 'rubbish that is dropped in a public place', it is an uncountable noun and does not have a plural form.

little 461

1

×	✓
× Although the room was little, it was big enough for me.	✓ Although the room was small, it was big enough for me.

The adjective ***little*** is normally used before a noun: 'a pretty little village', 'a silly little man'.

⇨ 16.1

2

×	✓
× There are too many people for too little jobs.	✓ There are too many people for too few jobs.

⇨ 640.3

3

×	✓
× I was worried a little about what she would say.	✓ I was a little worried about what she would say.

When we use ***a little*** as an adverb of degree, we place it before an adjective ('worried'), not after it. Compare: 'I sometimes worry ***a little*** about what will happen to her.'

live 462

×	✓
× My parents are living at 64 Kalluaki Street, Athens.	✓ My parents live at 64 Kalluaki Street, Athens.

⇨ 619.3

long: verb 463

×	√
× I'm longing for seeing my family again.	√ I'm longing to see my family again.

⇨ 841.5

look 464

×	√
× She always looks beautifully.	√ She always looks beautiful.

⇨ 28.1

×	√
× This is how the British High Commissioner's new $4 million residence will look like.	√ This is what the British High Commissioner's new $4 million residence will look like.

⇨ 371.2

look forward to 465

1

×	√
× I look forward for your next visit.	√ I look forward to your next visit.

We ***look forward to*** something, NOT ***for***.

2

×	√
× We look forward to see you again in August.	√ We look forward to seeing you again in August.

We ***look forward to doing*** something. This verb has three parts (*look* + *forward* + *to*) and the last part (***to***) is a preposition. ⇨ 837

look like 466

×	√
× She was unable to describe how the thief looked like.	√ She was unable to describe what the thief looked like.

⇨ 371.2

lot 467

1

×	√
× Some teenagers have lot of problems.	√ Some teenagers have a lot of problems.

We can say ***a lot of*** or ***lots of***, but NOT ***lot of*** or ***a lots of***.

2

× The university has cost the government alot of money.	√ The university has cost the government a lot of money.

A lot is written as two words. ⇨ 883.1

loud 468

× She spoke loud so that everyone could hear her.	√ She spoke loudly so that everyone could hear her.

We do not normally use ***loud*** as an adverb. Note, however, that we do use ***louder*** and ***loudest*** as adverbs: 'I wish she would speak *louder*.' Also, we sometimes use ***loud*** as an adverb when it is part of a phrase ('he read the letter *out loud*') or when it is modified ('she doesn't speak *loud enough*').

love 469

1

× I would love spending a week in Rome.	√ I would love to spend a week in Rome.

⇨ 839.6

2

× My brother loves music very much and wants to be a musician.	√ My brother loves music and wants to be a musician.

⇨ 843.2

luck 470

1

× Everybody wished me a good luck.	√ Everybody wished me good luck.

Luck is an uncountable noun and is not used with ***a/an***. ⇨ 2.1

2

× It was good luck for you that the train arrived late.	√ You were lucky that the train arrived late.

When we say why somebody is/was lucky, we use ***lucky*** (NOT ***luck***):

She's *lucky* that nobody saw her.
In the circumstances he's *lucky* to be alive.
We're *lucky* not having to pay any rent.

When there is a change of subject ('You' ... 'the train'), we use ***lucky*** + ***that***-clause: 'He was *lucky that* the driver managed to stop in time.'

luggage 471

× The customs officer made me open all my luggages.	√ The customs officer made me open all my luggage.

Luggage is an uncountable noun and does not have a plural form.

lunch 472

× Where shall we go to have a lunch?	√ Where shall we go to have lunch?

⇨ 532.3

machinery 473

× The new machineries will be installed over the next two years.	√ The new machinery will be installed over the next two years.

Machinery is an uncountable noun and does not have a plural form.

mad 474

× My two brothers are mad for football.	√ My two brothers are mad about football.

If we are very enthusiastic about something, we are ***mad about*** it, (NOT ***for*** it).
This expression is not used in formal styles.

made 475

× A lot of rubber is still made of latex.	√ A lot of rubber is still made from latex.

When the original material is still recognizable, we use ***made of***: 'The table is *made of* wood.' When the original material is no longer recognizable, we use ***made from***: 'Paper is *made from* wood.'

mail 476

× Please redirect my mails to the following address.	√ Please redirect my mail to the following address.

Mail is an uncountable noun and does not have a plural form.

make 477

1

× Bob Geldof made people to realize the seriousness of the situation in Africa.	√ Bob Geldof made people realize the seriousness of the situation in Africa.

We ***make*** someone ***do*** something, (NOT ***to do***): 'The police ***made*** everyone ***leave*** the building immediately.'

Note, however, that someone ***is made to do*** something: 'Everyone ***was made to leave*** the building immediately.'

⇨ 839.2,4

2

× The seating arrangement makes the pupils difficult to talk to each other.	√ The seating arrangement makes it difficult for the pupils to talk to each other.

⇨ 838.4

manage 478

× Did you manage finding someone to repair the car?	√ Did you manage to find someone to repair the car?

We ***manage to do*** something, (NOT ***doing***): 'I'm afraid I didn't ***manage to post*** your letter after all.' Compare: 'Did you ***succeed in finding*** someone to repair the car?'

mankind 479

1

× Mankind have spent centuries trying to find a solution.	√ Mankind has spent centuries trying to find a solution.

Mankind ('the human race') is an uncountable noun and takes a singular verb.

2

× Without these forests, the mankind could not survive.	√ Without these forests, mankind could not survive.

⇨ 782.5

many 480

1

× My family eats many vegetables.	√ My family eats a lot of vegetables.

Many is used mainly in questions and negative sentences: 'Did you see ***many people*** there?' 'She doesn't write ***many letters***.' In affirmative sentences, we normally use ***a lot of*** or ***plenty of***.

Note that the above rule does not apply when ***many*** is used in formal contexts: '***Many vegetables*** supply the body with essential nutrients.' Nor does it apply when ***many*** combines with ***so***, ***too***, ***as*** or ***more***: 'I get ***too many*** interruptions.'

⇨ 499.1

2

×	√
I can't go out because I have too many work to do.	I can't go out because I have too much work to do.

Many is used with plural count nouns, not uncountable nouns: 'not ***many*** cars' but 'not ***much*** traffic'.

⇨ 640.3

married 481

×	√
His daughter is married with a doctor.	His daughter is married to a doctor.

A person is ***married to*** someone, NOT ***with***.

marry 482

×	√
Did he really ask you to marry with him?	Did he really ask you to marry him?

We get ***engaged to*** someone but we ***marry*** someone, NOT ***with*** or ***to*** someone.

match 483

×	√
I want to buy some dark brown shoes to match with my new handbag.	I want to buy some dark brown shoes to match my new handbag.

Something ***matches*** something else, (WITHOUT ***with***). Compare: 'I want to buy some dark brown shoes to ***go with*** my new handbag.'

mathematics 484

×	√
I don't like mathematics at all. In fact, I hate them.	I don't like mathematics at all. In fact, I hate it.

Not all nouns that end in ***s*** are plural. ***Mathematics*** is uncountable. ⇨ 530

matured 485

× They are all matured students with relevant teaching experience.	√ They are all mature students with relevant teaching experience.

⇨ 577.2

may 486

× Without the dog to guide her, she may have been killed.	√ Without the dog to guide her, she might have been killed.

When we mention something in the past that was possible but did not happen, we use ***might have*** (NOT ***may have***). Compare: 'He doesn't have a map and so he ***may have*** got lost.' (= it is still possible that he has got lost)

maybe 487

× May be they've decided not to come.	√ Maybe they've decided not to come.

The adverb ***maybe*** (= perhaps) is written as one word. Compare: 'It ***may be*** that they've decided not to come.'

me 488

1

× I often ask me why I work so hard.	√ I often ask myself why I work so hard.

⇨ 590.3

2

× Me and Karen spend a lot of time together at the weekend.	√ Karen and I spend a lot of time together at the weekend.

'***Me*** and X' is sometimes heard in everyday conversation. However, most people regard this structure as uneducated.

mean 489

1

× Being a good parent means to make a child feel loved.	√ Being a good parent means making a child feel loved.

If we ***mean to do*** something, we intend to do it: 'I didn't ***mean to be*** rude.' When we want to say that something involves or entails something else, we use ***mean*** + ***-ing***: 'Her new job will ***mean selling*** her house and moving to London.'

2

×	✓
× Television provides a mean by which people discover what is happening in the world.	✓ Television provides a means by which people discover what is happening in the world.

⇨ 530.2

media 490

×	✓
× The medias, especially television, have a very powerful influence.	✓ The media, especially television, have a very powerful influence.

Media is the plural form of ***medium***. ⇨ 181.6. Many people use ***media*** as a singular form, but some careful users regard this as incorrect.

meet 491

×	✓
× On my way home I met with one of my old school friends.	✓ On my way home I met one of my old school friends.

If we meet someone by chance, we ***meet*** them, (WITHOUT ***with***). If the meeting has been arranged, either ***meet*** or ***meet with*** is possible: 'We are ***meeting (with)*** the contractors tomorrow.' ***Meet with*** is used mainly in American English.

mention 492

×	✓
× The newspaper report did not mention about the number of casualties.	✓ The newspaper report did not mention the number of casualties.

We ***mention*** something, (NOT ***about*** something). Compare: 'Nobody wanted to ***talk about*** the accident.'

million 493

×	✓
× To reach the planet would take million years.	✓ To reach the planet would take a million years.
× The total population is over a hundred millions.	✓ The total population is over a hundred million.
× More than two millions of trees have been destroyed.	✓ More than two million trees have been destroyed.

⇨ 538

mind 494

1

× I didn't mind to help her.	√ I didn't mind helping her.

If someone is willing to do something, they ***don't mind doing*** it (NOT ***to do*** it).

2

× Do you mind to open the parcel, please?	√ Would you mind opening the parcel, please?

When we want someone to do something, we say: '***Would you mind*** ...' (NOT '***Do you mind*** ...'). Compare: '***Do you mind*** not having any sisters or brothers?' (= How do you feel about ...?)

3

× Would you mind if I sit down?	√ Would you mind if I sat down?

When ***Would you mind*** is followed by an ***if***-clause, the verb in the ***if***-clause is normally in the past tense. Compare: '***Do you mind*** if we ***go*** home now?' '***Would you mind*** if we ***went*** home now?'

modal verbs 495

1

× An elephant can washes itself with its trunk. × She would not asked him for anything.	√ An elephant can wash itself with its trunk. √ She would not ask him for anything.

Modal verbs are followed by a bare infinitive:

You ***can*** + ***help*** me if you like.
It ***must*** + ***be*** getting late.
You ***should*** + ***ask*** Peter what he thinks.

Note that ***dare*** and ***need*** are used sometimes as modal verbs and sometimes as main verbs. As modal verbs, they take a bare infinitive in the normal way. Compare: 'You ***needn't*** + ***go***.' (modal verb + bare infinitive) 'You don't ***need*** + ***to go***.' (main verb + *to*-infinitive)

⇨ 198.2, 510.1

2

× She said that she could not to go straight home after school. × You must never to tell anyone about this.	√ She said that she could not go straight home after school. √ You must never tell anyone about this.

A modal verb is followed by a bare infinitive ('go', 'tell'), NOT a ***to***-infinitive ('to go', 'to tell'). The one exception is ***ought***, which is followed by a ***to***-infinitive: 'You ***ought to see*** a doctor straight away.'

3

× A small country like ours must alert to such dangers.	√ A small country like ours must be alert to such dangers.

A modal verb is normally followed by a main verb. ⇨ 96.2

money 496

× He just didn't have the money which were needed for his wife's operation.	√ He just didn't have the money which was needed for his wife's operation.

Money is an uncountable noun and takes a singular verb.

more 497

1

× Gas is usually more cheap than electricity.	√ Gas is usually cheaper than electricity.
× She arrived more late than we had expected.	√ She arrived later than we had expected.

One-syllable adjectives and adverbs usually form their comparatives with -*er* (NOT ***more***).

2

× The water in the canal was much more higher than usual.	√ The water in the canal was much higher than usual.
× I usually play more better when nobody is watching me.	√ I usually play better when nobody is watching me.

We do not use ***more*** with the -*er* form of an adjective or adverb. ⇨ 15.2, 27.2

3

× The course should provide more of practical sessions.	√ The course should provide more practical sessions.

⇨ 640.1

most 498

1

× Most of the Japanese girls prefer tall men.	√ Most Japanese girls prefer tall men.

⇨ 640.2

2

× The most of us eat meat about once a week.	✓ Most of us eat meat about once a week.

When ***most*** is followed by an ***of***-phrase, it is not used with ***the***. Compare: '***The majority of*** us eat meat about once a week.'

much 499

1

× He knows much about cars.	✓ He knows a lot about cars.
× She earns much money in her new job.	✓ She earns a lot of money in her new job.

Much is used mainly in questions and negative sentences: 'Did you get ***much*** help?' 'I don't know ***much*** about computers.' In affirmative sentences, we normally use ***a lot (of)*** or ***a great deal (of)***.

Note that the above rule does not apply when ***much*** is used in formal contexts: 'The proposal to increase income tax has met ***much*** resistance.' Nor does it apply when ***much*** combines with ***so***, ***too***, ***as*** or ***more***: '***Too much*** money is spent on weapons.'

⇨ 480.1

2

× She couldn't answer much questions.	✓ She couldn't answer many questions.

⇨ 640.3

3

× They do not have very much of money.	✓ They do not have very much money.

⇨ 640.1

4

× The first question was not much difficult.	✓ The first question was not very difficult.

Much is used before the comparative form of an adjective: 'He's ***much taller*** than me.' 'The second question was ***much more difficult*** than the first one.' Before the base form of an adjective, we normally use ***very***.

music 500

1

× I spend most of my free time listening to musics.	✓ I spend most of my free time listening to music.

Music is an uncountable noun and does not have a plural form.

2

×	✓
× He loves the music and playing the guitar.	✓ He loves music and playing the guitar.

When we mean 'music in general', we use ***music*** without a determiner.

⇨ 782.3

must 501

1

×	✓
× My coat must to be still in the hotel.	✓ My coat must be still in the hotel.

Must (a modal verb) is followed by a bare infinitive. ⇨ 495.2

2

×	✓
× In my last job I must wear a tie. × I was sure that she had recognized me and so I must talk to her.	✓ In my last job I had to wear a tie. ✓ I was sure that she had recognized me and so I had to talk to her.

We use ***must*** to refer to the present or future. To refer to the past, we use the past tense of ***have to***.

3

×	✓
× I think you must wait here until she returns.	✓ I think you should wait here until she returns.

When giving advice or making a suggestion, we use ***should***. We use ***must*** when the subject is not free to choose or decide: 'You ***must always stop*** when the lights are red.'

4

×	✓
× You mustn't come if you don't want to.	✓ You needn't come if you don't want to. ✓ You don't have to come if you don't want to.

When we want to say that an action is not obligatory, we use ***needn't*** or ***don't have to***, (NOT ***mustn't***).

5

×	✓
× The plane leaves Athens at 12 o'clock and must reach London about two hours later.	✓ The plane leaves Athens at 12 o'clock and should reach London about two hours later.

To make a prediction, we use ***should***. We use ***must*** for a deduction: 'If she drives a Porsche, she ***must have*** a lot of money.'

named 502

× His first wife was named as Cilla.	√ His first wife was called Cilla. √ The name of his first wife was Cilla.

We use ***named*** (= having the name) immediately after a noun: 'a horse ***named*** Black Rock'. Compare: 'The baby ***was named*** Steven James.' (= was given the name)

nationality 503

× His wife, Mareta, is from Finnish nationality.	√ His wife, Mareta, is of Finnish nationality.

A person is ***of*** a particular ***nationality***. Note that in everyday conversation it is more natural just to say 'His wife ***is/comes from*** Finland', or 'His wife ***is*** Finnish'.

nationality words 504

1

× Her husband is a typical English.	√ Her husband is typically English. √ Her husband is a typical Englishman.

We can say 'the English', meaning 'all the people of England', but we cannot say 'an English'. To refer to one person, we use the countable nouns ***Englishman*** and ***Englishwoman***. To refer to the group, we use ***the English***, which is always plural: 'Is it true that ***the English*** are not as romantic as ***the French***?'

COUNTRY	ADJECTIVE	GROUP NOUN	PERSON NOUN
Britain	British	the British	Briton (rare)
England	English	the English	Englishman, -woman
France	French	the French	Frenchman, -woman
Holland	Dutch	the Dutch	Dutchman, -woman
Ireland	Irish	the Irish	Irishman, -woman
Spain	Spanish	the Spanish	Spaniard (rare)
Wales	Welsh	the Welsh	Welshman, -woman

Note that, when there is a choice of structure, we often avoid using the person noun. For example, instead of saying 'She is a ***Welshwoman***', we would normally say 'She is ***Welsh***' or 'She is ***from Wales***'.

Note also that ***Briton*** is used very little except in news reports. Instead, we use phrases such as 'a ***British woman***', 'two girls ***from Britain***'. Similarly, ***Spaniard*** is not common and is rarely applied to a woman.

2

× I had never spoken to a Swedish before. × I found the Scottish very friendly.	√ I had never spoken to a Swede before. √ I found the Scots very friendly.

With some nationality words, both the group noun and the person noun are different from the adjective.

COUNTRY	ADJECTIVE	GROUP NOUN	PERSON NOUN
Denmark	Danish	the Danes	a Dane
Finland	Finnish	the Finns	a Fin
Poland	Polish	the Poles	a Pole
Scotland	Scottish	the Scots	a Scot, a Scotsman, -woman
Sweden	Swedish	the Swedes	a Swede
Turkey	Turkish	the Turks	a Turk

3

× Swiss are very fussy about hygiene.	√ The Swiss are very fussy about hygiene. √ Swiss people are very fussy about hygiene.

When we refer to all the people of a country, ***the*** is normally optional: '(*The*) ***Americans*** are very fond of baseball.'

However, we always use ***the*** if the nationality word ends in ***-sh***, ***-ss***, ***-ese*** or ***-ch***: '***The French*** are lucky to have such a beautiful country, and so are ***the British*** for that matter.'

4

× In the boat there were about sixty Vietnameses.	√ In the boat there were about sixty Vietnamese.

Most nouns of nationality have a singular form and a plural form: 'a ***Dane***' – 'two ***Danes***', 'a ***Frenchman***' – 'two ***Frenchmen***'. However, some of them have just one form: 'a ***Vietnamese***' – 'two ***Vietnamese***'. Nouns with just one form include: ***Burmese***, ***Chinese***, ***Japanese***, ***Portuguese***, ***Vietnamese*** and ***Swiss***.

nature 505

× We must try harder to stop these people from destroying the nature.	√ We must try harder to stop these people from destroying nature.

⇨ 782.5

near 506

1

× A police officer came near me and asked me to describe what I had seen.	√ A police officer came up to me and asked me to describe what I had seen.

When we approach someone, we ***go***, ***come***, ***walk***, etc., ***up to*** them, (NOT ***near*** or ***near to*** them).

2

× I drove the car to a near garage.	√ I drove the car to a nearby garage.

As an adjective meaning 'a short distance away', ***near*** may be used after a linking verb ('The garage is quite ***near***') but not immediately before a noun. In this position, we use ***nearby***.

Note that, unlike ***near***, ***nearest*** may be used immediately before a noun: 'I drove to the ***nearest garage***.'

3

× I sat down in the nearest chair to the door.	√ I sat down in the chair nearest (to) the door.

When the meaning of ***nearest*** is completed by a ***to***-phrase, we put ***nearest*** immediately after the noun. Compare: 'How far is the ***nearest petrol station***?' 'We'll stop at the ***petrol station nearest*** (***to***) the motorway.'

nearby 507

× The new supermarket is nearby the bank.	√ The new supermarket is near (to) the bank.

Nearby is not used as a preposition. Compare: 'We stayed in a ***nearby*** hotel'. (= adjective) 'My parents live ***nearby***, about a mile away'. (= adverb)

nearly 508

1

× The car nearly had hit a man on the pavement.	√ The car had nearly hit a man on the pavement.
× She nearly is too old to apply for the job.	√ She is nearly too old to apply for the job.

⇨ 29.1–2

2

× I slept very little and ate nearly nothing.	√ I slept very little and ate almost nothing.

Before ***no***, ***nobody***, ***nothing***, etc, we use ***almost***, (NOT ***nearly***). Compare: 'She knew ***almost/nearly everyone*** at the party.'

need: noun 509

1

× It is no need to lock the door.	√ There is no need to lock the door.

Note the structure: ***There*** + ***be*** + ***no need*** + ***to***-clause. Compare: '***It is not necessary*** to lock the door.'

2

× There is a general need of better communication.	√ There is a general need for better communication.

We talk about a ***lack/shortage of*** something but a ***need for*** something. Note, however, the phrase ***in need of***: 'The roof of the house is ***in need of*** repair.'

need: verb **510**

1

× You need not to sign the form if you prefer not to.	√ You need not sign the form if you prefer not to. √ You don't need to sign the form if you prefer not to.

In questions and negative sentences, ***need*** can be used as a full verb or as a modal (auxiliary) verb. As a modal verb, it is followed by a bare infinitive: 'You ***needn't worry***.' '***Need I pay*** now?' As a full verb, it is followed by a ***to***-infinitive: 'You don't ***need to worry***.' 'Do I ***need to pay*** now?' ⇨ 198.2 Note that in American English, 'don't need to' is far more common than 'needn't'.

2

× I need speak to her immediately.	√ I need to speak to her immediately.

In statements, ***need*** is used as a full verb and is followed by a ***to***-infinitive:

3

× The car is needing to be repaired before you can drive it.	√ The car needs to be repaired before you can drive it.

Need is not normally used in progressive tenses. ⇨ 627.3

4

× You needn't any money to get into the concert.	√ You don't need any money to get into the concert.

Needn't ('need not') is a modal verb and must be followed by a full verb: 'You ***needn't pay*** for the tickets until you get them.'

5

× We need that everyone takes more interest in their environment.	√ We need everyone to take more interest in their environment.

We ***need*** someone ***to do*** something. The verb ***need*** cannot be followed by a ***that***-clause. Compare: 'It is ***necessary that*** ...'

needless to say 511

1

× (incorrect)	√ (correct)
× Needless for me to say, these highly skilled workers are in great demand.	√ Needless to say, these highly skilled workers are in great demand.

Needless to say is a fixed expression. Compare: '*There is no need for me to say that* these highly skilled workers are in great demand.'

2

× (incorrect)	√ (correct)
× Needless to say that many people have complained about the new legislation.	√ Needless to say, many people have complained about the new legislation.

Needless to say (an adverbial expression), is followed by a comma and a main clause, NOT by a ***that***-clause.

⇨ 779.2

negative sentences 512

1

× (incorrect)	√ (correct)
× Sometimes our teacher not allow us to use a dictionary.	√ Sometimes our teacher does not allow us to use a dictionary.
× She told me that she not liked her job and wanted to change it.	√ She told me that she did not like her job and wanted to change it.

When there is no auxiliary verb (e.g. *have*, *can*, *must*), we form a negative with ***do*** + ***not***. Compare:

She wants to come with us.
She ***doesn't/does not*** want to come with us.

She liked the film.
She ***didn't/did not*** like the film.

Tense is shown by ***do*** and the main verb is a bare infinitive.

2

× (incorrect)	√ (correct)
× David doesn't likes small cars.	√ David doesn't like small cars.
× I don't understand why you didn't received the parcel.	√ I don't understand why you didn't receive the parcel.

After ***don't***, ***didn't***, ***does not***, etc, the main verb is always a bare infinitive ('like', 'receive').

3

× (incorrect)	√ (correct)
× My mother does never eat meat.	√ My mother never eats meat.

The auxiliary verb ***do*** is used before ***not*** but NOT before ***never***, ***rarely***, ***seldom***, etc. Compare: 'She ***doesn't answer*** my letters.' 'She ***never/rarely/seldom answers*** my letters.'

4

✗	✓
× Turning on the radio, I was surprised to not hear the faintest sound.	√ Turning on the radio, I was surprised not to hear the faintest sound.
× I prefer to not watch violent films.	√ I prefer not to watch violent films.

We put ***not*** and ***never*** in front of the ***to*** of a ***to***-infinitive (NOT after it).

5

✗	✓
× I think I can't afford a holiday this year.	√ I don't think I can afford a holiday this year.
× I suppose you don't know her address?	√ I don't suppose you know her address?

Verbs of thinking and feeling (e.g. *think*, *suppose*, *feel*) are often followed by a ***that***-clause. Instead of making the verb in the ***that***-clause negative, we normally make *think*, *suppose*, etc., negative.

Two common exceptions to this rule are ***hope*** and ***wish***: 'I ***hope she doesn't*** recognize me.' 'I ***wish you wouldn't*** do that.'

6

✗	✓
× Everybody couldn't understand what he was saying.	√ Nobody could understand what he was saying.
× All of the trees didn't have any leaves.	√ None of the trees had any leaves.
× Both of the children didn't want to go to school.	√ Neither of the children wanted to go to school.
× Almost all of the classrooms are not air-conditioned.	√ Hardly any of the classrooms are air-conditioned.

Some positive words have negative equivalents. Compare:

POSITIVE	NEGATIVE
all	none
almost (all/everyone/etc)	hardly (any/anyone/etc.)
both	neither
everybody	nobody
everything	nothing

Instead of using a positive word ('Everybody') with a negative verb ('couldn't'), we normally use the negative word ('Nobody') with a positive verb ('could').

7

✗	✓
× Nobody in the office could not give me the information.	√ Nobody in the office could give me the information.
× None of her children never visit her.	√ None of her children ever visit her.

Only one part of a clause can be negative. When the subject is negative (e.g. *nobody*, *nothing*, *none*), the verb is positive.

8

✗	✓
× Sitting at the back, I couldn't hear nothing at all.	√ Sitting at the back, I couldn't hear anything at all.
× Then he went into the bank, trying not to be seen by nobody.	√ Then he went into the bank, trying not to be seen by anybody.

Only one part of a clause can be negative. After a negative subject or negative verb, we use ***any***, ***anybody***, ***anything***, etc. ⇨ 733.2–4

9

✗	✓
× The bag was so heavy that I couldn't hardly lift it.	√ The bag was so heavy that I could hardly lift it.
× I won't never forget how kind you have been.	√ I won't ever forget how kind you have been.
	√ I will never forget how kind you have been.

Only one negative adverb may be used with a verb. Negative adverbs include ***not***, ***never***, ***barely***, ***hardly***, ***rarely***, ***scarcely*** and ***seldom***.

10

✗	✓
× Hardly I had sat down when the doorbell rang.	√ Hardly had I sat down when the doorbell rang.
× Not only computers are faster today, but they are also cheaper.	√ Not only are computers faster today, but they are also cheaper.

When a sentence begins with a negative meaning (e.g. 'hardly', 'not only'), the subject and verb change places. ⇨ 31.1, 169.5

neither 513

1

✗	✓
× Neither programmes was suitable for children.	√ Neither programme was suitable for children.
	√ Neither of the programmes was suitable for children.

⇨ 640.4

2

✗	✓
× Neither letter were properly addressed.	√ Neither letter was properly addressed.
! Neither of the governments are willing to give way.	√ Neither of the governments is willing to give way.

⇨ 44.13

3

× He hasn't written to me. Neither he has telephoned.	√ He hasn't written to me. Neither has he telephoned.

⇨ 169.5

neither ... nor ... 514

1

! Neither the bank nor the post office were open.	√ Neither the bank nor the post office was open.

⇨ 44.18

2

× Neither Helen nor David is not old enough to travel alone.	√ Neither Helen nor David is old enough to travel alone.

A clause normally has only one negative word. ⇨ 512.7

3

× She neither finds him handsome nor intelligent.	√ She finds him neither handsome nor intelligent.

The two units linked by ***neither*** … ***nor*** … must be grammatically equal.

⇨ 178.9

4

× Some people can neither read or write.	√ Some people can neither read nor write.

Neither is always followed by ***nor***. Compare: 'You can *either* wait *or* come back tomorrow.'

never 515

1

× None of her children never visits her.	√ None of her children ever visits her.

⇨ 512.7

2

× I won't never forget how kind you have been.	√ I won't ever forget how kind you have been. √ I'll never forget how kind you have been.

⇨ 512.9

3

×	✓
× They do never really cause us any trouble.	✓ They never really cause us any trouble.

⇨ 512.3

4

×	✓
× Never I had met such a lazy person before.	✓ Never had I met such a lazy person before.

⇨ 31.3

5

×	✓
× She said that she never had seen a ghost.	✓ She said that she had never seen a ghost.
× As a teacher, you never must lose your temper.	✓ As a teacher, you must never lose your temper.

⇨ 29.1

6

×	✓
× She advised me to never point my finger at anyone.	✓ She advised me never to point my finger at anyone.

We put ***never*** and ***not*** in front of the ***to*** of a ***to***-infinitive (NOT after it).

nevertheless 516

×	✓
× Most criminals realize that they may be caught nevertheless they are prepared to take the risk.	✓ Most criminals realize that they may be caught. Nevertheless, they are prepared to take the risk. ✓ Most criminals realize that they may be caught, but nevertheless they are prepared to take the risk.

⇨ 28.3

news 517

1

×	✓
× I've just received a very good news.	✓ I've just received some very good news.

News is an uncountable noun and is not used with ***a/an***. ⇨ 2.1

2

×	✓
× The news are always bad nowadays.	✓ The news is always bad nowadays.

News takes a singular verb. ⇨ 530.1

nice 518

×	✓
× I had always wanted a nice and comfortable bed.	✓ I had always wanted a bed that was nice and comfortable.

Adjectival expressions beginning ***nice and*** (e.g. 'nice and comfortable', 'nice and tidy') always go after the noun. Compare: 'I had always wanted a ***nice***, ***comfortable*** bed.'

night 519

×	✓
× It was very late in the night and the streets were empty.	✓ It was very late at night and the streets were empty.

We say 'in the daytime', 'in the morning', 'in the afternoon', 'in the evening' but ***at night***: 'I'd rather travel in the daytime than ***at night***.' 'Sometimes she works until eleven o'clock ***at night***.'

nobody/no one 520

1

×	✓
× Nobody were allowed to see him, not even his parents.	✓ Nobody was allowed to see him, not even his parents.
× Apart from us, no one else were asked to move.	✓ Apart from us, no one else was asked to move.

Nobody and ***no one*** (also spelt ***no-one***) take a singular verb. ⇨ 44.11

2

×	✓
× He closed the door quietly so that nobody wouldn't hear him.	✓ He closed the door quietly so that nobody would hear him.
× The man ran into the bank, taking care not to be seen by no one.	✓ The man ran into the bank, taking care not to be seen by anyone.

A clause normally has only one negative word. ⇨ 512.7–8

3

×	✓
× Almost no one believes in ghosts nowadays.	✓ Hardly anyone believes in ghosts nowadays.

⇨ 51.2

noise 521

×	✓
× There were a lot of noises in the classroom and I couldn't concentrate.	✓ There was a lot of noise in the classroom and I couldn't concentrate.

⇨ 529.2

no matter **522**

× No matter you have a lot of experience, qualifications are essential.	√ No matter how much experience you have, qualifications are essential.

No matter is always followed by ***how***, ***what***, ***who***, ***where***, etc: '***No matter what*** people say about Jill, I like her.' '***No matter where*** you go, you won't find a better hotel.'

none **523**

1

× None of the food were fit for human consumption.	√ None of the food was fit for human consumption.

When ***none of*** is followed by an uncountable noun ('food'), the verb is singular.

2

! None of these murders have been solved yet.	√ None of these murders has been solved yet.

When ***none of*** is followed by a plural count noun ('murders'), the verb may be either singular or plural. When we mean 'not a single one', the verb is singular: '***None of*** these essays ***is*** worthy of a distinction.'

When we mean 'all ... not', the verb is plural: '***None of*** the shops ***are*** open today.'

In formal styles, careful users generally prefer a singular verb.

3

! I can't lend you any money because I have none.	√ I can't lend you any money because I don't have any.

A positive verb ('have') + ***none*** sounds very formal or literary. Instead, we normally use a negative verb + ***any***.

4

× None of the two applicants had suitable qualifications.	√ Neither of the two applicants had suitable qualifications.

We use ***none*** when we are talking about three or more people or things. When there are just two people or things, we use ***neither***.

nor **524**

× He doesn't want to study, nor he wants a job.	√ He doesn't want to study, nor does he want a job.

⇨ 169.5

no sooner **525**

×	✓
× No sooner I had opened the door than the telephone rang.	✓ No sooner had I opened the door than the telephone rang.

⇨ 169.5

not **526**

1

×	✓
x I had not enough money to pay for a taxi.	✓ I did not have enough money to pay for a taxi.

⇨ 512.1

2

×	✓
× She told me to not feel nervous.	✓ She told me not to feel nervous.

⇨ 512.4

not only **527**

1

×	✓
× Not only computers are faster today, but they are also cheaper.	✓ Not only are computers faster today, but they are also cheaper.

⇨ 169.5

2

×	✓
× Not only did she tell lies but stole things.	✓ Not only did she tell lies but she stole things.

When two linked clauses have the same subject, it is normally possible to omit the subject from the second clause: 'She applied for the job but (she) didn't get it.'

However, when the first clause begins with ***not only***, the subject of the second clause cannot be omitted.

3

×	✓
× The pupils not only talked to each other but also to exchange answers.	✓ The pupils not only talked to each other but also exchanged answers.

⇨ 178.4

4

×	✓
× He not only owns a Mercedes but also a BMW.	✓ He owns not only a Mercedes but also a BMW.
× We should try to build a nation that not only will last for a century but forever.	✓ We should try to build a nation that will last not only for a century but forever.

⇨ 178.9

nothing 528

×	✓
× When I bought the dress, I didn't notice nothing wrong with it.	✓ When I bought the dress, I didn't notice anything wrong with it.

A clause normally has only one negative word. ⇨ 512.8

nouns: countable or uncountable ? 529

1

×	✓
× There is always a heavy traffic in the city centre.	✓ There is always heavy traffic in the city centre.
× The news are always bad nowadays.	✓ The news is always bad nowadays.

There are two main groups of noun: 'countable' and 'uncountable'. Both ***traffic*** and ***news*** are uncountable; they cannot be used with ***a/an*** and they always take a singular verb.

The meaning of a noun is often a good indicator of its group. Meanings which are normally uncountable include:

anything perceived as a mass: ***traffic, hair, equipment, grass***
materials: ***wood, cotton, plastic, rubber, cardboard***
liquids and gases: ***water, milk, oil, air, oxygen***
types of food: ***bread, cheese, rice, meat, beef***
concepts: ***knowledge, health, time, energy, noise, travel***
activities: ***reading, drawing, swimming, shopping***
types of institution: ***school, university, hospital***
sports and games: ***tennis, snooker, hopscotch, chess***
languages: ***English, French, Malay***

On the other hand, the name of anything that we can count is likely to be a countable noun: 'a ***toothbrush***', 'two ***chairs***', 'some ***pencils***'.

Many nouns in common use have both countable and uncountable meanings.

2

× This shampoo is ideal for people with dry hairs. × There were a lot of noises in the classroom and I couldn't concentrate.	√ This shampoo is ideal for people with dry hair. √ There was a lot of noise in the classroom and I couldn't concentrate.

Many nouns are countable in one meaning and uncountable in another meaning. For something that we perceive as a mass, we use the uncountable form: 'Where do you get your ***hair*** cut?' (NOT *hairs*)

For things that we perceive as individual units, we use the countable form: 'There's *a* ***hair*** in my soup.'

3

× After the explosion, the street was full of broken glasses.	√ After the explosion, the street was full of broken glass.

When a noun refers to a type of material, liquid or food, it is uncountable: 'The lenses are made of ***glass***.' 'Do you like ***chicken***?'

When a noun refers to an object, animal, or individual unit, it is countable:

I've broken two of my best ***glasses***.
I'd like *a* ***glass*** of milk.
I didn't know that they keep ***chickens***.

4

× More money should be spent on educations.	√ More money should be spent on education.

When a noun refers to a concept, it is normally uncountable: 'Private ***education*** is very expensive.'

When it refers to something specific (e.g. an actual event, place or experience), it is normally countable: 'She has had one of the best ***educations*** that money can buy.'

5

× In the old days, many children never went to a school. × We had a breakfast in the hotel restaurant.	√ In the old days, many children never went to school. √ We had breakfast in the hotel restaurant.

⇨ 532.2–3

6

× He obviously wanted us to take a pity on him.	√ He obviously wanted us to take pity on him.
× Apart from a few scratches, the rosewood chairs were in excellent conditions.	√ Apart from a few scratches, the rosewood chairs were in excellent condition.
× He was able to describe the woman in details.	√ He was able to describe the woman in detail.

In fixed and semi-fixed expressions, uncountable nouns are more usual than countable nouns, e.g. ***at night***, ***on average***, ***in detail***, ***in (good/ poor) condition***, ***by mistake***, ***under control***, ***take pity on***, ***lose interest (in)***.

⇨ 532.4

7

× The junior staff require further trainings.	√ The junior staff require further training.
× She has gone out to do some shoppings.	√ She has gone out to do some shopping.

Many nouns ending in ***-ing*** come from verbs, e.g. ***to train – training***; ***to fish – fishing***; ***to shop – shopping***. When these nouns refer to activities, they are uncountable: '***Jogging*** is very popular nowadays.' 'She is very good at ***drawing*** and ***painting***.'

When they refer to things, they are normally countable: 'Two of his ***paintings*** are hanging in the Tate Gallery.'

8

× The news are always bad nowadays.	√ The news is always bad nowadays.

Nouns ending in ***-s*** look like plural count nouns. However, a number of nouns ending in ***-s*** are uncountable.

⇨ 530.1

nouns which look plural 530

1

× The news are always bad nowadays.	√ The news is always bad nowadays.

Most nouns which end in ***-s*** are plural and take a plural verb: e.g. 'These ***trousers are*** too tight.' However, some nouns which end in ***-s*** are uncountable and take a singular verb. Most of these nouns are the names of sciences or diseases. The group includes: ***acoustics***, ***athletics***, ***economics***, ***linguistics***, ***mathematics***, ***measles***, ***mumps***, ***news***, ***physics***, ***statistics***.

Note that when ***acoustics***, ***economics***, ***mathematics***, and ***statistics*** are not used as the names of sciences, they are plural and take a plural verb: e.g. 'The ***acoustics*** of the auditorium ***are*** ideal for concerts.'

2

× Television provides a mean by which people discover what is happening in the world.	√ Television provides a means by which people discover what is happening in the world.

Many nouns have a plural form ending in ***-s*** and a singular form without ***-s***, e.g. ***books*** (plural) ***book*** (singular). With some nouns, however, both the plural form and the singular form end in ***-s***. This small group includes: ***barracks***, ***crossroads***, ***headquarters***, ***means*** (= method), ***series***, ***species***, ***works*** (= factory).

nouns which look singular 531

1

× The fields were full of cows and sheeps.	√ The fields were full of cows and sheep.

The plural form of most nouns ends in ***-s***, ***-es*** or ***-ies***: 'one cow', 'two cows'. However, some plural forms are irregular: 'one sheep', 'two sheep'.

⇨ 181.5–6

2

× The police is still looking for her.	√ The police are still looking for her.
× Some people says that punishments should be more severe.	√ Some people say that punishments should be more severe.

Police and ***people*** are plural nouns and take a plural verb.

3

× He is a British and comes from Liverpool.	√ He is British and comes from Liverpool.

⇨ 504.1

nouns used without a determiner 532

1

× I don't like things that are made of the plastic.	√ I don't like things that are made of plastic.
× All these opinions are based on the prejudice.	√ All these opinions are based on prejudice.
× It is sometimes said that the teachers have a very easy life.	√ It is sometimes said that teachers have a very easy life.

We do not use a determiner with uncountable nouns ('plastic', 'prejudice') or plural count nouns ('teachers') when they have general reference. ⇨ 782.3

2

× In the old days, many children did not go to a school.	√ In the old days, many children did not go to school.
× Young offenders should not be sent to a prison.	√ Young offenders should not be sent to prison.

Some nouns ('school', 'prison') can refer to a particular place or to a type of place. When they refer to a type of place, they are uncountable and do not have a determiner: 'Is Gloria still in ***hospital***?' 'Young offenders should not be sent to ***prison***.'

When they refer to a particular place, they are countable and, if used in the singular, require a determiner: 'We spent the afternoon at ***the hospital***, visiting Gloria.' '***The prison*** was designed to hold five hundred inmates.'

We normally use a determiner if the noun is modified. Compare:

Our children go to ***school*** at 8 o'clock.
Our children go to ***a very good school***.
He goes to ***a special school for slow learners***.

Nouns that are used in this way include: ***bed***, ***church***, ***class***, ***college***, ***gaol***, ***home***, ***hospital***, ***jail***, ***kindergarten***, ***prison***, ***school***, ***sea***, ***university***, ***work***.

Note that users of American English say *in the hospital* and *at the university* even when they are talking about a type of place: 'Is Gloria still ***in the hospital***?'

3

× We had a breakfast in the hotel restaurant.	√ We had breakfast in the hotel restaurant.

When a noun (e.g. 'breakfast') refers to a type of meal, it is uncountable and is normally used without a determiner: 'Ray and Helen have invited us out to ***dinner***.' 'Where shall we go for ***lunch*** today?'

When the noun refers to a particular meal, it is countable and, if used in the singular, must have a determiner: 'We've had a lovely evening and ***the dinner*** was delicious.'

We always use a determiner when there is an adjective before the noun. Compare: 'We usually have ***breakfast*** at about seven o'clock.' 'We usually have just ***a light breakfast*** on weekdays.'

4

× The driver lost the control of the car and it crashed into a tree.	√ The driver lost control of the car and it crashed into a tree.
× He obviously wanted us to take a pity on him.	√ He obviously wanted us to take pity on him.
× You cannot leave the country without a special permission.	√ You cannot leave the country without special permission.

When a noun is part of a fixed or semi-fixed expression, it often has no determiner. The phrases below show the types of pattern in which determiners (e.g. *a/an*, *the*, *this*, *my*) are frequently omitted.

1 PREPOSITION + NOUN
above/below ground, at night, at/for breakfast, at risk, at war, at home/school/work/sea, beyond description, beyond dispute/reproach, by air/post, by bicycle/bus/car/train, by force, for fun/pleasure, for sale, in conclusion, in danger, in detail, in disgrace, in hand, in doubt, in love, in/out of order, in peace, in/out of place, in private/public, in time, on fire, on holiday, in tune, in turn, on time, on top, out of/under control, out of danger, out of envy/greed/sympathy, out of pocket, past hope, under discussion, under oath, under observation, within reach, without cause, without doubt, without fail, without permission

2 PREPOSITION + NOUN + PREPOSITION
by means of, for fear of, in accordance with, in charge of, in expectation of, in honour of, in keeping with, in league with, in line with, in memory of, in place of, in recognition of, in touch with, in view of, on account of, on pain of, on top of, with reference/regard/respect to

3 VERB + NOUN (+ PREPOSITION)
declare war (on), do research (into), fall victim to, find fault (with), give cause for, give rise to, have confidence/faith (in), have difficulty (in), have respect (for), have trouble (with), lose/take control (of), lose/show/take interest (in), make friends (with), make fun (of), make peace (with), make progress, pay attention (to), show contempt (for), show signs of, take care of, take command of, take notice (of), take offence (at), take pity (on), take pleasure/pride in, take precedence over, take turns (at)

4 VERB + OBJECT + PREPOSITION + NOUN
bring (something) under control, force (someone) into submission, get (someone) into trouble, leave (someone) in peace, raise (something) for discussion, take (something) into account/consideration, take (someone) to court

5 VERB (+ ADVERB) + PREPOSITION + NOUN
come to grief, come up for discussion, get into trouble, go to bed/college/school/university, go to war, get/keep in touch, live in peace, stand on ceremony

nouns used as modifiers 533

1

×	✓
× Examinations results are very important.	✓ Examination results are very important.
× In my job I have to attend lots of committees meetings.	✓ In my job I have to attend lots of committee meetings.
× The tables arrangement made it difficult for the children to talk to each other.	✓ The table arrangement made it difficult for the children to talk to each other.

A noun used as a modifier (i.e. immediately before another noun) does not normally have a plural ending. Compare:

'a case for pencils' BUT 'a ***pencil*** case'
'a ring made of diamonds' BUT 'a ***diamond*** ring'
'results of examinations' 'BUT '***examination*** results'

Note, however, that some plural nouns keep their plural ending when used in this way, e.g. 'a ***goods*** train', 'a ***glasses*** case'. If we dropped the plural ending, we would produce a different meaning, e.g. 'a ***glass*** case', 'a ***good*** train'.

Nouns used in genitive structures also keep their plural ending: 'a ***girls'*** school', 'his ***parents'*** permission'.

2

× A government officer salary is about $2000 a month.	√ A government officer's salary is about $2000 a month.

When a noun that refers to a person ('officer') comes before another noun, the first noun normally ends with ***-'s/-s'***: 'a ***learner's*** dictionary', 'a ***child's*** toy', 'his ***mother-in-law's*** house'.

⇨ 694

3

× We had a three weeks holiday in Corfu.	√ We had a three-week holiday in Corfu.
× Every morning I have four 50 minutes lessons.	√ Every morning I have four 50-minute lessons.
× I didn't know that a five-years-old child could be so clever.	√ I didn't know that a five-year-old child could be so clever.

When a modifier consists of a number ('three') and a noun ('weeks'), the noun does not normally have a plural ending. Also, the parts of the modifier are joined with a hyphen (-) to form a compound. Compare:

Our holiday lasted three weeks. – A ***three-week*** holiday.
We walked for two miles. – A ***two-mile*** walk.
The child is five years old. – A ***five-year-old*** child.

Note that two different structures are easily confused: 'We had a ***three-week*** holiday in Corfu.' 'We had ***three weeks'*** holiday in Corfu.'
In the second sentence, ***three weeks'*** (*-s* + apostrophe) is a genitive phrase.

⇨ 694.4

4

× After half an hour journey we arrived at the hotel.	√ After half an hour's journey we arrived at the hotel.
× We have ten minute break between lessons.	√ We have ten minutes' break between lessons.

A genitive phrase of duration ends in *-'s/-s'*. Note the alternative: 'We have ***a ten-minute break*** between lessons.' In this sentence, 'ten-minute' is a compound modifier, not a genitive structure, and the noun 'minute' does not have a plural ending.

noun patterns **534**

× The forests are in danger to be destroyed.	√ The forests are in danger of being destroyed.
× In San Antonio I didn't have the chance of speaking much English.	√ In San Antonio I didn't have the chance to speak much English.

Nouns are used in a number of different patterns:

We cannot understand their ***refusal + to co-operate*** with us.
I had ***trouble + starting*** the car this morning.
She had ***difficulty + in obtaining*** a visa.
It was a great ***relief + to see*** my name on the list.
It's ***no good + talking*** to anyone but the manager.
It's a ***shame + that*** you cannot come to the wedding.
There's ***no point + (in) worrying*** about her.

Unfortunately, there are no rules to help us choose the correct pattern.

Nouns of similar meaning normally take the same patterns: 'He told us about his ***wish/ambition + to visit*** other countries.' 'It is a ***pity/shame + that*** you cannot come.'

But there are exceptions. Compare: 'We have no ***wish + to go*** there again.' 'We have no ***intention + of going*** there again.'

Special care is needed with nouns which have more than one meaning, because each meaning may take a different pattern: 'I didn't have a ***chance + to go*** shopping.' 'United have little ***chance + of winning*** the cup.'

Extra care is also needed when the noun is part of a phrasal expression: 'The company is ***in danger of + losing*** the contract.' 'She ***takes*** great ***pleasure in + helping*** people.'

In this book, common errors involving noun patterns are shown at the entry for the noun. If you cannot find what you are looking for, look up the noun in a good dictionary, paying particular attention to the examples of usage.

nouns with prepositions 535

× The price for oil will continue to increase.	√ The price of oil will continue to increase.
× There is a general need of better communication.	√ There is a general need for better communication.

Noun + preposition combinations are a common cause of error. Quite often, a noun takes the same preposition as the related adjective or verb:

You have to be very ***patient with*** small children.
He has no ***patience with*** people who are always complaining.

We were surprised that she ***participated in*** the performance.
Her ***participation in*** the performance came as a surprise.

However, there are many exceptions: 'They are very ***proud of*** their daughter's success.' 'They take great ***pride in*** their daughter's success.'

Nouns of similar meaning normally take the same preposition: 'Do you know the ***price of*** the tickets?' 'What will be the ***cost of*** the repair?'

But again there are exceptions: 'What was his ***reason for*** leaving so early?' 'Nobody knows the ***cause of*** the explosion.'

After some nouns, there is a choice of preposition. In a given context, however, only one of the combinations is likely to be correct:

There is an urgent ***need for*** food and medical supplies.
They are ***in*** urgent ***need of*** food and medical supplies.

We all know about the ***dangers of*** smoking.
Reckless drivers are a ***danger to*** society.

Errors involving noun + preposition combinations are shown in this book at the entry for the noun. If you cannot find what you are looking for, look up the noun in a good dictionary, paying particular attention to the examples of usage.

nowadays 536

×	√
× In nowadays marriage is going out of fashion.	√ Nowadays marriage is going out of fashion.

We do not use ***in*** before ***nowadays***.

number 537

1

×	√
× In recent years a large number of our equipment has been stolen from construction sites.	√ In recent years a large amount of our equipment has been stolen from construction sites.

Before an uncountable noun ('equipment'), we use ***amount of***. We use ***number of*** before the plural form of a countable noun: 'She has received ***a number of*** complaints.'

2

×	√
× A number of wooden platforms was built for the tortoises to lie on and bask in the sun.	√ A number of wooden platforms were built for the tortoises to lie on and bask in the sun.

After a phrase beginning ***a number of***, the verb is plural. ⇨ .3 below

3

×	√
× I suggest that the number of students in the class are reduced.	√ I suggest that the number of students in the class is reduced.

After a phrase beginning ***the number of***, the verb is singular. ⇨ .2 above

numbers 538

1

×	√
× The war lasted almost hundred years.	√ The war lasted almost a hundred years.

When the meaning is 'one hundred', 'one thousand', etc., we always use ***a*** (or ***one***) before the number word: '***a dozen*** eggs', '***a hundred*** guests', '***a thousand*** demonstrators', '***a million*** inhabitants'.

2

×	✓
× The total population is over a hundred millions.	✓ The total population is over a hundred million.
× We were travelling at about two hundreds kilometres per hour.	✓ We were travelling at about two hundred kilometres per hour.

When ***dozen***, ***hundred***, ***thousand*** and ***million*** are used as part of a number, they never have an ***s***: 'five ***thousand***', 'five ***thousand*** people'.

We give these words an ***s*** only when we use them to express an approximate idea of number, e.g. 'We've received ***hundreds*** of letters and ***thousands*** of telephone calls.' 'There were ***dozens*** of people at the party.'

3

×	✓
× You will need four litres of milk and two dozens of eggs.	✓ You will need four litres of milk and two dozen eggs.
× Over fifty thousands of tourists came here last year.	✓ Over fifty thousand tourists came here last year.

'A dozen', 'two dozen', 'three dozen', etc., are determiners and come immediately before the noun. The same is true for 'a hundred', 'two thousand', 'three million', etc.

Do not confuse '***a dozen*** plates', '***two hundred*** people' with '***dozens*** of plates', '***hundreds*** of people'. Only approximate numbers, e.g. ***dozens***, ***hundreds***, can be followed by an ***of***-phrase.

4

!	✓
! The composer was born exactly a hundred eighty years ago.	✓ The composer was born exactly a hundred and eighty years ago.

Users of British English say 'a hundred ***and*** five', 'three thousand ***and*** eighty', etc. In American English, however, ***and*** is not necessary.

obey 539

×	✓
× Some children are very naughty and never obey to their parents.	✓ Some children are very naughty and never obey their parents.

We ***obey*** someone or something (WITHOUT ***to***): 'There are ways of forcing people to ***obey*** the law.'

object 540

1

×	✓
× Some people object sudden changes.	✓ Some people object to sudden changes.

⇨ 841.2

2

× She objected to have to wait.	√ She objected to having to wait.

⇨ 837

obstacle 541

× Religion should not be seen as an obstacle for preserving multi-racial harmony.	√ Religion should not be seen as an obstacle to preserving multi-racial harmony.

Something is an ***obstacle to*** (doing) something: 'This latest scandal could well prove an ***obstacle to*** his re-election.'

obvious 542

× It was obvious for everyone that the man had been drinking.	√ It was obvious to everyone that the man had been drinking.

Something is ***obvious to*** someone, (NOT ***for***): 'By now it must surely be ***obvious***, even ***to*** his friends, that he is as guilty as the others.'

o'clock 543

1

× I set the alarm for 7 o'clock a.m.	√ I set the alarm for 7 a.m. √ I set the alarm for 7 o'clock.

We do not use ***o'clock*** and ***a.m./p.m.*** together.

2

× In Brunei it starts to get dark at about 6.00 o'clock.	√ In Brunei it starts to get dark at about 6 o'clock.

We can use ***o'clock*** after '6' (or 'six'), but not after '6.00'.

of 544

1

× Do you know the ninth symphony of Beethoven? × If the umbrella isn't yours, it must be of Peter.	√ Do you know Beethoven's ninth symphony? √ If the umbrella isn't yours, it must be Peter's.

With nouns that refer to people or animals (i.e. animate nouns), we normally form the genitive with ***-'s/-s'***: '***Henry's*** wife', 'my ***friend's*** house', 'a good ***learner's*** dictionary'. The same is true for pronouns ending ***-one*** or ***-body***: '***someone's*** gloves'.

The *of*-genitive is used mainly with inanimate nouns: 'the back ***of the car***', 'the sound ***of his voice***', 'the price ***of butter***', 'the cause ***of the fire***'.

2

× I took Martin and a friend of him to Teotihuacan.	√ I took Martin and a friend of his to Teotihuacan.

⇨ 590.2

3

× He collects very old vases of China.	√ He collects very old Chinese vases.

We do not normally use an ***of***-phrase ('of China') when there is a suitable adjective ('Chinese').

4

× He will be arriving at the airport of Manchester.	√ He will be arriving at Manchester airport.
× We often talk about the peace of the world.	√ We often talk about world peace.

We do not normally use an ***of***-phrase ('of Manchester') when the noun in the ***of***-phrase ('Manchester') can be used as a modifier (i.e. like an adjective).

5

! We stopped for a rest of ten minutes.	√ We stopped for ten minutes' rest. √ We stopped for a ten-minute rest.

When we mention the duration of something, we normally use one of the following patterns: 'We had ***two weeks' holiday*** in France.' 'We had ***a two-week holiday*** in France.'

Of-patterns (e.g. 'a holiday of two weeks' – 'two weeks of holiday') usually sound unnatural.

6

× I couldn't get the paint off of my hands.	√ I couldn't get the paint off my hands.

In American English and in some regional varieties of British English, 'off of' is quite common. In Standard British English, however, ***off*** is never followed by ***of***: 'The handle had come ***off*** her suitcase.' 'She tried to push me ***off*** the chair.'

7

× I arrived in England on the 14th of June, 1990.	√ I arrived in England on 14th June, 1990.

⇨ 199.2

8

× We were taken to see a play of Shakespeare.	√ We were taken to see a play by Shakespeare.

To refer to the person who wrote a play, painted a picture, etc., we use ***by***: 'a novel ***by*** D.H. Lawrence'.

9

× He is said to be the richest man of the world.	√ He is said to be the richest man in the world.

After a superlative (e.g. 'the ***richest*** man'), we use ***in*** + place: 'the ***busiest*** airport ***in Europe***', 'the ***oldest*** building ***in Rome***', 'the ***most intelligent*** child ***in the class***'.

10

× It was a hot night of August and I was lying in bed reading.	√ It was a hot night in August and I was lying in bed reading.

We say 'the month ***of*** August' but 'a night ***in*** August', 'a week ***in*** February', 'the last Sunday ***in*** July', etc.

11

× Altogether, I have lost almost 3 kilos of weight.	√ Altogether, I have lost almost 3 kilos in weight.

Something is a number of units ***in weight***, ***in length***, ***in height***, etc: 'The swimming pool is exactly 20 metres ***in length***.'

off 545

× There was a lot of sand flying off from the back of the lorry. × I couldn't get the paint off of my hands.	√ There was a lot of sand flying off the back of the lorry. √ I couldn't get the paint off my hands.

In Standard British English, ***off*** is never followed by ***from*** or ***of***. ⇨ 544.6

offspring 546

× A husband and wife should share the responsibility of bringing up their offsprings.	√ A husband and wife should share the responsibility of bringing up their offspring.

The plural form of ***offspring*** is ***offspring***. ⇨ 181.5

often 547

×	✓
× He hated his stepfather and often had thought about running away.	✓ He hated his stepfather and had often thought about running away.
× The lessons often are difficult to understand.	✓ The lessons are often difficult to understand.

⇨ 29.1–2

old 548

×	✓
× We were met by a boy of twelve years old.	✓ We were met by a boy of twelve.

The phrase ***x years old*** normally comes after the verb ***be***: 'Our house is over ***a hundred years old***.' It cannot be used in an ***of***-phrase. Compare: 'We were met by ***a twelve-year-old*** boy.' ⇨ 890.3

on 549

1

×	✓
× On last Sunday I went fishing with my father.	✓ Last Sunday I went fishing with my father.

We do not use ***on*** before a time expression beginning with ***last***, ***next***, ***this***, ***that***, ***every***: 'I'm seeing him again ***next week***.' 'She comes to London ***every Tuesday***.'

2

×	✓
× On this photograph you can see where we used to live.	✓ In this photograph you can see where we used to live.

Before things which have (or seem to have) three dimensions, such as a room, photograph or film, we use ***in***: '***In*** the next film, you will see how paper is made.' Before things which have two dimensions, such as a map, we usually use ***on***: '***On*** this map you can see where we used to live.'

on/upon 550

1

×	✓
× He died just ten minutes upon arriving at the hospital.	✓ He died just ten minutes after arriving at the hospital.

We use ***on/upon*** when two actions happen almost simultaneously or when one action happens very soon after the other. The first action often provides the reason for the second action: '***On*** hearing the crash, I rushed out into the street.'

We cannot use ***on/upon*** when the length of the interval between the two actions is mentioned ('just ten minutes'). ⇨ 864.3

2

×	√
× Sitting on the armchair was a man that I recognized.	√ Sitting in the armchair was a man that I recognized.

We sit or lie ***in*** something that encloses us. Compare: 'Would you like to sit ***on*** the floor or ***in*** your pushchair?'

once 551

1

×	√
× Once I will have more details, I shall contact you again.	√ Once I have more details, I shall contact you again.

⇨ 25

2

×	√
× I knew once a man who could eat glass.	√ I once knew a man who could eat glass.

⇨ 29.1

one 552

1

×	√
× He was wearing one blue shirt and grey trousers. × The old lady was taken away in one ambulance.	√ He was wearing a blue shirt and grey trousers. √ The old lady was taken away in an ambulance.

When number is not important or when the meaning is obviously 'one', we normally use ***a/an***.

2

×	√
× The film lasted an hour and one half.	√ The film lasted an hour and a half.

For fractions we normally use ***a/an***, not ***one***: 'half a kilo', 'two and a half kilos'.

3

×	√
× The food in New York was a very greasy one.	√ The food in New York was very greasy.

As a pronoun, ***one*** is used in place of a singular count noun: 'You can borrow my ***dictionary*** if you don't have *one*.' ***One*** cannot be used in place of an uncountable noun (e.g. 'food'). Compare: 'There is plenty of ***food*** left if you'd like *some*.'

4

×	√
× His new camera is very expensive one.	√ His new camera is a very expensive one. √ His new camera is very expensive.

When ***one*** (singular) is modified, the noun phrase must begin with a determiner:

I prefer ***the orange one***.
Give me ***that one over there***.
Have you got ***a smaller one***?

5

× Those chairs are quite comfortable but I prefer these ones.	√ Those chairs are quite comfortable but I prefer these.

We do not normally use ***one/ones*** after a word which itself can be used as a pronoun, e.g. 'these', 'Hilary's', 'Mrs Robinson's'. The two common exceptions to this rule are 'this one' and 'that one': 'Which hat do you like? ***This one*** or ***that one***?'

6

× One does not appreciate the importance of good health until you are ill.	√ One does not appreciate the importance of good health until one is ill.

In British English, to refer back to ***one*** (= 'people in general'), we use ***one/one's/oneself***, (NOT ***he/his/himself***, ***she/her/herself***, ***you/your/yourself***, etc.): 'In such circumstances, *one* is forced to defend *oneself*.' In American English, however, the use of ***he/his/himself*** to refer back to ***one*** is common: '*One* has to look after *his* health.'
Note that in both British and American English, the use of ***one*** to mean 'people in general' occurs only in formal styles. Even here, this usage can sound awkward and most people prefer to use one of the alternatives:

People don't appreciate the importance of good health until ***they*** are ill.
We don't appreciate the importance of good health until ***we*** are ill.
You don't appreciate the importance of good health until ***you*** are ill.

7

× Changi is one of the best airport in the world. × Keeping fish is just one of my hobby.	√ Changi is one of the best airports in the world. √ Keeping fish is just one of my hobbies.

When ***one*** is followed by an ***of***-phrase, the noun in the ***of***-phrase is plural: 'He is ***one of*** the finest players in the club.'

8

× One of the cars were badly damaged.	√ One of the cars was badly damaged.

After ***one*** + ***of***-phrase, the verb is always singular: '***One of*** the dogs ***is*** about to have puppies.'

only 553

1

× The contractor only offered to replace the cracked tiles.	√ The contractor offered to replace only the cracked tiles.

To avoid possible confusion, careful writers place ***only*** immediately before the part of a sentence that it refers to. Compare:

Only Helen studied medicine. (= nobody else studied medicine)
Helen *only* studied medicine. (= she didn't make medicine her profession)
Helen studied *only* medicine. (= she didn't study anything else)

Note that ***only*** sometimes follows the word or phrase that it refers to, especially when this is in final position: 'The contractor offered to replace the cracked tiles *only*.'

In everyday conversation, ***only*** normally comes in middle position. Intonation makes the meaning clear.
⇨ 29.1–4

2

× Only if the two sides talk to each other war can be avoided.	√ Only if the two sides talk to each other can war be avoided.

⇨ 31.2

3

× If he only would stop biting his fingernails!	√ If only he would stop biting his fingernails!

We do not separate ***if only*** when we express a wish or regret: '***If only*** I had asked her to marry me, she might still be here.'
⇨ 376

opinion 554

× According to my opinion, the quality of television programmes has deteriorated.	√ In my opinion, the quality of television programmes has deteriorated.

⇨ 11.2–3

opportunity 555

× Unfortunately, I didn't have the opportunity for saying goodbye to her.	√ Unfortunately, I didn't have the opportunity to say goodbye to her.

We usually say that someone has an ***opportunity to do*** something: 'The party will be a good ***opportunity to make*** some new friends.'

opposite 556

1

×	✓
× Our new showroom is opposite to the petrol station.	✓ Our new showroom is opposite the petrol station.
× She came in and sat down opposite from me.	✓ She came in and sat down opposite me.

When ***opposite*** means 'facing', it is not followed by ***to*** or ***from***.

2

×	✓
× The opposite house has an unusual blue roof.	✓ The house opposite has an unusual blue roof.

⇨ 16.3

3

×	✓
× The opposite to 'increase' is 'decrease'.	✓ The opposite of 'increase' is 'decrease'.

When two things are as different as they can be, we use ***the opposite of***, NOT ***to***.

or 557

1

×	✓
× She can neither read or write.	✓ She can neither read nor write.

After ***neither***, we use ***nor***. Compare: 'I shall ***either*** buy a new one ***or*** have the old one repaired.'

2

×	✓
× For most writers, a typewriter or a word processor are indispensable.	✓ For most writers, a typewriter or a word processor is indispensable.

⇨ 44.17–18

For more information about linking parts of a sentence with **or**, ⇨ 178

order 558

×	✓
× We ordered for the new software two months ago.	✓ We ordered the new software two months ago.

We ***order*** something, NOT ***for*** something. Compare: 'We placed an ***order for*** the new software two months ago.' Use ***for*** after the noun, but not after the verb.

other

559

1

×	✓
× They told me to take her to an other hospital.	✓ They told me to take her to another hospital.

When ***other*** comes after ***an***, we write ***another***, NOT ***an other***.

2

×	✓
× We have seen the same thing happening in several others countries.	✓ We have seen the same thing happening in several other countries.

When used as an adjective, ***other*** never has a plural ending. 'Do they have any *other* children?' It can have a plural ending when used as a pronoun: 'I like this photograph but I don't like the *others*.' Note also the use of ***others*** as a plural noun: 'She seems completely indifferent to the needs of *others*.'

3

×	✓
× Some people like hot weather; the others hate it.	✓ Some people like hot weather; others hate it.

When ***others*** refers to an unspecified group, it is used WITHOUT ***the***. Compare: 'One of my children is at university but *the others* are still at school.'

4

×	✓
× The sign showed the distance to the Equator, the North Pole and other major cities. × Mynahs, doves and other insects made this giant tree their home.	✓ The sign showed the distance to the Equator, the North Pole and major cities. ✓ Mynahs, doves and insects made this giant tree their home. ✓ Mynahs, doves and other birds made this giant tree their home.

Other is followed by the name of the set or group to which the things previously mentioned belong. Compare: '***Nissan***, ***Toyota*** and ***other Japanese car manufacturers*** may be forced to lower their prices.' '***Mercedes, Volkswagen*** and ***Japanese car manufacturers*** may be forced to lower their prices.'

ought

560

×	✓
× I think that you ought stay in bed and rest.	✓ I think that you ought to stay in bed and rest.

We say that someone ***ought to do*** something. Unlike all the other modal verbs, ***ought*** is followed by a *to*-infinitive. Compare: 'I think that you *should* stay in bed.'

outside 561

× I waited for her outside of the shop.	√ I waited for her outside the shop.

In British English, the preposition is always ***outside*** (WITHOUT ***of***). Compare: 'They were painting ***the outside of*** the building.' (*the* + noun + *of*)

In American English, ***outside of*** is sometimes used, but only in informal styles.

⇨ 400

outskirts 562

× I live on the outskirt of Madrid.	√ I live on the outskirts of Madrid.

Outskirts is a plural noun. ⇨ 603.1

over 563

× It cost me 60 over dollars just to get to the airport.	√ It cost me over 60 dollars just to get to the airport.

Over is placed before a number, NOT after it: 'All applicants must be ***over 30 years of age***.'

overalls 564

× In his dark blue overall, he looked like a workman.	√ In his dark blue overalls, he looked like a workman.

Workmen (e.g. painters, builders, plumbers) wear ***overalls***. This is a plural noun and does not have a singular form. ⇨ 603. An ***overall*** (countable noun) is worn by hospital staff, dentists, shop assistants, etc.

overseas 565

× Most of the students in my class are overseas.	√ Most of the students in my class are from overseas.

If we say 'most of the students in my class are ***overseas***', we mean that the class is almost empty because most of the students have gone to other countries. If we mean 'students who have come from other countries', we say '***overseas*** students' or 'students ***from overseas***'.

own 566

1

× My uncle in Malaysia is owning a lot of land.	√ My uncle in Malaysia owns a lot of land.

Own is not used in progressive tenses. ⇨ 627.3

2

× As a child, I always wanted to have an own bicycle.	√ As a child, I always wanted to have my own bicycle. √ As a child, I always wanted to have a bicycle of my own.

Own is used after a possessive determiner (***my***, ***your***, ***our***, etc), NOT after ***an*** or ***the***:

She is buying ***her own*** house.
The children have a room of ***their own*** to play in.
Is it a company car or is it ***your own***?

pair 567

1

× Each pair of trousers were too big.	√ Each pair of trousers was too big.

When we use a singular determiner (e.g. ***a/an***, ***this***, ***each***) with ***pair of***, the verb is normally singular. Compare: 'Nowadays, ***a pair of*** real leather shoes ***is*** very expensive.' '***My*** first ***pair of*** real leather shoes ***were/was*** made in Italy.'

2

× We also bought a pair of kitchen scissors, which is always very useful.	√ We also bought a pair of kitchen scissors, which are always very useful.

When ***a pair of*** + plural noun is followed by a relative clause, the verb in the relative clause is plural (i.e. the verb agrees with the plural noun).

3

× I still remember the time when I bought a pair of shoes in a sale. Everything was fine, except that it felt a little tight.	√ I still remember the time when I bought a pair of shoes in a sale. Everything was fine, except that they felt a little tight.

When we are talking about a set of two separate things, e.g. 'a pair of shoes', 'a pair of gloves', 'a pair of earrings', we normally use the plural forms ***they***, ***them***, ***their*** (NOT ***it***, ***its***).

4

×	✓
× I wear a pair of glasses only for reading.	✓ I wear glasses only for reading.

We do not normally use ***a pair of*** before a noun that has general reference. Compare: 'He hates wearing pyjamas.' (NOT '***a pair of*** pyjamas') 'Lying on the bed was ***a pair of*** blue silk pyjamas.'

pants 568

×	✓
× I had forgotten to pack a clean pants.	✓ I had forgotten to pack any clean pants.

Pants (British English = 'underpants'; American English = 'trousers') is a plural noun.

⇨ 603.2

paper 569

×	✓
× Each child was given a paper and a pencil.	✓ Each child was given some paper and a pencil.

When ***paper*** means 'the material that we write on', it is an uncountable noun and is not used with ***a/an***. ⇨ 2.1.
When ***paper*** means 'newspaper' or 'examination paper', it is countable: 'I bought ***a paper*** to find out what was happening.'

part 570

×	✓
× There are two parts in the magazine.	✓ There are two parts to the magazine.

We say that there are a number of ***parts to*** something, NOT ***in***. Compare: 'The magazine is ***in*** two ***parts***.'

participate 571

×	✓
× The country's size does not prevent it from participating at international competitions.	✓ The country's size does not prevent it from participating in international competitions.
× Two teams have refused to participate the games.	✓ Two teams have refused to participate in the games.

If we take part in something, we ***participate in*** it.

participation 572

× The public's active participations should be encouraged.	√ The public's active participation should be encouraged.

Participation is an uncountable noun and does not have a plural form.

participle clauses 573

× Walking down the road, the shops were just beginning to open.	√ Walking down the road, I noticed that the shops were just beginning to open.
× Ordered over a month ago, we expect the books to arrive any day now.	√ Ordered over a month ago, the books are expected to arrive any day now.

A participle clause does not normally have a subject. '***Turning on the light*** ...' (Who turned on the light?) '***Forced to abandon the ship*** ...' (Who was/were forced to abandon the ship?)

The 'missing' subject should come at the beginning of the main clause. 'Turning on the light, ***Lilly*** realized that the flat had been burgled.' 'Forced to abandon the ship, ***the crew*** swam for the shore.'

If the main clause does not begin with the 'missing' subject, the sentence will be illogical (e.g. shops cannot walk down the road).

passed 574

× I've been looking forward to this trip for the passed six months.	√ I've been looking forward to this trip for the past six months.

Passed is the past simple tense and past participle of the verb ***pass***: 'Six months have ***passed*** since our last meeting.' 'On the way to Newcastle, we ***passed*** Sheffield and Leeds.'

The adjective is ***past***. ⇨ 576

passive 575

1

× All successful applicants will notify by post.	√ All successful applicants will be notified by post.
× Since joining the company, he has never promoted.	√ Since joining the company, he has never been promoted.

In most clauses, the subject is the person or thing that does the action described by the verb: '***George*** has eaten all the bananas.'

The subject of this clause, ***George***, is the 'doer', the person or thing that does the action described by the verb (***has eaten***). The object of the clause is ***all the***

bananas. The object of a clause is the 'receiver' of the action. When the subject of a clause is the doer of the action (e.g. ***George***), we say that the clause and the verb phrase are 'active'.

Sometimes the subject of a clause is not the doer but the receiver: 'All the bananas ***have been eaten***.'

If it is necessary to mention the doer, we add a ***by***-phrase at the end of the clause: 'All the bananas ***have been eaten by George***.'

Clauses which begin with the receiver are called 'passive'. If we use a passive clause, the form of the verb phrase must also be passive. To make a passive verb phrase, we use ***be*** + past participle. Compare:

ACTIVE	We will notify all successful applicants by post.
PASSIVE	All successful applicants ***will be notified*** by post.
ACTIVE	Salesmen from all the regions attended the meeting.
PASSIVE	The meeting ***was attended*** by salesmen from all the regions.
ACTIVE	They have never promoted him.
PASSIVE	He ***has*** never ***been promoted***.

A passive clause cannot have an active verb phrase (e.g. 'will notify', 'has promoted').

2

× For the last two decades my country's economy has been base on agriculture.	√ For the last two decades my country's economy has been based on agriculture.
× This problem will be discuss in Section 3.	√ This problem will be discussed in Section 3.
× The meeting was attending by salesmen from all the regions.	√ The meeting was attended by salesmen from all the regions.

In a passive clause, the main verb is always a past participle ('based', 'discussed', 'attended'). The past participle of regular verbs ends in *-ed*. For the past participles of irregular verbs, ⇨ 419

3

× I want to know how these substances absorbed by the body.	√ I want to know how these substances are absorbed by the body.
× The polish can apply to any surface.	√ The polish can be applied to any surface.

To make the passive form of a simple tense, we use ***be*** + past participle:

The letter ***was sent*** last Tuesday.
She ***has been interviewed*** already.
The train ***could be delayed*** again.
Your keys ***might have been found*** by now.

4

×	✓
× These machines are using in many homes and offices.	✓ These machines are being used in many homes and offices.
× The company's workforce is gradually reduced.	✓ The company's workforce is gradually being reduced.

To make the passive form of a progressive tense, we use ***be*** + ***being*** + past participle: 'Her car ***is being repaired***.' 'The elephants ***were being fed***.'

5

×	✓
× The prison has been escaped several times.	✓ There have been several escapes from the prison.
× The summit was arrived at just before dawn.	✓ The summit was reached just before dawn.
	✓ We arrived at the summit just before dawn.

An intransitive verb (or a verb that is used with an intransitive meaning) cannot be made passive.

past 576

×	✓
× Many years have past since we last met.	✓ Many years have passed since we last met.
× These customs are past from generation to generation.	✓ These customs are passed from generation to generation.

Pass is a regular verb. To make the past simple tense and the past participle, we add -***ed***.

Past is used as an adjective ('the ***past*** six weeks'), adverb ('she ran ***past***'), preposition ('driving ***past*** the museum') and noun ('thinking about the ***past***').

⇨ 574

past participles 577

1

×	✓
× People who break the law should be punish.	✓ People who break the law should be punished.
× Try to make the interviewee feel relax.	✓ Try to make the interviewee feel relaxed.

The past participle form of a regular verb ends in -***ed***. We use this form as a verb ('punished') and as an adjective ('relaxed').

2

× Wrong	√ Right
× The shops are usually opened from 9 a.m. to 5 p.m.	√ The shops are usually open from 9 a.m. to 5 p.m.
× Replacing such a politically matured leader will not be easy.	√ Replacing such a politically mature leader will not be easy.

Sometimes we have to choose between an adjective (e.g. 'open'), and a past participle used as an adjective (e.g. 'opened'). To describe a state or quality, we normally use the adjective. We use the past participle when the meaning contains action: 'The shop ***is opened*** at 9 a.m.' (= somebody opens the shop at 9 a.m.)

past perfect tense: form 578

1

× Wrong	√ Right
× This type of thing had never happen before.	√ This type of thing had never happened before.

The simple form of the past perfect tense is ***had* ('*d*)** + past participle:

After the rain ***had stopped***, we went out.
I'***d*** already ***spoken*** to him before the meeting.
Had you ***seen*** her before last night?'

⇨ 626.1

2

× Wrong	√ Right
× The letter had sent to the wrong address.	√ The letter had been sent to the wrong address.

The passive form of the past perfect simple is ***had*** + ***been*** + past participle: 'The car ***had been moved*** by the police.' 'While he was asleep, his wallet ***had been stolen***.'

past perfect tense: use 579

1

× Wrong	√ Right
× My wife and I had come to England about six months ago.	√ My wife and I came to England about six months ago.
× In 1987 a number of new science subjects had been introduced.	√ In 1987 a number of new science subjects were introduced.
× How many trips to Europe had you made last year?	√ How many trips to Europe did you make last year?

To refer to a completed action which happened at a particular time or during a particular period in the past (e.g. 'six months ago', 'in 1987', 'last year'), we use the past simple tense ('came'), NOT the past perfect ('had come').

We use the past perfect tense to refer to an action which happened before another action in the past or before a particular time in the past, e.g. 'By the time I arrived, the match ***had*** already ***started***.' 'They ***had finished*** the job by 11 o'clock.'

2

×	✓
× Mr White, our sales manager, had worked for our company for 12 years.	✓ Mr White, our sales manager, has worked for our company for 12 years.
× For the last two years the room had been used as a laboratory.	✓ For the last two years the room has been used as a laboratory.
× We should focus our attention on the roads where accidents had already happened.	✓ We should focus our attention on the roads where accidents have already happened.
× Most of the books on these shelves had been used for ten years or more.	✓ Most of the books on these shelves have been used for ten years or more.

To refer to an action or period which began in the past and which has continued up to *now* (the moment of speaking), we use the present perfect tense ('has worked'), NOT the past perfect ('had worked').

'Mr White ***had worked*** (or ***worked***) for our company for 12 years' means that Mr White is no longer with the company. 'Mr White ***has worked*** for our company for 12 years' means that Mr White continues to work for the company.

past progressive tense: form — 580

1

×	✓
× When I first met Paul, he working as a chef in London.	✓ When I first met Paul, he was working as a chef in London.

To make the past progressive tense, we use ***was/were*** + ***-ing***: 'While I ***was waiting*** to see the dentist, I read an interesting article on child adoption.' 'What ***were*** you ***doing*** last night just before all the lights went out?'

2

×	✓
× While my car was repairing, I had to use my bicycle.	✓ While my car was being repaired, I had to use my bicycle.

The passive form of the past progressive tense is ***was/were*** + ***being*** + past participle: 'When we last stayed at the hotel, some of the rooms ***were being renovated***.' 'Water ***was being sprayed*** onto the logs to keep them wet.'

past progressive tense: use — 581

1

×	✓
× When he was a boy, my father was attending a boarding school.	✓ When he was a boy, my father attended a boarding school.

When we mention past actions and situations that last a long time, we normally use the past simple tense. We use the past progressive for shorter, temporary situations. Compare: 'In those days the people ***lived*** in small caves in the the mountainside.' 'For the first two weeks we ***were living*** in rented accommodation.'

We also use the past progressive to give background information: 'While I ***was attending*** the course, I made several new friends.'

2

× We were visiting the museum every morning.	√ We visited the museum every morning.

For a repeated action in the past, we normally use the past simple tense: 'The elephant ***roared*** three times and then collapsed.'

We use the past progressive when we want to say what was happening at a particular moment in the past: 'When I opened the door, the two children ***were jumping*** up and down on the bed.'

past simple tense: form **582**

1

× The science teacher seem to think we were lazy. × In 1956 the school change its name.	√ The science teacher seemed to think we were lazy. √ In 1956 the school changed its name.

The past simple form of a verb is nearly always different from its base form. Regular verbs take ***-d*** or ***-ed***.

2

× He sweared that he had not taken the money. × I ringed the bell three times but nobody came.	√ He swore that he had not taken the money. √ I rang the bell three times but nobody came.

The past simple tense of most irregular verbs is not formed with ***-d*** or ***-ed***.

⇨ 419

3

× I tryed to apologize but she refused to listen.	√ I tried to apologize but she refused to listen.

If the verb ends in ***-ly***, ***-ry***, ***-dy***, ***-fy***, etc (consonant + ***y***), we change the ***-y*** to *-**ied***: 'We ***studied*** the map very carefully.' 'The baby ***cried*** all night.'

4

× I payed a lot of money for the camera and I expect it to work. × Every year the doves layed eggs on the verandah.	√ I paid a lot of money for the camera and I expect it to work. √ Every year the doves laid eggs on the verandah.

If a regular verb ends in ***-ay***, ***-ey***, ***-oy***, etc (vowel + ***y***), we add *-**ed***: 'The children ***played*** in the garden.' 'We ***delayed*** our departure until the following morning.' However, ***pay***, ***lay*** and ***say*** are irregular: ***paid***, ***laid***, ***said***.

5

× We not wanted to listen to him any longer.	√ We did not want to listen to him any longer.

⇨ 512.1

6

× She did not paid any attention to us. × They didn't sold any cars last month.	√ She did not pay any attention to us. √ They didn't sell any cars last month.

⇨ 512.2

7

× They asked you when you can begin?	√ Did they ask you when you can begin?

⇨ 642.2

8

× What did she told you about me?	√ What did she tell you about me?

⇨ 642.4

past simple tense: use **583**

1

! I can't hire a car because I didn't pass my driving test. ! We're not going to the art gallery because we already went there.	√ I can't hire a car because I haven't passed my driving test. √ We're not going to the art gallery because we've already been there.

We often mention a past action because of the effect that it has *now* (at the moment of speaking). In British English, when we are talking more about the present than about the past, we use the present perfect, NOT the past simple. In informal American English, either tense may be used.

Note that we do not use the present perfect if the time of a past action is stated. With definite times, e.g. 'at two o'clock', 'yesterday', 'on Monday', 'last March', 'in 1987', 'two days ago', we use the past simple tense: 'I ***passed*** my driving test ***last December***.'

2

! Since getting married, she was much happier. ! In the last three years more and more people stopped smoking. ! This is the third time I visited London and so I know it quite well.	√ Since getting married, she has been much happier. √ In the last three years more and more people have stopped smoking. √ This is the third time I have visited London and so I know it quite well.

When we refer to something which began in the past and which has continued until *now* (the moment of speaking), we use the present perfect tense, NOT the past simple.

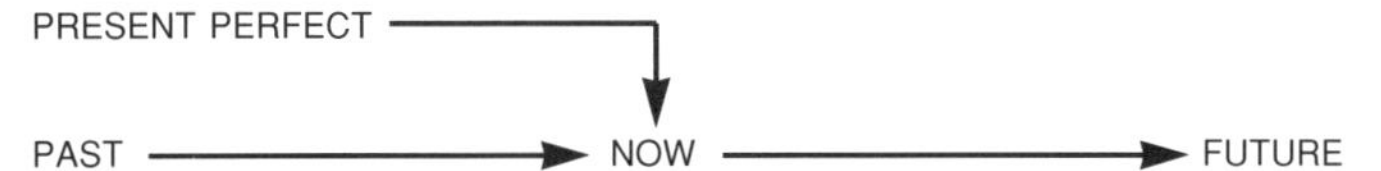

The present perfect is often used with expressions which mean or contain the meaning 'until now', e.g. *since, still, yet, ever, so far, recently, to date.*
Note that in informal American English, either tense may be used.

3

! Did you ever see the queen?	√ Have you ever seen the queen?
! The country's second university was just opened.	√ The country's second university has just been opened.

When we refer to an action which happens at an unspecified time before *now* (the moment of speaking), we use the present perfect tense, NOT the past simple. Compare: '*I **have seen*** that film ***before/already***.' 'I ***saw*** that film ***last Tuesday/a year ago***.'

The present perfect is often used with words which mean 'before now', e.g. *already, ever, never, just, before, recently.* With specific times, e.g. 'at two o'clock', 'yesterday', 'on Monday', 'last March', 'in 1987', 'two days ago', we use the past simple tense. Note that, in informal American English, either the present perfect or the past simple may be used with words meaning 'before now'.

4

× During my lifetime I saw many changes take place.	√ During my lifetime I have seen many changes take place.
× In the twentieth century, governments introduced laws to control the operation of industry.	√ In the twentieth century, governments have introduced laws to control the operation of industry.

When we mention a period of time that is still continuing at the moment of speaking (e.g. 'in the twentieth century', 'during my lifetime'), we use the present perfect tense, NOT the past simple.

Compare: 'I ***didn't have*** anything to eat this morning.' 'I ***haven't had*** anything to eat this morning.' In the first sentence, 'didn't have' (the past simple) tells us that the morning is over. In the second sentence, 'haven't had' (the present perfect) tells us that it is still morning.

5

× I just opened the door when the telephone rang.	√ I had just opened the door when the telephone rang.
× As soon as he saw what she did, he told the bus driver to stop.	√ As soon as he saw what she had done, he told the bus driver to stop.

When two actions happen at different times in the past, we use the past perfect for the action which happens first.

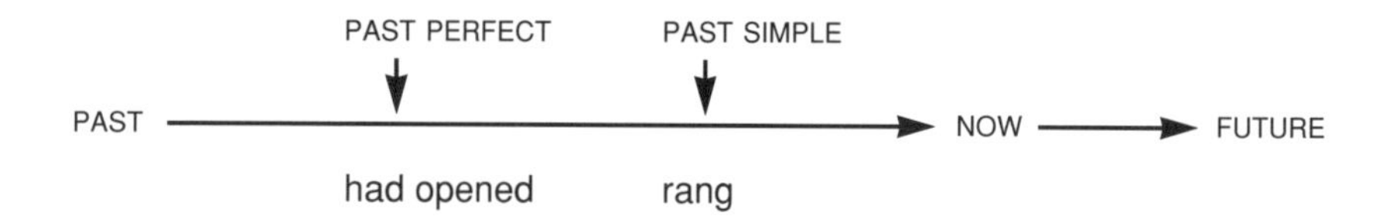

6

× By midday we sold more that 75 tickets. × I did not meet his wife before the night of the party and I was very impressed.	√ By midday we had sold more that 75 tickets. √ I had not met his wife before the night of the party and I was very impressed.

When we refer to a period of time which ends at a time in the past, we use the past perfect tense.

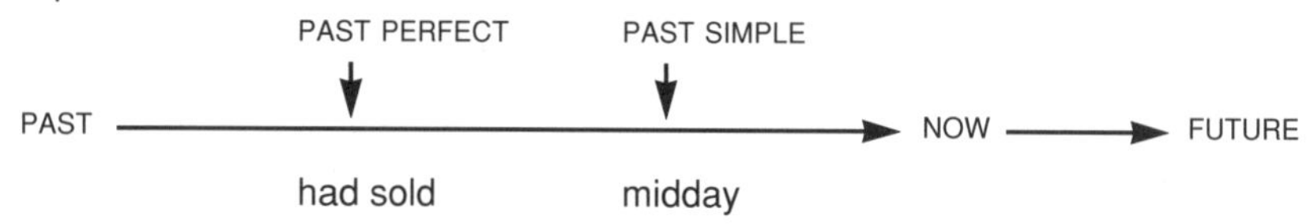

7

× I made the dinner when the telephone rang. × She didn't hear me because she played the guitar.	√ I was making the dinner when the telephone rang. √ She didn't hear me because she was playing the guitar.

To describe what was happening at a particular time in the past (or when something else happened), we use the past progressive tense: 'While I ***was opening*** the tin, I cut my finger.'

8

× Gianni returned to Italy on Friday but now he cannot go.	√ Gianni was returning to Italy on Friday but now he cannot go.

When we mention a previous plan or intention, we use the past progressive tense. Compare: 'I ***am going*** shopping this afternoon.' (= this ***is*** my intention) 'I ***was going*** shopping this afternoon.' (= this ***was*** my intention)

patience **584**

× To teach young children, you need a great patience.	√ To teach young children, you need great patience.

Patience is an uncountable noun and is not used with ***a/an***. ⇨ 2.1

pay 585

1

×	✓
× I payed a lot of money for the camera and I expect it to work.	✓ I paid a lot of money for the camera and I expect it to work.
× He had payed for all of us.	✓ He had paid for all of us.

Pay (infinitive), ***paid*** (past simple), ***paid*** (past participle).

2

×	✓
× He expected me to pay the drinks too.	✓ He expected me to pay for the drinks too.

We ***pay for*** the things that we buy: 'Whose turn is it to ***pay for*** the tickets?' 'I'm not going to ***pay*** $10 just ***for*** an ice-cream.'

3

×	✓
× If they become ill, the Government has to pay for the medical bills.	✓ If they become ill, the Government has to pay the medical bills.

We ***pay*** a bill, debt, fee, etc, WITHOUT ***for***: 'Do you have to ***pay*** income tax?' 'She can't afford to ***pay*** the tuition fees.'

4

×	✓
× Doctors usually get a very good pay.	✓ Doctors usually get very good pay.

Pay is an uncountable noun and is not used with ***a/an***.

⇨ 2.1

people 586

1

×	✓
× Some peoples who live in the city cycle to work.	✓ Some people who live in the city cycle to work.

People is normally used to refer to men, women, and children: 'Not many ***people*** can afford such luxuries.' In this meaning, it is a plural noun and cannot take an *-s* ending.

When ***people*** refers to a race or nation, it is a countable noun and can take an *-s* ending: 'It is time for the ***peoples*** of the world to unite.'

2

×	✓
× Since this people have no jobs, they don't have any money.	✓ Since these people have no jobs, they don't have any money.
× Some people says that punishments should be more severe.	✓ Some people say that punishments should be more severe.

⇨ 603.2,4

3

× Her husband is the most boring people I've ever met.	√ Her husband is the most boring person I've ever met.

The singular form of ***people*** is ***person***. ⇨ 589

per cent 587

× Fifty per cent of the machinery have to be replaced.	√ Fifty per cent of the machinery has to be replaced.

⇨ 44.10

permission 588

× You cannot leave the country without a special permission.	√ You cannot leave the country without special permission.

Permission is an uncountable noun and is not used with ***a/an***. ⇨ 2.1

person 589

× We all know persons who have gone to live abroad.	√ We all know people who have gone to live abroad.

Nowadays, the plural form of ***person*** is nearly always ***people***. ***Persons*** is used mainly in legal texts and public notices, eg 'Capacity – ***6 persons***'.

personal pronouns: use 590

1

× This report looks at teaching aids and how it helps teachers.	√ This report looks at teaching aids and how they help teachers.
× The jewellery was given to Mary, who sold them for $6,000.	√ The jewellery was given to Mary, who sold it for $6,000.

⇨ 42.1–2

2

× I took Martin and a friend of him to Teotihuacan.	√ I took Martin and a friend of his to Teotihuacan.

If a double genitive ends with a pronoun, we use ***mine***, ***yours***, ***his***, ***hers***, ***ours***, ***theirs*** (possessive pronouns), NOT ***me***, ***you***, ***him***, ***her***, ***us***, ***them***: 'These old shoes ***of mine*** are very comfortable.' 'Is he a friend ***of yours***?'

3

×	✓
× I often ask me why I work so hard.	✓ I often ask myself why I work so hard.
× Although we worked very hard, we enjoyed us.	✓ Although we worked very hard, we enjoyed ourselves.

When the subject and object refer to the same person or thing, we use a reflexive pronoun, ***myself***, ***herself***, etc. (NOT ***me***, ***her***, etc.).

Note that this is also the case even when the subject is not actually mentioned: 'There is no time (for us) to relax and enjoy ***ourselves***.' 'Help ***yourself*** to some cake.'

4

×	✓
× The majority of viewers are children and it is them who are exposed to such scenes of violence.	✓ The majority of viewers are children and it is they who are exposed to such scenes of violence.

Nowadays, even in formal styles, most people normally use the object forms ***me***, ***him***, ***her***, ***us***, ***them*** after the verb ***be***: 'Look! It's ***her*** again.' (NOT *she*) 'I didn't realize it was ***them***.' (NOT *they*)

However, there is one occasion when ***be*** is followed by the subject forms ***I***, ***he***, ***she***, ***we***, ***they***. These forms are used in formal styles when the personal pronoun is followed by a relative clause beginning with a subject pronoun: 'The workers idolized her, since it was ***she who*** had given them hope.'

5

!	✓
! Nowadays, anybody can use a computer if he or she really wants to.	✓ Nowadays, anybody who really wants to use a computer can do so.
! Each subscriber was told that he would receive a refund.	✓ All subscribers were told that they would receive a refund.

⇨ 42.4

6

×	✓
× Nobody is allowed to use the computer but I.	✓ Nobody is allowed to use the computer but me.

After a preposition we normally use ***me***, ***her***, ***him***, ***us***, ***them*** (object pronouns), NOT ***I***, ***she***, ***he***, ***we***, ***they*** (subject pronouns). ⇨ .7 below

7

×	✓
× My sister plays the piano much better than I.	✓ My sister plays the piano much better than me.
	✓ My sister plays the piano much better than I do.

After ***than*** or ***as***, we normally use ***me***, ***her***, ***him***, ***us***, ***them*** (object pronouns), especially in informal styles. In formal styles, we normally use ***I***, ***she***, ***he***, ***we***, ***they*** (subject pronouns) + verb.

8

! We have no objection to you paying a deposit now and the balance later.	√ We have no objection to your paying a deposit now and the balance later.
! I fully understand him not wanting to pursue the matter.	√ I fully understand his not wanting to pursue the matter.
× These errors are the result of they trying to translate.	√ These errors are the result of their trying to translate.

In formal styles, we normally use a possessive determiner (e.g. ***my***, ***our***, ***their***) before an *-ing* form. In informal styles, however, an object pronoun (e.g. ***me***, ***you***, ***them***) is very common. A subject pronoun (e.g. ***I***, ***we***, ***they***) is always incorrect.

9

× Rape is a very serious crime and they should be sent to prison.	√ Rape is a very serious crime and rapists should be sent to prison.

We cannot use a pronoun ('they') unless the person or thing that it refers to is mentioned somewhere in the context.

10

× My friends lent me some books. They were very helpful.	√ My friends lent me some books, which were very helpful. √ My friends were very helpful and lent me some books.

In the error sentence above, it is not clear whether the pronoun 'They' refers to 'some books' or to 'My friends'. A reader should not have to guess the word or phrase that a pronoun refers to. ⇨ 610.5

personal pronouns: wrongly included 591

1

× The people without their own shops they were selling their things on the pavement.	√ The people without their own shops were selling their things on the pavement.
× The research it will investigate some major traffic problems.	√ The research will investigate some major traffic problems.

We cannot use a pronoun as the subject of a verb if the verb has a subject already. A verb can have only one subject. This type of error often occurs when the head of the subject ('people') is a long way from the verb ('were selling'). ⇨ 669.1

2

× The second group Spitzer calls it 'social dynamite'.	√ The second group Spitzer calls 'social dynamite'.

To emphasize a direct object, we sometimes move it to the beginning of a clause. Compare: 'I found ***her first book*** very interesting.' '***Her first book*** I found very interesting.'

When a clause begins with a direct object, we do not use a pronoun object after the verb (e.g. 'it'). A verb can have only one direct object.

3

×	√
× The computer is very easy to use it.	√ The computer is very easy to use.
× The book is certainly worth reading it.	√ The book is certainly worth reading.
× Is this parcel too heavy to send it by air?	√ Is this parcel too heavy to send by air?

Compare the following patterns:

Pattern A It is difficult to move ***a piano***.
Pattern B ***A piano*** is difficult to move.

In Pattern A, the object ('a piano') is in its normal position, after the verb.

In Pattern B, 'a piano' has become the grammatical subject, but it is also the logical object of 'to move'. When a verb has a logical object, it cannot have a grammatical object as well. The incorrect inclusion of an object pronoun is very common in Pattern B sentences.

4

×	√
× The music is very good to listen to it.	√ The music is very good to listen to.

Compare the following patterns:

Pattern A It is easy to get to ***my house***.
Pattern B ***My house*** is easy to get to.

In Pattern A, 'my house' is the grammatical object of the preposition 'to'.

In Pattern B, 'my house' has become the grammatical subject, but it is also the logical object of 'to'. When a preposition has a logical object, it cannot have a grammatical object as well. The incorrect inclusion of an object pronoun is very common in Pattern B sentences.

5

×	√
× He gave me two cookery books, which I find them very useful.	√ He gave me two cookery books, which I find very useful.

For information about the use of personal pronouns in relative clauses, ⇨ 669

persuade 592

×	√
× I finally persuaded her staying another day.	√ I finally persuaded her to stay another day.

We ***persuade*** someone ***to do*** something: 'How did you ***persuade*** him ***to change*** his mind?'

phenomenon 593

× We still don't have explanations for such phenomenons.	√ We still don't have explanations for such phenomena.

The plural form of ***phenomenon*** is ***phenomena***.

phone/telephone 594

1

× I have to phone to my parents to tell them where I am.	√ I have to phone my parents to tell them where I am.

We ***phone/telephone*** someone, NOT ***to*** someone: 'I'll ***phone you*** again on Tuesday.'

2

x My telephone's number is 343474.	√ My telephone number is 343474.

⇨ 694.5

phrasal verbs 595

1

× The fan was very noisy and so I turned off it.	√ The fan was very noisy and so I turned it off.
× Our parents brought up us to respect elderly people.	√ Our parents brought us up to respect elderly people.

With many phrasal verbs, there is a choice of word order:

Pattern A I ***turned off*** the fan.
She ***put on*** her shoes.

Pattern B I ***turned*** the fan ***off***.
She ***put*** her shoes ***on***.

However, when the direct object is a pronoun, only Pattern B is possible: 'I ***turned*** it ***off***.' 'She ***put*** them ***on***.'

2

× The woman was handing free samples of a new type of chocolate bar out.	√ The woman was handing out free samples of a new type of chocolate bar.

When there is a long direct object (e.g. 'free samples of a new type of chocolate bar'), the parts of a phrasal verb stay together, as in Pattern A. ⇨ .1 above

Note, however, that if a long direct object contains a movable qualifier (e.g. a relative clause), two patterns are possible: 'They have ***brought out*** a new battery which never needs recharging.' 'They have ***brought*** a new battery ***out*** which never needs recharging.'

In the second pattern, the adverb ('out') is placed immediately after the head of the direct object ('battery') and the qualifier comes last.

piano 596

! How long have you been playing piano?	√ How long have you been playing the piano?

⇨ 783.6

piece 597

× The two pieces of cracked tiles were replaced.	√ The two cracked tiles were replaced.

⇨ 823.4

pierce 598

× Fortunately, the dog's teeth were not sharp enough to pierce into my skin.	√ Fortunately, the dog's teeth were not sharp enough to pierce my skin.

When a pointed object is pushed into something, it ***pierces*** it (WITHOUT ***into***): 'A long nail had ***pierced*** one of the front tyres.'

pity 599

1

× Why do so few people feel a pity for the deaf?	√ Why do so few people feel pity for the deaf?

When ***pity*** means 'a feeling of sympathy and sorrow', it is an uncountable noun and is not used with ***a/an***: 'I feel ***pity*** for people who have no home of their own.' 'We should take ***pity*** on them.' ⇨ 2.1 Compare: 'It's ***a pity*** that you have to leave so soon.' (= it is unfortunate that) 'What ***a pity***!'

2

× Seeing him in tears, I immediately took pity for him.	√ Seeing him in tears, I immediately took pity on him.

We ***feel pity for*** someone but we ***take pity on*** someone: 'He hopes that you will ***take pity on*** him and forget the money you lent him.'

please 600

1

× Please I would like to know the exact dates of your trip.	√ Please let me know the exact dates of your trip. √ Please would you let me know the exact dates of your trip.

Please is normally used in imperative clauses ('Please let …') and interrogative clauses ('Please would you let … ?').

2

× Please, when you have time, write to me again.	√ Please write to me again when you have time. √ When you have time, please write to me again.

Please should not be separated from its verb.

3

× I shall be please to pay for the postage and packing.	√ I shall be pleased to pay for the postage and packing.

⇨ 14.1

pleased 601

× I hope she is pleased about the present we gave her.	√ I hope she is pleased with the present we gave her.

If we like a new possession (e.g. a gift or a purchase), we are ***pleased with*** it: 'George is very ***pleased with*** his new lawnmower.' Compare: 'We're both ***pleased about/at*** not having to sell our house after all.'

pleasure 602

× It gives me a great pleasure to send you this little gift.	√ It gives me great pleasure to send you this little gift.

When ***pleasure*** means 'a feeling of happiness', it is an uncountable noun and is not used with ***a/an***: 'Our children give us enormous ***pleasure***.' ⇨ 2.1
Compare: 'It's been ***a pleasure*** having you stay with us.' (= an enjoyable experience)

plural nouns 603

1

× My new trouser was covered in white paint.	√ My new trousers were covered in white paint.
× Trees help to create a peaceful surrounding.	√ Trees help to create peaceful surroundings.

Even when we are talking about just one pair of trousers, we say ***trousers***, NOT 'trouser'. ***Trousers*** is a plural noun and does not have a singular form.

The following list contains nouns which are always plural and nouns which are plural when used in a particular meaning.

arms (weapons), ***arrears***, ***belongings***, ***binoculars***, ***braces***, ***briefs*** (underpants or knickers), ***clothes***, ***clergy***, ***congratulations***, ***contents***, ***costs*** (money that the loser of a legal action has to pay), ***credentials***, ***customs*** (e.g. at an airport), ***damages*** (compensation awarded to the winner of a legal action), ***directions*** (instructions), ***dregs***, ***earnings***, ***essentials***, ***expenses*** (money that people spend while doing their work), ***glasses*** (spectacles), ***goods***, ***greens*** (vegetables), ***grounds***, ***headquarters***, ***jeans***, ***knickers***, ***lodgings***, ***looks*** (appearance), ***manners*** (behaviour), ***morals***, ***odds***, ***outskirts***, ***overalls***, ***pains*** (effort), ***panties***, ***pants***, ***particulars*** (details), ***people***, ***pincers***, ***police***, ***pliers***, ***premises*** (a building), ***proceeds***, ***prospects***, ***provisions*** (food supplies), ***pyjamas***, ***qualifications***, ***qualms***, ***quarters*** (lodgings), ***refreshments***, ***regards*** (good wishes), ***remains***, ***scales*** (as in 'bathroom scales'), ***scissors***, ***shears***, ***shortcomings*** (faults or weaknesses), ***shorts***, ***slacks***, ***spectacles***, ***sunglasses***, ***supplies***, ***surroundings***, ***talks***, ***thanks***, ***tights***, ***travels***, ***the tropics*** (the hottest part of the world), ***trousers***, ***trunks*** (as in 'swimming trunks'), ***tweezers***, ***underpants***, ***valuables***, ***whereabouts***.

2

× All you need is plenty of paper and a sharp scissors.	√ All you need is plenty of paper and some sharp scissors.

A plural noun (e.g. 'scissors') cannot be used with determiners which have a singular meaning, e.g. *a/an*, *another*, *each*, *either*, *every*, *this*, *that*.

3

× I bought three jeans for just $60.	√ I bought three pairs of jeans for just $60.

A number cannot come immediately in front of ***jeans***, ***scissors***, ***sunglasses***, etc. Instead, we normally use a construction with ***pair/s***:

NUMBER +	PAIR/S +	OF-PHRASE
two	pairs	of binoculars
four	pairs	of tennis shorts

⇨ 567

4

× The jails are so crowded that the police does not arrest people for minor offences.	√ The jails are so crowded that the police do not arrest people for minor offences.

A plural noun ('police') always takes a plural verb ('do').

5

×	✓
× Her husband is a typical English.	✓ Her husband is typically English. ✓ Her husband is a typical Englishman.

⇨ 504

poetry 604

×	✓
× I didn't know that Shakespeare wrote poetries too.	✓ I didn't know that Shakespeare wrote poetry too.

Poetry is an uncountable noun and does not have a plural form. Compare: 'I didn't know that Shakespeare wrote ***poems*** too.'

point 605

1

×	✓
× I grabbed the gun and pointed it to him.	✓ I grabbed the gun and pointed it at him.

We ***point*** an object (e.g. a gun or camera) ***at*** someone or something (NOT ***to***). Compare: 'She ***pointed to*** the NO SMOKING sign.'

2

×	✓
× Some people do not see the point to learn a foreign language.	✓ Some people do not see the point of learning a foreign language.

If we understand the purpose of doing something, we ***see the point of*** doing it.

3

×	✓
× It's no point asking Philip to help you. × There was little point to take the car back to the same garage.	✓ There's no point in asking Philip to help you. ✓ There was little point in taking the car back to the same garage.

If an action has no useful purpose, we say that there is ***no point in*** doing it.

⇨ 833.3

point of view 606

×	✓
× We should also consider this matter in the child's point of view.	✓ We should also consider this matter from the child's point of view.

The phrase is ***from*** a particular ***point of view*** (NOT ***in***): '***From*** a practical ***point of view***, the first proposal has several advantages.' Compare: '***In my opinion***, the first proposal has several advantages.'

police 607

1

×	✓
× The jails are so crowded that the police does not arrest people for minor offences.	✓ The jails are so crowded that the police do not arrest people for minor offences.

Police is a plural noun and takes a plural verb.

⇨ 603

2

×	✓
× A police was standing outside the bank.	✓ A police officer was standing outside the bank.

Police is a plural noun. To refer to a member of the police force, we use ***policeman***, ***policewoman*** or ***police officer***.

pollution 608

×	✓
× Should we let our children inherit a world full of pollutions?	✓ Should we let our children inherit a world full of pollution?

Pollution is an uncountable noun and does not have a plural form.

poor 609

×	✓
× She has spent most of her life helping the poors.	✓ She has spent most of her life helping the poor.

⇨ 19.1

possessive determiners 610

1

×	✓
× Pupils sometimes suffer in a test when the questions are written in a language which is not his mother tongue.	✓ Pupils sometimes suffer in a test when the questions are written in a language which is not their mother tongue.
× I visited the local library with her collection of rare books.	✓ I visited the local library with its collection of rare books.

⇨ 42

2

×	✓
× Thank you for all your help that you have given me with my studies.	✓ Thank you for all the help that you have given me with my studies.

⇨ 667.2

3

× Why does she keep hitting herself on her head?	√ Why does she keep hitting herself on the head?

When we refer to a part of someone's body, we normally use ***his***, ***her***, etc.:

She had cuts all over ***her*** hands.
His nose was bleeding.
I've hurt ***my*** back again.

However, when the person is the object of the clause and the part of the body follows in a prepositional phrase, we use ***the***:

	OBJECT +	PREPOSITIONAL PHRASE
I tapped	the woman	on ***the*** shoulder.
I grabbed	the boy	by ***the*** arm.
The ball hit	him	in ***the*** stomach.

We also use ***the*** in related passive structures: 'He had been punched on ***the*** nose by an angry housewife.' 'All of a sudden, I was grabbed by ***the*** arm.'

4

! I would never treat my relative like that.	√ I would never treat a relative (of mine) like that. √ I would never treat one of my relatives like that.

If we say 'my relative', we suggest that we have just one relative. Compare: 'Is he ***your friend***?' 'Is he ***a friend of yours***?' ⇨ 694.3

5

× A student may not understand a lecturer if his English is weak.	√ A student whose English is weak may not understand a lecturer. √ A student may not understand a lecturer whose English is weak.

A reader should never have to guess the word or phrase that a determiner refers to. In the first sentence above, we cannot tell whether 'his' refers to 'student' or 'lecturer'. ⇨ 590.10

possibility 611

× We are currently considering the possibility to buy our own house.	√ We are currently considering the possibility of buying our own house.

We talk about the ***possibility of doing*** something: 'The company is looking into the ***possibility of employing*** more staff.' Compare: 'Will it be ***possible to employ*** more staff?'

poverty 612

×	√
× The government's primary goal is to reduce the poverty.	√ The government's primary goal is to reduce poverty.

⇨ 782.3

prefer 613

1

×	√
× Does he really prefer sausages than meat?	√ Does he really prefer sausages to meat?

We ***prefer*** one thing ***to*** another thing, NOT ***than***. Compare: 'Does he really ***like*** sausages ***more than*** meat?'

2

×	√
× I'd prefer going in my own car, if you don't mind.	√ I'd prefer to go in my own car, if you don't mind.

⇨ 839.6

3

×	√
× She is preferring to type the letter herself.	√ She prefers to type the letter herself.

Prefer is not used in progressive tenses.

⇨ 627.3

prepositions: general 614

1

×	√
× In spite of the driver didn't stop, we managed to get the number of the car.	√ Although the driver didn't stop, we managed to get the number of the car. √ In spite of the driver not stopping, we managed to get the number of the car.

⇨ 882.7

2

×	√
× I told to the policeman everything I had seen.	√ I told the policeman everything I had seen.

⇨ 387.3

3

×	√
× I drove to the hotel where she was staying at.	√ I drove to the hotel where she was staying.

⇨ 668

4

×	✓
× Besides to like children, a good teacher has to have a lot of patience.	✓ Besides liking children, a good teacher has to have a lot of patience.

When a verb follows a preposition, we use the *-ing* form. ⇨ 837

5

×	✓
× It is one of the most popular cars of the world.	✓ It is one of the most popular cars in the world.
× For my surprise, the box was empty.	✓ To my surprise, the box was empty.
× In the whole, the pupils seem to like their teacher.	✓ On the whole, the pupils seem to like their teacher.

Many fixed expressions begin with a preposition, e.g. ***in*** *the world*, ***to*** *my surprise*, ***on*** *the whole*, ***under*** *investigation*, ***at*** *great expense*. Unfortunately, there are no general rules to help us choose the correct preposition for a particular expression and each phrase has to be learned separately. Fixed phrases in common use can be found in a good dictionary at the entry for the noun (e.g. *in the world* will be found at *world*).

For more information about the use of prepositions, ⇨ 21, 535, 841

present **615**

1

×	✓
× The football was a present of my grandfather.	✓ The football was a present from my grandfather.

A ***present*** (noun) is ***from*** the person who gives it to us, NOT ***of***.

2

×	✓
× The editor presented the winner of the competition a cheque for $100.	✓ The editor presented the winner of the competition with a cheque for $100.

We ***present*** (verb) someone ***with*** something: 'At her retirement party, Judy was ***presented with*** a black leather handbag.'

3

×	✓
× I had never been present to such an important event before.	✓ I had never been present at such an important event before.

A person is ***present*** (adjective) ***at*** an event, NOT ***to***.

4

×	✓
× During the meeting several of the present teachers said that more money should be spent on books.	✓ During the meeting several of the teachers present said that more money should be spent on books.

⇨ 16.3

present perfect tense: form **616**

1

× The company has open a new shop on Jalan Sultan.	√ The company has opened a new shop on Jalan Sultan.
× For the last two decades my country's economy has been base on agriculture.	√ For the last two decades my country's economy has been based on agriculture.

The present perfect simple always ends with a past participle.

They ***have opened*** a new shop. ACTIVE
A new shop ***has been opened***. PASSIVE

Someone ***has stolen*** his watch. ACTIVE
His watch ***has been stolen***. PASSIVE

2

× For the past two years I have working as a teacher.	√ For the past two years I have been working as a teacher.

The form of the present perfect progressive is ***have/has*** + ***been*** + ***-ing***: 'I ***have been waiting*** here for nearly an hour.' 'How long ***have*** you ***been living*** here?'

present perfect tense: use **617**

1

× I have seen the film in London last week.	√ I saw the film in London last week.
× In France the death penalty has been abolished in 1981.	√ In France the death penalty was abolished in 1981.

When we mention something which took place at a particular time in the past (e.g. 'last week', 'in 1981', 'yesterday', 'two months ago'), we use the past simple tense, NOT the present perfect. ⇨ 583.1–4

2

× By the time we reached the classroom, the first lesson has almost ended.	√ By the time we reached the classroom, the first lesson had almost ended.
× Unfortunately, the car has been sold before I arrived.	√ Unfortunately, the car had been sold before I arrived.
× In New York I took the subway by myself although I have been told that it was dangerous.	√ In New York I took the subway by myself although I had been told that it was dangerous.

When two things happen at different times in the past, we use the past perfect tense for the one which happens first: 'After we ***had painted*** the ceiling, we ***painted*** the walls.' 'Once I ***had eaten*** something, I ***began*** to feel better.'

Note that the past perfect tense is formed with ***had*** + past participle, NOT ***have/has***.

3

× Everything has been fine until yesterday.	√ Everything had been fine until yesterday.

To refer to a situation that no longer exists, we use the past tense or the past perfect tense. Compare: 'She ***looked*** much happier ***last week***.' 'She ***had looked*** much happier ***until last week***.'

We use the present perfect if the situation still exists: 'She ***has looked*** much happier ***since last week***.' (= she still looks happy)

present progressive tense: form — 618

× I already looking forward to your next visit.	√ I am already looking forward to your next visit.
× They still waiting for you to reply.	√ They are still waiting for you to reply.

The form of the present progressive tense is ***am/are/is*** + ***-ing***:

I ***am (****I****'m) going*** out tonight.
You ***are (****You****'re) listening*** to the BBC World Service.
Are you ***writing*** to George?
She ***is (****She****'s) leaving*** tomorrow.
They ***are (****They****'re)*** not ***coming*** back until next Wednesday.

present progressive tense: use — 619

1

× I am studying law since 1987.	√ I have been studying law since 1987.
× He is working here for almost 12 years.	√ He has been working here for almost 12 years.

When we mention an action or situation which began in the past and which is still continuing *now* (at the moment of speaking), we use the present perfect progressive tense. Compare: 'I ***am learning*** English at the Bell School.' 'I ***have been attending*** the Bell School for the last two years.'

The first sentence focuses on what is happening *now*; there is no link with the past. The second sentence also tells us what is happening *now*, but the focus is on a period of time which links *now* with the past.

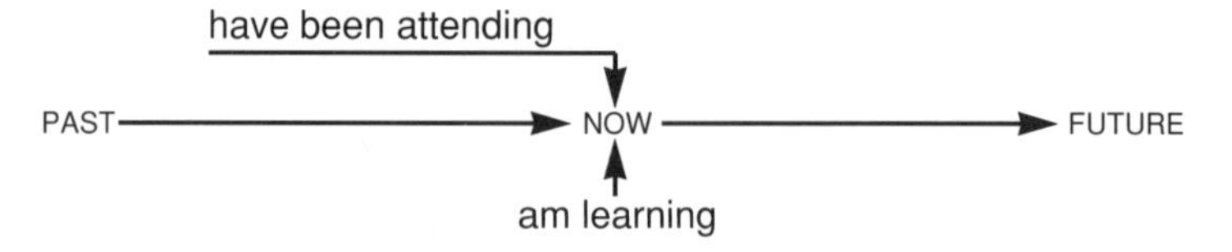

If the verb is not normally used in progressive tenses (⇨ 627.3), we use the present perfect simple: 'I ***have known*** Hilary since she was a child.'

The present perfect tense is very common with time adverbials that connect *now* with the past. These include: ***since***, ***already***, ***yet***, ***ever***, ***still***, ***so far***, ***recently***, ***to date***, ***during/for/in/over the last/past*** *(six weeks)*.

2

×	✓
× Every year she is making two trips to Singapore.	✓ Every year she makes two trips to Singapore.
× Some of my friends are not letting their children watch the television on their own.	✓ Some of my friends do not let their children watch the television on their own.

When we mention something which happens repeatedly or habitually, we normally use the present simple tense: 'We normally ***spend*** our holidays in France.' 'Babies always ***cry*** when they are hungry.'

3

×	✓
× A lot of people in Southeast Asia are speaking three languages.	✓ A lot of people in Southeast Asia speak three languages.
× My parents are living at 64 Kalluaki Street, Athens.	✓ My parents live at 64 Kalluaki Street, Athens.

When we use the present progressive tense ('are living'), we suggest that the situation is temporary: 'At the moment we ***are living*** in rented accommodation, but next month we'll be moving into our new house.'
When we are talking about a situation that is permanent, we use the present simple ('live').

4

×	✓
× People who are not eating properly are often catching colds.	✓ People who do not eat properly often catch colds.

When we make a statement that is always true, we use the simple form of the present tense, not the progressive form. Compare: 'It ***takes*** a long time to learn a foreign language.' 'It ***is taking*** them a long time to answer our letter.'

5

×	✓
× I am wondering whether you can mark my homework.	✓ I was wondering whether you could mark my homework.

In enquiries and requests, we often use past tense forms in places where present tense forms might be expected. Past tense forms sound more tentative and polite: 'We ***were hoping*** that you ***might agree*** to sponsor us.'

present simple tense: form **620**

1

×	✓
× If anyone happen to find the watch, please contact Miss Goh.	✓ If anyone happens to find the watch, please contact Miss Goh.
× It is not clear what the writer mean by 'stricter punishment'.	✓ It is not clear what the writer means by 'stricter punishment'.

After a third person singular subject (e.g. *he*, *Mrs Jones*, *anyone*, *the writer*, *the girl you spoke to yesterday*), we use the ***-s*** form of the verb.

2

×	√
× My husband watch television every night.	√ My husband watches television every night.
× The main problem is that the radio do not work.	√ The main problem is that the radio does not work.

After a third person singular subject, we add ***-es*** to verbs ending in ***-ch***, ***-sh***, ***-s***, ***-x*** or ***-o*** (e.g. *teach*, *wash*, *guess*, *fix*, *do*, *go*). Compare: 'He ***washes*** his hair twice a week but I ***wash*** mine every day.'

3

×	√
× A baby always crys when it is hungry.	√ A baby always cries when it is hungry.

After a third person singular subject, if the verb ends in a consonant + ***-y***, we change the ***-y*** to ***-ies***: 'I ***try*** to help him whenever I can, but he never ***tries*** to help me.'

If the verb ends in a vowel + ***-y***, we add ***-s*** in the normal way: 'She often ***buys*** me presents but she never ***pays*** the rent.'

4

×	√
× Sometimes our teacher not allow us to use a dictionary.	√ Sometimes our teacher does not allow us to use a dictionary.
× I like not very noisy music.	√ I don't like very noisy music.

⇨ 512.1

5

×	√
× My husband doesn't speaks English at all.	√ My husband doesn't speak English at all.

⇨ 512.2

6

×	√
× How much it costs?	√ How much does it cost?

⇨ 642.2

7

×	√
× How long does it takes to get from London to Oxford?	√ How long does it take to get from London to Oxford?

⇨ 642.4

present simple tense: use **621**

1

×	✓
× I write to you to thank you for my birthday present.	✓ I am writing to you to thank you for my birthday present.
× You look busy. What do you do?	✓ You look busy. What are you doing?
× Following a fall in revenues, the company's workforce is gradually reduced.	✓ Following a fall in revenues, the company's workforce is gradually being reduced.

When we refer to something that is happening at the moment of speaking, we use the present progressive tense. Compare: 'Alex ***is having*** breakfast in the kitchen.' (= now; at this moment), 'Alex ***has*** breakfast in the kitchen.' (= usually; every morning)

2

×	✓
× Perhaps she comes to see you tonight.	✓ Perhaps she will come to see you tonight.
× I meet you outside the cinema at seven o'clock.	✓ I'll meet you outside the cinema at seven o'clock.

There are many ways of referring to the future in English. However, the present simple tense is NOT used for this purpose unless we are talking about a timetable, programme or schedule:

The train ***leaves*** at half past five.
The film ***begins*** at seven o'clock sharp.
We ***leave*** Hong Kong on Tuesday evening and ***arrive*** in London the following morning.

The present simple is also used for future reference in subordinate clauses: 'When she ***gets*** back, I'll tell her that you called.' 'If you ***arrive*** before eight o'clock, there will still be some food left.' ⇨ 25, 163.2

3

×	✓
× I am a bank clerk for over 10 years now.	✓ I have been a bank clerk for over 10 years now.
× I live in Athens since I was two years old.	✓ I have lived in Athens since I was two years old.
× For the last three weeks the shop is closed.	✓ For the last three weeks the shop has been closed.

To refer to something which began in the past and which has continued up to *now* (the moment of speaking), we use the present perfect tense, NOT the present simple.

4

×	√
× This year my sister visits me three times.	√ This year my sister has visited me three times.
× This is the second time that a group of children from Cambridge comes to France.	√ This is the second time that a group of children from Cambridge has come to France.
× This is the first time that I eat mushrooms.	√ This is the first time that I have eaten mushrooms.

When the period of time is not over yet (e.g. 'this year') or when the meaning is 'ever; in all my life up to now', we use the present perfect tense.

5

×	√
× I can't believe that I pass all the examinations.	√ I can't believe that I have passed all the examinations.
× I don't know what happens to the CD but it sounds terrible.	√ I don't know what has happened to the CD but it sounds terrible.

To talk about something which has happened at some (unstated) time *before now*, we use the present perfect tense. The present perfect suggests a close connection between what has happened and the present situation, e.g. 'I ***have passed*** all the examinations.' (= I am very happy *now*) 'Something ***has happened*** to the CD player.' (= the sound is terrible *now*)

prevent 622

×	√
× The size of our population does not prevent us to take part in international competitions.	√ The size of our population does not prevent us from taking part in international competitions.

If we make it impossible for someone to do something, we ***prevent*** them ***from doing*** it: 'My parents tried to ***prevent*** me ***from getting*** married.'

price 623

×	√
× He thinks that the price for oil is bound to increase.	√ He thinks that the price of oil is bound to increase.

We talk about the ***price of*** something, NOT ***for*** something.

proceed 624

×	√
× The speaker proceeded on to explain why foreign investment was essential.	√ The speaker proceeded to explain why foreign investment was essential.

We ***proceed to do*** something, WITHOUT ***on***. Compare: 'The speaker ***went on to explain*** why foreign investment was essential.'

progress 625

×	✓
× The doctors say that he is making a good progress and will not need an operation.	✓ The doctors say that he is making good progress and will not need an operation.

Progress is an uncountable noun and is not used with ***a/an***. ⇨ 2.1

progressive tenses: form 626

1

×	✓
× They still waiting for you to reply.	✓ They are still waiting for you to reply.
× When I first met Paul, he working as a chef in London.	✓ When I first met Paul, he was working as a chef in London.

To make a progressive tense, we use ***be*** + ***-ing***. Examples:

She ***is writing*** a report. (present progressive)
She ***was writing*** a report. (past progressive)
She ***has been writing*** a report. (present perfect progressive)
She ***had been writing*** a report. (past perfect progressive)

Note also the pattern: modal verb + ***be*** + ***-ing***: 'She ***may/must be writing*** a report.' 'She ***may/must have been writing*** a report.'

2

×	✓
× The company's workforce is gradually reduced.	✓ The company's workforce is gradually being reduced.
× While my car was repairing, I had to use my bicycle.	✓ While my car was being repaired, I had to use my bicycle.

To make the passive form of a progressive tense, we use ***be*** + ***being*** + past participle. Only two tenses are normally used in this way: 'The report ***is being written***.' (present progressive passive) 'The report ***was being written***.' (past progressive passive)

progressive tenses: use 627

1

×	✓
× Every year she is making two trips to Singapore.	✓ Every year she makes two trips to Singapore.

When we mention a habit or a regularly repeated action, we normally use a simple tense: 'The sun ***rises*** in the east and ***sets*** in the west.'

2

×	✓
× Most of the children are living quite near the school.	✓ Most of the children live quite near the school.
× When he was a boy, my father was attending a boarding school.	✓ When he was a boy, my father attended a boarding school.

When we are talking about a situation that is permanent, we use a simple tense. A progressive tense suggests that the situation is temporary. Compare: 'He ***is*** normally very serious but today he ***is being*** silly.'

3

× Computers are useless unless you are knowing how to use them.	√ Computers are useless unless you know how to use them.
× Whether or not I pass is depending on how hard I work.	√ Whether or not I pass depends on how hard I work.

Know and ***depend*** belong to a group of verbs which, in one or more of their meanings, are not used in progressive tenses. These meanings are all connected with states, for which reason the verbs are sometimes called 'stative' verbs:

Honey ***comes from*** bees.
Paula ***comes from*** Italy.
That black hat ***doesn't suit*** you at all.
He actually ***believes*** that eggs grow on trees.
I ***like*** oranges but I ***don't like*** grapefruit.

Verbs that are sometimes used wrongly in progressive tenses are listed below. The list includes verbs of perception (e.g. *see*, *hear*, *taste*), verbs of thinking (e.g. *know*, *wonder*, *realize*), verbs which express likes and dislikes (e.g. *like*, *prefer*, *hate*), and verbs which express relationships (e.g. *be*, *have*, *belong*, *own*).

agree, appear, be (× She is being lonely), ***believe, belong, can't bear, care, come from*** (× I am coming from Switzerland), ***concern, consider, consist, contain, cost, depend, deserve, dislike, doubt, envy, equal, exist, expect, fear, feel*** (= believe), ***fit, forget, forgive, guess*** (= suppose), ***hate***, ***have*** (× I am having two sisters), ***hear***, ***hold*** (= be able to contain), ***hope***, ***imagine***, ***include***, ***intend***, ***interest***, ***keep on***, ***know***, ***look*** (= appear), ***lack***, ***like***, ***look***, ***love***, ***matter***, ***mean***, ***measure*** (= have a particular measurement), ***not mind***, ***need***, ***notice***, ***owe***, ***own***, ***please***, ***possess***, ***prefer***, ***realize***, ***recognize***, ***refuse***, ***regret***, ***remember***, ***resemble***, ***see***, ***seem***, ***smell***, ***sound***, ***suit***, ***suppose***, ***suspect***, ***taste***, ***think*** (= believe), ***understand***, ***want***, ***weigh***, ***wish***, ***wonder***

Note that some of these verbs also have active meanings and therefore may also be used in progressive tenses. Compare:

This soup ***tastes*** absolutely awful! (state)
He ***is tasting*** the soup to see if it needs more salt. (action)

I ***think*** that nuclear weapons should be abolished. (state)
Please don't disturb me now. ***I'm thinking***. (action)

Note also that the ***-ing*** form of a stative verb can be used in participle clauses: '***Knowing*** *that she was angry with me*, I avoided her.' 'He denies ***knowing*** *anything about the report*.'

When an ***-ing*** form is used by itself (i.e. without ***be***), it has no tense.

promise 628

1

×	√
He promised returning the book by today.	He promised to return the book by today.

We ***promise*** (not/never) ***to do*** something, NOT ***doing*** something.

2

×	√
I promised to your parents that I would take care of you.	I promised your parents that I would take care of you.

We ***promise*** someone (NOT ***to*** someone) ***to do/that we will do*** something.

⇨ 390.3

proof 629

1

×	√
The tape recordings contained proofs of his involvement.	The tape recordings contained proof of his involvement.

When ***proof*** means 'evidence', it is uncountable and does not have a plural form.

2

×	√
We must have a proof that these drugs are harmless.	We must have proof that these drugs are harmless.

When ***proof*** means 'evidence', it is not used with ***a/an***. ⇨ 2.1

property 630

×	√
The sign on the door said 'LOST PROPERTIES'.	The sign on the door said 'LOST PROPERTY'.

When ***property*** means 'possessions', it is an uncountable noun and does not have a plural form: 'You are advised not to leave bags or personal ***property*** unattended.' Compare: 'She owns several ***properties*** in the south of France.'

propose 631

×	√
The organizing committee proposed each contestant to be given a prize.	The organizing committee proposed that each contestant should be given a prize.

⇨ 839.9

prospect 632

1

×	✓
× I feel very excited about the prospect to go to England.	✓ I feel very excited about the prospect of going to England.

If we look forward to doing something, we feel happy about the ***prospect of doing*** it.

2

×	✓
× We talked about the team's prospect and whether they could win the championship again.	✓ We talked about the team's prospects and whether they could win the championship again.

When we mean 'chances of success', we use the plural noun ***prospects***.

⇨ 603

protection 633

×	✓
× In view of the threat on his life, he has asked the police for a 24-hour protection.	✓ In view of the threat on his life, he has asked the police for 24-hour protection.

Protection is an uncountable noun and is not used with ***a/an***. ⇨ 2.1

proud 634

×	✓
× I felt very proud for myself.	✓ I felt very proud of myself.

We feel ***proud of*** someone.

provide 635

×	✓
× Vegetables provide us many vitamins.	✓ Vegetables provide us with many vitamins.
× We were each provided a packed lunch.	✓ We were each provided with a packed lunch.

We ***provide*** someone ***with*** something. Compare: 'The government *provides* free health care (for everyone).' 'The government *provides* everyone *with* free health care.'

In the passive, these patterns look like this: 'Free health care is *provided* (for everyone).' 'Everyone is *provided with* free health care.'

purpose **636**

× The main purpose to have senior masters in a school is to assist the deputy principal.	√ The main purpose of having senior masters in a school is to assist the deputy principal.

We talk about the ***purpose of*** (***doing/having***) something.

pyjamas **637**

× I rushed out to buy a new pyjama and a toothbrush.	√ I rushed out to buy some new pyjamas and a toothbrush.

Pyjamas is a plural noun. ⇨ 603

qualification **638**

× Your salary depends on your qualification and experience.	√ Your salary depends on your qualifications and experience.

To refer to all the examination passes, skills and achievements that make someone suitable/unsuitable for a particular job, we use ***qualifications*** (a plural noun): 'It's almost impossible to get a job nowadays unless you have the necessary *qualifications*.' ⇨ 603

qualms **639**

× Most lawyers have no qualm about earning interest on their clients' money.	√ Most lawyers have no qualms about earning interest on their clients' money.

If we feel uncertain about whether it is right to do something, we have ***qualms about*** doing it: 'I've always had *qualms about* borrowing money from people.' ***Qualms*** is a plural noun. ⇨ 603

quantifiers **640**

1

× I asked him why some of animals looked sick.	√ I asked him why some of the animals looked sick.

We can say 'some animals' or 'some of the/these/my/their/John's animals', but NOT 'some of animals'. When we use ***some of*** instead of ***some***, the next word is normally a determiner. Similarly, compare:

I bought *a few stamps*.
A few of these stamps are torn. (NOT 'A few of stamps')

Most horses like being brushed.
Most of their horses are imported. (NOT *Most of horses*)

I gave *each child* a balloon.
I gave *each of the children* a balloon. (NOT *each of children*)

We do not use a determiner when the next word is a pronoun: '*Some of them* are still in bed.'

Quantifiers which are used in this way include: *all, any, both, each, either, enough, (a) few, half, (a) little, less, many, more, most, much, neither, one/two/three etc., several, some*.

⇨ .2 below

2

×	✓
× Adult programmes should be shown late at night when most of the children are in bed.	✓ Adult programmes should be shown late at night when most children are in bed.

We use an *of*-phrase after ***most*** when we wish to specify exactly who or what we are referring to: '*Most of the cars parked outside the hotel* had chauffeurs.'

Otherwise, we put ***most*** immediately in front of the noun: '*Most cars* have four wheels.' (NOT 'Most of the cars')

General quantifiers which are used in this way include: *all, any, enough, (a) few, (a) little, less, many, more, most, much, several, some*.

3

×	✓
× There was very few traffic on the road.	✓ There was very little traffic on the road.
× There are too many people for too little jobs.	✓ There are too many people for too few jobs.

We can say 'very few cars' but NOT 'very few traffic'. ***Few*** is used only with words which have a plural meaning. On the other hand, we can say 'too little work' but NOT 'too little jobs'. ***Little*** is used only with words which have an uncountable meaning.

Since ***few*** and ***little*** are similar in meaning, we sometimes think of them as a pair. Altogether, there are five of these pairs:

+ PLURAL	+ UNCOUNTABLE
a few	a little
few	little
fewer	less
many	much
a number of	an amount of

Note also that ***a great/good deal of*** is used only with uncountable nouns.

⇨ 202.1

4

× Each students were given a new dictionary.	√ Each student was given a new dictionary. √ Each of the students was given a new dictionary.
× Neither books were very interesting.	√ Neither book was very interesting. √ Neither of the books was very interesting.

When the noun comes immediately after ***each***, ***every***, ***either*** and ***neither***, it is always singular. When these words are followed by an *of*-phrase, the noun in the *of*-phrase is always plural.

5

× Each of the six Asean countries were represented at the conference.	√ Each of the six Asean countries was represented at the conference.
× Neither letter were properly addressed.	√ Neither letter was properly addressed.

⇨ 44.13

6

× We gave all them a present.	√ We gave them all a present. √ We gave all of them a present.

We can say 'them all' or 'all of them', but NOT 'all them'. ***All***, ***both*** and ***each*** normally go immediately after a personal pronoun. Before a personal pronoun, we use ***all of***, ***both of***, etc. Compare: 'They've invited ***us both*** to dinner at their house.' 'They've invited ***both of us*** to dinner at their house.'

When we use the ***of*** structure ('both of us'), the quantifier ('both') is emphasized.

7

× When we reached the shops, we found that they all were closed.	√ When we reached the shops, we found that they were all closed.
× They each were delighted with the photographs.	√ They were each delighted with the photographs.

We normally put ***all***, ***both*** and ***each*** immediately before the main verb: 'My brothers ***both*** work for Gibson Mortimer.'

However, when the main verb is ***be*** (and there are no auxiliary verbs), we put ***all***, ***both*** and ***each*** immediately after it: 'My brothers are ***both*** accountants.'

8

× We all have seen a road accident at some time in our lives.	√ We have all seen a road accident at some time in our lives.
× I asked the girls if they each could describe the man.	√ I asked the girls if they could each describe the man.

When the verb phrase has two or more parts ('have seen', 'could describe'), ***all***, ***both*** and ***each*** normally go immediately after the first part, i.e. after the first auxiliary verb.

quantity 641

×	✓
× Drink large quantity of water and seek medical attention immediately.	✓ Drink large quantities of water and seek medical attention immediately.

⇨ 823.3

questions 642

1

×	✓
× Where you are going tonight?	✓ Where are you going tonight?
× You did not watch the programme?	✓ Didn't you watch the programme?

In questions, the subject and auxiliary verb normally change places. The auxiliary verb goes immediately before the subject.

Not normally becomes ***-n't*** and is added to the end of the auxiliary verb: 'Is***n't*** he coming with us?' 'Why have***n't*** you finished yet?'

Note that in spoken ***wh***-questions, the auxiliary verb is often contracted: 'Where***'ve*** they sent him?' 'When***'s*** she coming?'

2

×	✓
× You like Italian food?	✓ Do you like Italian food?
× How long it takes to send a letter to France?	✓ How long does it take to send a letter to France?
× What meant you to say?	✓ What did you mean to say?

When there is no auxiliary verb, we put ***do/does/did*** in front of the subject. The main verb is a bare infinitive ('like', 'take', 'mean').

3

×	✓
× Who did tell you that?	✓ Who told you that?
× How many drivers did finish the race?	✓ How many drivers finished the race?

When the ***wh***-word or ***wh***-phrase is the subject, we do not normally use ***do/does/did***. Compare:

Mr Wilson signed the contract.	SUBJECT
Who signed the contract?	SUBJECT
What/Which contract did Mr Wilson sign?	OBJECT
Why/When/Where did he sign the contract?	ADVERBIAL

When the ***wh***-word or ***wh***-phrase is the subject, we use ***do/does/did*** only when we wish to express great interest or curiosity: 'If the children didn't eat the chocolate, who *did* eat it?'

4

× Does he likes his new school?	√ Does he like his new school?
× Where will she lives?	√ Where will she live?

When the verb phrase begins with an auxiliary verb, the main verb cannot be finite. It is either a bare infinitive or a participle.

Where ***did/can*** she ***go***? (*do*/modal + bare infinitive)
Where ***has*** she ***gone***? (*have* + *-ed*)

Where ***can*** she ***have gone***? (modal + *have* + *-ed*)
Where ***is*** she ***going***? (*be* + *-ing*)

Where ***can*** she ***be going***? (modal + *be* + *-ing*)
Where ***has*** she ***been going***? (*have* + *been* + *-ing*)
Where ***can*** she ***have been going***? (modal + *have* + *been* + *-ing*)

5

× Can you tell me where can I buy some postcards?	√ Can you tell me where I can buy some postcards?

⇨ 389.1

6

× How many children do Angela have?	√ How many children does Angela have?

⇨ 44.14

7

× Do they have some children?	√ Do they have any children?

⇨ 733.1

question tags 643

1

× She earns a lot of money, isn't it?	√ She earns a lot of money, doesn't she?
× They made the film in Venice, isn't it?	√ They made the film in Venice, didn't they?

In some languages, the form a question tag never changes. In English, a question tag matches the subject and verb in the previous clause.

The pronoun in the question tag matches the subject of the previous clause: Compare: '***This book*** is rather expensive, isn't ***it***?' '***These books*** are rather expensive, aren't ***they***?'

If there is an auxiliary verb in the previous clause, we use the same auxiliary in the question tag. Compare: 'They ***are*** coming tomorrow, ***aren't*** they?' 'They ***can*** come tomorrow, ***can't*** they?'

If there is no auxiliary verb in the previous clause, we use ***do*** in the question tag. Compare: 'They ***come*** once a week, ***don't*** they?' 'They ***came*** yesterday, ***didn't*** they?'

However, if the only verb in the previous clause is ***be***, we use ***be*** in the question tag: 'His wife ***is*** a doctor, ***isn't*** she?

2

×	✓
× She never invites you to her house, doesn't she?	✓ She never invites you to her house, does she?
× You won't be angry, won't you?	✓ You won't be angry, will you?

If the previous clause is negative, the question tag is normally positive. If the previous clause is positive, the question tag is normally negative. Compare: 'You've been to London before, ***haven't*** you?' 'You haven't been to London before, ***have*** you?'

Note, however, that a positive tag sometimes follows a positive clause and that a negative tag sometimes follows a negative clause. These sequences are mainly used to express surprise, disbelief, anger, etc.: 'You've been to London before, have you?' (= I am surprised to know that you have been to London before)

quick 644

×	✓
× I got dressed quick and ran downstairs.	✓ I got dressed quickly and ran downstairs.

The adverb is nearly always ***quickly***. ***Quick*** is normally used as an adjective: 'a ***quick*** shower', 'a ***quick*** meal'. It is used as an adverb mainly in compounds (e.g. '***quick***-frozen', '***quick***-drying') and in very informal styles.

quiet 645

×	✓
× I closed the door as quiet as I could.	✓ I closed the door as quietly as I could.

Quiet is an adjective: 'She has a very ***quiet*** voice.' The adverb is ***quietly***: 'She speaks very ***quietly***.'

quite 646

1

×	✓
× He looks quite older than his wife.	✓ He looks rather older than his wife.

We can say 'He looks ***quite*** old' but NOT '***quite*** older'. Before a comparative form (-*er*), we use ***rather***. Compare: 'He looks ***quite a lot older*** than his wife.'

2

× After living in the jungle for two years, he quite became accustomed to it.	√ After living in the jungle for two years, he became quite accustomed to it.

Quite normally goes immediately before the word that it modifies. ⇨ .3 below

3

× I had applied for a job in Santander, a quite big town in Spain.	√ I had applied for a job in Santander, quite a big town in Spain.

Quite normally goes immediately before ***a/an***: 'On the whole, it was ***quite a*** good performance.'

4

× The problems that concord presents to the learner of English are quite many.	√ The problems that concord presents to the learner of English are quite numerous.

Most quantifiers, including ***many***, cannot be modified by ***quite***. The quantifiers which can be modified by ***quite*** are ***enough*** *(of)*, ***a lot*** *(of)*, ***a few*** *(of)*, ***a number*** *(of)*, ***an amount*** *(of)*.

raise 647

1

× The price of oil has raised considerably.	√ The price of oil has risen considerably.

Raise (past tense and past participle ***raised***) is a transitive verb and takes an object: 'The government is unlikely to ***raise taxes*** just before an election.' When we need an intransitive verb, we use ***rise*** (past tense ***rise***, past participle ***risen***).

⇨ 688

2

× The government wishes to raise up the standard of football in the country.	√ The government wishes to raise the standard of football in the country.

⇨ 840

rarely 648

1

× I rarely have seen her looking really happy.	√ I have rarely seen her looking really happy.

⇨ 29.1

2

× Rarely you see these birds during the daytime.	√ Rarely do you see these birds during the daytime. √ You rarely see these birds during the daytime.

⇨ 31.1

rather 649

1

! They visit me rather frequently and usually stay for lunch.	√ They visit me quite/fairly frequently and usually stay for lunch.

Rather is mainly used in 'negative' expressions:

His clothes are always ***rather dirty***.
These shoes are ***rather too big***.
She feels ***rather lonely***.

When ***rather*** is used in 'positive' expressions, it usually means 'more than one would expect': 'George is a real misery but his wife, Edna, is ***rather jolly***.'

2

× I would rather to stay indoors until the rain stops.	√ I would rather stay indoors until the rain stops.

We say that a person ***would rather do*** something, NOT ***to do*** something: 'I like badminton but I'***d rather play*** tennis.' Compare: 'I would ***prefer to stay*** indoors until the rain stops.'

3

× I'd rather you meet me at the airport. × I would rather you don't use the Volvo this afternoon.	√ I'd rather you met me at the airport. √ I would rather you didn't use the Volvo this afternoon.

When ***would rather*** is followed by a clause, the verb in the clause is either in the past tense or in the past perfect tense. We use the past tense ('met', 'didn't use') to refer to the present or future. We use the past perfect to refer to the past: 'I'***d rather*** you ***hadn't told*** her our address.'

The above also applies to ***would sooner***: 'I'***d sooner*** you ***kept*** this a secret.' (NOT 'keep')

reach 650

× By the time we reached to the classroom, the lesson had already begun.	√ By the time we reached the classroom, the lesson had already begun.

We ***reach*** a place, WITHOUT ***to***. Compare: 'By the time we ***got to*** the classroom, the lesson had already begun.'

ready 651

×	✓
× I'll be ready for leaving by five o'clock.	✓ I'll be ready to leave by five o'clock.

We say that someone is ***ready to do*** something.

real 652

×	✓
× At the detention centre, these offenders are made to work real hard.	✓ At the detention centre, these offenders are made to work really hard.

In American English, ***real*** is sometimes used instead of ***really***, especially in spoken English. In British English ***real*** is an adjective: 'a real pleasure'.

realize 653

×	✓
× Most parents realize about the importance of education.	✓ Most parents realize the importance of education.

We ***realize*** something (NOT ***about*** something).

really 654

×	✓
× It was really a hot day.	✓ It was a really hot day.

When ***really*** means 'very', it goes immediately before the adjective or adverb that it modifies.

reason 655

1

×	✓
× Is there a good reason of his absence?	✓ Is there a good reason for his absence?
× He explained his reasons of leaving the army.	✓ He explained his reasons for leaving the army.

We talk about the ***reason/s for*** (***doing***) something. Compare: 'What was the ***cause of*** the fire?'

2

×	✓
× The main reason that I am against the proposal is that too much money is involved.	✓ The main reason why I am against the proposal is that too much money is involved.

A relative clause after ***reason/s*** begins with ***why***, NOT ***that***.

3

× Our main reason for sending our children to England to study is because we have relatives there.	√ Our main reason for sending our children to England to study is that we have relatives there.

Careful users say that the ***reason*** (for something) is ***that*** + clause, (NOT ***because*** + clause).

reassure **656**

× The doctor reassured that my problem was not serious.	√ The doctor reassured me that my problem was not serious.

We ***reassure someone*** + *that*-clause.

⇨ 390

recall **657**

× Can you recall back the time when you were at school?	√ Can you recall the time when you were at school?

⇨ 840

recent and recently **658**

! In recent years, more and more elderly people were seen on television.	√ In recent years, more and more elderly people have been seen on television.

After ***recently*** and phrases such as 'in recent months', 'during recent years', 'over recent decades', etc., we normally use the present perfect tense.

⇨ 583.2

recommend **659**

1

× I asked him if he could recommend me a good garage.	√ I asked him if he could recommend a good garage.

Recommend does not normally have an indirect object ('me'). If it is necessary to include an indirect object, we introduce it with ***to***: 'I've just been to see the dentist that you *recommended* (***to me***).'

2

× The committee recommends to upgrade the candidate to a Third Class Honours degree.	√ The committee recommends upgrading the candidate to a Third Class Honours degree.

We ***recommend doing*** something, NOT ***to do***.

refer 660

× In this report we will refer the two primary schools as P1 and P2.	√ In this report we will refer to the two primary schools as P1 and P2.

We ***refer to*** someone or something: 'During her talk she kept ***referring to*** Albert Schweitzer.'

reflexive pronouns 661

1

× Everybody was laughing and enjoying themselfs. × I suppose you are all asking yourself where we are going to take you.	√ Everybody was laughing and enjoying themselves. √ I suppose you are all asking yourselves where we are going to take you.

When we mention just one person, we use ***-self***. When we mention two or more people, we use ***-selves***.

SINGULAR	PLURAL
myself	ourselves
yourself	yourselves
himself herself oneself itself	themselves (NOT 'themselfs' or 'theirselves')

2

× My brother-in-law designed himself the house.	√ My brother-in-law designed the house himself.

When we use a reflexive pronoun to mean 'without help from anyone', we normally put it at the end of the clause: 'George does all the cooking ***himself***.' 'She decided to write the letter ***herself***.'

3

× My brother and myself are both keen on fishing.	√ My brother and I are both keen on fishing.

A reflexive pronoun can emphasize the subject of a verb ('Mrs Kennedy ***herself*** will be attending the meeting.') If it is not used for emphasis, it cannot be used in subject position.

refrain 662

× I couldn't refrain to listen to their conversation.	√ I couldn't refrain from listening to their conversation.

We ***refrain from doing*** something, NOT ***to do***.

refuse 663

1

× She offered me some money but I refused.	√ She offered me some money but I refused it.

When ***refuse*** means 'to not accept something that we are offered', it is a transitive verb. Compare: 'I asked her to help me, but she ***refused***.'

2

× I asked him to drive more slowly, but he refused me.	√ I asked him to drive more slowly, but he refused.

When ***refuse*** means 'to not do (or to say that we will not do) what someone has asked us to do', it is normally intransitive: 'I keep telling him to see a doctor, but he ***refuses***.'

regarding 664

× I am writing to you regarding about nominations for this year's University medals.	√ I am writing to you regarding nominations for this year's University medals.

Use either ***regarding*** OR ***about***, but not both together. ***Regarding*** is used only in formal styles.

regret 665

1

× He suddenly regretted to have run away from home.	√ He suddenly regretted having run away from home.

If we feel sorry about something that has already happened, we ***regret doing*** it: 'We shall always ***regret selling*** the house.' 'Do you ever ***regret*** not ***going*** to university?'

We use a ***to***-infinitive after ***regret*** when we are about to give someone some bad news: 'I ***regret to inform*** you that your application for a bank loan has been unsuccessful.' This pattern is used only in formal styles.

2

× We regret for any inconvenience caused.	√ We regret any inconvenience caused.

We ***regret*** something, NOT ***for*** something.

regular verbs 666

1

× In 1956 the school change its name.	√ In 1956 the school changed its name.

To form the past simple tense and past participle of a regular verb, we normally add *-d* or *-ed*.

2

× I tryed to apologize but she refused to listen.	√ I tried to apologize but she refused to listen.

With verbs ending in *-ly*, *-ry*, *-dy*, *-fy*, etc., we form the past simple tense and past participle by changing the *-y* to *-ied*: 'We ***studied*** the map very carefully.' 'The baby ***cried*** all night.'

relative clauses: general 667

1

× The school is about seven miles from the sea, which is surrounded by houses and government flats.	√ The school, which is surrounded by houses and government flats, is about seven miles from the sea.
× My school holidays finished on 2nd September which lasted two weeks.	√ My school holidays, which lasted two weeks, finished on 2nd September.

A relative clause goes immediately after the noun to which it refers, or as close to the noun as possible.

2

× Thank you for all your help that you have given me with my studies.	√ Thank you for all the help that you have given me with my studies.

We often use a relative clause to define a previous noun: 'Have you seen the car (***that***) ***she drives***?'

In such cases, the previous noun cannot be used with a possessive determiner (e.g. 'your'). A possessive determiner defines a noun and we cannot define a noun which has already been defined.

× ***Their*** house ***that they live in*** has five bedrooms.
√ ***The*** house ***that they live in*** has five bedrooms.

× ***My*** car ***that I drive*** is difficult to park.
√ ***The*** car ***that I drive*** is difficult to park.

3

× School leavers, especially who have failed their examinations, often have difficulty in getting a job.	√ School leavers, especially those who have failed their examinations, often have difficulty in getting a job.

We cannot use a relative clause immediately after words such as ***especially***, ***particularly***, ***namely***, ***including***, ***chiefly***, ***mainly*** or ***notably***. These words introduce a new noun phrase, which is 'in apposition' with the previous one. The new noun phrase must have a head (e.g. 'those'): 'Most of our customers, ***especially those who appreciate good service***, keep coming back year after year.'

relative clauses: prepositions **668**

1

× I drove straight to the hotel where she was staying at.	√ I drove straight to the hotel where she was staying.

When we use a relative clause to identify a building or place, we have a choice of structure:

I drove straight to the hotel ***that/which*** she was staying ***at***.
I drove straight to the hotel ***at which*** she was staying.
I drove straight to the hotel ***where*** she was staying.

If we begin the relative clause with ***where***, we do NOT use a preposition of place (*at*, *in*, *on*, etc.). ⇨ 866.3

2

× There is also a student counsellor with whom we can discuss personal problems with.	√ There is also a student counsellor with whom we can discuss personal problems.
× These managers have improved the performance of all the companies for which they have worked for.	√ These managers have improved the performance of all the companies for which they have worked.

In formal styles, we sometimes place a preposition right at the beginning of the relative clause, immediately before the relative pronoun (e.g. '***with*** whom', '***for*** which'). In such cases, the preposition must not be repeated.
Compare: 'Is this the woman ***to whom you gave my address***?' (formal)
'Is this the woman (***that***) ***you gave my address to***?' (informal)

relative clauses: pronouns **669**

1

× The man who was sitting next to me he had blood on his shirt.	√ The man who was sitting next to me had blood on his shirt.

A main clause can have just one subject, NOT two. After a relative clause, we do not repeat the subject with a personal pronoun ('he').

SUBJECT	VERB	OBJECT	ADVERBIAL
The man ***who was sitting next to me***	had	blood	on his shirt.

2

× It was the same man he had stolen my wallet.	√ It was the same man who had stolen my wallet.

To connect a relative clause to a previous noun, we use a relative pronoun (*who*, *which*, *that*, etc). Compare:

It was the same man. He had stolen my wallet.
It was the same man ***who had stolen my wallet***.

I went to get my umbrella. It was still in the car.
I went to get my umbrella, ***which was still in the car***.

3

× I shall show you the letter which it arrived today.	√ I shall show you the letter which arrived today.

A relative clause can have just one subject, NOT two. We do not repeat the subject ('which') with a personal pronoun ('it'). 'I'm trying to find a shop ***which sells flowers***.' (NOT 'which it') 'Is that the girl ***who comes from Georgia***? (NOT 'who she')

4

× He gave me two cookery books, which I find them very useful.	√ He gave me two cookery books, which I find very useful.
× I am returning the two diskettes that you lent them to us.	√ I am returning the two diskettes that you lent to us.

A relative clause can have only one direct object. When we use ***which***, ***that*** or ***who/m*** as an object pronoun, we do not repeat the object with a personal pronoun (e.g. *them*, *her*, *him*). 'Is this the magazine ***that Helen bought***?' (NOT 'bought it') 'The other girl, ***whom I recognized***, said nothing.' (NOT 'recognized her')

⇨ .5 below

5

× Several of the people we had invited them did not speak English.	√ Several of the people we had invited did not speak English.

When the relative pronoun is the object of the relative clause, we sometimes omit it. Compare: 'Are these the shoes ***that you intend to buy***?' (object included) 'Are these the shoes ***you intend to buy***? (object omitted)

Although the object pronoun (*that*, *which*, *who/m*) may be missing, it is nevertheless 'understood' and we do not repeat the object with a personal pronoun (e.g. *them*, *her*, *him*). 'The woman ***he marries*** will need a lot of patience.' (NOT 'marries her') 'Have you seen the house ***they have just bought***?' (NOT 'bought it')

6

× It has 180 pages, which all of them have colour photographs.	√ It has 180 pages, all of which have colour photographs.
× The coat had two pockets of which both of them were full of money.	√ The coat had two pockets, both of which were full of money.

A quantifier (e.g. *all*, *each*, *several*, *many*, *both*, *two*) normally comes right at the beginning of a relative clause and is followed by ***of*** + relative pronoun: 'The children, ***some of whom*** I knew, seemed pleased to see me.' 'We stayed in two hotels, ***neither of which*** was very clean.'

7

×	✓
× I looked at him who was sitting next to me.	✓ I looked at the man who was sitting next to me.

A relative clause cannot refer back to a personal pronoun ('him').

8

×	✓
× She married someone called Sandro, who she met and won her heart soon after she arrived in the country.	✓ She married someone called Sandro, who she met and who won her heart soon after she arrived in the country.

When two relative pronouns are both subjects, the second one can be omitted: 'I met her husband, ***who*** comes from Italy and (***who***) works in a bank.'

When two relative pronouns are both objects, the second one can be omitted: 'He introduced me to his wife, ***who*** he met in England and (***who*** he) married in France.'

However, when one relative pronoun is an object ('***who*** she met') and the other is a subject ('***who*** won her heart'), the second one cannot be omitted.

relative clauses: verbs **670**

1

×	✓
× The woman is waiting to see you looks rather angry.	✓ The woman (who is) waiting to see you looks rather angry.
× The car was parked outside the bank was a Mercedes.	✓ The car (which was) parked outside the bank was a Mercedes.

To identify the person or thing that we are talking about, we often use a relative clause: 'The woman ***who is waiting to see you*** looks rather angry.' 'The car ***which was parked outside the bank*** was a Mercedes.'

If an identifying relative clause begins with a relative pronoun + ***be*** + participle, the relative pronoun + ***be*** can usually be omitted. The clause (sometimes called a 'reduced relative') then begins with a participle: 'The woman ***waiting to see you*** looks rather angry.' 'The car ***parked outside the bank*** was a Mercedes.'

The 'missing words' ('who is', 'which was') are understood.

2

×	✓
× It was always the brightest students who was asked to answer the question.	✓ It was always the brightest students who were asked to answer the question.
× He said that he didn't have the money which were needed for the operation.	✓ He said that he didn't have the money which was needed for the operation.

In the first sentence above, the relative pronoun 'who' refers back to 'the brightest students'. Since 'students' is plural, the verb in the relative clause must be plural ('were'). In the second sentence, the relative pronoun 'which' refers back to 'money'. Since 'money' is an uncountable noun, the verb in the relative clause must be singular ('was').

3

×	√
× Some countries do not have enough skilled workers, which cause serious problems.	√ Some countries do not have enough skilled workers, which causes serious problems.

A relative clause sometimes refers back to the idea or fact which is expressed in the first part of the sentence ('Some countries do not have enough skilled workers'). In such cases, the verb in the relative clause is singular. Compare: 'Some countries do not have enough skilled workers and this causes serious problems.'

4

×	√
× I intend to sell the car to the first person who will make a reasonable offer.	√ I intend to sell the car to the first person who makes a reasonable offer.
× Anyone who will get all the answers correct will receive a special prize.	√ Anyone who gets all the answers correct will receive a special prize.

When we are talking about something which may happen in the future, the verb in the relative clause is normally in the present simple tense ('makes', 'gets').

relax 671

1

×	√
× Finns like to relax themselves in the sauna.	√ Finns like to relax in the sauna.
× I tried to keep calm and relax myself.	√ I tried to keep calm and relax.

Relax is not used with reflexive pronouns (*myself*, *yourself*, etc.): 'Just sit down and ***relax*** for ten minutes.'

2

×	√
× Try to make the interviewee feel relax.	√ Try to make the interviewee feel relaxed.

⇨ 14.1

relief 672

×	√
× I asked the doctor for something to relief the pain.	√ I asked the doctor for something to relieve the pain.

Relief is a noun. The verb is ***relieve***.

⇨ 882.5

remember 673

× Wrong	√ Right
× Remember taking an umbrella in case it rains.	√ Remember to take an umbrella in case it rains.
× Did you remember posting the letter?	√ Did you remember to post the letter?

If we ***remember*** something that we have done, we ***remember doing*** it: 'I ***remember coming*** here with my parents when I was a child.'

If there is something we have to do, we try to ***remember to do*** it: '***Remember to bring*** your swimming costume tomorrow.'

remind 674

1

× Wrong	√ Right
× I wish you had reminded me of sending him a birthday card.	√ I wish you had reminded me to send him a birthday card.

We ***remind*** someone ***to do*** something: '***Remind*** me ***to buy*** some milk while we are out.'

2

× Wrong	√ Right
× I am writing this letter to remind you our arrangements.	√ I am writing this letter to remind you of our arrangements.

A person or thing ***reminds*** someone ***of*** something: 'The advertisement ***reminded*** me ***of*** my holiday in France.'

repeat 675

× Wrong	√ Right
× We wish to repeat again what we said in our first letter.	√ We wish to repeat what we said in our first letter.

⇨ 840

replace 676

× Wrong	√ Right
× I should like you to replace it for a new one.	√ I should like you to replace it with a new one.

We ***replace*** someone/something ***with*** someone/something else. Compare: 'The manager offered to ***exchange*** the faulty camera ***for*** a different model.'

reply 677

1

×	✓
× It was almost two months before they replied my letter.	✓ It was almost two months before they replied to my letter.

We ***answer*** a letter but ***reply to*** a letter ⇨ 841.2

2

×	✓
× She replied me that there was no hot water available.	✓ She replied that there was no hot water available.

We do not put an indirect object ('me') between ***reply*** and a ***that***-clause.
⇨ 390.2

3

×	✓
× I have written to her three times but she hasn't replied back.	✓ I have written to her three times but she hasn't replied.

Reply contains the meaning 'back'. Compare: 'I have written to her three times but she hasn't ***written back***.' ⇨ 840

report 678

×	✓
× The meeting of Foreign Ministers in Djakarta is reported about in today's newspapers.	✓ The meeting of Foreign Ministers in Djakarta is reported in today's newspapers.

⇨ 841.1

reputation 679

×	✓
× The company has a good reputation about after sales service.	✓ The company has a good reputation for after sales service.

A person or organization has a ***reputation for*** something: 'The new Prime Minister has a ***reputation for*** getting things done.'

request 680

×	✓
× Last April I wrote to you requesting for a refund.	✓ Last April I wrote to you requesting a refund.

We ***request*** something (WITHOUT ***for***). Compare: 'Last April I wrote to you ***asking for*** a refund.' ⇨ 841.1

research 681

1

× They are doing a research into the teaching of Arabic by computer.	√ They are doing research into the teaching of Arabic by computer.

Research is an uncountable noun and is not used with ***a/an***. ⇨ 2.1

2

× Despite all the researches, there is still no cure for the disease.	√ Despite all the research, there is still no cure for the disease.

Research is an uncountable noun and does not have a plural form.

resemble 682

× Her father resembled to a man that I used to work for.	√ Her father resembled a man that I used to work for.

Someone/something ***resembles*** another person/thing (WITHOUT ***to***). Compare: 'Her brother bore a close ***resemblance to*** a man that I used to work for.' We use ***to*** after the noun, but not after the verb. ⇨ 841.1

resign 683

× I resigned myself to spend the holiday on my own.	√ I resigned myself to spending the holiday on my own.

⇨ 837

responsible 684

× Young people are responsible to take care of their elders.	√ Young people are responsible for taking care of their elders.
× Why should a woman be responsible of all the household chores?	√ Why should a woman be responsible for all the household chores?

A person is ***responsible for*** someone or (***doing***) something.

result 685

× I got quite a good result in the last examinations.	√ I got quite good results in the last examinations.

We normally talk about examination ***results*** (plural): 'Whether or not I go to university depends on my A-level *results*.'

return 686

× Wrong	√ Right
× I shall return back to Athens at the end of August.	√ I shall return to Athens at the end of August.

Return contains the meaning 'back'. Compare: 'I shall ***go back*** to Athens at the end of August.'

⇨ 840

ring 687

× Wrong	√ Right
× I ringed the bell three times but nobody came.	√ I rang the bell three times but nobody came.

Ring (infinitive), ***rang*** (past simple), ***rung*** (past participle).

rise 688

× Wrong	√ Right
× I rose the child off the ground.	√ I raised the child off the ground.
× I hope they don't rise prices again.	√ I hope they don't raise prices again.

Rise (past simple ***rose***, past participle ***risen***) is an intransitive verb and does not take an object: 'The aircraft slowly ***rose*** into the air.' 'Food prices are likely to ***rise*** again.'

When we need a transitive verb, we use ***raise*** (past simple and past participle ***raised***).

⇨ 647

risk 689

× Wrong	√ Right
× I didn't want to risk to lose all my money.	√ I didn't want to risk losing all my money.

We ***risk doing*** something (NOT ***to do*** something): 'These people ***risk getting*** caught and sent to prison.'

rubbish 690

1

× Wrong	√ Right
× People should not leave their rubbishes in the street.	√ People should not leave their rubbish in the street.

Rubbish is an uncountable noun and does not have a plural form.

2

× Wrong	√ Right
× All the rubbish have been removed.	√ All the rubbish has been removed.

Rubbish takes a singular verb.

run 691

× We run to the window to see what was happening.	√ We ran to the window to see what was happening.

Run (infinitive), ***ran*** (past simple), ***run*** (past participle).

rush 692

× Shouting and waving my arms, I rushed to the man who was attacking her.	√ Shouting and waving my arms, I rushed at the man who was attacking her.

If we run towards someone in a way that suggests violence, we ***rush at*** them. Compare: 'Ambulances ***rushed to*** the scene of the accident.'

-'s/-s': wrongly omitted 693

1

× Childrens shoes are very expensive nowadays.	√ Children's shoes are very expensive nowadays.
× In the afternoon we were taken to visit a girls school.	√ In the afternoon we were taken to visit a girls' school.
× A government officer salary is about $2000 a month.	√ A government officer's salary is about $2000 a month.

When we classify or define something, we often add **-'s/-s'** to the noun that comes immediately before. This first noun is usually animate: 'a ***child's*** bicycle', 'a ***fisherman's*** cottage', '***lamb's*** wool'.

2

× We were met at the airport by a friend of Pablo.	√ We were met at the airport by a friend of Pablo's.

In double genitive structures, the noun in the ***of***-phrase has an ***-'s/-s'*** ending: 'That new car ***of Peter's*** has very good brakes.' 'A friend ***of John's*** has invited us to lunch.'

3

× After half an hour journey we arrived at the hotel.	√ After half an hour's journey we arrived at the hotel.

⇨ 533.4

-'s/-s': use 694

1

x Two of my mothers' rings were missing.	√ Two of my mother's rings were missing.

If the noun is singular, we normally add ***-'s*** (NOT ***-s'***): '***Tom's*** house', 'his ***wife's*** birthday', 'Mr ***Smith's*** address'.

A noun which ends in ***-s'*** is usually plural. Compare: 'We have never been to our daughter***'s*** school.' (= we have one daughter) 'We have never been to our daughter***s'*** school.' (= we have more than one daughter). Note, however, that irregular plurals take ***-'s***: 'a ***children's*** library'.

Singular forms that end in ***s*** can usually take either ***-'s*** or just an apostrophe ('): 'Mr ***Jones's*** address', 'Mr ***Jones'*** address'.

2

× The curtains' colour had faded in the sun.	√ The colour of the curtains had faded in the sun.
× All the cases were put in the car's boot.	√ All the cases were put in the boot of the car.

We do not normally add ***-'s/-s'*** to an inanimate noun ('curtains', 'car'). Instead, we use an ***of***-phrase: 'the end ***of the road***', 'the outskirts ***of the town***', 'the back ***of the door***'.

Note however that time expressions usually take ***-'s/-s'***: 'six ***weeks'*** work', 'a ***month's*** salary in advance'.

3

! The boat belongs to my father's friend.	√ The boat belongs to a friend of my father's. √ The boat belongs to one of my father's friends.

⇨ 610.4

4

× We're having a two weeks' holiday in July.	√ We're having a two-week holiday in July. √ We're having two weeks' holiday in July.

When the head of a genitive phrase is plural ('weeks'), it cannot follow a singular determiner ('a'). Instead, we use either a compound modifier ('a ***two-week*** holiday') or a genitive phrase without ***a/an***: ('***two weeks'*** holiday'). ⇨ 533.3

5

× I have always enjoyed taking part in school's plays.	√ I have always enjoyed taking part in school plays.

We do not normally use an ***-'s/-s'*** ending when the noun can be used as a modifier (i.e. like an adjective). ⇨ 533.1

sale 695

× CLOSING DOWN SALES 12-16 June	√ CLOSING DOWN SALE 12-16 June

When a shop reduces its prices for a limited period, it has ***a sale*** (WITHOUT ***-s***). When all the shops in a town have a sale, we talk about ***the sales***: 'Have you been to ***the sales*** yet?' The plural form ***sales*** also refers to the number of things that are sold over a certain period: 'In the last six months, ***sales*** have almost doubled.'

salt 696

× Some people never put the salt on their food.	√ Some people never put salt on their food.

⇨ 782.3

same 697

1

× For the last ten years I have worked for same company.	√ For the last ten years I have worked for the same company.

Same is nearly always used with ***the***: 'These two photographs are ***the same***.' 'This one is ***the same*** as that one.' Occasionally, it is used with a demonstrative (*this*, *that*, *these*, *those*): 'At ***that same*** meeting an agreement was reached on the issue of strategic arms.'

2

× She does not have the same ability than her sister.	√ She does not have the same ability as her sister.
× He got out at the same station I did.	√ He got out at the same station as I did.

The same is normally followed by ***as***: 'Her guitar is ***the same as*** mine.' 'She has ***the same*** guitar ***as*** I have.' Before a clause, we can use either ***as*** or ***that***: 'She made ***the same*** excuse ***as/that*** she made the last time.'

satisfied 698

× None of us was satisfied about the quality of the food.	√ None of us was satisfied with the quality of the food.

If we think that something is good enough, we are ***satisfied with*** it.

say 699

×	√
× She said the doctor that she was unable to sleep.	√ She told the doctor that she was unable to sleep.

⇨ 390.2

scarcely 700

1

×	√
× There scarcely was enough time to say anything.	√ There was scarcely enough time to say anything.

⇨ 29.2

2

×	√
× Scarcely we had left the garage when the car broke down again.	√ Scarcely had we left the garage when the car broke down again. √ We had scarcely left the garage when the car broke down again.

⇨ 31.1

scenery 701

×	√
× We stopped at the top of the hill to admire the sceneries.	√ We stopped at the top of the hill to admire the scenery.

Scenery is an uncountable noun and does not have a plural form.

school 702

1

×	√
× Before I go to work, I have to take my children to their school. × My children are always hungry when they come home from the school.	√ Before I go to work, I have to take my children to school. √ My children are always hungry when they come home from school.

⇨ 532.2

2

×	√
× Their children are quite young and are still schooling.	√ Their children are quite young and are still at school.

Most children of school age are ***at school*** or ***go to school***: 'Lucy is too young to *go to school*.'

scissors 703

×	✓
All you need is lots of paper and a sharp scissors.	All you need is lots of paper and some sharp scissors.

Scissors is a plural noun. ⇨ 603

scorn 704

×	✓
Instead of being grateful, he scorned at my offer of help.	Instead of being grateful, he scorned my offer of help.

If we reject something because we feel that it is ridiculous, we ***scorn*** it, (WITHOUT ***at***). Compare: 'Any serious effort to reach a peace settlement is not to be ***laughed at***.'

search 705

×	✓
I spent the whole morning searching the ring.	I spent the whole morning searching for the ring.

If we try to find something, we ***search for*** it. Compare: 'I ***searched*** all my pockets, but the ring wasn't there.' 'The police stopped and ***searched*** our car.'

see 706

×	✓
During the examination, I saw one of the students to pass a piece of paper to another one.	During the examination, I saw one of the students pass a piece of paper to another one.

⇨ 839.3–5

seek 707

×	✓
We mustn't stop seeking for a solution to this problem.	We mustn't stop seeking a solution to this problem.

We ***seek*** someone or something (WITHOUT ***for***). Compare: 'We mustn't stop ***looking/searching for*** a solution.'

seem 708

1

×	✓
Most of the children were seeming rather bored.	Most of the children seemed rather bored.

Seem is not used in progressive tenses. ⇨ 627.3

2

× The boy seemed that he was in a hurry.	√ It seemed that the boy was in a hurry. √ The boy seemed to be in a hurry.

When ***seem*** and ***appear*** are followed by a ***that***-clause, we use ***it*** as an empty subject: '***It*** + seems/appears + ***that these new cars are very popular***.'

When these verbs have a real subject, we follow them with a ***to***-clause: '***These new cars*** + seem/appear + ***to be very popular***.'

3

× In my opinion seems to be something wrong with her.	√ In my opinion there seems to be something wrong with her.

Seem must always have a subject. When we mention the existence of something, we use ***there*** as an empty subject.

⇨ 787.1

seldom 709

1

× These snakes seldom are dangerous.	√ These snakes are seldom dangerous.

⇨ 29.2

2

× Seldom we receive any complaints.	√ Seldom do we receive any complaints. √ We seldom receive any complaints.

⇨ 31.1

sent 710

× She asked me to sent her my address.	√ She asked me to send her my address.

Send (infinitive), ***sent*** (past simple), ***sent*** (past participle).

sentence structure: incomplete 711

1

× All television programmes that are shown during the early part of the evening.	√ All television programmes that are shown during the early part of the evening should be suitable for children.

To be complete, every statement must have a subject and a predicate. In other words, after we have mentioned the subject, we have to say something about it:

SUBJECT	PREDICATE
The film	had been censored.
The film that I saw last night	had been censored.
The film that I saw while I was in Sabah	had been censored.

2

×	√
× We were unable to visit her. Because we did not have her address.	√ We were unable to visit her because we did not have her address.
× I shall write to you again. As soon as I know if I can come.	√ I shall write to you again as soon as I know if I can come.

In most varieties of written English, a subordinate clause (e.g. 'Because we did not have her address') cannot be used on its own as a sentence. A subordinate clause provides or develops a part of a sentence, telling us *when*, *why*, *which*, *what*, etc.

3

×	√
× Nowadays is very expensive to run a car.	√ Nowadays it is very expensive to run a car.
× In some countries are very strict laws.	√ In some countries there are very strict laws.

Apart from imperatives (e.g. 'Shut the door, please'), every sentence must have a subject. The 'empty' subjects ***it*** and ***there*** are sometimes wrongly omitted.
⇨ 423, 787

4

×	√
× School examination results always very important.	√ School examination results are always very important.

Every sentence must have a verb. The linking verb ***be*** is sometimes wrongly omitted, leaving the sentence incomplete. ⇨ 96.1

several 712

×	√
× Several of suspects have been released on bail.	√ Several of the suspects have been released on bail.

⇨ 640.1

shall ('ll) 713

1

×	√
× They shall be in Glasgow by now.	√ They will be in Glasgow by now.

We sometimes use ***shall*** in statements about the future, but only after a first-person subject: '***I/we shall*** be very pleased to see you.'

After a second-person or third-person subject (and usually after a first-person subject), we use ***will*** or ***'ll***: 'You ***will be*** amazed to see how much he has grown.' 'This time next week they***'ll be*** back in France.'

Compare the use of ***shall*** in orders and instructions: 'Students ***shall*** remain seated until the end of the examination.' 'No alterations ***shall*** be made to the property without the prior consent of the landlord.'

This imperative use of ***shall*** occurs only in very formal styles, and is not common in American English.

2

× Shall you be coming back this evening?	√ Will you be coming back this evening?

In questions, we use ***shall*** with a first person subject: '***Shall I/we*** invite the Harrisons to the party?' With second and third person subjects, we use ***will***: '***Will you/she*** be going past the post office?' Compare: '***Will you*** invite them or ***shall I***?'

The same is true for indirect/reported questions: 'He hasn't decided where ***he will go***.' (NOT ***shall go***).

3

! Next week I shall return to France.	√ Next week I am returning to France. √ Next week I'll be returning to France. √ Next week I am going to return to France. √ Next week I return to France.

⇨ 873.5

4

× As soon as I shall have a job, I want to buy a car.	√ As soon as I have a job, I want to buy a car.

In an adverbial clause of time, we normally use the present simple tense to refer to the future (NOT ***shall*** or ***will***). ⇨ 25

5

× If I shall see her tonight, I shall give her your message.	√ If I see her tonight, I shall give her your message.

In a conditional clause, we normally use the present simple tense to refer to the future (NOT ***will*** or ***shall***). ⇨ 163.2

6

× I shall be grateful if you will reply as soon as possible.	√ I should/would be grateful if you would/could reply as soon as possible.

⇨ 163.8

shame 714

×	√
× We should not be shamed to discuss these things with our children.	√ We should not be ashamed to discuss these things with our children.

Shame is a noun or a verb. The adjective is ***ashamed***: 'I felt terribly ***ashamed*** of myself.' 'There's nothing to be ***ashamed*** of.'

she 715

1

×	√
× He eats a lot more than she.	√ He eats a lot more than her/than she does.

⇨ 590.7

2

×	√
× The girl who had found the purse she was given a reward.	√ The girl who had found the purse was given a reward.

⇨ 591.1

sheep 716

×	√
× The fields were full of cows and sheeps.	√ The fields were full of cows and sheep.

The plural form of ***sheep*** is ***sheep***. ⇨ 181.5

shopping 717

1

×	√
× She said she was going out to do some shoppings.	√ She said she was going out to do some shopping.

Shopping is an uncountable noun and does not have a plural form.

2

×	√
× On Saturday morning I usually go for shopping.	√ On Saturday morning I usually go shopping.

⇨ 331.3

shorts 718

×	√
× Everybody except me was wearing a short.	√ Everybody except me was wearing shorts.

Shorts is a plural noun. ⇨ 603

should 719

1

× If I hadn't been there, the child should have drowned.	√ If I hadn't been there, the child would have drowned.

In conditional sentences, we normally use ***would*** (NOT ***should***). We can use ***should*** instead of ***would*** only after a first-person subject: 'If he had been there, I *would/should* have seen him.'

When ***should*** comes after a second-person or third-person subject, it means 'ought to': '*You should* get more sleep.' '*The child should* have stayed out of the water.'

2

× The train should arrive at 8.25, but it was almost an hour late.	√ The train should have arrived at 8.25, but it was almost an hour late.

When we are talking about the past, we use ***should*** + perfect infinitive.

⇨ 393.2

3

× Some young people think that anyone with grey or white hair should be senile.	√ Some young people think that anyone with grey or white hair must be senile.

To express our logical interpretation of a situation or action, we use ***must*** (NOT ***should***): 'If she owns a Mercedes, she *must* be very rich.' 'If she has accepted your invitation, she *must* like you.'

similar 720

× The house is quite similar with the one I lived in before.	√ The house is quite similar to the one I lived in before.

A person or thing is ***similar to*** another person or thing.

simple tenses 721

1

× I write to ask you if you can meet me at the airport.	√ I am writing to ask you if you can meet me at the airport.
× I have learned English for almost two years.	√ I have been learning English for almost two years.

When we mention an action that is still happening at the moment of speaking (or at some time in the past or future), we normally use a progressive tense (the ***be*** + *-ing* form).

2

×	✓
× She didn't hear me because she played the guitar.	✓ She didn't hear me because she was playing the guitar.
× At the back of the office, someone typed a letter.	✓ At the back of the office, someone was typing a letter.

When we wish to say that something happens over an extended period of time (i.e. it does not happen instantly), we normally use a progressive tense. The progressive tense draws attention to the duration or repetition of an action. Compare: 'Someone ***sneezed***.' (= they sneezed just once) 'Someone ***was sneezing***.' (= they sneezed several times)

since **722**

1

×	✓
× The company was in India since 1951.	✓ The company has been in India since 1951.

When a time expression begins with ***since***, we normally use the present perfect tense (NOT the past simple). ⇨ 583.2

2

×	✓
× I hadn't heard from him since at least two years.	✓ I hadn't heard from him for at least two years.

When we mention the length of a period, we use ***for***: 'She was in hospital ***for six weeks***.' 'Can you wait ***for twenty minutes***?'

Since marks the beginning of a period which continues up to *now* (the moment of speaking): 'I haven't seen him ***since October***.'

3

×	✓
× Many things have changed since the last ten years.	✓ Many things have changed over/during the last ten years.

When we mention the period of time within which something happens, we use ***over*** or ***during***. Compare: 'Many things have changed ***since*** I was a boy.'

4

×	✓
× I bought the calculator since three months.	✓ I bought the calculator three months ago.

When we mention the time when something happened in relation to *now* (the moment of speaking), we use ***ago***: 'I came to England ***three months ago***.'

5

× Since we were late, so we decided to go by taxi.	√ Since we were late, we decided to go by taxi. √ We were late, so we decided to go by taxi.

We do not use ***since*** and ***so*** together in the same sentence. To link two clauses, we use just one conjunction (NOT two). ⇨ 169.2

slacks 723

× He had bought himself a new slacks.	√ He had bought himself some new slacks. √ He had bought himself a new pair of slacks.

Slacks is a plural noun. ⇨ 603

slang 724

× We were told not to use slangs in our essays.	√ We were told not to use slang in our essays.

Slang is an uncountable noun and does not have a plural form.

sleep 725

1

× I told him to turn on the light as I was not sleeping.	√ I told him to turn on the light as I was not asleep.

To refer to a state, we use the adjective ***asleep*** (OPPOSITE ***awake***).

2

× Before I sleep, I always read a book.	√ Before I go to sleep, I always read a book.

When we pass from one state into another, we ***go to sleep*** or ***fall asleep*** (OPPOSITE ***wake up***).

smell 726

1

× The dustbin had not been emptied and smelled awfully.	! The dustbin had not been emptied and smelled awful. √ The dustbin had not been emptied and there was an awful smell.

The verb ***smell*** is followed by an adjective (NOT an adverb), ⇨ 28.1. Note, however, that the verb + adjective construction is used mainly in informal styles. In formal styles, we normally use ***smell*** as a noun, e.g. 'The cheese had a most unusual *smell*.'

2

×	✓
× She asked me if I was smelling gas.	✓ She asked me if I could smell gas.

Smell is not normally used in progressive tenses, ⇨ 627.3. When we want to say that we are able to smell something, we use ***can/could***: 'I *can smell* something burning.'

smile — 727

×	✓
× When he arrived home, his mother opened the door and smiled to him.	✓ When he arrived home, his mother opened the door and smiled at him.

We ***smile at*** someone.

smoke — 728

×	✓
× I could hardly see anything because of all the smokes.	✓ I could hardly see anything because of all the smoke.

Smoke is an uncountable noun and does not have a plural form.

snow — 729

×	✓
× The streets and the houses were covered in snows.	✓ The streets and the houses were covered in snow.

When ***snow*** means 'soft white flakes which fall from the sky in cold weather', it is an uncountable noun and does not have a plural form.

so — 730

1

×	✓
× If a country has no natural resources, so it has to rely on imports.	✓ If a country has no natural resources, it has to rely on imports.
× Since I couldn't sleep, so I got up and went downstairs.	✓ Since I couldn't sleep, I got up and went downstairs.
	✓ I couldn't sleep, so I got up and went downstairs.

If the first clause begins with a conjunction (eg *if*, *since*, *as*, *because*), the next clause cannot begin with ***so***. ⇨ 169.2

2

× I was not used to driving in so heavy traffic.	√ I was not used to driving in such heavy traffic.
× I had never received so expensive presents.	√ I had never received such expensive presents.

At the beginning of a noun phrase, we normally use ***such***: 'I didn't know that Sweden could have ***such warm weather***.' 'It was ***such a good film*** that I watched it again.'

So is normally used at the beginning of an adjective/adverbial phrase: 'Why do I always feel ***so tired***?' 'The traffic was ***so heavy*** that nobody could move.' It is used at the beginning of a noun phrase only when the next word is a quantifier (e.g. *few*, *many*, *much*): 'How do you manage to save ***so much money***?'

3

× Some people are so proud and refuse to accept charity.	√ Some people are very proud and refuse to accept charity.

When we use ***so*** before an adjective or adverb, the sentence normally continues with a ***that***-clause: 'Some people are ***so proud that*** they refuse to accept charity.' 'He snores ***so loudly that*** he keeps me awake.'

Sometimes, especially in informal styles, the ***that***-clause is 'understood' or expressed indirectly: 'You are ***so*** untidy (that you keep losing things)!' 'If you weren't ***so*** untidy, you wouldn't keep losing things.'

When there is no ***that***-clause, ***so*** + adjective normally expresses strong personal emotion: 'Have you seen their little girl? She's ***so pretty***!'

4

× The train was so crowded so we had to stand up all the way.	√ The train was so crowded that we had to stand up all the way.

After ***so*** + adjective/adverb, we use a ***that***-clause. Compare: 'The train was very crowded and ***so*** we had to stand up all the way.'

5

× I'm sure that your next party will be so good as your last one.	√ I'm sure that your next party will be as good as your last one.

In comparisons, we normally use ***as*** ... ***as***: 'Your handwriting is ***as bad as*** mine.' After ***not***, we can use either ***as*** ... ***as*** or ***so*** ... ***as***, but ***as*** ... ***as*** is more common. Compare:

Your feet are ***as*** big ***as*** mine.	POSITIVE
Are your feet ***as*** big ***as*** mine?	QUESTION
Your feet are not ***as/so*** big ***as*** mine.	NEGATIVE

so far 731

1

×	✓
There was very little progress so far.	There has been very little progress so far.

With ***so far***, we normally use the present perfect tense. ⇨ 583.2

some 732

1

×	✓
The shop on the corner sells some milk.	The shop on the corner sells milk.
My brother has a large collection of some stamps.	My brother has a large collection of stamps.

When we refer to things in general, we do not use ***some***. We use ***some*** to refer to an indefinite quantity. Compare:

> Butter is made from ***milk***.
> Don't forget to buy ***some milk***.

> Most people like ***bananas***.
> I bought six oranges and ***some bananas***.

When an uncountable noun ('milk') or a plural count noun ('bananas') has general reference, it does not have a determiner. ⇨ 782.3

2

×	✓
I stopped the car to rest for some minutes.	I stopped the car to rest for a few minutes.

When we mean 'not many', we use ***a few*** + plural count noun. Compare:

> Speaker A: I need ***some*** envelopes.
> Speaker B: How many?
> Speaker A: Oh, just ***a few***.

3

×	✓
For some reasons, it was always the brightest students who were invited to answer the questions.	For some reason, it was always the brightest students who were invited to answer the questions.

When we use a countable noun after ***some***, it is normally plural: 'I've got to write *some letters* this evening.'

Sometimes, however, especially in spoken English, we use the strong form of ***some*** (/sʌm/) with a singular count noun: 'I've just had a phone call from ***some woman*** in Luton.' 'I suppose I'll have to fill in ***some form*** or other.'

In these sentences ***some*** is similar to ***a/an***, the difference being that ***some*** has the extra meaning 'I don't know who/which'. Unlike ***a/an***, ***some*** + singular count noun is also used to express scorn, impatience, anger, etc.:

> She's getting married to ***some man*** that she met on holiday.
> Knowing Clive, he's bound to have ***some excuse*** or other.
> ***Some idiot*** has parked right in front of our drive.

4

× (incorrect)	√ (correct)
× Do they have some children?	√ Do they have any children?
× The driver wouldn't let some more people get on the bus.	√ The driver wouldn't let any more people get on the bus.

In questions and negative contexts we normally use ***any***. ⇨ 733.1–2

5

× (incorrect)	√ (correct)
× Some of houses had already been pulled down.	√ Some of the houses had already been pulled down.

⇨ 640.1

6

× (incorrect)	√ (correct)
× Some of the people never eat meat.	√ Some people never eat meat.

⇨ 640.2

some/some- 733

1

× (incorrect)	√ (correct)
× Do they have some children?	√ Do they have any children?
× Have you told someone about the letter?	√ Have you told anyone about the letter?

In questions, we normally use ***any*** or an ***any***-word (i.e. *anybody*, *anyone*, *anything*, *anywhere*, *anyhow*):

Are there ***any*** matches in the drawer?
Did ***anyone*** tell you what to do?
We're not going ***anywhere*** tonight.

However, when we expect (or hope to receive) a 'yes' answer, we use ***some*** or a ***some***-word: 'They did give you ***something*** to eat, didn't they?'
For this reason, we often use ***some***, ***someone***, etc, in offers and requests: 'Would you like ***some*** milk?' 'Could you give me ***some*** milk, please?'

2

× (incorrect)	√ (correct)
× The driver wouldn't let some more people get on the bus.	√ The driver wouldn't let any more people get on the bus.
× As I didn't have something special to do, I went with him.	√ As I didn't have anything special to do, I went with him.

We normally use ***some*** or a ***some***-word in positive contexts. In negative contexts we normally use ***any*** or an ***any***-word. Compare:

They gave me ***something*** to read.
They did***n't*** give me ***anything*** to read.

Everybody wanted ***some*** cake.
Nobody wanted ***any*** cake.

3

× They refused to give me some more time.	√ They refused to give me any more time.
× He denied telling someone about what he had seen.	√ He denied telling anyone about what he had seen.

With words that have a negative meaning we normally use ***any*** or an ***any***-word, ⇨ .2 above. In addition to *not*, *never*, *nobody*, etc, whose negative meaning is obvious, there are words like ***refuse*** ('*not* agree') and ***deny*** ('*not* admit') whose negative meaning is less obvious.

Words and phrases with a 'hidden' negative meaning include:

> ***barely***, ***deny***, ***fail***, ***forbid***, ***forget***, ***hardly***, ***impossible***, ***improbable***, ***incapable***, ***on no account***, ***no sooner***, ***prohibit***, ***rarely***, ***reluctant***, ***scarcely***, ***seldom***, ***unable***, ***under no circumstances***, ***unless***, ***unlikely***, ***unnecessary***, ***unwilling***, ***without***

These are normally used with ***any*** or an ***any***-word.

4

× My parents were too poor in those days to give me some money.	√ My parents were too poor in those days to give me any money.
× I felt too full to eat something else.	√ I felt too full to eat anything else.

The structure ***too*** + adjective/adverb + ***to***-infinitive has a negative meaning. Compare: 'She was ***too*** frightened to say ***anything***.' 'She did***n't*** say ***anything*** because she was too frightened.'
In a negative context, we use ***any***, ***anything***, etc.

5

× Tell me if you see something unusual.	√ Tell me if you see anything unusual.

In contexts which contain ***if*** or the meaning 'if', we normally use ***any*** or an ***any***-word: '***If anyone*** has seen this man, they should contact the police.' '***Anyone*** arriving late was sent to the headmaster's office.'

somebody/someone **734**

1

× She thinks that someone have been watching her.	√ She thinks that someone has been watching her.

Somebody and ***someone*** take a singular verb. ⇨ 44.11

2

× Have you told someone about the letter?	√ Have you told anyone about the letter?
× I would never borrow money from somebody.	√ I would never borrow money from anybody.

In questions and negative contexts we normally use ***anybody***/***anyone***.

⇨ 733.1–2

3

! Someone had left his or her suitcase on the train.	√ Someone had left their suitcase on the train.

⇨ 42.4

something 735

1

× He is afraid that something have gone wrong.	√ He is afraid that something has gone wrong.

Something takes a singular verb.

⇨ 44.11

2

× The boy said that he hadn't done something wrong.	√ The boy said that he hadn't done anything wrong.
× I felt too full to eat something else.	√ I felt too full to eat anything else.
× Tell me if you see something unusual.	√ Tell me if you see anything unusual.

⇨ 733.2,4,5

sometime 736

× Sometime all the buses are full and I have to walk.	√ Sometimes all the buses are full and I have to walk.

When we mean 'occasionally', we use ***sometimes*** (with an -***s***). ***Sometime*** (without -***s***) means 'at an unknown or unspecified time': 'If you keep trying, you're bound to pass your driving test *sometime*.' 'She'll be arriving *sometime* in August.'

sometimes 737

× At Chinese New Year, children sometimes are given money in a small red envelope.	√ At Chinese New Year, children are sometimes given money in a small red envelope.

⇨ 29.1

somewhere 738

× He asked me if I had seen his wife somewhere.	√ He asked me if I had seen his wife anywhere.

⇨ 733.5

soon 739

× The baby soon will be one year old.	√ The baby will soon be one year old.
× My clothes soon were dry again and I went home.	√ My clothes were soon dry again and I went home.
× People soon will be living on the moon.	√ People will soon be living on the moon.

⇨ 29.1–3

sooner 740

1

× I would sooner to have my own business than work for somebody else.	√ I would sooner have my own business than work for somebody else.

We say that a person ***would sooner do*** something (NOT ***to do*** something): 'I'd ***sooner stay*** at home than come to this hotel again.' Compare: 'I'd ***prefer to stay*** at home than come to this hotel again.'

2

× I'd sooner you don't tell anyone about this.	√ I'd sooner you didn't tell anyone about this.

⇨ 649.3

sorry 741

1

× He wants everyone to feel sorry about him.	√ He wants everyone to feel sorry for him.

If we feel pity for someone, we feel ***sorry for*** them: 'I feel ***sorry for*** children who have nowhere to play.'

2

× I'm sorry for all the mistakes in this letter.	√ I'm sorry about all the mistakes in this letter.

When we apologize, we normally say that we are ***sorry about*** something: 'I'm ***sorry about*** the delay in answering your fax.'

3

× I'm sorry to not answer your letter before.	√ I'm sorry for not answering your letter before.

We use ***sorry*** + present infinitive to apologize for something that we are doing *now* (at the moment of speaking) or for something that we are just about to do:

'I'm ***sorry to disturb*** you, but you are wanted on the telephone.' 'I'm ***sorry to trouble*** you, but I wonder if you could help me.'

To apologize for something that we did *before now*, we can use one of several patterns:

I'm ***sorry about/for waking*** you up last night.
I'm ***sorry that/if I woke*** you up last night.
I'm ***sorry to have woken*** you up last night.

A perfect infinitive ('to have woken') is used mainly in formal styles.

sort of 742

× These sort of people should not be given a licence.	√ These sorts of people should not be given a licence.

⇨ 436

so that 743

! I have my own car now so that it's easier to get around.	√ I have my own car now, so it's easier to get around.

When we mention the result of an action or situation, we normally use ***so*** or ***and so***: 'The petrol gauge showed empty ***and so*** we stopped at the next service station.' Also, when it is obvious that the second clause expresses result, we can just use ***and***: 'The car is very old ***and*** nobody wants to buy it.'

So that is normally used to express the purpose of an action: 'We hired a car *so that* it would be easier to get around.'

It is possible to use ***so that*** to express result: 'At that moment all the lights went out, *so that* the whole house was plunged into darkness.' However, this usage is not common and occurs mainly in formal styles.

Note that there is a comma before ***so that*** when it expresses result, but no comma when it expresses purpose.

sound 744

× His voice sounded very strangely.	√ His voice sounded very strange.

⇨ 28.1

spaghetti 745

× I hope you like spaghettis.	√ I hope you like spaghetti.

Spaghetti is an uncountable noun and does not have a plural form.

speak 746

×	✓
× A lot of people in Southeast Asia are speaking three languages.	✓ A lot of people in Southeast Asia speak three languages.

⇨ 619.3

specially 747

×	✓
× Pollution is a serious problem, specially in industrial areas.	✓ Pollution is a serious problem, especially in industrial areas.
× The programme has been designed with young children specially in mind.	✓ The programme has been designed with young children especially in mind.

When we mean 'above all', we use ***especially***:

I don't like going to bed late, ***especially*** when I have to get up early.
Sixth-form students ***especially*** should find the book very useful.
He's good at all ball games, ***especially*** tennis and football.

We use ***specially*** to emphasize that something is done for one particular purpose or person:

She's come all the way from Brussels ***specially to see you***.
The camera has been ***specially designed*** for underwater photography.
He wrote this song ***specially for Helen***.

spectacles 748

×	✓
× The doctor said that I probably needed a new spectacles.	✓ The doctor said that I probably needed (some) new spectacles.

Like ***glasses***, ***spectacles*** is a plural noun. ⇨ 603

spend 749

1

×	✓
× On St Valentine's Day some Japanese girls spend almost half their salary for chocolate.	✓ On St Valentine's Day some Japanese girls spend almost half their salary on chocolate.

We ***spend*** a sum of money ***on*** the thing that we buy.

2

×	✓
× Since she retired, she spends most of her time just on relaxing and enjoying herself.	✓ Since she retired, she spends most of her time just relaxing and enjoying herself.

We ***spend*** a period of time ***doing*** something (WITHOUT ***on***): 'He ***spends*** all his free time reading.'

3

× After three days we had already spend most of our money.	√ After three days we had already spent most of our money.

Spend (infinitive), ***spent*** (past simple), ***spent*** (past participle).

sport **750**

1

× I am not very good at sports.	√ I am not very good at sport.

When ***sport*** means 'sport in general', it is an uncountable noun and does not have a plural form. We use ***sport*** as a countable noun to refer to a particular sport: 'My favourite ***sports*** are tennis and hockey.' 'Do you like water ***sports***?'

⇨ 529.4

2

× Two miles away, there is a new sport centre.	√ Two miles away, there is a new sports centre.

In British English, the form that is used before a noun is ***sports***: 'a ***sports*** centre', 'a ***sports*** car', etc.

staff **751**

× The principal introduced me to some of her teaching staffs.	√ The principal introduced me to some of her teaching staff.
× The average teaching load of an academic staff is 10 contact hours a week.	√ The average teaching load of an academic staff member is 10 contact hours a week.

Staff refers to all the people that work for an organization:

She has 40 ***staff*** under her.
She has ***a staff*** of 40.
The staff are pleased with their salary increase.

To refer to one or more individual people, we normally use ***member/s of***: 'Three ***members of staff*** are on sick leave.' In formal styles, we also use ***staff member/s***.

stand **752**

× I couldn't stand to have to sit behind a desk all day.	√ I couldn't stand having to sit behind a desk all day.

We ***cannot stand doing*** something (NOT ***to do***).

start 753

× I could see that she was starting getting angry.	√ I could see that she was starting to get angry.

⇨ 839.8

still 754

1

× The rest of my family still is in France.	√ The rest of my family is still in France.

⇨ 29.2

2

× I cannot still believe that the exams are over.	√ I still cannot believe that the exams are over.

When the verb phrase is negative, ***still*** normally goes immediately before the first auxiliary verb.

3

× Until now I still like the song.	√ (Even now) I still like the song.

⇨ 829.3

stop 755

1

× When he saw the teacher looking at him, he stopped to cheat.	√ When he saw the teacher looking at him, he stopped cheating.

Stop is followed by a ***to***-infinitive for one meaning and by an ***-ing*** form for another meaning. 'She ***stopped to speak*** to him' tells us why she stopped. 'She ***stopped speaking*** to him' tells us what she stopped doing. Compare: 'When I saw how tired he was, I ***stopped to help*** him.' 'When I realized how ungrateful he was, I ***stopped helping*** him.

2

× Governments all over the world are trying to stop industry to pollute the environment.	√ Governments all over the world are trying to stop industry (from) polluting the environment.

If we prevent someone from doing something, we ***stop*** them (***from***) ***doing*** it. Compare: 'The policeman ***stopped*** the driver ***to check*** his licence.'

3

× I couldn't stop from thinking that there was trouble ahead.	√ I couldn't stop thinking that there was trouble ahead.

We cannot use ***from*** after ***stop*** unless ***stop*** has an object ⇨.2 above. Note the alternative: 'I couldn't ***stop myself (from) thinking*** that there was trouble ahead.'

stress 756

× She stressed on the importance of keeping the lenses spotlessly clean.	√ She stressed the importance of keeping the lenses spotlessly clean.

We ***stress*** something (WITHOUT ***on***). Compare: 'Her piano teacher lays particular ***stress on*** the need to practise regularly.' Use ***on*** after the noun, but not after the verb.

strict 757

× Some parents complain if teachers are too strict to their children.	√ Some parents complain if teachers are too strict with their children.

A parent or teacher is ***strict with*** a child (NOT ***to***).

succeed 758

× I eventually succeeded to open the drawer.	√ I eventually succeeded in opening the drawer.

We ***succeed in doing*** something. Compare: 'I eventually ***managed to open*** the drawer.'

such 759

1

× I had never been in a such difficult situation.	√ I had never been in such a difficult situation.

Such goes immediately before ***a/an***, not after it: 'You're lucky to have ***such a*** kind husband.'

2

× The alleged offences include such crimes like theft and shoplifting.	√ The alleged offences include such crimes as theft and shoplifting.

To introduce examples of something, we use ***such*** + noun + ***as*** (NOT ***like***). Note the alternative: 'The alleged offences include crimes ***such as*** theft and shoplifting.'

such that 760

×	√
It should be possible to schedule the examination timetable such that the eight papers are more evenly spread.	It should be possible to schedule the examination timetable so that the eight papers are more evenly spread.

We use ***such that*** to describe the degree and effect of something: 'The severity of the earthquake was ***such that*** tremors were felt over 50 miles away.' 'The extent of the damage is ***such that*** the whole building will have to be pulled down.' ***Such that*** refers back to a noun ('severity', 'extent').

When we talk about the purpose or desired outcome of an action, we use ***so that***: 'The desks were spread out ***so that*** the students couldn't cheat.'

suddenly 761

×	√
I heard footsteps suddenly outside the door.	I suddenly heard footsteps outside the door. Suddenly, I heard footsteps outside the door.

⇨ 29.1

suggest 762

1

×	√
He suggested to meet us outside the cinema.	He suggested meeting us outside the cinema.

We ***suggest doing*** something (NOT ***to do***).

2

×	√
I suggest you to try to get some sleep.	I suggest (that) you try to get some sleep.

We ***suggest*** (***that***) someone ***do*** something. Compare: 'I *advise you to try* to get some sleep.'

3

×	√
He suggested me that I should take the examination again.	He suggested to me that I should take the examination again.

With ***suggest*** we always use ***to*** before an indirect object. Compare: 'He *advised me* that I should take the examination again.'

suit 763

× Apart from being very expensive, the coat doesn't suit to you.	√ Apart from being very expensive, the coat doesn't suit you.

If a coat, hat, colour, etc, makes someone look smart or attractive, it ***suits*** them (WITHOUT ***to***): 'Bright colours ***suit*** some people, but they don't ***suit*** me.'

superior 764

1

× The new ZX1000 is superior than earlier models.	√ The new ZX1000 is superior to earlier models.

When it is necessary to mention a person or thing after ***superior***, we use a ***to***-phrase (NOT ***than***). ⇨ 392

2

× Just because something is expensive, it is not necessarily more superior.	√ Just because something is expensive, it is not necessarily superior.

Superior has a comparative meaning already and is not normally used with ***more***. ⇨ 15.4

supply 765

× Who is supplying these people such terrible weapons?	√ Who is supplying these people with such terrible weapons?

We ***supply*** a person or organization ***with*** something. Compare: 'Who is ***supplying*** these weapons?'

suppose 766

1

× The jumper was suppose to be made of pure wool.	√ The jumper was supposed to be made of pure wool.

⇨ 577.1

2

× I suppose you don't know her address?	√ I don't suppose you know her address?

⇨ 512.5

supposing 767

×	✓
× Supposing if a doctor discovers that a patient is critically ill, is the doctor compelled to inform the patient of the diagnosis?	✓ Supposing a doctor discovers that a patient is critically ill, is the doctor compelled to inform the patient of the diagnosis?

Supposing is never used with ***if***. The same is true for ***suppose***: '*Suppose* she asks me where you are, what shall I say?'

sure 768

×	✓
× She feels sure to be offered the job.	✓ She feels sure of being offered the job.

⇒ 135

swear 769

×	✓
× He sweared that he had not taken the money.	✓ He swore that he had not taken the money.

Swear (infinitive), ***swore*** (past simple), ***sworn*** (past participle).

swim 770

1

×	✓
× I swimmed towards her as fast as I could.	✓ I swam towards her as fast as I could.

Swim (infinitive), ***swam*** (past simple), ***swum*** (past participle).

2

×	✓
× At one time I used to go for swimming every morning.	✓ At one time I used to go swimming every morning.

⇒ 331.2–3

take 771

1

×	✓
× He asked me if I had took any photographs.	✓ He asked me if I had taken any photographs.

Take (infinitive), ***took*** (past simple), ***taken*** (past participle).

2

× She opened the refrigerator and took a bottle of milk.	√ She opened the refrigerator and took out a bottle of milk.

When ***take*** contains the idea of movement, it is normally used with an adverb or prepositional phrase:

Take these books ***away***.
They ***took*** the injured player ***off*** on a stretcher.
You'll need some steps if you want to ***take*** the curtains ***down***.
I ***took*** her ***to the station***.

talk 772

1

× What were you talking her about?'	√ What were you talking to her about?'

We ***talk to*** someone (about something). Compare: 'What were you ***telling her*** about?'

2

! I talked with Gloria about her new job.	√ I talked to Gloria about her new job.

Users of British English ***talk to*** someone (about something). Compare: 'I had a ***talk with*** Gloria about her new job.' Users of American English ***talk to*** or ***with*** someone (about something).

taste 773

× The soup was tasting very salty.	√ The soup tasted very salty.

Taste is not normally used in progressive tenses. ⇨ 627.3

teach 774

× Who teached you to play the piano?	√ Who taught you to play the piano?

Teach (infinitive), ***taught*** (past simple), ***taught*** (past participle).

tell 775

1

× The policeman told that we could go back into the building.	√ The policeman told us that we could go back into the building. √ The policeman said that we could go back into the building.

⇨ 390.1

2

×	✓
× I told to the policeman everything I had seen.	✓ I told the policeman everything I had seen.

⇨ 390.3

3

×	✓
× I told him don't drive so fast.	✓ I told him not to drive so fast.

We ***tell*** someone **(*not*)** ***to do*** something.

⇨ 388

tenses: general — 776

×	✓
× All of the classrooms were provided with blackboards but only one of them has an OHP.	✓ All of the classrooms were provided with blackboards but only one of them had an OHP. ✓ All of the classrooms are provided with blackboards but only one of them has an OHP.
× He talks about the same things every time I met him.	✓ He talks about the same things every time I meet him. ✓ He talked about the same things every time I met him.

When we describe or report a situation, we choose either a '*then*' point of view or a '*now*' point of view. If we choose a '*then*' point of view, we use past tenses (e.g. 'were provided' + 'had'). If we choose a '*now*' point of view, we use present tenses (e.g. 'are provided' + 'has'). The mixing of present and past forms (e.g. 'were provided' + 'has') can be very confusing for the reader.

than — 777

×	✓
× She does not have the same ability than her sister.	✓ She does not have the same ability as her sister.
× Personality is just as important than appearance.	✓ Personality is just as important as appearance.

We use ***than*** after comparative adjectives and adverbs: 'Personality is ***more important than*** appearance.' 'They arrived ***sooner than*** we had expected.'

We also use ***than*** after ***more/less/fewer*** + noun: 'She has ***less ability than*** her sister.'

We do not use ***than*** after ***the same*** or ***as***.

thank 778

1

×	✓
× I should like to thank to the doctors and nurses who attended me during my recent illness.	✓ I should like to thank the doctors and nurses who attended me during my recent illness.

We ***thank*** someone (WITHOUT ***to***). Compare: 'I should like to send my ***thanks to*** the doctors and nurses …'

2

×	✓
× Thank you about the invitation. × Thank you for you agree to see me.	✓ Thank you for the invitation. ✓ Thank you for agreeing to see me.

We ***thank*** someone ***for*** (***doing***) something.

that: conjunction 779

1

×	✓
× She went home because that she was not feeling well. × The second paragraph explains that how students can benefit from using a computer.	✓ She went home because she was not feeling well. ✓ The second paragraph explains how students can benefit from using a computer.

If there is already a conjunction ('because') or ***wh***-word ('how') at the beginning of a subordinate clause, we do not use ***that***. Compare:

He told me + ***that*** I should do it.
He told me + ***how*** I should do it.
× He told me + ***that how*** I should do it.

2

×	✓
× As we all know that there are many good reasons for planting new trees. × Needless to say that these new products are in great demand.	✓ As we all know, there are many good reasons for planting new trees. ✓ Needless to say, these new products are in great demand.

Sometimes we begin a sentence with an adverbial:

Of course, there is no way of knowing what he will do.
Naturally, we cannot afford to take chances.
As you know, there are several ways of tackling this problem.

In written English, the adverbial usually ends with a comma and is followed by a main clause. The adverbial cannot be followed by a ***that***-clause.

3

× I promised to go with her that she wouldn't be nervous.	√ I promised to go with her so that she wouldn't be nervous.

To introduce a clause of purpose, we use ***so that*** (NOT ***that*** by itself).

⇨ 22.3

4

× The secret police are not as powerful that they used to be.	√ The secret police are not as powerful as they used to be.

A comparative clause begins with ***as*** (NOT ***that***). Note the construction (***not***) ***as*** ... **as** ... . 'He kicked the ball ***as*** hard ***as*** he could.' 'My examination results were ***not as*** good ***as*** they might have been.'

5

× It is almost six months that you last wrote to me.	√ It is almost six months since you last wrote to me.

To refer to the beginning of a period that began in the past and continues up to the moment of speaking, we use ***since***.

We can use a ***that***-clause after a point of time, e.g. 'It was this time last week ***that he had the accident***.' 'It's tomorrow ***that we have to hand in the assignment***.'

6

× Politicians should recognize the fact people will not tolerate unemployment indefinitely.	√ Politicians should recognize the fact that people will not tolerate unemployment indefinitely.
× It is possible the suitcase may have been taken by mistake.	√ It is possible that the suitcase may have been taken by mistake.

Many nouns, verbs and adjectives may be followed by a ***that***-clause. In the majority of cases, especially in informal styles, the word ***that*** may be omitted:

There is a good *chance* + (*that*) she may be late.
I *said* + (*that*) we couldn't wait any longer.
He is *sorry* + (*that*) he cannot attend the meeting.

After some nouns, verbs and adjectives, however, ***that*** cannot be omitted:

I object to the ***idea*** + ***that*** none of our staff can be trusted.
She ***repeated*** + ***that*** she had no intention of resigning.
It is ***essential*** + ***that*** they receive the report by next Friday.
Most people accept the ***fact*** + ***that*** smoking is dangerous.

To avoid possible error, it is advisable to include ***that*** at the beginning of a ***that***-clause, especially in formal styles.

⇨ 838.7

that: determiner/pronoun 780

1

× The school's outdoor facilities are better than that of many country clubs.	√ The school's outdoor facilities are better than those of many country clubs.

⇨ 207.1

2

× They asked him to return the book but he refused to do that.	√ They asked him to return the book but he refused to do so.

⇨ 235.1

that: relative pronoun 781

1

× My youngest child, that is only three, has started going to kindergarten.	√ My youngest child, who is only three, has started going to kindergarten.

If a relative clause tells us which person the speaker is talking about, it can begin with ***who*** or ***that***: 'Do you recognize the woman ***who/that has just come in***?'

On the other hand, if a relative clause simply adds a comment or detail, it cannot begin with ***that***: 'I lent the book to a friend of mine, ***who still has it***.'

The same applies to relative clauses which refer to things. We use ***which*** or ***that*** in defining clauses: 'The books ***which/that you ordered*** have now arrived.'

In non-defining clauses, we use ***which***: 'We rented a house in Chelsea, ***which is in London***.

2

× The shirt was fine until this morning that I decided to wash it.	√ The shirt was fine until this morning, when I decided to wash it.

If a relative clause identifies the morning, day, year, etc., that it refers to, it is possible to use ***when*** or ***that***, e.g. 'The shirt was fine until ***the morning when/that*** I decided to wash it.' In this sentence, the relative clause tells us *which* morning.

If the relative clause simply adds a comment or detail, we use ***when***.

3

× The record is by a French singer that I forget his name.	√ The record is by a French singer whose name I forget.

In a relative clause, we replace a possessive determiner ('his') with ***whose*** and put it with its noun at the beginning of the clause. Compare:

He is a teacher. His wife is having a baby.
He is the teacher ***whose wife*** is having a baby.
He is a teacher. You met his wife at the ante-natal clinic.
He is the teacher ***whose wife*** you met at the ante-natal clinic.

the: use **782**

1

× Brunei is the oil-producing country.	√ Brunei is an oil-producing country.

Since there are many oil-producing countries, we cannot say that Brunei is 'the oil-producing country'. When we mean 'one of many', we use ***a/an***. Compare:
'He lives in ***a*** house on Duke Street.' (There are many houses on Duke Street.)
'He lives in ***the*** house on Duke Street.' (There is just one house on Duke Street.)

Note that it is possible to say 'Brunei is ***the*** oil-producing country' if ***the*** is emphasized. This would mean that, of all the oil-producing countries, Brunei is the most important. When ***the*** is emphasized, it is always pronounced /ðiː/.

2

× Each school is surrounded by the brick wall.	√ Each school is surrounded by a brick wall.

When we mention someone or something for the first time, we normally use ***a/an***, not ***the***. When we mention the same person or thing again, we use ***the***.
'This story is about ***a*** little girl who got lost in ***a*** forest. ***The*** girl had gone into ***the*** forest to pick flowers.'

We use ***the*** for the first mention only when we are sure that the listener/reader will understand which person or thing we are talking about, e.g. 'Look at ***the*** moon!' 'Close ***the*** door, please.'

3

× It is often said that the teachers have a very easy life.	√ It is often said that teachers have a very easy life.
× The magazine is about the personal computers.	√ The magazine is about personal computers.
× Some people say that the butter is not good for you.	√ Some people say that butter is not good for you.
× The government's primary goal is to reduce the poverty.	√ The government's primary goal is to reduce poverty.

We do not use ***the*** with plural count nouns ('teachers', 'computers') or uncountable nouns ('butter', 'poverty') when they have general reference. Compare:

Teachers are always being criticized.	GENERAL REFERENCE
The teachers that I know work very hard.	SPECIFIC REFERENCE
Sales of ***butter*** have fallen dramatically.	GENERAL REFERENCE
Where did you put ***the butter***?	SPECIFIC REFERENCE

The same rule applies when the noun is modified:

New Zealand butter is exported to many countries.	GENERAL REFERENCE
Butter kept in the refrigerator will last longer.	GENERAL REFERENCE
The butter in the refrigerator is from New Zealand.	SPECIFIC REFERENCE

The same rule also applies when the noun phrase begins with a quantifier such as ***all***, ***many***, ***most***: '***Most children*** enjoy parties.' (GENERAL REFERENCE) '***Most of the children*** enjoyed the party.' (SPECIFIC REFERENCE)

Note that with singular count nouns, ***the*** is used both for general reference and for specific reference: '***The computer*** is a wonderful invention.' (GENERAL REFERENCE) '***The computer*** hasn't been turned on yet.' (SPECIFIC REFERENCE)

4

×	✓
× The driver lost the control of the car and crashed into a tree.	✓ The driver lost control of the car and crashed into a tree.
× At what time do you normally have the breakfast?	✓ At what time do you normally have breakfast?
× In some countries, children do not go to the school.	✓ In some countries, children do not go to school.

⇨ 532.2–4

5

×	✓
× Without these forests, the mankind could not survive.	✓ Without these forests, mankind could not survive.
× We must try harder to stop these people from destroying the nature.	✓ We must try harder to stop these people from destroying nature.

Most uncountable nouns are used without ***the*** for general reference and with ***the*** for specific reference (⇨ .3 above). Some uncountable nouns, however, are never used with ***the***. The reference of nouns such as ***mankind*** and ***nature*** (the world of animals, plants, etc) is always general.

6

×	✓
× I started playing the football when I was five.	✓ I started playing football when I was five.

We do not use ***the*** before the name of a sport or game.

7

×	✓
× The red is my favourite colour.	✓ Red is my favourite colour.

We do not use ***the*** before the name of a colour.

8

×	✓
× When I was a baby, I almost died of the pneumonia.	✓ When I was a baby, I almost died of pneumonia.

We do not use ***the*** before the name of an illness.

9

×	✓
× You should also visit the Aberdeen, which is the oldest fishing port in Hong Kong.	✓ You should also visit Aberdeen, which is the oldest fishing port in Hong Kong

The is not normally used with the name of a town, city, state, county or country, e.g. *Aberdeen*, *Cambridge*, *New York*, *Texas*, *Paris*, *Brazil*, *Egypt*, *Saudi Arabia*.

The is used if the name contains a plural noun, e.g. *the Netherlands, the Philippines.*

⇨ 783.9

10

× The train leaves from the Victoria Station.	√ The train leaves from Victoria Station.
× We arrived at the Orly Airport just before two o'clock.	√ We arrived at Orly Airport just before two o'clock.
× We spent the whole day shopping in the Oxford Street.	√ We spent the whole day shopping in Oxford Street.
× I studied at the Leeds University.	√ I studied at Leeds University.

Names that end with a common noun do not normally begin with ***the***. Examples:

London ***Airport***, *British* ***Airways***, *Westminster* ***Bridge***, *Coventry* ***Cathedral***, *Guy's* ***Hospital***, *Leeds City* ***Library***, *Buckingham* ***Palace***, *Hyde* ***Park***, *Bristol* ***Polytechnic***, *Bedford* ***Road***, *Waterloo* ***Station***, *Sesame* ***Street***, *Exeter* ***University*** (BUT ***The*** *University of Exeter*).

⇨ 826.2

The main exceptions to this rule are the names of oceans, seas, rivers, canals and deserts.

⇨ 783.11

11

× The next week we are going on a trip to Stratford.	√ Next week we are going on a trip to Stratford.

Unfortunately, there are no general rules for the use of ***the*** in time expressions and each expression has to be learned individually.

WITHOUT **THE**	WITH **THE**
next week/Monday	*(on) the next/following day*
last week/Monday	*the week before/after*
on Monday	*on the last/second Monday in September*
at present	*at the present time/moment*
in recent years	*for/in/over/during the last few/three years*

12

× The letter was posted on February the 2nd.	√ The letter was posted on February 2nd.

⇨ 199.2

13

× He just stood there with the hands in his pockets.	√ He just stood there with his hands in his pockets.

When we mention a part of someone's body, we normally use ***his***, ***her***, etc: 'The children had no shoes on ***their feet***.'

⇨ 610.3

the: wrongly omitted **783**

1

×	√
× I spoke to same man who had sold me the machine.	√ I spoke to the same man who had sold me the machine.
× He looked at my passport and asked me about purpose of my visit.	√ He looked at my passport and asked me about the purpose of my visit.

When we specify which person or thing we are talking about, we use ***the*** in front of the noun. Compare:

Children like sweets.
The two younger children had already gone to bed.

There has been a big increase in ***production***.
There has been a big increase in ***the production of saloon cars***.

Nobody can survive without *food*.
The food that we took with us lasted three days.

2

×	√
× Before we left, we gave children some presents.	√ Before we left, we gave the children some presents.
× In New York food was too rich for me.	√ In New York the food was too rich for me.
× Her keys were still inside car.	√ Her keys were still inside the car.

When we are sure that the listener/reader will understand which person or thing we are referring to, we use ***the*** in front of the noun. This means that we use ***the*** when we have mentioned the person or thing before. It also means that we use ***the*** when the person or thing is obvious from the situation.

3

×	√
× I asked him why some of animals looked sick.	√ I asked him why some of the animals looked sick.

⇨ 640.1

4

×	√
× The church was oldest building in the town.	√ The church was the oldest building in the town.
× It was most interesting story I had ever heard.	√ It was the most interesting story I had ever heard.

⇨ 15.3

5

×	√
× My apartment is on tenth floor.	√ My apartment is on the tenth floor.

We always use ***the*** before an ordinal number ('tenth').

6

! How long have you been playing piano?	√ How long have you been playing the piano?

In British English, we normally say that someone plays ***the*** piano, guitar, etc.
In American English, ***the*** is optional.

7

× She has spent her life helping disabled.	√ She has spent her life helping the disabled.

With an adjective used as a noun, we use ***the***: '***The injured*** have been taken to hospital.' 'More needs to be done to help ***the poor***.'

8

× Swiss are very fussy about hygiene.	√ The Swiss are very fussy about hygiene. √ Swiss people are very fussy about hygiene.

⇨ 504.3

9

× A lot of the foreign workers come from Philippines.	√ A lot of the foreign workers come from the Philippines.

If a name contains a plural noun, it normally begins with ***the***, e.g. *the Bahamas, the British Isles, the West Indies, the Netherlands, the United Arab Emirates, the United States (of America), the US/USA, the Himalayas, the French Alps, the Houses of Parliament, the Dark Ages.*

10

× Let me know when you arrive in UK.	√ Let me know when you arrive in the UK.

If the name of a country contains ***kingdom***, ***republic***, ***state*** or ***union***, it begins with ***the***, e.g. *the United Kingdom, the UK, the People's Republic of China, the United States (of America), the US/USA.*

11

× They're making a film about River Nile. × Our route will take us across part of Sahara Desert.	√ They're making a film about the River Nile. √ Our route will take us across part of the Sahara Desert.

The names of canals, rivers, seas, oceans and deserts (but NOT lakes) begin with ***the***, e.g. *the Suez Canal, the (River) Thames, the Mediterranean (Sea), the South China Sea, the Indian Ocean, the Kalahari (Desert).*

12

× In New York Hilton I was able to get Japanese food.	√ In the New York Hilton I was able to get Japanese food.

The names of hotels normally begin with ***the***, e.g. *the Sheraton*, *the Savoy*, *the Holiday Inn*, *the Mandarin*, *the Waldorf-Astoria*. We do not use ***the*** if the name has a genitive form (-*'s*), e.g. *Claridge's*.

their 784

× I know a lot about Japan but I have never been their.	√ I know a lot about Japan but I have never been there.

⇨ 786.1

then 785

1

× After having a bath, then he got dressed.	√ After having a bath, he got dressed.
× When a child is very young, then the mother should not go out to work.	√ When a child is very young, the mother should not go out to work.

When ***then*** means 'afterwards' or 'at that time', we do not use it after a time clause. We use ***then*** after a time clause (and after an ***if***-clause) when it means 'as a result or consequence': 'Once you've been to their house, ***then*** you'll know the true meaning of hospitality.'

2

× I read another ten pages of the book then I went to sleep.	√ I read another ten pages of the book and then I went to sleep.

Then ('after that') is an adverb. It expresses a time connection between two actions, but it does not link them grammatically. For this, we use a conjunction.

⇨ 28.3

there: use 786

1

× They have decided to sell there house.	√ They have decided to sell their house.

There is an adverb of place: 'We stopped in Rome and spent two days ***there***.' When we need a determiner, we use ***their***: 'The children had got ***their feet*** wet.'

2

× I've read a lot about Japan but I have never been to there.	√ I've read a lot about Japan but I have never been there.

We do not normally use ***to*** before ***there***.

⇨ 802.2

3

× There has been several complaints about the design of the building.	√ There have been several complaints about the design of the building.
× Inside the room there were a table and two chairs.	√ Inside the room there was a table and two chairs.

When ***there*** is used as an empty subject, the real subject goes after the verb ***be***. The verb agrees with the real subject.

EMPTY SUBJECT	+	BE	+	REAL SUBJECT
There		was		a loud bang.
There		were		two loud bangs.

When the real subject has two or more parts, the verb agrees with the first part:

EMPTY SUBJECT	+	BE	+	REAL SUBJECT
There		was		an orange and two apples.
There		were		two apples and an orange.

4

× Throughout the whole lesson, there was not a single discipline problem arose.	√ Throughout the whole lesson, there was not a single discipline problem. √ Throughout the whole lesson, not a single discipline problem arose.

After ***there is***, ***there were***, etc, the real subject cannot be followed by a finite verb ('arose'). For example, we can say '***There was*** someone ***knocking*** on the door' but we cannot say '***There was*** someone ***knocked*** on the door'.

5

× There's no good trying to work if you feel tired.	√ It's no good trying to work if you feel tired.
× Of course I can bring some CDs. There's no trouble at all.	√ Of course I can bring some CDs. It's no trouble at all.

Common expressions beginning ***there is no*** include:

There's no/little point (in) having a car if you can't drive.
Don't worry. *There is no cause/reason* to be alarmed.
There is no/little doubt that someone is not telling the truth.
I'm afraid that *there is no question* of giving you a refund.
Is there no chance of getting someone to help you?

Common expressions beginning ***it is no*** include:

It's no good employing people who do not want to work.
It's no trouble (at all) looking after a child like James.
It is no use having money if you cannot spend it.
It's no/little wonder that she always looks tired.

there: wrongly omitted

787

1

× In some countries are very strict traffic laws.	√ In some countries there are very strict traffic laws.
× Once pupils discover that a subject can be interesting is usually a big improvement in their work.	√ Once pupils discover that a subject can be interesting, there is usually a big improvement in their work.

When we say that someone or something exists or that something happens, we normally use ***there*** as an empty subject.

Unfortunately, ***there are*** several mistakes.
There is someone I would like you to meet.
I'm sure ***there must be*** a more simple explanation.
Suddenly, ***there was*** a very loud bang.

In this pattern, ***there*** has no meaning. It merely fills the subject position and makes the sentence complete.

Note that ***there*** is often used in this way before *seem to be* and *appear to be*: '***There seems/appears to be*** something wrong with the plug.'

2

! An index is at the back of the book.	√ There is an index at the back of the book. √ At the back of the book (there) is an index.

When we say that someone or something exists and is in a particular place, we normally use ***there*** as an empty subject. '***There*** was a large black cat under the table.'

If we mention the place at the beginning of the sentence, ***there*** is optional: 'Under the table (***there***) was a large black cat.'

therefore

788

1

× She did not recognize him with a beard therefore she walked straight past him.	√ She did not recognize him with a beard. Therefore, she walked straight past him. √ She did not recognize him with a beard and (therefore) she walked straight past him.

⇨ 28.3

2

×	✓
× Since these people have no jobs, therefore they have no money.	✓ Since these people have no jobs, they have no money.
	✓ These people have no jobs and therefore they have no money.

We do not use ***therefore*** after a clause beginning with *since*, *as*, *because*, *seeing as/that* (i.e. after a clause of reason).

these 789

×	✓
× These photograph was taken at my grandparents' house.	✓ These photographs were taken at my grandparents' house.
	✓ This photograph was taken at my grandparents' house.
× Who is reponsible for the maintenance of these equipment?	✓ Who is reponsible for the maintenance of this equipment

⇨ 207

they 790

1

×	✓
× Tourists like to come here because they are so many things to see.	✓ Tourists like to come here because there are so many things to see.
× They will always be a feeling of failure.	✓ There will always be a feeling of failure.

When we mention the presence or existence of someone or something, we use the empty subject ***there***, NOT ***they***.

2

×	✓
× The people at the back of the room they could not hear anything.	✓ The people at the back of the room could not hear anything.

⇨ 591.1

3

×	✓
× We can do the job faster than they.	✓ We can do the job faster than them/than they can.

⇨ 590.7

thief 791

×	✓
× The two thiefs were never caught.	✓ The two thieves were never caught.

⇨ 181.4

think 792

1

× She is thinking that she must have upset you.	√ She thinks that she must have upset you.

When ***think*** introduces an opinion (i.e. when it is followed by a ***that***-clause), it is not used in progressive tenses. ⇨ 627.3. Compare: 'They ***are thinking of/about*** holding the conference in Malta.' (= intention) 'They ***think that*** Malta is an ideal place for a conference.' (= opinion)

2

× I think we cannot wait any longer.	√ I don't think we can wait any longer.

⇨ 512.5

3

× At first I thought to put the money in the bank.	√ At first I thought about putting the money in the bank.

If we consider doing something, we ***think about/of*** doing it: 'Have you ever ***thought about/of*** starting your own business?'

this 793

1

× On this straight roads you can drive much faster.	√ On these straight roads you can drive much faster.

⇨ 207.1

2

× While awaiting my flight at Belgrade airport, I fell into conversation with this doctor from Nigeria.	√ While awaiting my flight at Belgrade airport, I fell into conversation with a doctor from Nigeria.

In informal styles, we sometimes use ***this/these*** when we mention somebody or something for the first time: 'I was just about to leave the shop when ***this woman*** came up to me and asked if I could give her some money to buy a loaf.'

This 'first mention' use of ***this/these*** is unacceptable in formal styles.

those 794

× All junk food, especially those sold at the canteen, should be avoided.	√ All junk food, especially that sold at the canteen, should be avoided.

⇨ 207.2

thousand 795

×	✓
× The castle is nearly thousand years old.	✓ The castle is nearly a thousand years old.
× Over fifty thousands of tourists came here last year.	✓ Over fifty thousand tourists came here last year.

⇨ 538

threaten 796

×	✓
× She threatened making him stay in his bedroom all day.	✓ She threatened to make him stay in his bedroom all day. ✓ She threatened him with having to stay in his bedroom all day.

We ***threaten to do*** something. Alternatively, we ***threaten*** someone ***with*** something.

throw 797

×	✓
× Some of the guests threw rice to the married couple.	✓ Some of the guests threw rice at the married couple.

We ***throw*** something ***at*** the person or thing that we want to hit.

thus 798

×	✓
× The discovery of oil also increased the amount of employment. Thus, as an independent country, Brunei has joined several political organizations.	✓ The discovery of oil also increased the amount of employment. (*new paragraph*) As an independent country, Brunei has joined several political organizations ...

We use ***thus*** (only in formal styles) to show that what we are about to say is the logical result or conclusion of what we have just mentioned:

> In 1986, women working full-time had an average income of $16,843, while full-time male workers earned $25,894. *Thus* for every dollar earned by men, women earned about 65 cents.
>
> Since socialization is based on all social experience, this process actually occurs everywhere. For this reason, socialization involves inconsistencies; even within the family we may receive different information from various family members. *Thus* socialization is not a simple process of learning, but a complex balancing act in which individuals encounter a wide range of ideas in the process of forming their own distinctive personality.
>
> (from *Sociology* by John J Maconis, Prentice Hall)

We cannot use ***thus*** to introduce a new topic or to link ideas that are unrelated.

tightly

799

×	✓
× I pulled the string tightly.	✓ I pulled the string tight.

⇨ 28.2

time

800

1

×	✓
× It's time you answer their letter.	✓ It's time you answered their letter.
× It is high time that the Wildlife Department addresses the problem of animal ownership.	✓ It is high time that the Wildlife Department addressed the problem of animal ownership.

After the phrase ***it's (about/high) time (that)***, we use the past tense, NOT the present tense. Both simple and progressive forms are possible: 'It's time you ***had*** a haircut.' 'It's about time we ***were leaving***.'

2

×	✓
× She spends all her time just on relaxing and enjoying herself.	✓ She spends all her time just relaxing and enjoying herself.

We ***spend time*** (or 'two days', 'a week', etc) ***doing*** something (WITHOUT ***on***): 'Simon has ***spent the last six months travelling*** around India.' Compare: 'She ***spent*** $300 ***on*** a new camera.'

3

×	✓
× I have donated blood for 25 times.	✓ I have donated blood 25 times.
× The battery can be recharged for five times.	✓ The battery can be recharged five times.

We do something ***three times***, ***ten times***, etc (WITHOUT ***for***).

4

×	✓
× This is my second time to visit England.	✓ This is the second time (that) I have visited England.

When ***time*** means 'occasion', it is followed by a ***that***-clause. Compare: 'It's ***time to stop*** work and go home.'

5

×	✓
× On the next time you see her, give her my regards.	✓ The next time you see her, give her my regards.

We say ***the first time***, ***the second time***, etc (WITHOUT ***on***).

tired **801**

× I'm tired to hear the same old excuses.	√ I'm tired of hearing the same old excuses.

We say that a person is ***tired of*** (***doing***) something.

to: preposition **802**

1

× I look forward to receive your next letter. × She objected to have to wait so long.	√ I look forward to receiving your next letter. √ She objected to having to wait so long.

To has two different functions. Sometimes it is an infinitive marker: 'I should like ***to know*** what you think.'

At other times it is a preposition and takes an ***-ing*** form, NOT an infinitive: 'She has resigned herself ***to living*** alone.'

In the following phrases, ***to*** is a preposition:

> ***be/get accustomed to***, ***face up to***, ***get down to***, ***get round to***, ***keep to***, ***lead up to***, ***look forward to***, ***object to***, ***own up to***, ***resign (oneself) to***, ***resort to***, ***sink to***, ***take to*** ('It's amazing how quickly the child ***took to*** swimming'), ***be/get used to***, ***in addition to***, ***owing to***, ***subject to***, ***with regard to***, ***with a view to***.

⇨ 837

2

× I ran to downstairs and opened the front door. × We have a small house next to a lake and we go to there every summer.	√ I ran downstairs and opened the front door. √ We have a small house next to a lake and we go there every summer.

After verbs of motion (e.g. 'go', 'run'), we do not normally use ***to*** before adverbs of place (e.g. *here*, *there*, *inside*, *home*, *downstairs*, *overseas*):

> They took me ***upstairs*** to see their new bathroom.
> We often go ***overseas*** for our holidays.
> It was a nice day and so I decided to walk ***home***.

3

× Some road signs are difficult to the driver to understand.	√ Some road signs are difficult for the driver to understand.

We introduce the subject of a ***to***-clause with ***for***: 'It was too dark ***for me*** to see anything.' 'It would be better ***for you*** to stay at home today.'

4

× She walked to me and asked me my name.	√ She walked up to me and asked me my name.

If someone comes towards us and stops in front of us, they come ***up to*** us, ***over to*** us or ***across to*** us. Compare: 'She always ***comes to*** me for help.'

5

× The policeman got out of the car and started coming to me.	√ The policeman got out of the car and started coming towards me.

When we are talking about direction, we use ***towards***. We use ***to*** for destination. Compare: 'The vehicle was last seen travelling ***towards*** Glasgow.' 'How long will it take to drive ***to*** Glasgow?'

toast 803

× We had a very light breakfast – just a cup of coffee and a toast.	√ We had a very light breakfast – just a cup of coffee and a piece of toast.

Like ***bread***, ***toast*** is an uncountable noun and is not used with ***a/an***. Instead of saying 'a toast', we say 'a piece/slice of toast'. ⇨ 2.1–2

too 804

1

× He was too ill that he couldn't get out of bed.	√ He was too ill to get out of bed. √ He was so ill that he couldn't get out of bed.
× She shouted too loudly that the children began to cry.	√ She shouted so loudly that the children began to cry.

After a ***too***-phrase, we can use a ***to***-infinitive clause (but NOT a ***that***-clause of result): 'The suitcase was ***too heavy*** + (for me) ***to lift***.'

We use a ***that***-clause of result after a phrase beginning with ***so*** or ***such***: 'The suitcase was ***so heavy*** + ***that I couldn't lift it***.' 'It was ***such a heavy suitcase*** + ***that I couldn't lift it***.'

2

× It was a too difficult question.	√ The question was too difficult.

Too is normally used before predicative adjectives: 'The table was ***too small***.' 'He is ***too quick*** (to criticize people).'

We do not use ***too*** before an adjective that is followed by a noun. In this position, we use ***very***: 'It was a ***very difficult question***.' However, ***very*** does not have the same meaning as ***too***. ⇨ .3 below

In formal styles we sometimes use the structure: ***too*** + adjective + ***a/an*** + noun: 'It was ***too*** difficult ***a*** question to answer.'

3

×	✓
× My new shoes were too expensive.	✓ My new shoes were very expensive.
× I was too frightened but Laila just laughed.	✓ I was very frightened but Laila just laughed.

If something is ***too*** expensive, we do not buy it. When we use ***too*** before an adjective or adverb, we mean 'to an excessive degree' or 'to a degree that has a negative result'. Compare:

We arrived ***too*** late and missed the train.
We arrived ***very*** late but we still caught the train.

The question was ***too*** difficult and I couldn't answer it.
The question was ***very*** difficult, but I managed to answer it.

Too many and ***too much*** are used in the same way. Compare: 'Our new typist makes ***too many*** mistakes.' (= more than we can accept) 'Our new typist makes ***a lot of*** mistakes.' (= more than we expect)

4

×	✓
× She was too shocked to say something.	✓ She was too shocked to say anything.

⇨ 733.4

5

×	✓
× I am almost too old to apply for the job and my lack of qualifications doesn't help too.	✓ I am almost too old to apply for the job and my lack of qualifications doesn't help either.

In negative contexts we use ***either***, NOT ***too***.

⇨ 53.2

too: wrongly omitted — 805

×	✓
× I was tired to walk any further.	✓ I was too tired to walk any further.

Before a ***to***-clause which expresses a negative result ('I could not walk any further'), we use ***too*** + adjective/adverb: 'She is ***too ill*** + to go to work.' 'He is still ***too young*** + to go to school.'

too many — 806

1

×	✓
× Our team did well last season; we had too many good players.	✓ Our team did well last season; we had a lot of good players.

⇨ 804.3

2

×	✓
× I can't go out because I have too many work to do.	✓ I can't go out because I have too much work to do.

⇨ 640.3

too much 807

1

×	✓
In my opinion, these people are too much confident in man's abilities.	In my opinion, these people are too confident in man's abilities. In my opinion, these people have too much confidence in man's abilities.

We use (*far/much*) ***too much*** before a noun. Before an adjective or adverb, we use (*far/much*) ***too***. Compare: 'In my opinion, these people have ***too much*** money.' 'In my opinion, these people are ***too*** rich.'

2

×	✓
For each photograph that is accepted, I get too much money.	For each photograph that is accepted, I get a lot of money.

⇨ 804.3

3

×	✓
Where I live, there are too much factories.	Where I live, there are too many factories.

⇨ 640.3

traffic 808

×	✓
There is always a heavy traffic in the city centre.	There is always heavy traffic in the city centre.

Traffic is an uncountable noun and is not used with ***a/an***. ⇨ 2.1

training 809

×	✓
Some of the junior staff require further trainings.	Some of the junior staff require further training.

Training is an uncountable noun and does not have a plural form.

translate 810

×	✓
Her novels have been translated to many languages.	Her novels have been translated into many languages.

We ***translate*** something ***into*** another language.

transport 811

× Unless there is a better public transport, the number of cars will continue to increase.	√ Unless there is better public transport, the number of cars will continue to increase.

Transport is an uncountable noun and is not used with ***a/an***. ⇨ 2.1

travel 812

× During his travel in the Far East, he caught malaria.	√ During his travels in the Far East, he caught malaria.

When someone moves from place to place within a region, we talk about their ***travels***. This is a plural noun and refers to a number of trips or journeys.
⇨ 603

trouble 813

× I hope that this inquiry will not cause you any troubles.	√ I hope that this inquiry will not cause you any trouble.

When ***trouble*** means 'extra work and inconvenience', it is an uncountable noun and does not have a plural form.

We use the plural noun ***troubles*** to refer to someone's personal problems: 'Having managed to pay her debts, she thought that all her ***troubles*** were over.' We also use ***troubles*** to refer to political or social conflict: 'Whether this new agreement will put an end to the ***troubles*** in the Middle East remains to be seen.'

trousers 814

× My new trouser was covered in white paint.	√ My new trousers were covered in white paint.

Trousers is a plural noun. ⇨ 603

try 815

1

× If it isn't sweet enough, try to add a little sugar.	√ If it isn't sweet enough, try adding a little sugar.

When we attempt to do something, we ***try to do*** it: 'I ***tried to move*** the piano on my own, but it was too heavy.'

When we do something in the hope that it will improve a situation, we ***try doing*** it: 'If your hair is very dry, ***try using*** a different shampoo.'

2

×	✓
× I tryed to apologize but she refused to listen.	√ I tried to apologize but she refused to listen.

Try (infinitive), ***tried*** (past simple), ***tried*** (past participle). ⇨ 666.2

type of 816

1

×	✓
× The manager said that the shop was not responsible for these type of faults.	√ The manager said that the shop was not responsible for these types of fault/s.

⇨ 436.1

2

×	✓
× This type of shoes is made of pure leather.	√ This type of shoe is made of pure leather. √ Shoes of this type are made of pure leather.

⇨ 436.2

UK 817

×	✓
× How long did you stay in UK?	√ How long did you stay in the UK?

⇨ 783.10

uncountable nouns 818

1

×	✓
× People should not leave their rubbishes in the street. × We offer a full range of laboratory equipments.	√ People should not leave their rubbish in the street. √ We offer a full range of laboratory equipment.

A noun with an uncountable meaning (e.g. *rubbish*, *equipment*, *furniture*) does not have a plural form.
For information about meanings which are uncountable, ⇨ 529

2

×	✓
× I love the smell of a fresh bread. × They couldn't give me a detailed information. × We need another information before we can reach a decision. × I can't go out because I have too many work to do.	√ I love the smell of fresh bread. √ They couldn't give me any detailed information. √ We need more information before we can reach a decision. √ I can't go out because I have too much work to do.

Uncountable nouns cannot be used with determiners which have a singular or plural meaning. These include: ***a/an***, ***another***, ***both***, ***each***, ***few***, ***two***, ***several***, ***many***, ***these/those***.

Determiners that are commonly used with uncountable nouns include: ***some/any***, ***the***, ***this/that***, ***all***, ***enough***, ***less***, ***little***, ***more***, ***most***, ***much***, ***no***. The use of ***a/an*** with an uncountable noun is a particularly common error.

⇨ 2.1–2

3

×	✓
× The government's primary goal is to reduce the poverty.	✓ The government's primary goal is to reduce poverty.
× You cannot leave the country without a special permission.	✓ You cannot leave the country without special permission.

We do not use a determiner (e.g. *the*, *a/an*) before an uncountable noun which has general reference:

Music often helps me to relax.
She has a special interest in ***history***.
Plants will not grow without ***light*** and ***water***.

A particularly common error is the use of ***the*** before uncountable nouns that are the names of general concepts, e.g. *poverty*, *education*, *jealousy*. Compare: '***Poverty*** can cause a family to disintegrate.' 'Chapter Two deals with ***the poverty of single-parent families***.'

We use ***the*** with an uncountable noun only when it has specific reference.

⇨ 782.3

4

×	✓
× The cargo handling equipment are mostly of Japanese origin.	✓ The cargo handling equipment is mostly of Japanese origin.

After an uncountable noun ('equipment'), the verb is always singular.

understand 819

1

×	✓
× She was obviously not understanding you.	✓ She obviously didn't understand you.

Understand is not used in progressive tenses. ⇨ 627.3

2

×	✓
× As you understand, I don't have very much free time.	✓ As you know, I don't have very much free time.

Understand is not normally used in a comment clause at the beginning of a sentence. Compare: 'The owners may not agree to sell the house, ***you understand***.'

Note the common exception: '***As I understand it***, the owners have decided not to sell the house after all.'

underwear 820

× An increasing number of clothes designers are specializing in underwears.	√ An increasing number of clothes designers are specializing in underwear.

Underwear is an uncountable noun and does not have a plural form.

unique 821

× Her first novel displays a very unique sense of humour.	√ Her first novel displays a unique sense of humour.

When ***unique*** means 'the only one of its kind', it is ungradable and cannot be used with *more*, *very*, *rather*, etc. ⇨ 15.4

Note that nowadays, especially in informal styles, many people use ***unique*** as a gradable adjective meaning 'unusual' or 'extraordinary': 'The way he'd arranged the garden was ***rather unique***.'

Some careful users consider this to be incorrect.

unit 822

× Two units of secondhand air-conditioners for sale.	√ Two secondhand air-conditioners for sale.

We can use ***unit*** as a unit noun only when it is followed by an uncountable noun, e.g. 'How much does ***one unit of electricity*** cost?' ⇨ 823.4

unit nouns 823

1

× Do not put more than two kilos clothes in the machine.	√ Do not put more than two kilos of clothes in the machine.

A unit noun ('kilo') is followed by an ***of***-phrase: 'two litres of milk', 'eight ounces of butter', 'three packets of envelopes', 'a pocketful of loose change'.

⇨ .2 below

2

× Only a handful people managed to finish the race.	√ Only a handful of people managed to finish the race.

We can say 'a few people' (determiner + noun) but we cannot say 'a handful people'. ***Handful***, ***spoonful***, ***fistful***, etc, are unit nouns and are followed by an ***of***-phrase: 'a spoonful of sugar', 'two handfuls of rice'.

3

× Drink large quantity of water and seek medical attention immediately.	√ Drink large quantities of water and seek medical attention immediately.

When we use ***quantity*** as a unit noun, we can say *a (large/small) quantity of* or *(large/small) quantities of* (plural), but not 'quantity of'. ***Amount*** is used in the same way.

4

× The two pieces of cracked tiles were replaced.	√ The two cracked tiles were replaced.

We can say 'two pieces of bread' but we cannot say 'two pieces of cracked tiles'. ***Piece*** is used only with uncountable nouns: 'a piece of cheese', 'three pieces of paper'. Unit nouns which are used only with uncountable nouns include: ***bit***, ***drop***, ***knob***, ***lump***, ***piece***, ***pinch***, ***pool***, ***scrap***, ***sheet***, ***shred***, ***slice***, ***speck***, ***spot***, ***trace***, ***unit***. Examples: 'a pinch of salt', 'two slices of bread', 'ten sheets of paper', 'a hundred units of electricity'.

5

× The two sheets of writing paper was still on her desk.	√ The two sheets of writing paper were still on her desk.

The verb agrees with the unit noun ('sheets'), not the noun in the ***of***-phrase. Compare: 'The ***sheet*** of writing paper ***was*** still on her desk.'

United Kingdom 824

× In parts of United Kingdom there is a lot of unemployment.	√ In parts of the United Kingdom there is a lot of unemployment.

⇨ 783.10

United States 825

× I would love to visit United States.	√ I would love to visit the United States.

⇨ 783.9–10

university 826

1

× When I leave school, I want to go to a university.	√ When I leave school, I want to go to university.

We use ***a***, ***the***, etc, only when we are talking about a particular university: 'Boston has ***a*** very good ***university***.' 'Does this bus go to ***the university***?'

⇨ 532.2

2

× My brother is studying at the Hull University.	√ My brother is studying at Hull University. √ My brother is studying at the University of Hull.

When we put the place name first, we do not use ***the***: 'Hull University.' We use ***the*** when the place name comes last (in an ***of***-phrase): 'the University of Hull'.

⇨ 782.10

unless 827

1

× He refuses to invite her again unless she will apologize.	√ He refuses to invite her again unless she apologizes.

⇨ 163.2

2

× It is impossible to obtain a credit card unless you do not have a steady income.	√ It is impossible to obtain a credit card unless you have a steady income.

Unless means 'if … not'. Compare: 'It is impossible to obtain a credit card *if* you *do not* have a steady income.'

3

× She said that unless if he moved the car, she would call the police.	√ She said that unless he moved the car, she would call the police.

We can begin a clause with ***unless*** or with ***if***, but not with both of them. Note the alternative: 'She said that *if* he didn't move the car, she would call the police.'

unlikely 828

× It is unlikely for the meeting to end before twelve.	√ It is unlikely that the meeting will end before twelve.

In *it*-sentences, ***unlikely*** is followed by a ***that***-clause.

until/till 829

1

× I shall not know what I am doing next year until I will get my results.	√ I shall not know what I am doing next year until I get/have got my results.

⇨ 25

2

× I was told to return to the office until 4 p.m.	√ I was told to return to the office by 4 p.m.

When we mention a deadline, we normally use ***by***: 'Applications must reach our office ***by*** Wednesday 12th March.' (= no later than Wednesday 12th March) Compare: 'I waited ***until*** 2 p.m. and then I went home.'

3

× Until now I still like the song.	√ I still like the song.

We do not use ***until now*** with ***still***. As a time adverb, ***still*** means 'up to now'. However, if we wanted to express a strong sense of surprise, we could say: '*Even now*, I ***still*** like the song.'

upstairs 830

× We carried him to upstairs and laid him on a bed.	√ We carried him upstairs and laid him on a bed.

⇨ 802.2

us 831

× At the party we met some old friends of us.	√ At the party we met some old friends of ours.

⇨ 590.2

USA 832

× My first computer was made in USA.	√ My first computer was made in the USA.

⇨ 783.9–10

use 833

1

× My grandfather still remembers the time when most people use to come here by ship.	√ My grandfather still remembers the time when most people used to come here by ship.

When we are talking about something that happened repeatedly in the past, or about a past situation that lasted a long time, we use ***used to***: 'Before I got married, I ***used to*** think that men were childish. Now I know they are.'

2

× The water seems very cold at first, but after a few minutes you get use to it.	√ The water seems very cold at first, but after a few minutes you get used to it.

After a while we ***get used to*** (doing) something that was at first strange or unpleasant: 'It took me a long time to ***get used to*** working on a Saturday.'

3

× It is no use to speak to someone who refuses to listen.	√ It is no use speaking to someone who refuses to listen.

If something is pointless, it is ***no use doing/having*** it: 'It's *no use having* a camera if you don't have a film.'

⇨ 605.3

used to 834

1

× Before they were caught, they were used to live in the jungle. × The school was used to be called St George's.	√ Before they were caught, they used to live in the jungle. √ The school used to be called St George's.

It is very easy to confuse ***be/get used to*** (***doing***) something and ***used to do*** something.

When we are talking about something that happened repeatedly in the past, or about a past situation that lasted a long time, we use ***used to*** (WITHOUT ***be/get***): 'When we were children, we *used to* spend a lot of time with our grandparents.'

We use ***be/get used to*** when we mean 'accustomed to' something: 'I'*m used to having* milk in my tea.'

Compare: 'Until recently, these young apes *used to live* in the jungle and they *are* still not *used to living* with people.'

2

! Did he really used to be a chef?	√ Did he really use to be a chef?

To refer to a past habit, we always use the spelling ***used to*** in affirmative sentences: 'People *used to* think that the earth was flat.'

In questions and negative/emphatic sentences, however, both ***used to*** and ***use to*** are found: '*Did* people really *use(d) to* think that the earth was flat?' 'Nowadays, we know that the earth is round, but we *didn't use(d) to*.'

Although both spellings appear in everyday usage, ***use to*** is generally preferred. Furthermore, some people insist that ***did/didn't*** must be followed by an infinitive and therefore regard ***used to*** as incorrect.

Note that in spoken English the two forms sound exactly the same: /ˈjuːst tə/.

3

× I must admit that I am not used to speak to a machine.	√ I must admit that I am not used to speaking to a machine.

The ***to*** in ***be/get used to*** is a preposition and takes an ***-ing*** form: 'I shall never ***get used to living*** in a polluted environment.'

Compare: 'Before coming to England, my father ***used to manage*** a restaurant.'

⇨ 802.1

usual 835

× In some countries it is usual that people have a siesta in the afternoon.	√ In some countries it is usual for people to have a siesta in the afternoon.

It is ***usual/unusual*** (***for*** someone) ***to do*** something: 'It's ***unusual for*** Brian ***to arrive*** late.'

vegetable 836

× My parents grow their own vegetable.	√ My parents grow their own vegetables.

Vegetable is a countable noun, usually plural: 'Fruit and ***vegetables*** are good for you.'

verbs: after a preposition 837

× I look forward to see you again. × Instead of to buy books, I borrow them from the library. × My grandfather didn't know about my parents wanted a divorce.	√ I look forward to seeing you again. √ Instead of buying books, I borrow them from the library. √ My grandfather didn't know about my parents wanting a divorce.

When a verb comes after a preposition, we always use the *-ing* form:

I'm not happy ***about leaving*** them alone in the house.
He tried to prevent me ***from buying*** it.
She took the purse ***without*** even ***thanking*** me.

To test whether a word or phrase is a preposition, substitute the words that come next with ***that***. If the sentence is still grammatical, the word or phrase is a preposition: 'I look forward ***to that***.' (***to*** is a preposition here) 'I look forward ***to seeing*** you again.' (preposition + *-ing form*)

If the sentence is no longer grammatical, the word or phrase is not a preposition: × I'd like ***to that***.' (***to*** is NOT a preposition here) 'I'd like ***to see*** you again.' (*to*-infinitive)

Remember that a preposition can consist of one word (e.g. *about, by, despite*), two words (e.g. *owing to, because of, instead of*), three words (e.g. *as well as, in addition to, in favour of, in spite of*), or four words (e.g. *in the event of, for the sake of, with a view to*).

Note also that the preposition may be separated from the verb: 'I'm tired ***of*** her always ***complaining*** about everything.' 'They are ***against*** visitors ***being*** allowed in without a permit.'

verb patterns 838

1

×	✓
× I tried to go to sleep but the man kept disturbing.	✓ I tried to go to sleep but the man kept disturbing me.

We can say 'The train ***arrived*** at six o'clock' but we cannot say 'The train ***reached*** at six o'clock'. ***Reach*** must have an object: 'The train reached ***Frankfurt/the station*** at six o'clock.'

Verbs like ***reach*** are called 'transitive'. Verbs like ***arrive***, which are used without an object, are called 'intransitive.'

Note that some verbs can be used either with or without an object: 'They are ***playing*** (badminton) in the garden.' 'I wish they would stop ***interrupting*** (us).'

Also, some verbs may require an object in one meaning but not in another meaning: 'She ***runs*** her own business.' (TRANSITIVE) 'If you want to catch the bus, you'd better ***run***.' (INTRANSITIVE)

A good dictionary lists all the meanings of a verb, and tells us whether each meaning is transitive, intransitive, or both.

2

×	✓
× During the examination period there is no time to relax and enjoy.	✓ During the examination period there is no time to relax and enjoy yourself.
× I should like to familiarize with the latest teaching methods.	✓ I should like to familiarize myself with the latest teaching methods.

Enjoy is a transitive verb and must have an object. When the subject and object of a transitive verb refer to the same person or thing, we use a reflexive pronoun as the object, e.g. *myself, herself, themselves*: 'She tripped and fell, but ***she*** didn't ***hurt herself***.'

Sometimes, especially in imperative clauses, the subject is not actually mentioned: 'Don't forget to ***introduce yourself*** to everybody.'

Verbs which often have a reflexive pronoun as object, sometimes called 'reflexive verbs', include:

> ***absent***[1], ***adapt***, ***ask***, ***avail***[1], ***behave***, ***blame***, ***busy***[1], ***compose***, ***content***[1], ***cut***, ***deceive***, ***dress***, ***dry***, ***enjoy***, ***excel***, ***exert***, ***express***, ***familiarize***, ***fool***, ***free***, ***hurt***, ***injure***, ***introduce***, ***kill***, ***look after***, ***please***, ***pride***[1], ***wash***
>
> [1] The object of these verbs is always a reflexive pronoun.

3

×	√
× She doesn't like when people criticize her.	√ She doesn't like it when people criticize.
× I would appreciate if you could send me the name and address of your agent in France.	√ I would appreciate it if you could send me the name and address of your agent in France.

Like is a transitive verb and must have an object. When the clause lacks a real object, we use ***it*** as an empty object: 'She doesn't like + ***it*** + when people criticize her.' 'You will regret + ***it*** + if anyone finds out.'

The need for ***it*** becomes clear when we turn the two clauses round: × 'When people criticize her, she doesn't ***like***.' 'When people criticize her, she doesn't ***like it***.'

Verbs which often take ***it*** as an empty object include: ***appreciate***, ***enjoy***, ***hate***, ***like***, ***love***, ***regret***.

4

×	√
× Some people find to stop smoking difficult.	√ Some people find it difficult to stop smoking.
× The seating arrangement makes the pupils difficult to talk to each other.	√ The seating arrangement makes it difficult for the pupils to talk to each other.

Some verbs may be followed by an object + complement:

	VERB	+	OBJECT	+	COMPLEMENT
We	found		the hotel		very comfortable.
The news	made		her		rather sad.

However, if the object is a clause (e.g. 'to stop smoking'), we have to use a different pattern:

	VERB	+	IT	+	COMPLEMENT	+	TO-CLAUSE
He	finds		it		difficult		to stop smoking.
They	made		it		impossible		to leave the company.

If the verb in the ***to***-clause has a subject, we put it into a ***for***-phrase:

	VERB	+	IT	+	COMPLEMENT	+	TO-CLAUSE
They	made		it		impossible		*for Jones* to leave the company.

Verbs that often appear in this pattern include ***believe***, ***consider***, ***find***, ***make***, ***think***.

5

×	√
× I went up to the policeman and gave the wallet I had found.	√ I went up to the policeman and gave him the wallet I had found.

Some transitive verbs have meanings which require two objects, a direct object and an indirect object:

	VERB	INDIRECT OBJECT	DIRECT OBJECT
I	gave	him	the wallet I had found.
She	lent	us	enough money to get home.

Verbs which are often used in this pattern include:

ask, ***book***, ***bring***, ***buy***, ***charge***, ***cost***, ***fetch***, ***get***, ***give***, ***grant***, ***hand***, ***leave*** ('My grandmother left me all her jewellery'), ***lend***, ***make***, ***offer***, ***owe***, ***pass***, ***pay***, ***promise***, ***read***, ***refuse***, ***save***, ***sell***, ***send***, ***show***, ***take***, ***teach***, ***tell***, ***throw***, ***write***

Note that when the indirect object is much longer than the direct object, the direct object comes first:

		DIRECT OBJECT	INDIRECT OBJECT
I	gave	it	to the policeman.
We	bought	hats	for all the children at the party.

When the indirect object comes last, it is introduced by ***to*** or ***for***. ⇨ 387.1

6

×	✓
× The doctor reassured that it was not serious.	✓ The doctor reassured me that it was not serious.
× She replied me that there was no hot water.	✓ She replied that there was no hot water.

After some reporting verbs (e.g. *reassure*) we always mention the 'hearer'. After other reporting verbs (e.g. *reply*), we do not mention the hearer. ⇨ 390.1–2

7

×	✓
× They always ignore that their country attacked us first.	✓ They always ignore the fact that their country attacked us first.

Ignore cannot go immediately in front of a ***that***-clause. It belongs to a small group of verbs which are followed by a noun phrase + ***that***-clause: 'They must ***face*** + ***the fact*** + ***that*** our products are far superior.' 'We cannot ***ignore*** + ***the possibility*** + ***that*** these machines could lose us our jobs.'

The head of the noun phrase is always an abstract noun, e.g. *fact*, *possibility*, *danger*, *belief*, *suspicion*. Note also that the conjunction ***that*** at the beginning of the ***that***-clause cannot be omitted.

Verbs and verbal expressions often used in this pattern include:

account for, ***allow for***, ***comment on***, ***complain about***, ***dwell on/upon***, ***face*** (= accept), ***ignore***, ***object to***, ***pay attention to***, ***recognize***, ***reject***, ***substantiate***, ***support***

verb 1 + verb 2 839

1

×	✓
× Some students cannot afford paying these prices.	✓ Some students cannot afford to pay these prices.
× I enjoy to speak foreign languages.	✓ I enjoy speaking foreign languages.
× She never lets other children to play with her toys.	✓ She never lets other children play with her toys.

A main verb is often followed by a second verb. The second verb may come immediately after the first verb:

I ***want*** + ***to write*** a letter.
I ***refuse*** + ***to listen*** to any more excuses.
We both ***enjoyed*** + ***seeing*** you again.

On the other hand, the two verbs may be separated:

I ***found*** + your younger brother + ***sitting*** in the library.
His doctor ***advised*** + him + ***to go*** on a diet.
We ***spent*** + the whole holiday + ***sitting*** on the beach.

The second verb can be either a ***to***-infinitive, a bare infinitive, or an ***-ing*** form. The choice of form depends on the first verb, which is the 'control unit'. Compare:

They ***forced*** me ***to wait*** outside.
They ***made*** me ***wait*** outside.
They ***kept*** me ***waiting*** outside.

Force is followed by a ***to***-infinitive, ***make*** by a bare infinitive, and ***keep*** by an ***-ing*** form.

In some cases, the first verb can be followed by either of two different forms. The problem is knowing which form is correct in a particular context. Compare:

I ***hate*** + not ***having*** anyone to talk to.
I would ***hate*** + ***to hurt*** her feelings.

I wish I could ***stop*** + ***smoking***.
I ***stopped*** + ***to buy*** a newspaper.

They ***made*** + him + ***wait*** for over an hour.
He was ***made*** + ***to wait*** for over an hour.

In this book, common errors in the use of verb + verb combinations are shown at the entry for the first verb. If you cannot find the verb that you are looking for, look it up in a good dictionary.

2

×	√
× The police made everyone to leave the building immediately.	√ The police made everyone leave the building immediately.
× I would rather to stay indoors until the rain stops.	√ I would rather stay indoors until the rain stops.

The verbs ***let***, ***make*** and ***have*** (when used as a causative verb) are followed by an object + bare infinitive, NOT a ***to***-infinitive:

She wouldn't ***let*** + me + ***read*** the letter.
First of all, they ***make*** + you + ***fill*** in a long form. ⇨ .4 below
I ***had*** + him + ***wait*** outside until I was ready.

Had better and ***would rather*** also take a bare infinitive: 'I think you ***had better*** + ***apologize*** to her.' 'I ***would rather*** + ***live*** in Leeds than in London.'

3

×	√
× I heard someone to say that the driver was drunk.	√ I heard someone say/saying that the driver was drunk.

In active clauses, ***see***, ***watch***, ***feel***, ***hear***, ***overhear***, ***notice*** and ***observe*** may be followed by an object + bare infinitive or by an object + ***-ing*** form but NOT by an object + ***to***-infinitive. ⇨ .5 below

Note, however, that a ***to***-infinitive is sometimes possible in passive clauses: 'She was heard ***to say/saying*** that the chairman should resign.' ⇨ .4 below

4

× We were made leave our bags at the front of the shop.	√ We were made to leave our bags at the front of the shop.
× He was heard say that he intended to resign.	√ He was heard to say/saying that he intended to resign.

In active clauses, some verbs are followed by an object + bare infinitive: 'She ***made*** + him + ***rewrite*** the letter.' 'Her brother ***helped*** her ***tie/to tie*** her shoelaces.'

In passive clauses, however, these verbs cannot be followed by a bare infinitive. ***Make*** and ***help*** are followed by a ***to***-infinitive: 'He was ***made*** + ***to rewrite*** the letter.' 'She was ***helped*** + ***to tie*** her shoelaces.'

See and ***hear*** are followed by a ***to***-infinitive or *-ing* form: 'He has been ***seen*** + ***to leave/leaving*** the office at two o'clock.' 'She was ***heard*** + ***to say/saying*** that the chairman should resign.'

⇨ .5 below

5

! All of a sudden, I felt something hard hitting me in the back.	√ All of a sudden, I felt something hard hit me in the back.
! I saw the mouse popping back into the hole.	√ I saw the mouse pop back into the hole.

See, ***watch***, ***feel***, ***hear***, ***overhear***, ***notice*** and ***observe*** may be followed by an object + bare infinitive or by an object + *-ing* form. However, the two patterns have slightly different meanings.

A bare infinitive suggests that the action happens just once: 'I saw the car ***crash*** into a lamppost.' 'I heard the clock ***strike*** one.'

An *-ing* form suggests that the action happens repeatedly or over a length of time: 'I could hear someone ***drilling*** holes in the wall.'

A bare infinitive also suggests that the action is observed from start to finish: 'I watched him ***sign*** the contract.'

An *-ing* form suggests that the action is observed, but not necessarily from start to finish: 'I watched the workmen ***restoring*** the cathedral.'

6

× I hate to live here. I can't wait to go back home.	√ I hate living here. I can't wait to go back home.
× I would like asking you a few more questions.	√ I would like to ask you a few more questions.

Hate, ***dread***, ***like***, ***love*** and ***prefer*** may be followed by a ***to***-infinitive or by an *-ing* form. However, the two patterns are used in slightly different ways.

When we are talking about an existing situation or something which happens repeatedly, we normally use an *-ing* form: 'I ***hate*** + ***living*** here.' 'I ***like*** + ***going*** for long walks.'

When we are talking about an imaginary situation or a future event, we normally use a ***to***-infinitive: 'I would ***hate*** + ***to live*** in a big city.' 'Would you ***like*** + ***to go*** for a walk?'

7

× When he saw the teacher looking at him, he stopped to cheat.	√ When he saw the teacher looking at him, he stopped cheating.

Stop, ***go on***, ***remember***, ***forget***, ***regret*** and ***try*** are followed by a ***to***-infinitive for one meaning and by an *-ing* form for another meaning. Information about the use of these verbs can be found at their individual entries.

8

× 'It's starting raining again,' she said. × The government has begun considering the possibility of further tax relief.	√ 'It's starting to rain again,' she said. √ The government has begun to consider the possibility of further tax relief.

Begin, ***start***, ***continue*** and ***cease*** can be followed by a ***to***-infinitive or by an ***-ing*** form. Very often, it doesn't matter which form we use, e.g. 'Everybody started ***to laugh/laughing***.' However, a ***to***-infinitive is more common and there are two situations in which an ***-ing*** form is either unusual or incorrect.

After the ***-ing*** form of ***begin***, ***start***, ***continue*** and ***cease***, we use a *to*-infinitive. We avoid having two ***-ing*** forms together. Compare: 'The grass ***had started*** + ***to turn/turning*** brown.' 'The grass ***was starting*** + ***to turn*** brown.' (NOT ***turning***)

When the following verb refers to a mental activity or to a feeling (e.g. *think*, *understand*, *see*, *realize*, *believe*, *feel*), we normally use a ***to***-infinitive. Compare: 'She ***began to hit/hitting*** me with one of her shoes.' 'I ***began*** + ***to think*** she didn't like me. (NOT ***thinking***)

9

× I suggest your wife to talk to the manager.	√ I suggest that your wife should talk to the manager.

We can ***advise*** someone ***to do*** something but we cannot ***suggest*** someone ***to do*** something. When the verb after ***suggest*** has its own subject ('your wife'), ***suggest*** takes a ***that***-clause.

The same rule applies to ***demand***, ***insist*** and ***propose***, with which learners tend to make the same error. The ***that***-clause after these verbs normally contains either a modal verb + bare infinitive, or just a bare infinitive: 'I suggest that your wife (***should***) ***talk*** to the manager.'

The main verb in the ***that***-clause can also be finite, especially in British English: 'I suggest that your wife ***talks*** to the manager.'

10

× She felt that she could never to go home again.	√ She felt that she could never go home again.

A modal verb (e.g. *could*, *must*, *should*, *will*) is followed by a bare infinitive, (NOT a *to*-infinitive).

⇨ 495.2

verbs with adverbs 840

× I shall return back to Athens at the end of August.	√ I shall return to Athens at the end of August.

We ***come back*** or ***go back*** to a place, but we ***return*** to a place (WITHOUT ***back***). Verbs like ***return*** which are sometimes used wrongly with an adverb include:

> ***boost*** (NOT ***boost up***), ***continue*** (NOT ***continue on***), ***cut*** (meaning 'reduce'; NOT ***cut down***), ***cope*** (NOT ***cope up***), ***list*** (NOT ***list down/out***), ***lower*** (NOT ***lower down***), ***proceed*** (NOT ***proceed on***), ***raise*** (NOT ***raise up***), ***recall*** (NOT ***recall back***), ***repeat*** (NOT ***repeat again***), ***reply*** (NOT ***reply back***), ***return*** (NOT ***return back***), ***slim*** (NOT ***slim down***)

verbs with prepositions 841

1

× The driver had entered into the opposite lane by mistake.	√ The driver had entered the opposite lane by mistake.
× I always answer to your letters as soon as I can.	√ I always answer your letters as soon as I can.

Some verbs take a preposition while other verbs do not. Compare: 'We ***arrived at*** the station at 3 o'clock.' 'We ***reached*** the station at 3 o'clock.'

Verbs like ***reach*** which do not take a preposition are listed below. The list is not complete. It contains only those verbs which are sometimes used wrongly with an unwanted preposition.

> ***answer*** (NOT ***answer to***)[1], ***approach*** (NOT ***approach to***), ***ask*** (NOT ***ask to***)[1], ***attack*** (NOT ***attack against***), ***discuss*** (NOT ***discuss about***), ***combat*** (NOT ***combat against***), ***comprise*** (NOT ***comprise of***), ***discuss*** (NOT ***discuss about***), ***emphasize*** (NOT ***emphasize on/upon***), ***enter*** (NOT ***enter in/into***)[1], ***explain*** (NOT ***explain about***), ***highlight*** (NOT ***highlight on***), ***investigate*** (NOT ***investigate into***), ***lack*** (NOT ***lack of***), ***leave*** (NOT ***leave from***)[1], ***marry*** (NOT ***marry with***), ***meet*** (NOT ***meet with***)[1], ***mention*** (NOT ***mention about***), ***obey*** (NOT ***obey to***), ***order*** (NOT ***order for***), ***phone*** (NOT ***phone to***), ***reach*** (NOT ***reach at/to***), ***remember*** (NOT ***remember about***)[1], ***report*** (NOT ***report about***)[1], ***request*** (NOT ***request for***), ***resemble*** (NOT ***resemble to***), ***stress*** (NOT ***stress on***), ***telephone*** (NOT ***telephone to***), ***visit*** (NOT ***visit to***)

Note that although these verbs do not take a preposition, many of the corresponding nouns do take a preposition. Compare: 'The police are ***investigating*** the cause of the accident.' 'The police are conducting an ***investigation into*** the cause of the accident.'

[1] These verbs also have meanings which require a preposition e.g. 'The two computer companies have ***entered into*** a new agreement.' These meanings may be found in a good dictionary.

2

×	✓
× Some people object sudden changes. × I'll be lucky if I ever succeed to achieve this ambition.	✓ Some people object to sudden changes. ✓ I'll be lucky if I ever succeed in achieving this ambition.

We ***dislike*** (doing) something but we ***object to*** (doing) something. We ***manage*** to do something but we ***succeed in*** (doing) something. Verbs like ***object*** and ***succeed*** which take a preposition are listed below. The preposition that is sometimes wrongly omitted is shown in brackets.

VERB + PREPOSITION

agree (*with*), ***apologize*** (*to/for*), ***apply*** (*to/for*)[1], ***approve*** (*of*)[1], ***arrive*** (*at/in*), ***ask*** (*for*)[1], ***belong*** (*to*), ***complain*** (*to/about*), ***depart*** (*from*), ***depend*** (*on/upon*), ***dream*** (*about/of*), ***insist*** (*on*), ***listen*** (*to*), ***look*** (*at/for*), ***object*** (*to*), ***participate*** (*in*), ***pay*** (*for*)[1], ***persist*** (*in*), ***refer*** (*to*), ***rely*** (*on*), ***reply*** (*to*), ***succeed*** (*in*), ***sympathize*** (*with*), ***think*** (*about/of*), ***wait*** (*for*), ***write*** (*to*)[1]

[1] These verbs also have meanings for which a preposition is not required, e.g. '***Apply*** the glue evenly to both surfaces.' These meanings may be found in a good dictionary.

3

×	✓
× They will provide you everything you need. × Let us consider some of the factors which discourage these people to get married.	✓ They will provide you with everything you need. ✓ Let us consider some of the factors which discourage these people from getting married.

We ***give*** a person something but we ***provide*** a person ***with*** something. We ***encourage*** a person ***to do*** something but we ***discourage*** a person ***from doing*** something. Verbs like ***provide*** and ***discourage*** which take an object + preposition are listed below.

VERB + OBJECT + PREPOSITION

accuse someone ***of*** (doing) something, ***blame*** someone ***for*** (doing) something, ***congratulate*** someone ***on*** (doing) something, ***deter*** someone ***from*** (doing) something, ***discourage*** someone ***from*** (doing) something, ***dissuade*** someone ***from*** (doing) something, ***excuse*** someone ***for*** (doing) something, ***forgive*** someone ***for*** (doing) something, ***keep*** someone ***from*** (doing) something, ***prevent*** someone ***from*** (doing) something, ***provide*** someone ***with*** something, ***stop*** someone ***from*** (doing) something, ***suspect*** someone ***of*** (doing) something, ***trick*** someone ***into*** doing something

4

×	✓
× These irresponsible people do not care for dropping litter. × Businessmen invest vast amounts on these industries.	✓ These irresponsible people do not care about dropping litter. ✓ Businessmen invest vast amounts in these industries.

Verb + preposition combinations are a common cause of error. The choice of preposition is often a matter of idiom rather than logic.

Verbs of similar meaning often take the same preposition. We ***benefit/profit from*** something, we ***rely/depend on*** someone, and we ***defend/protect/rescue*** someone ***from*** something. On the other hand, although we ***confuse*** someone ***with*** someone else, we ***mistake*** someone ***for*** someone else. We ***agree with*** something, but we ***approve of*** something.

Another difficulty is knowing which preposition to use for a particular meaning. People who have problems try to ***deal with*** them, whereas people who buy and sell motor cars ***deal in*** them. We ***complain of*** a sore throat but we ***complain about*** people who cut down trees.

In this book, errors concerning the choice of preposition after a verb are shown at the entry for the verb. If you cannot find the verb that you are looking for, look it up in a good dictionary, paying particular attention to the examples of usage.

5

× I'm longing for having more news of you.	√ I'm longing to have more news of you.

Most verb + preposition combinations may be followed by an *-ing* form:

She *insists on* + *doing* the job herself.
I don't *believe in* + *wasting* money.
When are we going to *talk about* + *getting* married?

However, we do not use a preposition + *-ing* form if the same meaning can be expressed by a ***to***-infinitive. Compare:

√ I'm *longing for* + a good holiday.
× I'm *longing for* + *having* a good holiday.
√ I'm *longing* + *to have* a good holiday.

√ He has *applied for* + leave.
× He has *applied for* + *going* on leave.
√ He has *applied* + *to go* on leave.

√ I ***helped*** him ***with*** + his homework.
× I ***helped*** him ***with*** + ***doing*** his homework.
√ I ***helped*** him + ***to do*** his homework.

very 842

1

× He was sitting behind a very enormous desk.	√ He was sitting behind an (absolutely) enormous desk.

⇨ 405.1

2

× Your co-operation is very appreciated.	√ Your co-operation is much/greatly appreciated.

⇨ 405.3

3

× His hair was very in need of a good wash.	√ His hair was (very) much in need of a good wash.

⇨ 405.4

4

× He looked very funny that I couldn't help laughing.	√ He looked so funny that I couldn't help laughing.
× It was a very good film that we watched it again.	√ It was such a good film that we watched it again.

Before a clause of result, we normally use a ***so/such*** phrase (NOT ***very***).

⇨ 24.2–3

5

× Unfortunately, I was very old to enter the competition.	√ Unfortunately, I was too old to enter the competition.

Before a *to*-clause, we use ***too*** + adjective: 'Paul is still ***too young to go*** to school.' 'It is never ***too late to apologize*** to someone.'

very much 843

1

× Our new teacher is very much different.	√ Our new teacher is very different.
× They seemed pleased very much to see us.	√ They seemed very pleased to see us.

To intensify an adjective ('different') or a past participle that is used as an adjective ('pleased'), we use ***very***. We use ***very much*** in connection with a verb:

He ***misses*** his parents ***very much***.
I ***don't like*** sweet things ***very much***.
We ***very much look forward*** to seeing you again.

2

× My brother loves music very much and wants to be a musician.	√ My brother loves music and wants to be a musician.

We do not use ***very much*** with verbs which have 'very much' as part of their meaning, e.g. *love*, *adore*, *treasure*.

3

× I like very much playing tennis.	√ I like playing tennis very much.

⇨ 29.6

visit 844

1

× We also want to visit to the British Museum.	√ We also want to visit the British Museum.

We ***visit*** a place, WITHOUT ***to***. Compare: 'We also want to pay ***a visit to*** the British Museum.'

2

× I shall never forget my visit in Hong Kong.	√ I shall never forget my visit to Hong Kong.

We talk about a ***stay in*** a place but a ***visit/trip to*** a place.

wait 845

× I was sitting in a cafe, waiting my friend.	√ I was sitting in a cafe, waiting for my friend.

We ***wait for*** someone or something (to do something).

wake 846

! When I waked up, it was still dark outside.	√ When I woke up, it was still dark outside.

Speakers of British English use ***wake*** (infinitive), ***woke*** (past simple), ***woken*** (past participle). ***Waked*** is used by speakers of American English.

want 847

1

× She doesn't want that you stay in the house on your own.	√ She doesn't want you to stay in the house on your own.

We ***want*** someone ***to do*** something. ***Want*** cannot be followed by a ***that***-clause.

2

× I want for you to give me my money back.	√ I want you to give me my money back.

We ***want someone*** to do something, (NOT ***for*** someone).

3

× These plants will want to be watered once a week.	√ These plants will want watering once a week.

When ***want*** means 'require', it is followed by an ***-ing*** form: 'The engine may ***want stripping*** down.' Compare: 'These plants will ***need watering/to be watered*** once a week.'

4

× There were so many flies in the kitchen that I was not wanting to eat anything.	√ There were so many flies in the kitchen that I didn't want to eat anything.

Want is not used in progressive tenses.

⇨ 627.3

-ware **848**

× Some computer softwares can be very expensive.	√ Some computer software can be very expensive.

Nouns ending in ***-ware*** are uncountable and do not have a plural form.

warn **849**

× She warned him don't go near the dog.	√ She warned him not to go near the dog.

⇨ 388

was **850**

1

× Nobody told me that you was waiting for me. × I didn't know you was interested in tropical fish.	√ Nobody told me that you were waiting for me. √ I didn't know you were interested in tropical fish.

When the subject is ***you***, we always use ***were***:

SINGULAR	PLURAL
I was	we were
you were	you were
he/she/it was	they were

2

! If the country's economy was to improve, many of these social problems would disappear.	√ If the country's economy were to improve, many of these social problems would disappear.

In formal styles, when we are talking about an unreal situation, we use ***were*** instead of ***was***. In such cases, the clause normally begins with ***if***, ***though***, ***as if*** or ***as though***: '***If she were*** to resign, the company would collapse.' 'She treated me ***as if I were*** a complete stranger.'

In informal styles, both ***was*** and ***were*** are common. However, some careful users insist that ***was*** is always incorrect.

water 851

×	√
× Plants cannot grow without some water.	√ Plants cannot grow without water.
× I have never liked washing in a cold water.	√ I have never liked washing in cold water.

Water is an uncountable noun. When it has general reference, it is used without a determiner.

⇨ 2.1

way 852

×	√
× I don't like his superior way to talk to people.	√ I don't like his superior way of talking to people.

When ***way*** means 'style', it is normally followed by ***of*** + *-ing*: 'The flowers are just his *way of saying* thank you.'

wealth 853

×	√
× One of the richest men in Hong Kong has decided to share some of his wealths.	√ One of the richest men in Hong Kong has decided to share some of his wealth.

Wealth is an uncountable noun and does not have a plural form.

we 854

×	√
× Some of their players were much taller than we.	√ Some of their players were much taller than us/than we were.

⇨ 590.7

wear 855

1

×	√
× My brother is quite tall and is wearing glasses.	√ My brother is quite tall and wears glasses.

When we are talking about something that a person normally ***wears***, we use the present simple tense. Compare: 'I usually *wear* glasses, but today I'*m wearing* contact lenses.'

⇨ 619.3

2

× I weared the skirt just three times.	√ I wore the skirt just three times.

Wear (infinitive), ***wore*** (past simple), ***worn*** (past participle).

wear/-wear 856

× All the children's wears have been reduced.	√ All the children's wear has been reduced.

Wear is an uncountable noun and does not have a plural form. Note that nouns ending in ***-wear*** are also uncountable, e.g. *footwear, swimwear.*

weather 857

× What a terrible weather, I thought, as the rain fell on my head.	√ What terrible weather, I thought, as the rain fell on my head.

Weather is an uncountable noun and is not used with ***a/an***. ⇨ 2.1

week 858

× I had just returned to work after a two weeks holiday.	√ I had just returned to work after a two-week holiday.

⇨ 533.3

welcomed 859

× Bring as many friends as you like. Everyone is welcomed.	√ Bring as many friends as you like. Everyone is welcome.

⇨ 577.2

welfare 860

× He has spent his whole life looking after the welfares of the disabled.	√ He has spent his whole life looking after the welfare of the disabled.

Welfare is an uncountable noun and does not have a plural form.

well 861

×	✓
× The child's table manners were not very well.	✓ The child's table manners were not very good.
× I was in a really well mood that day.	✓ I was in a really good mood that day.

Well is normally an adverb: 'She plays tennis very ***well***.' When used as an adjective, it means 'in good health': 'She doesn't feel ***well***.'

were 862

×	✓
× The letter were sent to the wrong address.	✓ The letter was sent to the wrong address.

After first and third person singular subjects, we normally use ***was***.

Note that in certain types of subordinate clause, ***were*** may be used instead of ***was***. These clauses always express an unreal situation: 'If I ***was/were*** in your position, I'd apply.' 'He wishes he ***was/were*** ten years younger. ⇨ 850

what 863

1

×	✓
× I asked him what did he want.	✓ I asked him what he wanted.
× I don't know what am I going to do.	✓ I don't know what I am going to do.

⇨ 389.1

2

×	✓
× Children should eat things what are good for them.	✓ Children should eat things that are good for them.

What is not used as a relative pronoun and cannot be used instead of ***that***, ***which*** or ***who***. Compare: 'Do you know ***what*** she wants?' 'Do you know the man ***that*** she is talking to?'

3

!	✓
! We cannot decide what trees to plant.	✓ We cannot decide which trees to plant.

When the number of possibilities or alternatives is restricted, we use ***which***: '***Which*** would you prefer, tea or coffee?' '***Which*** European countries have you visited?'

We use ***what*** when there is no restriction: '***What*** family would ever choose to live in a house like that?'

In informal styles, many people use ***what*** instead of ***which***: '***What*** would you prefer, tea or coffee?' Careful users regard this usage as ungrammatical.

4

×	✓
× What happen to the balloon when you let it go?	√ What happens to the balloon when you let it go?
× There is no need to repeat what have been said already.	√ There is no need to repeat what has been said already.

When ***what*** is the subject of a clause, it takes a singular verb. Compare:

What are you making? (OBJECT)
What have they been doing? (OBJECT)
What makes you think that you are right? (SUBJECT)

In the first two questions, ***what*** is the object and does not affect the verb. In the last question, ***what*** is the subject and the verb has to agree with it.

when — 864

1

×	✓
× Please tell me when can I come and see you.	√ Please tell me when I can come and see you.

⇨ 389.1

2

×	✓
× When I shall come to see you, I'll bring my guitar with me.	√ When I come to see you, I'll bring my guitar with me.

⇨ 25

3

×	✓
× When arriving home, I wrote down everything I had seen.	√ On arriving home, I wrote down everything I had seen.

When two actions happen at the same time or when one action happens very soon after the other, we use ***on/upon*** + ***-ing***.

We use ***when*** if the ***-ing*** form has a progressive meaning, e.g. '***When filling*** in the form, remember to use capital letters.' (= when you are filling in the form)

⇨ 550.1

whenever — 865

×	✓
× Whenever you'll need to copy something, you can use this machine.	√ Whenever you need to copy something, you can use this machine.

⇨ 25

where 866

1

× Can you tell me where is the gymnasium?	√ Can you tell me where the gymnasium is?

⇨ 389.1

2

× I drove straight to the hotel where she was staying at.	√ I drove straight to the hotel where she was staying.

⇨ 668.1

3

× I spent the next week in Perth, where Patrick lives there.	√ I spent the next week in Perth, where Patrick lives.

In a relative clause, we do not use ***there*** after the relative adverb ***where***.

4

× We went back to her house, where was much warmer.	√ We went back to her house, where it was much warmer.

Where is an adverb. It can never be the subject (or object) of the verb in a relative clause. Compare: 'We went back to her house. It was much warmer ***there***.' 'We went back to her house, ***where*** it was much warmer.'

whether 867

× Please let me know whether you are still coming to England or you have changed your plans.	√ Please let me know whether you are still coming to England or whether you have changed your plans.

When two linked clauses have different subjects or verb forms, we use ***or whether*** before the second clause (NOT ***or*** on its own.)
Compare:

I don't know ***whether*** I should buy a car ***or*** (***whether*** I should) hire one.
I don't know ***whether*** I should buy a car ***or whether*** Mary should buy one.

I wonder ***whether*** he has bought a car ***or*** (***whether*** he has) hired one.
I wonder ***whether*** he has bought a car ***or whether*** he is travelling by train.

We cannot say: 'I wonder ***whether*** he is leaving tonight ***or*** he will stay until tomorrow.'

which 868

1

×	✓
× He asked me which football team did I support.	✓ He asked me which football team I supported.

⇨ 389.1

2

×	✓
× The girl which sits next to me in class comes from Brazil.	✓ The girl who/that sits next to me in class comes from Brazil.
× My uncle has six children, all of which are still single.	✓ My uncle has six children, all of whom are still single.

In relative clauses, we use ***which*** to refer to things, NOT to people.
To refer to people, we normally use ***who*** or ***that*** (⇨ 781.1), but after a preposition (*of*, *with*, *from*, etc), we use ***whom***.

3

×	✓
× Each team had to build a model aeroplane which weight had to be less than 10 kilos.	✓ Each team had to build a model aeroplane whose weight had to be less than 10 kilos.
	✓ Each team had to build a model aeroplane, the weight of which had to be less than 10 kilos.

When we need a *wh*-word meaning 'his/her/its/their', we use ***whose***. Compare: 'I was talking to a ***girl. Her*** father teaches at your school.' 'I was talking to a ***girl whose*** father teaches at your school.'

When we are talking about a thing ('model aeroplane'), we can use ***of which*** instead of ***whose***. Note the difference in word order: 'whose weight' – 'the weight of which'.

When we are talking about a person, we can use ***of whom*** instead of ***whose***: 'I was talking to a ***girl***, the father ***of whom*** teaches at your school.'

4

×	✓
× She told me something which I'm sure it will surprise you.	✓ She told me something which I'm sure will surprise you.
× I've come about the refrigerator which I bought it here two weeks ago.	✓ I've come about the refrigerator which I bought here two weeks ago.

⇨ 669.3–4

5

×	✓
× It has 180 pages, which all of them have colour photographs.	✓ It has 180 pages, all of which have colour photographs.

⇨ 669.6

6

× I shall never forget the day which the hotel collapsed.	√ I shall never forget the day on which the hotel collapsed.

When a relative clause provides details about a time or place, it can begin with a preposition + ***which***, but NOT with ***which*** on its own:

These are the hours ***during which*** the traffic is heaviest.
Compare: 'The traffic is heaviest ***during*** these hours.'

This is the office ***in which*** I work.
Compare: 'I work ***in*** this office.'

A preposition + ***which*** is used mainly in formal styles. In less formal styles, we normally use ***when/where*** or ***that***: 'I shall never forget the day ***when/that*** the hotel collapsed.'

⇨ 781.2

who 869

1

× I asked him who should I talk to about the matter.	√ I asked him who I should talk to about the matter.

⇨ 389.1

2

× Our friends took us to see several old castles, who are the pride of France.	√ Our friends took us to see several old castles, which are the pride of France.

We use ***who*** to refer to people, NOT to things. To refer to things, we normally use ***which*** or ***that***. ⇨ 781.1

3

× I telephoned all his friends, none of who could tell me where he was.	√ I telephoned all his friends, none of whom could tell me where he was.

After a preposition (e.g. 'of'), we use ***whom***. Note that this usage occurs mainly in formal styles. Compare: 'I telephoned all his friends ***but none of them*** could tell me where he was.'

whom 870

1

× We tried to find out whom was responsible for the damage. × I cannot remember whom she said wanted to see you.	√ We tried to find out who was responsible for the damage. √ I cannot remember who she said wanted to see you.

When the *wh*-word is the subject of a verb, we use ***who***:

Who is coming to the meeting?
Do you know *who is coming* to the meeting?
Is that the woman *who came* to the meeting?
Do you remember *who* (she said) *came* to the meeting?

When the *wh*-word is the object of a verb, we may use ***who*** or ***whom***. ***Whom*** is used in formal styles.

Who/whom did you *see* at the meeting?
I'd be interested to know *who/whom* you *saw* at the meeting.
She described some of the people *who/whom* she *had seen* at the meeting.

2

×	✓
× Whom are you going to the party with?	✓ Who are you going to the party with?

We use ***whom*** after a preposition: '*To whom* should the letter be addressed?'

However, this construction (preposition + ***whom***) is used only in formal styles. Normally, we begin a question with ***who*** and put the preposition at the end: '*Who* should I address the letter *to*?'

why **871**

×	✓
× I don't understand why do so many tourists come here.	✓ I don't understand why so many tourists come here.

⇨ 389.1

wife **872**

×	✓
× Some wifes prefer to go out to work.	✓ Some wives prefer to go out to work.

⇨ 181.4

will ('ll) **873**

1

×	✓
× I'll telephone you when I will reach London.	✓ I'll telephone you when I reach London.

In an adverbial clause of time, we normally use the present simple tense to refer to the future (NOT ***will*** or ***shall***). ⇨ 25

2

×	✓
× If you will visit the caves, remember to take a torch with you.	✓ If you visit the caves, remember to take a torch with you.

In a conditional clause, we normally use the present simple tense to refer to the future (NOT ***will*** or ***shall***). ⇨ 163.2

3

× I will be grateful if you will reply as soon as possible.	√ I should/would be grateful if you would/could reply as soon as possible.

⇨ 163.8

4

× When I bought the computer, I thought it will be very easy to use.	√ When I bought the computer, I thought it would be very easy to use.

When the reporting verb is in the past tense ('thought'), we use the past form of a modal verb ('would'). ⇨ 391.4

5

! I'm too busy to see him this week and next week I will return to France.	√ I'm too busy to see him this week and next week I'm returning/I'll be returning/I'm going to return/I return to France.

'Next week I *will/shall return* to France' sounds like a sudden decision that is made at the moment of speaking. ⇨ 333.2

To show that the decision was made in the past (i.e. before the moment of speaking), we normally use a progressive form ('I'm returning' or 'I'll be returning') or ***going to***.

To show that a future action has been scheduled, we normally use the present simple tense ('I return').

6

× Will I help you to do that?	√ Shall I help you to do that?

With question forms (e.g. offers, requests), we use ***shall*** with a first person subject. We use ***will*** with second and third person subjects: '***Will you*** help me?'

wish 874

1

× I wish my legs will stop aching. × I often wish that my work shoes are as comfortable as my sports shoes.	√ I wish my legs would stop aching. √ I often wish that my work shoes were as comfortable as my sports shoes.

When we are thinking about the present or the future, the verb after ***wish*** is in the past tense. Compare:

I don't know her address.
I wish I ***knew*** her address.

I can't play the piano.
I wish I ***could*** play the piano.

I have to work tomorrow.
I wish I *didn't* have to work tomorrow.

Note also: 'I wish I ***was/were*** you.' 'He wishes he ***was/were*** back home.' After ***wish***, we often use ***were*** instead of ***was***, especially in formal styles.

2

× I wish I would know her address.	√ I wish I knew her address.

When there is no change of subject after ***wish***, we cannot use ***would***. Compare: '***I wish she would*** stop working so hard.' '***She wishes she had*** someone to help her.' (NOT 'would have')

3

× I wish you told me that you needed help.	√ I wish you had told me that you needed help.

When we are thinking about the past, the verb after ***wish*** is in the past perfect tense. Compare:

I've left my watch back in the hotel.
I ***wish I hadn't left*** my watch back in the hotel.

I didn't apply for the job.
I ***wish I had applied*** for the job.

4

× After wishing to the couple good luck, we all left.	√ After wishing the couple good luck, we all left.

We ***wish*** someone happiness, good luck, etc (WITHOUT ***to***). Compare: 'Please give my best wishes ***to*** all my old friends in the office.'

5

× I am wishing that I you could hear her play.	√ I wish that I you could hear her play.

Wish is not normally used in progressive tenses. ⇨ 627.3

with 875

1

× He will be travelling to London with the plane.	√ He will be travelling to London by plane.
× I decided to try to follow the car with my bicycle.	√ I decided to try to follow the car on my bicycle.
× They escaped with a car that was waiting outside the bank.	√ They escaped in a car that was waiting outside the bank.

We do not use ***with*** when we talk about how we travel. When we refer to a type of transport, we use ***by*** + noun. When we refer to a particular vehicle, the preposition varies:

by train (or 'on the train')	on a train
by bus (or 'on the bus')	on a bus
by car/taxi	in a car/taxi
by plane	in/on a plane
by bicycle	on a bicycle
by boat	in a boat
by ship	on a ship

⇨ 126.2

2

×	√
The best way to lose weight is with eating less food.	The best way to lose weight is by eating less food.

When we refer to the means by which something is done or achieved, we use ***by*** + ***-ing*** form: 'You will never get people to like you ***by showing off***.'

within **876**

×	√
I have to be home within 9 o'clock.	I have to be home by 9 o'clock.

When we are talking about a deadline, we normally use ***by***. Compare: '***Within*** a week you should be back on your feet again.' (= before a week has passed)

without **877**

×	√
She left without she even said goodbye.	She left without even saying goodbye.
You can't have a party without to invite your brother.	You can't have a party without inviting your brother.

Without is a preposition and is followed by an ***-ing*** form.

⇨ 837

women **878**

×	√
There was only one women on the committee.	There was only one woman on the committee.

Women (with an ***e***) is the plural of ***woman*** (with an ***a***).

⇨ 181.5

wonder **879**

×	√
I sometimes wonder that my mother is really happy.	I sometimes wonder whether my mother is really happy.

When ***wonder*** means 'ask oneself', it is not followed by a ***that***-clause. The clause begins with ***whether/if*** or a question word, e.g. *who, how, when*: 'I ***wonder how*** they managed to escape.'

We use a ***that***-clause after ***wonder*** when it means 'to be surprised': 'I ***don't wonder that*** the child wanted to leave home.' Note also: 'It's ***no wonder that*** you feel tired.' 'It's ***a wonder that*** you can stay awake.'

wood 880

×	✓
Most Finns prefer wood furniture, although it's more expensive.	Most Finns prefer wooden furniture, although it's more expensive.

To describe something that is made of ***wood***, we normally use the adjective ***wooden***: 'a ***wooden*** spoon', 'a ***wooden*** stool'.

wool 881

×	✓
The first thing I bought in England was a warm wool coat.	The first thing I bought in England was a warm woollen coat.

When we describe something that is made of wool, we normally use the adjective ***woollen***: '***woollen*** gloves', 'a ***woollen*** blanket'.

word classes (also called 'parts of speech') 882

1

×	✓
My grandmother dead before I born.	My grandmother died before I was born.
I am agree that too much money is spent on weapons.	I agree that too much money is spent on weapons.

To be able to use a word correctly, we have to know which word class it belongs to. Once we know this, we have a good idea of the work that it can do in a sentence (and of the work that it cannot do). For example, 'dead' is an adjective and cannot do the work of a verb. On the other hand, 'agree' is a verb and cannot do the work of an adjective. Information about the class of a word can be found in a learner's dictionary.

Note that most words belong to more than one word class:

A *crowd* of reporters was blocking the exit.	(noun)
They all *crowded* into the room.	(verb)
The room became very *crowded*.	(adjective)

2

×	✓
A small country like ours must alert to such dangers.	A small country like ours must be alert to such dangers.
I amazed when I heard that he was out of prison.	I was amazed when I heard that he was out of prison.

Each of the major word classes contains subclasses. For example, within the class of verbs, there are some which must always have an object (transitive verbs), some which can never have an object (intransitive verbs), and some which may or may not have an object (transitive/intransitive verbs). ⇨ 838.1

Alert can be used as an adjective, as a noun or as a verb. As a verb, it belongs to the transitive subclass and cannot be used without an object: 'We must ***alert people*** to the dangers of smoking.'

Amaze is also a transitive verb: 'The news that he was out of prison ***amazed me***.'

Note that words which have more than one meaning often belong to more than one subclass: 'Did you buy ***a paper*** this morning? ('newspaper' = countable noun) 'Give me a pen and ***some paper***.' ('writing material' = uncountable noun)

Information about a word's subclasses can be found in a learner's dictionary.

3

× He was very anger with me.	√ He was very angry with me.

Words which belong to more than one word class often have different forms:

NOUN	ADJECTIVE	ADVERB	VERB
danger	dangerous	dangerously	endanger
anger	angry	angrily	anger

The different forms and classes of a word can be found in a learner's dictionary.

4

× We should like to apologize for any inconvenient caused.	√ We should like to apologize for any inconvenience caused.
× He is a very importance man.	√ He is a very important man.

Words ending in ***-ance/-ence*** and ***-ant/-ent*** are sometimes confused. Compare:

NOUNS	ADJECTIVES
absence	absent
confidence	confident
convenience	convenient
importance	important
insistence	insistent
intelligence	intelligent
presence	present
relevance	relevant

Note, however, that words ending in ***-ant*** which refer to people are nouns, e.g. *assistant*, *attendant*, *defendant*, *dependant*.

5

× I adviced her to report the matter to the police.	√ I advised her to report the matter to the police.
× The doctors just managed to safe the child's life.	√ The doctors just managed to save the child's life.

Some words are so similar in form that they are often confused. Note the following pairs of nouns and verbs:

NOUNS	VERBS
advice /s/	advise /z/
device /s/	devise /z/
safe /f/	save /v/
belief /f/	believe /v/
relief /f/	relieve /v/
licence[1]	license
proof /f/	prove /v/
practice	practise[2]

⇨ 35

[1]In American English, the noun is *license*.
[2]In American English, the verb is *practice*.

Other pairs have the same written form but have different spoken forms. For example, the nouns ***excuse***, ***house*** and ***use*** end with a voiceless consonant (/s/) but as verbs they end with a voiced consonant (/z/). Words such as ***conduct***, ***export*** and ***insult*** have a stress on the first syllable when they are nouns. As verbs, the stress falls on the second syllable.

6

×	√
× AEROBIC FOR WOMEN – Tuesdays and Fridays, 3 pm – 4 pm	√ AEROBICS FOR WOMEN – Tuesdays and Fridays, 3 pm – 4 pm

Words ending in ***-ic*** and ***-ics*** are sometimes confused. Compare:

NOUNS	ADJECTIVES
acoustics	acoustic
aerobics	aerobic
athletics	athletic
economics	economic
gymnastics	gymnastic
linguistics	linguistic

Note, however, that nouns which refer to people end in ***-ic*** (without ***-s***), e.g. *critic, diabetic, fanatic.* When used for plural reference, they take an ***-s*** in the normal way: 'a critic', 'several critics'.

7

×	√
× In spite of he had very little money, he offered to pay for me.	√ Although he had very little money, he offered to pay for me. √ In spite of having very little money, he offered to pay for me.
× Although all these problems, I have continued to work on my thesis.	√ In spite of all these problems, I have continued to work on my thesis. √ Although I have had all these problems, I have continued to work on my thesis.

Prepositions and conjunctions are sometimes confused, especially those pairs which express similar meanings:

CONJUNCTIONS	PREPOSITIONS
although	in spite of/despite
and	as well as/besides
because	because of
while	during

To introduce a clause which has a finite verb ('had'), we use a conjunction:

Although it was raining, I didn't get wet. (NOT ***In spite of***)
While we were having dinner, we talked about politics. (NOT ***during***)
We had to slow down ***because there was ice on the road***. (NOT ***because of***)

To introduce a noun phrase, we use a preposition:

In spite of the rain, I didn't get wet. (NOT ***although***)
During dinner, we talked about politics. (NOT ***while***)
We had to slow down ***because of*** the ice on the road. (NOT ***because***)

Note that most prepositions (but NOT ***during***) may also introduce an ***-ing*** clause: '***In spite of not feeling well***, she still came to work.' 'Cycling is good exercise, ***as well as saving you money***.'

word division 883

1

× I got your letter eventhough it went to my old address.	√ I got your letter even though it went to my old address.

Some two-word and three-word phrases are often written incorrectly, as one word instead of two, or as two words instead of three. Note the following common errors:

INCORRECT	CORRECT
alot (of)	a lot (of)
ashame	a shame (but ashamed)
eventhough	even though
incharge (of)	in charge (of)
inorder to	in order to
inspite of	in spite of
inturn	in turn

2

× He can not come because his wife is ill.	√ He cannot come because his wife is ill.

One word is sometimes written incorrectly as two words. Note the following common errors:

INCORRECT	CORRECT
an other	another
can not	cannot
may be	maybe (= perhaps)
where as	whereas

3

×	✓
× Nowadays every one agrees that cigarettes are bad for you.	✓ Nowadays everyone agrees that cigarettes are bad for you.
× Everyone of us received a letter of thanks.	✓ Every one of us received a letter of thanks.

The pronouns ***anyone***, ***everyone***, ***everybody***, ***everything*** are written as one word. Compare: '***Everyone*** was interviewed.' (= pronoun) 'Nine people have applied for the job and ***every one*** of them is going to be interviewed.' (= determiner + pronoun)

Anywhere and ***everywhere*** (adverbs) are always written as one word. For the difference between ***everyday*** and ***every day***, ⇨ 273.

4

×	✓
× Passengers may request seats in the smoking or non-smoking zones when they check-in.	✓ Passengers may request seats in the smoking or non-smoking zones when they check in.

When a phrasal verb (e.g. 'check in') is used as a verb, its parts are written as separate words. A noun formed from a phrasal verb is written as a single word, sometimes with a hyphen and sometimes without a hyphen: 'I'll meet you at the ***check-in*** an hour before departure time.' 'He's having another of his nervous ***breakdowns***.'

These nouns have the same form when used as modifiers: 'There was a long queue at the ***check-in*** desk.' 'They operate a 24-hour ***breakdown*** service.'

5

×	✓
× The church is full of seventeenth century paintings.	✓ The church is full of seventeenth-century paintings.

When an adjective consists of two or three words, the words are normally linked with a hyphen: 'an ***ice-cold*** drink', 'a ***first-class*** degree', a ***five-year-old*** child', 'a ***seven-mile*** run'.

Hyphenated forms are very common before a noun. After a linking verb such as ***be***, we generally use phrases instead (i.e. no hyphens). Compare:

She has a ***two-month-old*** baby.
Her baby is ***two months old***.

I would like an ***ice-cold*** drink.
The drink was ***ice cold***.

Also, compare: 'We visited a ***thirteenth-century*** monastery.' 'The monastery was built ***in the thirteenth century***.'

work 884

1

×	✓
× Our teachers give us a lot of works.	✓ Our teachers give us a lot of work.

In its common meanings, ***work*** is uncountable and does not have a plural form.

2

×	✓
× I was just getting ready to go to my work.	✓ I was just getting ready to go to work.

⇨ 532.2

worry 885

1

×	✓
× Don't worry for anything. I've made all the arrangements.	✓ Don't worry about anything. I've made all the arrangements.

We ***worry about*** someone or something. Note also: 'I'm ***worried that*** the parcel may have been sent to the wrong address.'

2

×	✓
× I am worry about her health.	✓ I am worried about her health.

⇨ 14.1

worse/worst 886

1

×	✓
× He was the worse pilot I had ever flown with.	✓ He was the worst pilot I had ever flown with.
× When I turned it on again, the picture was even worst.	✓ When I turned it on again, the picture was even worse.

Worse is a comparative form: 'My hair looks ***worse*** now than before I had it cut.' ***Worst*** is a superlative form: 'This is ***the worst*** haircut I have ever had.'

2

×	✓
× The pollution gets more worse every day.	✓ The pollution gets worse every day.

⇨ 15.2

worth 887

1

×	✓
× A wedding in a Greek village is really worth to be seen.	✓ A wedding in a Greek village is really worth seeing.
× It's not worth to get upset about it.	✓ It's not worth getting upset about it.

Worth is followed by an ***-ing*** form, NOT by a ***to***-infinitive.

2

×	√
× The book is certainly worth reading it.	√ The book is certainly worth reading.

⇨ 591.3

3

×	√
× One pound worths about three dollars.	√ One pound is worth about three dollars.
× They wanted $9000 for the car but it didn't worth it.	√ They wanted $9000 for the car but it wasn't worth it.

Worth is not used as a verb.

⇨ 882.1

would ('d) 888

1

×	√
× I am busy today but I would have some free time tomorrow.	√ I am busy today but I should have some free time tomorrow.

When we mean that something is probable or likely to happen, we use ***should*** (or ***ought to***), NOT ***would***.

2

×	√
× Nowadays, most people would spend their money instead of saving it.	√ Nowadays, most people spend their money instead of saving it.

When we mention something which happens regularly in the present, we use the present simple tense (NOT ***would***): 'Most evenings we *sit* and watch the television.'

We use ***would*** when we mention something which happened regularly in the past: 'In the days before television, people ***would sit*** and listen to the radio.'

3

×	√
× If I would have a lot of money, I would buy my parents a house with a garden.	√ If I had a lot of money, I would buy my parents a house with a garden.
× If I would have answered one more question, I would have passed.	√ If I had answered one more question, I would have passed.

We do not normally use ***would*** or ***would have*** in an *if*-clause. ⇨ 163.4,6

4

×	√
× If you would have nowhere to stay, there is an excellent youth hostel.	√ If you should have nowhere to stay, there is an excellent youth hostel.

When we mention an unlikely possibility in an *if*-clause, we use ***should*** (NOT ***would***). Note the alternative: '***Should you have*** nowhere to stay …'

5

✗	✓
× I hope that you would come and see me again soon.	√ I hope that you will come and see me again soon.

⇨ 369.1

write 889

1

! / ✓	
! I wrote the British Council to ask about courses in Britain.	√ I wrote to the British Council to ask about courses in Britain.

Users of British English ***write to*** someone or somewhere. In American English, ***to*** is optional.

2

✗	✓
× She wrote to me a long letter about her stay in New York.	√ She wrote me a long letter about her stay in New York.

⇨ 387.1

3

✗	✓
× I write to you to thank you for my birthday present.	√ I am writing to you to thank you for my birthday present.

⇨ 621.1

year 890

1

✗	✓
× Successful candidates will be appointed initially on a three-years contract.	√ Successful candidates will be appointed initially on a three-year contract.
× I didn't know that a five-years-old child could be so clever.	√ I didn't know that a five-year-old child could be so clever.

⇨ 533.3

2

✗	✓
× I visit my parents about two or three times in a year.	√ I visit my parents about two or three times a year.

⇨ 383.1

3

✗	✓
× I can take optional retirement at fifty-five years.	√ I can take optional retirement at fifty-five.
× A child of five years cannot be expected to know such things.	√ A child of five cannot be expected to know such things.

When we refer to someone's age, we do not use ***years*** unless the phrase ends with ***old*** or ***of age***. Compare:

Our daughter is ***five years old***.
Our daughter is ***five years of age***.
We have a ***five-year-old*** daughter.

Our daughter is ***five***.
We have a daughter ***of five***.
When our daughter was born, I was ***twenty-nine***.

⇨ 548

yes 891

×	✓
× 'She doesn't like meat.' – 'Yes, she doesn't.'	✓ 'She doesn't like meat.' – 'No, she doesn't.'
× Yes, I don't go running in my badminton shoes.	✓ No, I don't go running in my badminton shoes.

When we want to confirm that a negative statement or belief is correct, we use ***no*** (NOT ***yes***). 'He can't swim.' '***No***, he can't.' (= I agree with you)

Similarly, to answer a negative question, we use ***no*** to confirm the speaker's belief (NOT ***yes***): 'Can't he swim?' (= my belief is that he can't swim) '***No***, he can't.' (= your belief is correct)

Compare: 'Can't he swim?' '***Yes***, of course he can.' (= your belief is incorrect)

yesterday 892

1

×	✓
× Yesterday night I went to a party.	✓ Last night I went to a party.

We say ***yesterday morning/afternoon/evening*** but ***last night***.

2

×	✓
× The meeting was held on yesterday afternoon.	✓ The meeting was held yesterday afternoon.

We do not use a preposition before ***yesterday*** or phrases beginning with ***yesterday***.

yet 893

1

×	✓
× Although the situation has improved, yet there are still too many people without jobs.	✓ Although the situation has improved, there are still too many people without jobs.
× Despite the fact that the fighting has ended, yet a peace settlement is a long way off.	✓ Despite the fact that the fighting has ended, a peace settlement is a long way off.

We do not use ***yet*** after ***although***, ***despite*** or ***in spite of***.

2

×	✓
× My children are yet at kindergarten.	✓ My children are still at kindergarten.
× When I woke up, I realized that the plane was yet on the ground.	✓ When I woke up, I realized that the plane was still on the ground.

When we want to say that a situation remains or remained unchanged, we use ***still***: 'She is ***still*** having piano lessons.' 'When I left home to go to university, my father was ***still*** a very fit man.'

We use ***yet*** mainly in questions and negative clauses to refer to an expected event: 'The plane hasn't landed ***yet***.' 'Have they come back from Australia ***yet***?'

Yet (= up until the moment of speaking) is normally used with the present perfect tense. It usually goes at the end of a clause.

you 894

×	✓
× Please tell me more about you.	✓ Please tell me more about yourself.

⇨ 590.3

yourself 895

×	✓
× You should both be proud of yourselfs.	✓ You should both be proud of yourselves.

The plural form of ***yourself*** is ***yourselves***. ⇨ 661.1

List of entries involving system errors